John Lodge, Mervyn Archdall

The peerage of Ireland; or, A genealogical history of the present nobility of that kingdom

John Lodge, Mervyn Archdall

The peerage of Ireland; or, A genealogical history of the present nobility of that kingdom

ISBN/EAN: 9783337184841

Printed in Europe, USA, Canada, Australia, Japan

Cover: Foto ©Andreas Hilbeck / pixelio.de

More available books at **www.hansebooks.com**

THE
PEERAGE OF IRELAND:

OR,

A GENEALOGICAL HISTORY

OF THE

PRESENT NOBILITY

OF THAT

KINGDOM.

WITH ENGRAVINGS OF THEIR PATERNAL COATS OF ARMS.

Collected from Public Records, authentic Manuscripts, approved Historians, well-attested Pedigrees, and personal Information.

BY JOHN LODGE, ESQ.

Deputy Keeper of the Records in Birmingham Tower, Deputy Clerk and Keeper of the Rolls, and Deputy Register of the Court of Prerogative.

REVISED, ENLARGED AND CONTINUED TO THE PRESENT TIME;

BY MERVYN ARCHDALL, A. M.

RECTOR OF SLANE IN THE DIOCESS OF MEATH, MEMBER OF THE ROYAL IRISH ACADEMY, AND AUTHOR OF THE MONASTICON HIBERNICUM.

VOL. V.

DUBLIN:

JAMES MOORE, 45, COLLEGE-GREEN.

M DCC LXXXIX.

TO

THE RIGHT HONOURABLE

GEORGE-FREDERICK NUGENT,

VISCOUNT DELVIN

HEIR APPARENT TO THE RIGHT HONOURABLE

THOMAS NUGENT

EARL OF WESTMEATH,

THE FIFTH VOLUME OF

THE PEERAGE OF IRELAND,

IS RESPECTFULLY INSCRIBED BY

MERVYN ARCHDALL.

Vol. V.—Corrections and Additions.

Page 41, *note line* 19, *for* Canelagh *read* Ranelagh. *p.* 75, *l.* 9, *for* sat in *read* was attainted by. *p.* 75, *l.* 19, *dele* in 1689 was attainted by K. James's parliament in Ireland. *p.* 87, *l.* 27, *read* E. How and B. of Langar in July. *p.* 89, *l.* 39, *for* viruen *read* irruens. *p.* 90, *l.* 14, *for* of *read* to. *p.* 158, *l.* 1, *after* He *read* married Deborah, daughter of Thomas Baker. *p.* 204, *l.* 19, *for* Hapson *read* Hopson. *p.* 224, *l.* 22, *after* honours; *add* 12 January 1789 he married the daughter of the late General Skinner, and niece to the Countess of Abingdon. *p.* 253, *l.* 26, *after* Orrery *add* her Ladyship died 1 May 1788. *p.* 279. *l.* 4, *read* Edward who died 20 April. *p.* 294, *l.* 17, *after* unmarried *add* he sat first in the house of peers 15 April 1789.

PEERAGE

OF

IRELAND.

VISCOUNTS.

TRACY, Viscount TRACY.

THE furname of TRACY was taken by this family from a maternal anceftor, defcended from the Tracies, Barons of Barnftaple in the county of Devon, who in the year 1066 accompanied the Conqueror in his expedition to England, and were denominated from the town of Traci in Normandy.—The honour and Barony of Barnftaple, Jahel, the fon of Alured de Totneis had formerly enjoyed, but it became the inheritance of Henry de Traci by the gift of K. Stephen; which Henry being an excellent foldier, and the only perfon in the county of Devon, who ftood firm to that King, did him confiderable fervice in thofe weftern parts, 'till at length laying fiege to Cari-caftle, Robert, Earl of Gloucefter forced him to fubmiffion.— But by paternal defcent his Lordfhip derives from the royal blood of the Saxon Kings of England, namely, from Goda, youngeft daughter of K. Ethelred (fon of K. Edgar) fifter to K. Edward the Confeffor, and Walter de Maunts (or

TRACY, Viscount TRACY.

De Maigne) a noble Norman, whose son Ralph was Earl of Hereford in the reign of his uncle, the Confessor; and in 1051 raising forces in that county, joined Leofric, Earl of Mercia, and Siward, Earl of Northumberland against Goodwin, Earl of Kent, who, under pretence of restraining the Welch, had entered into rebellion against his Prince; but those Earls joining the King at Gloucester, and Goodwin perceiving an equal power to oppose him, submitted to an amicable treaty, to be holden in London. After this, with Earl Odo, he was made admiral of above fifty ships, and sent against Harold, Earl Goodwin's son, who then infested the English coast; but when the Conqueror was settled on the throne, he deprived him of his Earldom; and his son Harold, at the time of the general survey of the possessions of lands in England, begun by the Conqueror 14 of his reign and finished the 20th [1]; possessing several Lordships, and fixing his chief residence at Sudeley, was Lord thereof, and of Todingtune in the county of Gloucester.

He founded the little priory of Ewyas for Benedictine Monks, the castle whereof and other lands he secured by his marriage with Maud, daughter of Hugh Lupus, Earl of Chester, (by his wife Ermentruda, daughter of Hugh de Claremont in Beauvoys [2]), by whom he left two sons, John de Sudeley, his successor in that barony; and Robert, surnamed D'Ewyas, from his residence there, who possessed a very great estate, part of which was Lydiard in the county of Wilts, and leaving an only child Sibylla, she was first married to Robert de Tregoz (after to Roger de Clifford) their son Robert gave it the name of Lydiard-Tregoz, and from them many honourable families in England descended.

John de Sudeley, Lord of Sudeley, by marriage with Grace, daughter of Traci, Baron of Barnstaple, had two sons, Ralph, Baron of Sudeley, founder of the Priory of Erdbury in Warwickshire, and progenitor of the Sudeleys, Barons of Sudeley, whose heirs male failed in John, Lord Sudeley, in the reign of Edward III. and the title was conveyed by his eldest sister Joan, to the family of her husband Sir William Butler (Boteler, of the family of Wemme) who were thereupon summoned Peers of England; after whose extinction, it hath also given the title of Baron from the

---

[1] Lodge's Collections.   [2] Idem.

the first year of Q. Mary, 1554, to the family of his Grace the Duke of Chandos.

William, the younger son, was named Traci from his mother, (a usual custom in that age, for younger sons to assume their mothers surnames) and he, or some of his posterity differenced their coat-armour from the elder house of Sudeley, by adding an escallop, sable, between the bendlets, as now used.—This William de Traci lived in the reign of Henry II. and held lands of his brother Ralph, by the service of one Knight's fee; which probably was the manor of Todingtune, for it appears by Domesday-book, that it was held by the Lord Sudeley of the manor of Sudeley; in the time of Edward I. the Tracies are expresly said to be possessed of it; and this William, in a deed, perfected by Otwell, Lord of Sudeley .(son and heir to the said Ralph) is called his uncle *.—To him succeeded his son Oliver, who is mentioned among the knights in Gloucestershire, that paid scutage in 2 of K. John; and his son William in 1263 being made sheriff of that county by the Barons, in opposition to Sir Macy de Beseicke, a Frenchman, was assaulted by him as he was holding his court, and imprisoned in the castle of Gloucester; whither the Barons sending Sir Roger Clifford, and Sir John Giffard to his rescue, they took the castle, with Macy in it, and seized all his goods.———In 1289 (17 Edw. I.) he is recorded among the Knights of the same county; and, with Ralph de Sudeley his kinsman, is said to command under that King, in his victorious expeditions to Scotland.

He left issue Sir William Tracy of Todington, who in 1298 (27 Edw. I.) was in ward to Laurence Tresham, being then certified to hold 40l. a year lands, and on that account qualified to receive the honour of Knighthood.— In the beginning of Edward II. reign he was at the tournament

Sir William.
Sir Oliver.
Sir William.
Sir William.

---

* *Fuller*, in his Worthies of England, makes this Sir William Traci of Toddington (whom he characterizes for a man of high birth, state and stomach; a favourite of the King, and his daily attendant) to be one of the four, who 13 December 1170 (17 Hen-II.) were concerned in the assassination of Thomas Becket, Archbishop of Canterbury, for his violent invasion of his sovereign's prerogative: but he had mistaken him for his contemporary Sir William Traci of Wollacomb in Devonshire, who lies there buried under a monument, with his effigies and armour engraven thereon; and this mistake was probably occasioned by Sir William Traci of Toddington's removal into that county in his old age, where he had large possessions, and who dying there about the year 1180, is supposed to lie buried in the church of Mort,

nament held at Dunstaple, as appears by an old draught of a Knight in armour, bearing a standard with the arms of the family [1]; 12 of that King he was sheriff of the county of Gloucester, and again in the 17, jointly with John Bermansel, an office in those times of great authority and jurisdiction.—He left issue a son Henry, and a daughter Margery, married to John, son of John Archer of Umberslade in the county of Warwick, who dying in 1299, (28 Edw. I.) left two sons, John, and Thomas, whose descendant Thomas in 1747 was created Lord Archer, Baron of Umberslade; which title became extinct in 1777.

Henry.   Henry Tracy, Esq. who succeeded at Todington, was
Henry.   the father of another Henry, whose son Thomas was she-
Thomas. riff of Gloucestershire in 1359 (34 Edw. III.) and so continued four years successively, says Sir Robert Atkins, in his Survey of that county; but Dr. Fuller, in his Worthies,
Sir John. makes John Tracy his son to be the sheriff, whom he also places in that office Anno 1363 (38 Edw. III.) and for 5 years after. Which John represented the said county in the parliaments, held at Westminster 32. 37. 40. and 43. Edw. III. and both authors agree that he was then a Knight; and sheriff again in 1370, (45 Edw. III.)—In 1362 he gave the advowson of the church of Todington and an acre of land to the abbey of Hales; and was suc-
Henry. ceeded by his son Henry, father of John Tracy of Tod-
John. ington, who was sheriff in 1379 (2 Richard III.), and left
William. William Tracy, who bore the same office in 1395, as did
William. his son William in 1416 (5 Hen. V.) and was one of those persons of quality in the county of Gloucester, who, bearing ancient arms from his ancestors and holding lands by tenure, had summons in 1418 to serve K. Henry V. in person for defence of the realm.—He married Alice, elder daughter and coheir to Sir Guy De-la-Spine (De Spineto) Lord of Coughton *, and had issue William his heir; John, living 27 Hen. VI. and Alice, married to Hugh Culme

---

* He was knight for Warwickshire in the parliaments of K. Richard II. and Escheator of that county and of Leicestershire; whose father William held notable employments in the former county in Edward III's reign, and was grandson to William De-la-Spine, who married Johanna, daughter and coheir to Sir Simon de Cotton (now called Coughton) the lineal heir male of Ralph, son of William de Cotton; who were all persons of great account, and flourished at that place before the reign of Henry II. So that Lord Tracy may quarter the arms of those two families.

[1] Lodge Collect.

Culme of Moland in Devonshire, ancestor by her to Sir Thomas Culme (or Cullum) of Haftede in Suffolk, created a Baronet 18 June 1660.

William Tracy, Esq. the elder son, in 12 Hen. VI. was returned by the King's commissioners, one of the gentry of the county of Gloucester, of which he was high sheriff 22 and 23 of that reign, he left his estate to his son William, who served the same office in 1449 (29 Hen. VI.) and in 1456 was a commissioner of array.—He married Margery, daughter of Sir John Pauncefoot, and left two sons Henry and Richard; the elder of whom married Alice, daughter and coheir to Thomas Baldington of Adderbury in the county of Oxford, Esq. and had issue three sons and two daughters, viz. William his heir; Richard; and Ralph, a monk, who was buried in Todington church near the pulpit, with his mother, as is expressed by an inscription in brass.

Sir William Tracy of Todington, the eldest son, being honoured with knighthood, was sheriff of his county in 1513, (5 Hen. VIII.); was a person of distinguished parts and sound learning, and is memorable for being one of the first that embraced the reformed religion in England, as appears by his last will, dated in 1530 (22 Hen. VIII.) *

He

---

* This will was condemned, as *Heretical*, in the Bishop of London's court, and an order on that account issued to Parker, Chancellor of Worcester, to raise his body, according to the law of the church; who too officiously burning the corpse, was two years after sued by the heirs of Sir William, fined 400l. and turned out of his Chancellorship.—The preamble to the will runs thus:

" In the name of God, Amen. I William Tracy of Todington
" in the county of Gloucester, Esq. make my testament and last
" will, as hereafter followeth.——First, and before all other things,
" I commit myself to God, and to his mercy, believing, without
" any doubt or mistrust, that, by his grace and the merits of Jesus
" Christ, and by the virtue of his passion and resurrection, I have
" and shall have, remission of all my sins, and resurrection of body
" and soul, according as it is written, *I believe that my Redeemer*
" *liveth, and that at the last day I shall rise out of the earth, and in*
" *my flesh shall see my Saviour*. This, my hope, is laid up in my
" bosom.—And touching the wealth of my soul, the faith that I
" have taken and rehearsed is sufficient (as I suppose) without any
" other man's works or merits. My ground and belief is, that
" there is but one God, and one Mediator between God and man,
" which is Jesus Christ; so that I accept none in heaven or in earth
" to be mediator between me and God, but only Jesus Christ; all
" others to be but as petitioners in receiving of grace, but none able
" to give influence of grace; and therefore will I bestow no part of
" my

He married Margaret, second daughter of Sir Thomas Throckmorton of Corse-Court in the county of Gloucester *, and had issue two daughters, and three sons, William, ancestor to the Lord Tracy; Richard; and Robert, who left no children.

Family of Stanway, Barts. Richard, the second son, had by his father's gift, the manor of Stanway in the county of Gloucester, part of the possessions of the abbey of Tewkfbury, granted to him by the crown upon the dissolution of monasteries.—He was well educated, and wrote several learned and judicious treatises in defence of his father's faith †.

In

" my goods for that intent, that any man shall say or do to help
" my soul, for therein I trust only to the promises of Christ. *He*
" *that believeth and is baptized, shall be saved; and he that believeth*
" *not shall be damned.*—As touching the burying of my body, it
" availeth me not whatsoever be done thereto; for St. Augustine
" faith, *De Cura agenda pro Mortuis*, that the funeral pomps are
" rather the solace of them that live, than the wealth and comfort
" of them that are dead; and therefore I remit it wholly to the dis-
" cretion of my executors.——And touching the distribution of my
" temporal goods, my purpose is, by the grace of God, to bestow
" them to be accepted as the fruits of faith; so that I do not sup-
" pose that my merit shall be by the good bestowing of them, but
" my merit is the faith of Jesus Christ only, by whom such
" works are good; according to the words of our Lord, *I was hun-*
" *gry, and thou gavest me meat*, &c. and it followeth, *That ye have*
" *done to the least of my brethren, ye have done it to me:* And ever
" we should consider that true saying, That a good work maketh
" not a good man, but a good man maketh a good work, for faith
" maketh a man both good and righteous; for a righteous man liv-
" eth by faith, and whatsoever springeth not of faith, is sin."

* Who died in 1472 (12 Edw. IV.) by his wife Margaret, daughter and coheir to Sir Robert Olney of Weston in the county of Buckingham, descended from John de Throckmertona, Lord of Throckmorton in Worcestershire 1130, of which the family was possessed long before the entrance of the Normans, and had enriched themselves by the marriage of Eleanor, younger daughter and coheir to Sir Guy De-la-Spine, and sister to the great-grandmother of this Sir William Tracy.

† Among which was that remarkable one, entitled, *Preparations to the Cross*, written experimentally (say the *Decem Scriptores*) having suffered much in his estate for his father's reputed heretical will: He also wrote prophetically in 1550 (two or three years before Q. Mary's reign) another treatise, *To teach one to Die*, which was annexed to the former when reprinted, and falsely ascribed by the Editor to John Frith; being one of the three, found in the belly of a cod, brought in 1626 to be sold in the market of Cambridge, wrapped in canvass, which probably had been devoured by that voracious fish, out of the pocket of some shipwrecked seaman: On which occasion the wits of that University diverted themselves; one of them in his verses having this distich;

If fishes thus do bring us books, then we
May hope to equal Bodley's library.

TRACY, Viscount TRACY.

In 2 Eliz. he was sheriff of the county of Gloucester, and by Barbara, third and youngest daughter of Sir Thomas Lucy of Cherlecote by his wife Elizabeth, daughter of Sir Richard Empson of Easton-Neston in the county of Northampton [1], had three daughters, and as many sons, Paul, Nathaniel, and Samuel; the eldest of whom succeeding, served the same office of sheriff, 28 Eliz. and 8 James I. which King conferred on him the dignity of a Baronet 29 June 1611, being the thirtieth created from the institution of the order.—He married Anne, daughter of Sir Ralph Shakerley *, by whom he had twenty children, ten of each sex, viz. Richard his successor; Paul (whose son of his name died 1 June 1618, and was buried under a white marble in the chancel of Bansted-church, Surry, bearing the figure of a child in swadling clothes, with this inscription;

> Here under lieth the corpse of Paule Tracy, who
> Died the 1st day of June 1618, sonne of Paule
> Tracy esquier, and Margaret his wief, sonne of
> Sir Paule Tracy of Stanway in the county of
> Gloucester, Baronet, and Margaret, the daughter
> Of Philip Moss, esquier, of Cannon in the
> County of Surry. 1619) [2];

Shakerley; Alexander; William; Nathaniel; Thomas; Nathaniel; John; Vicesimus (so called from being the twentieth child); Anne, married to Edward Hall of the county of Worcester, Esq.; Lucia, to Bray Aylworth of Aylworth in the county of Gloucester, Esq.; Alice; Hesther; Elizabeth; two of the name of Susan; Barbara; Margaret; and another.—The surviving Susan was married to William Price of Winchester, Esq. one of the grooms of the King's privy chamber, and dying 13 March 1632, before she had been married full 14 weeks, was buried in St. Martin's church in the fields, London, under a very fair table, fastened to a pillar near the pulpit, curiously adorned with emblems of mortality, and a very long inscription,

---

* So the Baronetage of England hath it; but on the grave-stone of Paul Tracy in Bansted church, she is said to be Margaret, daughter of Philip Moss of Cannon in Surry, Esq. and he is also said to marry Anne, daughter of Sir Ambrose Nicholas, Lord Mayor of London, and widow to William Dutton of Shireburne in Gloucestershire, Esq.

[1] Lodge Collect. [2] Idem.

inscription, that part of which over the figure of Death, is an addrefs to the ladies, as follows;

> Ibimus omnes.
> Ladies, when you
>   Your pureſt Beauties ſee,
> Think them but Tenants
>   To Mortality;
> There's no Content on Earth,
>   Joys ſoon are fled,
> Heathful to Day we live,
>   To morrow dead.
> I was as you are now,
>   Young, fair and clear;
> And you ſhall one Day be
>   As you ſee me here.

Sir Richard Tracy, the ſecond Baronet, was knighted in his father's life-time, and in 1628 was ſheriff of the county of Gloucester. He married Anne, third daughter of Sir Thomas Coningſby of Hampton-court in the county of Hereford, by Philippa, ſecond daughter of Sir William Fitz-William, L. D. of Ireland, and had iſſue three ſons, Humphry; Richard; and John, who all ſucceeded to the title.

Sir Humphry, the third Baronet, was ſheriff of Gloucefterſhire in 1639, and for his loyalty to K. Charles I. had his eſtate ſequeſtered, for the poſſeſſion of which he paid 1600l. compoſition money *——He died without iſſue in 1651, being ſucceeded by his brother Richard, who left the title to his brother John, the fifth Baronet, who deceaſing in 1677 alſo without iſſue, the title became extinct, and he left the manor of Stanway, with all his eſtate, to Ferdinando Tracy, the ſecond ſon of John, Viſcount Tracy, as will follow.

We

---

* Mr. Sandford, in his Genealogical Hiſtory of the Kings of England, page 15, obſerves, that the monument of Robert, Duke of Normandy, eldeſt ſon of K. William the Conqueror, ſet up in St. Peter's church at Gloucester, ſtood firm, until the parliament having garriſoned that city againſt K. Charles I. the rebellious ſoldiers tore it to pieces; but the parcels thereof (ready to be burnt) were by the care of a loyal perſon (this Sir Humphry) bought of the ſoldiers, and privately laid up till the Reſtoration, when they were repaired and beautified with gold and colours at the charge of that worthy perſon (but rather his brother, for he was then dead) who added a wire ſkreen, in form of an arch, for its future preſervation.

We now return to William, eldest son of Sir William **William.** Tracy, who made the memorable will. He succeeded at Todington, and marrying the daughter of Sir Simon Digby of Coles-hill in the county of Warwick, was father of John (or Henry) Tracy, who married Elizabeth, second **John.** daughter of John, the first Lord Chandos of Sudeley (ancestor to the Duke of Chandos) died in 1551, and was buried at Todington, having issue five sons, John; Giles; Edward; Francis; Nicholas; and a daughter Eleanor, married to Anthony Kington of Quenington, Esq.—Sir **Sir John.** John Tracy of Todington, the eldest son, on 1 March 1572 was appointed by his uncle Edmond, Lord Chandos, overseer of his last will, in which he left him the best gelding he would chuse among all his geldings; and in 1574 Q. Elizabeth, in her progress to Bristol, knighted him, 20 of whose reign he was sheriff of the county of Gloucester, and in the 39 its representative in parliament.— He deceased in 1591, and was buried at Todington, where his effigies is in the chancel; and having married Anne, daughter of Sir Thomas Throckmorton of Corse-court, Knt. by his wife Margaret, daughter and coheir to Thomas Whittington of Pauntly in Gloucestershire, Esq. had issue five sons and two daughters who survived, viz. John, his heir; Thomas; William, who married Mary, daughter of Sir John Conway of Arrow, and sister to Edward, Lord Conway; Anthony; Henry; Dorothy, first married to Edmund, son and heir to Edmund Bray of Barrington in Gloucestershire, Esq. and secondly to Sir Edward Conway of Arrow in Warwickshire, created Lord Conway; and Mary, (the youngest of his fifteen children) was born 18 May 1581, three days after which her mother died; she was married first, when 19 years old, to Mr. William Hoby, by whom she had two sons, who died unmarried, the elder in his 23 year, and the younger in his 14 [1]; and secondly to Sir Horatio Vere, Baron of Tilbury, one of the greatest generals of his age; and dying 25 December 1671, she was buried 10 January at Castle-Heveningham in Essex *.

Sir

---

* She had issue by him, who was buried in Westminster-abbey 8 May 1635, five daughters his coheirs, Elizabeth, married to John Holles, Earl of Clare; Mary, first married to Sir Roger Townshend of Raynham in Norfolk, ancestor to the Marquess Townshend of Raynham, and secondly to Mildmay, Earl of Westmorland; Catharine,

[1] Lodge Collect.

Sir John, 1 Viscount.

Sir John Tracy, who succeeded, was knighted by K. James I. served the office of sheriff for the county of Gloucester in 1609; and for his great merits and accomplishments, was advanced by letters patent, dated 12 January 1642, to the dignity of Viscount Tracy of Rathcoole.— His Lordship [1] married Anne, daughter of Sir Thomas Shirley of Isfield in Sussex, Knt. by whom he left

Sir Robert, 2 Viscount.

Sir Robert, the second Viscount, who was knighted by K. Charles I. represented the county of Gloucester in several parliaments; and married to his first wife Bridget, third daughter of John Lyttleton of Frankley-court in Worcestershire, Esq. who died 25 July 1601, by his wife Meriel, daughter of Sir Thomas Bromley, Lord Chancellor of England, by whom he had John, his successor in the honour; and Anne, married to William Somerville of Edston in Warwickshire, Esq. and by him, who died 13 December 1676, had eleven sons and five daughters.—His Lordship's second wife was Dorothy, daughter of Thomas Cox of Castleditch in the county of Hereford, Esq. and by her he had Robert Tracy, Esq. who being bred to the law, went out serjeant in that profession 6 November 1700, having been 3 October 1699 by K. William deservedly made one of the justices of the King's Bench, which he surrendered 13 November 1700, and was advanced to the same station in the court of Common Pleas; being also by Q. Anne, 25 September 1710 appointed, with Sir Thomas Trevor, and Baron Scrope, commissioners of the great seal of England, until it was delivered (17 October) to Sir Simon Harcourt; and again 15 April 1718, with Sir John Pratt, and Sir James Montague, Baron of the Exchequer, upon the resignation of the Lord Chancellor Cowper.—His ill state of health obliging him to quit his employment 26 October 1726, his Majesty, in recompence of his services, settled on him 1000l. a year for life.—He married Anne, eldest daughter of William Dowdeswell of Pool-court in Worcestershire, Esq. and had two daughters, and three sons, Robert; Richard; and William, the eldest of whom left a son Thomas Tracy, Esq. of Severn-Hampton in the county of Gloucester, who in April 1746 married the daughter

tharine, first to Oliver, son and heir to Sir John St. John of Lydiard in Wilts, Bart. and secondly to John, Lord Paulet; Anne, to Thomas, Lord Fairfax (which title is extinct); and Dorothy, to John, son and heir to Sir John Wolstenholme, Bart.

[1] Ulster's Office.

daughter and heir to ——— Dowdeswell, Esq. who brought him an estate of 400ol. per ann. and had issue Dowdeswell his heir, born 19 March 1746-7 who also became heir to his grandfather; the daughters were, Anne, first married to Charles Dowdeswell of Forthampton-court in Gloucestershire, Esq. and secondly to Thomas Wylde, Esq. commissioner of excise, and member in several parliaments for the city of Worcester, who died 12 April 1740; and Dorothy, married 10 April 1725 to John Pratt, Esq. eldest son of Sir John Pratt, chief justice of the King's Bench, and died 23 March 1726 in child-birth.

The Judge lies buried under a neat monument in the parish church of Dodbrooke, with this memorial;

> Near this Place
> Lies interred the Body
> Of the Honble. Robert Tracy Esq;
> Son of the Right Honble. Robert, late
> Lord Viscount Tracy, of Todington.
> He was a Judge 26 Years
> In the courts of Westminster,
> But being struck with the Palsy,
> In the Year 1726, resigned a Commission,
> Which he had so long executed
> With the greatest Knowledge,
> Moderation and Integrity;
> To the Honour
> Of his Prince,
> And the universal Satisfaction
> Of his Fellow-Subjects.
> Obiit 11 Sept. Anno 1735
> Ætat. 80.
> Benefacere magis quam Conspici.

John, the third Viscount Tracy [a], married Elizabeth, eldest surviving daughter of Thomas, the first Lord Leigh of Stoneley, by whom he had two sons, William his heir; and Ferdinando Tracy, Esq. who being (as before observed) left by Sir John Tracy, Bart. heir to his estate, became seated at Stanway; and marrying the daughter of Sir Anthony Keck commissioner of the great seal, was there succeeded by John his only son possessor of a large estate, who married Anne, daughter of Sir Robert Atkyns of Saperton

John, 3 Viscount.

[a] Ulster's Office.

ton in the county of Gloucester, made in 1689 [1] chief Baron of the exchequer (who died in 1710, by his second wife Anne, daughter of Sir Thomas Dacres of Hertfordshire) and deceasing 19 April 1735, had several children; of whom Robert [2], the eldest son, (was chosen to parliament in April 1734 for Tewksbury, and in 1747 for Worcester; 7 August 1735 he married the eldest daughter of Sir Roger Hudson, Knt.); John Tracy Keck of Lincoln's-Inn, Esq. (counsellor at law, the second son was Cursitor Baron of the Exchequer, and in 1770 succeeded his youngest brother Thomas, in his estate of Great-Tew, in the county of Oxford [3], 8 October 1735 he married the daughter of Mr. Lindsey [4]); Anthony [5], married in August 1736 the Lady Susan Hamilton, sister of James, Duke of Hamilton); and Thomas (who 26 January 1737 entered into his Majesty's army as an ensign of foot; in April 1746 he married the daughter and heir to ―― Dodwell, Esq. and had a son, born in March 1746-7, who died young; he was a member of parliament for the county of Gloucester, and dying 24 June 1770 was interred at Stanway, leaving his elder brother John his heir [6].

William, 4 Viscount.

William, [7] the fourth Viscount Tracy, married to his first wife Frances, [8] daughter of Leicester Devereux, Viscount Hereford, by whom he had an only daughter Elizabeth [9], married first to Robert, son and heir apparent to Sir Robert Burdet of Bramcote in Warwickshire, Bart. who dying 7 January 1715, a fortnight before his father, left her with child of Sir Robert Burdet, Bart. born 28 May 1716, (who in November 1739 married the only daughter of the late Sir Charles Sedley of Nuthall in Nottinghamshire, Bart. and was chosen to parliament in 1748 for the borough of Tamworth; she married secondly Ralph Holden of Aston in the county of Derby, Esq. [10]). His Lordship's second wife was Jane [11], third and youngest daughter of Sir Thomas Leigh, who died before his father Thomas, the second Lord Leigh, by his second wife Jane, daughter of Patrick, the nineteenth Lord of Kerry, and by her he had issue, Thomas-Charles his successor [12], and Anne, [13] married 23 November 1710 to Sir William Keyt of Old-Stratford upon Avon in Warwickshire, Bart. member

[1] Lodge.   [2] Ulster's Office.   [3] Lodge Collect.
[4] Idem.   [5] Douglas's Peerage of Scotland, 326.
[6] Ulster's Office.   [7] Idem.   [8] Idem.   [9] Idem.
[10] Lodge.   [11] Ulster.   [12] Atkins's Gloucestershire.
[13] Idem.

ber of parliament for Warwick (whose ancestor Sir John Keyt of Ebrington in Gloucestershire, was advanced to that dignity 22 December 1660) and was mother of Sir Thomas-Charles Keyt, Bart. born in 1712; John; William, who died an infant; Robe   Agnes; Anne, who died an infant; and Elizabeth [1].

Thomas-Charles, the fifth Viscount Tracy, was Lord of the manors of Todington and Hales, and possessed a large estate; the latter of which came into the family in the reign of James I. and was an abbey, founded in 1246 by Richard Plantagenet, Earl of Cornwall, King of the Romans, youngest son of K. John: And the former hath continued in the name of Tracy, from the beginning of the reign of Edward I.—His Lordship rebuilt and decently adorned the old building of the vicarage of Todington at his own expence.—On 27 December 1712 he married first Elizabeth, eldest daughter of William Keyt, Esq. who died before his father Sir William Keyt of Ebrington in the county of Gloucester, Bart. and by her, who was born 11 September 1689, and died in 1720, he had issue William, who was educated in the University of Oxford, and died without issue in 1740 [2]; Thomas-Charles, who succeeded to the honour; and Jane, married 7 October 1743 to Capel Hanbury of Ponty-pool in the county of Monmouth, Esq. representative in the British parliament for that county, she died 13 August 1744 having had one son.—His Lordship married secondly Frances, eldest daughter of Sir John Packington of Westwood in the county of Worcester, Bart. by his wife Frances, eldest daughter of Sir Henry Parker of Honington in the county of Warwick, Bart. and he deceased 4 June 1756 [3] leaving issue by his said wife, who died 23 April 1751, four sons and four daughters, viz. John, [4] made warden of All-Souls College in Oxford; Robert; and Packington, died young; Henry, (in the army, and married 12 December 1767 to a daughter of —— Weaver, Esq.); daughter Frances, bed-chamber woman to the Queen [5]; Anne, (married 23 June 1757 to John Smith of Comb-hay in Somerset, Esq. member of parliament for Bath, and by him who died in 1763 had issue one son); Dorothy, and Elizabeth, died young [6].

Thomas-

---

[1] Lodge.   [2] Ulster's Office.   [3] Lodge Collect.
[4] Ulster.   [5] Idem.   [6] Idem.

BULKELEY, Viscount BULKELEY.

Thomas-Charles, 6 Viscount.

Thomas-Charles, the sixth and present Viscount Tracy, married 10 February 1755 Harriet, daughter of Peter Bathurst of Clarendon-Park in the county of Wilts, Esq. by his second wife Lady Selina Shirley, daughter of Robert, Earl Ferrers [1].

TITLE.] Thomas Charles Tracy, Lord Viscount Tracy of Rathcoole in the county of Dublin.

CREATION.] So created 12 January 1642, 18 Car. I.

ARMS.] Topaz, an escallop in the chief point, diamond, between two bends, ruby.

CREST.] On a cap of maintenance ruby, turned up, ermine, an escallop, diamond, between two wings erect, topaz.

SUPPORTERS.] Two falcons, proper, their beaks and bells, gold.

MOTTO.] MEMORIA PII ÆTERNA.

SEATS] Todington in the county of Gloucester, 80 miles from London; Hales-abbey near Winchcomb in the same county, a very large house, heretofore the habitation of the abbots, as appears by many religious figures and inscriptions in the rooms.

BULKELEY, Viscount BULKELEY.

16 Robert.

William.

THIS ancient and noble family is descended from Robert Bulkeley, Lord of the Manor of Bulkeley in the county palatine of Chester, in the reign of K. John, and was succeeded by his son William, who had five sons, viz. Robert; Willcock, of Petty-hall in that county (whose son Richard married

[1] Lodge.

married Mary, daughter of Hugh Venables, Baron of Kinderton, and had an only son of his own name); Roger, of Orton-Madock in Cheshire; Ralph (seated at Rudal-Heath in the same county, but died without issue); and David, from whom the Bulkeleys of Bickerton in Cheshire descended.

Robert, of Bulkeley, the eldest son, married a daughter of Thomas Butler of Warrington in Cheshire, by whom he had two sons and four daughters, viz. William his heir; and Peter, ancestor to the Bulkeleys of Wore in Shropshire, and Broxton in Cheshire: the daughters were, Alice married to —— Weaver; Maude to —— Hampton; Jane to John Larkton; and Margaret to Gruffyth Vychan ap Jer Gruffyth ap Jervorth Goch. Robert.

William, the eldest son, was living at Bulkeley in the year 1302, and was twice married, first to Maud, daughter of Sir John Davenport, Knt. by whom he had five sons, viz. William, living at Bulkeley in 1314 (but his line terminated in a grand-daughter, Alice, wife to Thomas Holford of Holford in Cheshire); Robert, of whom presently; Roger (to whom his father gave the manor of Norbury in Cheshire, and which became the surname of his descendants); Thomas (seated at Alpraham in Cheshire, in right of his wife Alice, daughter and coheir to Matthew Alpraham, of Alpraham, by whom he left a daughter and sole heir Hellen, married to Sir Thomas Ardern of Aldford in Cheshire, Knt.); and Peter. William married secondly Alice, daughter of Bryan St. Piere, and had one son Richard, to whom he gave the manor of Prestland in Cheshire, whereupon he assumed that surname, and which his descendants continued to use. William.

Robert, the second son of William, became seated at Eaton in Cheshire; he was sheriff of the county in 1341, and married Isabel, daughter of Philip Egerton of Malpas in Cheshire, and by her had a daughter Cecily, married to Thomas Weaver of Cheshire, and two sons, Robert, from whom the Bulkeleys of Eaton descend; and Richard, ancestor to the Viscount Bulkeley [1]. Robert.

Robert Bulkeley of Eaton, Esq. (styled *Junior* during his father's life) served the office of sheriff for Cheshire in 1341, 15 Edw. III. and had two sons, John; and Robert, whose only child Ellen was married to William, son of Robert Family of Eaton.

---

[1] Supplement to Collins's Peerage.

bert Wetenhall, by whom she had two daughters, Lettice, married to William Praers of Baddeleigh (whose daughter and heir Agnes was wife to Richard Bromley of Chedleton, Esq. 9 Hen. IV.); and Agnes, first married to Matthew Domville, and secondly to John Piggot.—John Bulkeley of Eaton, Esq. living 20 Rich. II. was father of Sir William Bulkeley of Eaton, Chief Justice of Chester in the reign of Henry IV. who was also living 30 Hen. VI. and marrying Margaret, daughter of Sir Richard Molyneux of Sephton, by Elizabeth his wife, sister to Thomas, Earl of Derby, had issue four sons and four daughters, viz.

(1) Thomas, who succeeded at Eaton.
(2) Arthur, living 25 Hen. VIII. who left issue, Richard; William; Thomas; and Edward.
(3) Richard living in 1439, and
(4) Ralph, who married the daughter and heir of —— Vernon of Whitcroft in Cheshire, and of Parwick in Derbyshire, with whom he had those lands, and by her was father of William Bulkeley, an officer under the Lord Audley, and master of the wardrobe, who for his services had his estate confirmed to him, by the name of William *the Hunter*; and his son Richard, who died 6 Hen. VII. obtaining the Lordship of Stanlowe in Staffordshire by the marriage of Joan, daughter and heir to Richard Sherratt, Lord of Cheddleton and Stanlowe, his posterity was denominated from thence; he had issue William, who died young; and Humphry his successor, who 16 Henry VIII. married Joan, daughter of —————— Egerton and had William his heir, on whom he entailed his estates in Derbyshire and Staffordshire; he was succeeded by his son Thomas, who in 1573, married Catharine, daughter of Ralph Holingshead of Baddesley, Esq. and had issue Arthur, Alexander, Timothy, and Fortune.—Arthur the eldest married Joyce, daughter of Ralph Ashenhurst of Ashenhurst, Esq. and had five sons and three daughters of whom John the eldest, married first Elenor, daughter of Thomas Bennyon, Esq. by whom he had three daughters, viz. Anne, Mary, and Alice.—He married secondly Sarah, daughter of Edward Manwaring of Whitmore, Esq. and by her had three sons and two daughters, viz. Thomas; Arthur, (who married Elizabeth, daughter of James

¹ Lodge.

James Fox of Manchester, merchant, son of Sir Patrick Fox of Westmeath, Knt. and had four daughters, Elenor married to —— Palmer; Elizabeth, to —— Jackson of the county of Meath; Sarah to —— Butler of the county of Kilkenny; and Margaret to —— Lamprey of Dublin, by whom she had Arthur, high sheriff of the city of Dublin in 1755); John; Elenor; and Sarah.—Thomas, who succeeded, married Alice, daughter of Godfrey Froggett of Staley merchant, and had John his heir, living in 1675 and many other children [1].

The daughters were Maud, (married to Thomas Holford of Holford, Esq. living 29 Hen. VI. by whom she had Sir George Holford, great-grandfather to Christopher, whose only daughter Mary was the wife of Sir Hugh Cholmondeley, ancestor to the Viscount Cholmondeley of Kells); Petronilla, (to Richard Brett of Dunham, Esq.); Catharine (to Randal Brereton of Malpas, Esq. and was mother of Sir Randal, Chamberlain of Chester, made a Banneret at the siege of Tournay); and ——, to John Minshull of Minshull, Esq. all in the county of Chester.

Thomas Bulkeley, Esq. who succeeded his father Sir William at Eaton, married Jane, daughter of Sir Geffrey Warburton, and had three sons and two daughters, viz. Thomas, who married Eleanor, daughter of Sir William Brereton, of Brereton, by his wife Maud, daughter of John Dutton of Dutton, relict of Sir William Booth of Dunham-Massey, Bart. and by her, who remarried with Hugh Cholmondeley, Esq. had a son Thomas, who died without issue by his wife Elizabeth, daughter of Thomas Venables, Esq.; Robert, whose son William died unmarried; William, whose two sons, Robert, and Richard died without issue; Genet, or Joan, married to Roger Puleston of Kimbrall, Esq.; and Elizabeth, to John Frobisher of Chirke in Flintshire, Esq. This branch of the family being brought to its period, we return to

Richard, second son of Robert Bulkeley of Eaton and Agnes his wife, ancestor to the Lord Bulkeley.—He married Agnes, daughter and coheir to Roger Cheadle of Cheadle in the county of Chester, Esq. 1307, by whom he had Richard his heir, and three daughters, Clementia, Alice, and Margery married to Sir Lawarin Warren of Poynton in the said county.—Richard, who succeeded, took to wife Alice, daughter of Sir Ralph Bostock, and had

Richard.

Richard.

[1] Lodge.

William. had William Bulkeley of Cheadle, Esq. who in the reign of Henry VI. being constable of Beaumaris in the Isle of Anglesey, prevented the Duke of York from landing there in his return from Ireland, to join the Earl of Warwick against the King. He married Ellen, daughter of Guilliam ap Griffith of Pentrie, Esq. and died in 1484, (2 Rich. III.) having issue six sons and four daughters, viz. Rowland of Beaumaris; William of Burgat in Hantshire (who by the daughter and heir of Sir John Popham, had Robert his heir, who married Anne, daughter of John Pointz of Acton in Gloucestershire, and had issue three sons, of whom Robert the eldest, living in 1565, married Joan, daughter of William Gascoigne of Carrington, Esq. and was ancestor, by his son William, to the family at Burgat); Hugh; Richard; Edward or Edmund, who died young; William; Genet, married to Hugh Lewellen; Ellen, to Robert Meredyth; Alice; and Agnes.

Rowland. Rowland Bulkeley of Beaumaris, Esq. married Alice, daughter and heir to William Beconsal of Beconsal in Lancashire, Esq. by his wife the daughter and heir to —— Ashton, and had five sons and two daughters, viz. Richard his heir; Thomas; John; William of Porthamel in the Isle of Anglesey; Hugh; Henry; Robert; Ellen, (the first wife of Sir William Norreys of Espeake in Lancashire, whose son and heir William was slain in Muscelburgh-fight, without issue); and Margaret, married 12 June 1531 to George Booth of Dunham in Cheshire, Esq. to whom she was first wife, and died childless.

Family of Porthamell. William Bulkeley of Porthamell, the fourth son, married Ellen, daughter and heir to Richard ap Meredyth ap Thomas of Porthamell, in whose right he became seated there, and had issue Rowland his successor; Richard, Robert, Hugh, and John, who died without issue; Thomas and William, both of Lanvechell; Catharine; Ellen, married to John Owens of Llandyffnan; and Anne, to Rowland ap Rys Wyn of Llanidowe.—Rowland, the eldest son married Alice, daughter of John Conway of Portriathan, and had Richard; Thomas; John who left no issue; William; Hugh; Henry, and Ellen, the wife of Daniel, son of Sir Richard Bulkeley, Knt.—Richard, who succeeded, married Margaret, daughter of William Lloyd, and had issue Rowland; William; Richard; Hugh; Ellen; Mary; Margaret; Elizabeth; and Anne, married to Thomas Dutton of Caernarvon, Esq.—Rowland

land was living at Porthamell in the year 1600, and marrying Jane, daughter and heir to Robert Bulkeley of Grynlyn, Esq. had William his successor, who took to wife Mary, daughter of Dr. Launcelot Bulkeley, Archbishop of Dublin, and had two sons, ——, and Launcelot, who both died unmarried; Rowland who succeeded, (and was father of Francis Bulkeley of Porthamell, Esq. who died without issue); Margaret, Alice, Jane, all died unmarried; and Griffild, the wife of Robert Lloyd of Placenewyd in the county of Denbigh, Esq. by whom she had Edward Lloyd, who died issueless; Frances, who died unmarried; Alice, married to the Rev. Stephen Vaughan of Kilkenny; Dorothy, to Richard Connel of the same city, Esq.; and Mary, to Michael Boyle, Gent.

Sir Richard. Sir Richard Bulkeley, who succeeded his father Rowland at Beaumaris, was honoured with Knighthood, and made Chamberlain of North-Wales in 1534 (26 Hen VIII.) and marrying Catharine, daughter to Sir William Griffith of Penryn in the county of Caernarvon, junior chamberlain of North-Wales, had four sons and two daughters, Richard; Rowland; John; Thomas; Eleanor, second wife of John Ardern of Hawarden in Cheshire, Esq. living in 1568; and Jane, married to Maurice Gwyn (or Wynne) of Gwyther in Caernarvonshire, Esq. and was mother of Sir John Wynne, created a Baronet 29 June 1611.

Sir Richard. Sir Richard Bulkeley of Beaumaris and of Cheadle, the eldest son, was knighted 1576; served in parliament, for the county of Anglesey in the reigns of Q. Mary, and Q. Elizabeth; to the latter of whom he proved an excellent soldier and faithful servant on several occasions; and was also chamberlain of North-Wales.—He married to his first wife Margaret, daughter of Sir John Savage of Rock-Savage in Cheshire; and to his second wife Anne (or Agnes) daughter of Thomas Needham of Shenton, Esq. by whom he had eight sons and two daughters, viz. Launcelot, Arthur, Tristram, who all died young; George, Edward, both died without issue; Launcelot, Archbishop of Dublin, of whom presently; Arthur, (Vicar of Coydan in 1596, 38 Eliz., who marrying Jane, daughter and heir to Rhyse Wyn ap William ap Price of Coydan, had issue William; Thomas, who married Elizabeth, daughter of John Brereton of Eglesham; and Catharine, wife to Peter Hanmer of Carvalach, Esq.—William, the elder son, married first Agnes, daughter of William Williams of Coghwithlan, by whom he had two sons, William and Arthur; and secondly Anne, daughter of David Lloyd of Llodyard in Anglesey, by whom he had a daughter Anne. William, who succeeded, married first Margaret, daughter of Richard Parry, Bishop of St. Asaph, by whom he had four sons and one daughter, viz. Richard, ancestor to the Bulkeleys of Coydan; Rev. Launcelot Bulkeley, John, Charles, and Ellen; and by his second wife, the daughter of ———— Gayner, he had two daughters, Mary and Catharine); Tristram the youngest son of Sir Richard, married Anne, daughter of Jenkyn ap Griffith ap Lhuellyn, and had two sons and four daughters, John, who died childless; William, who married Anne, daughter and heir to Owen Griffith of Dreaven; Agnes, wife to Hugh, second son of Pierce Lloyd of Gathodoge; Mary; Jane; and Genet.—Sir Richard's two daughters were Grizel, (married to Sir Henry Power of Bersham in Denbighshire, constable of the castle of Maryborough, Knight Mareschal of Ireland, governor of Leix, privy counsellor, and created Viscount Valentia 1 March 1620, who dying without issue 25 May 1642, was succeeded in that title by Sir Francis Annesley; and she departing this life at Chapel-Izod 8 September 1641, was buried the 17 in St. Patrick's church, Dublin); and Mary, married to James Eaton of Dudleston in the county of Salop, Esq.

Family of Bulkeley. Baronets.

Doctor Launcelot Bulkeley, the sixth son, was admitted a Commoner in Brazen-Nose College, Oxford, in 1587, the 18 year of his age, and taking his degree of A. M. in 1593, was 13 November that year ordained deacon by Hugh Bellot, Bishop of Bangor, and the same day instituted to the rectory of Landyffnan, to which was added 4 March following *That* of Llandegvan, otherwise Beaumaris, of which the Lord Bulkeley is patron.—On 25 March 1594 the same Bishop conferred on him priest's orders in his cathedtal; after which being made archdeacon of Dublin, he took the degree of D. D. in that university; and by letters patent, dated 11 August 1619, was promoted to that archiepiscopal see; soon after which he was called into the privy council; and 15 April 1624 appointed one of the commissioners for the preservation of the peace in the provinces of Leinster and Ulster, during the L. D. Falkland's absence to visit and settle the new plantations in the north. †—He deceased at his palace of Tallaght

† Whilst he sat in this See, he purchased the estate of Dunlavan, Tervant, Merginstown, certain houses and lands in Rathcoole, with other hereditaments in the counties of Dublin and Wicklow.

laght 8 September 1650, in the 82 year of his age, and was buried in St. Patrick's cathedral; and having married Alice, daughter of Rowland Bulkeley of Beaumaris, Esq. had issue by her *, who was buried with him in February 1654, two sons and two daughters, viz. the Rev. William Bulkeley, archdeacon of Dublin; Rev. Richard Bulkeley, D. D. of Bawne, who died about the beginning of the troubles of 1641, and left three orphans under the tuition of their uncle William; Mary, married to William Bulkeley of Porthamell, Esq. as before specified; and Griffild, to the Rev. Ambrose Aungier ¹.

William, the eldest son, D. D. and archdeacon of Dublin, lived at Miltown, which, with many other houses and castles, belonging to the protestant nobility and gentry, in the counties of Dublin and Wicklow, were burned in 1641, to prevent the English from planting any garrison in those parts; and it appears from the depositions concerning the murders and losses of the protestants, that he also lost in rents 530l. a year; in stock, 450l. in buildings at Old-Bawne, which were wasted and destroyed, 3000l. in rents, tithes, &c. at Dunlavan and elsewhere, 6315l. that his father, the Archbishop, lost in cattle, houses burnt and rents, 370l. and the orphans of his brother, 503l. 18s.— He was a person of great virtue and piety; one, who made it his employ only to serve the church; and his diversion only to improve and adorn his estate with plantations, which from a rude, desolate and wild land, he brought to a most delightful patrimony †.—He married Elizabeth,

---

* The commissioners of government having published an order to prevent the killing of lambs, on account of the great decay and scarcity of sheep, upon the pain of ten shillings for each lamb, to be paid as well by the killer as the eater; she petitioned the government for licence to eat lamb, by reason of her great age, and weakness of body: In consideration whereof her petition was granted, and she had a licence 17 March 1652, to kill and dress so much as should be necessary for her own use and eating, not exceeding three lambs in the whole for that year: And the same day she had their permission to take such studds for her own use as did of right belong to her; having received an order 18 February preceding, to possess her lands about Rathcoole garrison, and to dispose of the same to her best advantage, paying contribution, provided she planted them with English tenants.

† As assignee to Sir James Craige, he had a grant from K. Charles I. 5 March 1627, to him, his heirs and assignes, of the towns and lands of Tesnavan, otherwise Steghneven, Drumie, Lisnakill, Loghansion, Oldbawne, otherwise Shanbawne, Killtallowan, Cappoge, &c. in the counties of Dublin and Wicklow, to hold in Capite, by knight's service.

¹ See Packenham, Countess of Longford.

Elizabeth,[1] daughter [*] of Henry Mainwaring of Kilkenny, Esq. master in chancery, who died 1 March 1635, and was buried in St. Mary's chapel in the cathedral church of St. Canice by his second wife Elizabeth, daughter of Ralph Skipwith of Parkbury in the county of Hertford, Esq. and 3 December 1670, being in the 73 year of his age, he made his will, and died the next year, having issue by her, who deceased in 1679, three sons and three daughters, viz. Sir Richard; Arthur, who died unmarried in 1666; Launcelot, who also died a batchelor; Alicia,[2] married to Henry Martin, Esq. †; Mary, (to Launcelot Dowdall of Mountown in Meath, Esq. and died 3 December 1668, having two sons, Bulkeley, who died unmarried; and Launcelot, who left no issue by his wife Levina, daughter of John Philips of Newtown-Lemavady in the county of Derry, Esq.); and Agnes, first married to Edward Chichester, Esq. grandson of Edward, Viscount Chichester; secondly to Roger Masterson of Prospect and Monyseed in the county of Wexford, Esq and by him had an only son Henry, whom by his will, dated 15 February 1679, he left under the care of his uncle Sir Richard Bulkeley.

Which Sir Richard, who succeeded at Old-Bawne, was also seated at Dunlavan in the county of Wicklow, where he had a fair estate ‡, and being a man of great merit and goodness,

---

[*] She brought into the family divers castles, houses and gardens near to, and within the precinct of the Dominican Abbey of Black Friars in Kilkenny; the impropriate rectories of Bananogh, otherwise Castledough, Dysert, and Kilferah, with the glebes thereof, &c. in the county of Kilkenny.

† He was son and heir to Anthony, Bishop of Meath, by Catharine, daughter of Sir Robert Newcomen, Bart. and his issue were Henry Martin, Esq.; Launcelot, and Elizabeth, who both died unmarried; and Alicia, first married to Thomas Whitfield, Esq. by whom she had no issue, and secondly to Rev. William Moore of Ballyknew in the county of Wexford, by whom she had three sons and two daughters, and died in September 1737.

‡ Upon his representation to the King, that the town of Dunlavan lay near the mountains of the county of Wicklow, and that there was a great want in that part of the country of Markets and fairs, to which the inhabitants of the said mountains and other parts adjacent might resort, to buy such things as they wanted, and to sell such commodities as they had to spare; and that the said town was a place very convenient for those uses; his Majesty, 24 March 1661, granted

[1] Mentioned in her grandmother's will.
[2] In his father's will.

goodness, was honoured with the dignity of a Baronet, by privy seal, dated at Whitehall 24 September, and by patent [1] 9 December 1672.—In 1659 he married first Catharine, daughter and coheir to John Bysse, Esq. chief Baron of the Exchequer, and by her, who died in 1664, in the 21 year of her age, had two sons, Richard and John. His second wife was Dorothy, [2] daughter of —— Whitfield, Esq. by whom he had no issue, and dying in 1685, she remarried with William Worth, Esq. Baron of the Exchequer, died 12 January 1704, and was buried in St. Patrick's church.

Sir Richard Bulkeley, the second Baronet, had his education in the universities of Dublin and Oxford, taking his degree of A. B. in the latter 21 May 1680; and (as he tells us himself) was a person of good understanding and reason, which in divers respects were much improved by the imperfect symmetry and deformity of his body; for, in the course of his childhood his faculties were so extraordinary, that in a few years he acquired a very great measure of learning, and was blessed with so great memory, that his learning and knowledge were therein most securely treasured up.—At 16 years of age (he says) he had a large stock of human learning, and faculties of soul scarcely equalled; wit, fancy, and apprehension extraordinary; but a memory almost miraculous.——Yet, with all this fund of reason and literature, he was strangely deluded and led away by the unreasonable infatuations of a set of enthusiastical pretenders to prophecy, who first appeared among the *French Camisars* and *Huguenots*; with whom he engaged so deeply, that not only his estate partly supplied their extravagancies; but he prostituted his excellent pen in defence of their frenzy, and misapplied his great capacity and good sense, by submitting them to their groundless delusions; and was only prevented by death from selling his estate to distribute among them.—In the 25 year of his age he succeeded

---

granted him a Wednesday market, and two fairs to be held on the second Tuesday in May, and the second Tuesday after Michaelmas, each to continue for two days; which grant on 1 June 1692 was renewed to his son Sir Richard, with the alteration of the day, viz. a weekly Friday market for live cattle, and a Saturday market for the accommodation of the inhabitants of the town and neighbourhood.——For whose greater convenience the Right Honourable James Tynte, heir to the family, built a beautiful market-house,

[1] Rot. Anno 24 Car. II. 3 p. D.
[2] Mentioned in his grandfather's will.

ceeded his father, and was F. R. S. but died in 1710, and lies buried in his impropriate church of Ewell in Surry (where he had a handsome house, which was purchased from his heirs by Sir William Lewen, Lord Mayor of London, in 1718) under a black marble under the altar, with his coat-armour thereon engraven, and this inscription;

Here lyeth the Body of
Sir RICHARD BULKELEY, Bart.
Who departed this Life,
April the 7th. 1710,
in the 47th Year
Of his Age.

And also LUCY his Wife,
Who departed this Life
October the 9th. 1710 in the 47th
Year of her Age.

She was daughter of Sir George Downing of Hatley in the county of Cambridge, Bart.; but by her, who in August 1710 remarried with the aforesaid William Worth, Esq. having an only son, who died an infant, the title ceased; and his brother John, who died 18 July 1699, in the 38 year of his age, having married Elizabeth, daughter of Henry Whitfield, Esq. had one son who died an infant, and one daughter Hester, who became heir to the estate, and was married 15 April 1702 to James Worth Tynte, Esq. (younger son of the said Mr. Baron Worth) member of parliament for Youghall, and one of his Majesty's privy council; and she deceasing 9 August 1723, had two sons, Henry, buried at St. Patrick's 5 February 1709; and William, buried there 20 August 1710.

We now return to the issue of Sir Richard Bulkeley of Beaumaris, by his first wife Margaret Savage, which were six sons and five daughters, viz. Sir Richard his successor; John (who by Margaret, daughter of ――― Morgan, had a son Charles and a daughter Margaret); Daniel (who married Ellen, daughter of Rowland Bulkeley of Porthamell, and had four sons sons and two daughters, Richard, Rowland, Thomas, John, Margaret, and Ellen); William, Thomas, Charles, died without issue; Jane, married to Robert ap Hugh Creythin; Margaret, and Ellen died unmarried;

married; Elizabeth, married to Owen Holland, Esq.; and Catharine, to Griffith ap John Griffith of Lyn.

Sir Richard Bulkeley, who succeeded at Beaumaris, was knighted, and by K. James's instructions to William, Lord Compton, president of Wales, dated 12 November 1617, was appointed of council to his Lordship for that principality.—He died 28 June 1621, and was buried at Beaumaris with his ancestors; having married first Catharine, daughter of Sir William Davenport of Broomhall in the county of Chester; and secondly Mary, daughter of William, Lord Borough of Gainsborough in the county of Lincoln, (grandfather of Thomas, Lord Borough, who died L. L. of Ireland) by his wife Catharine, daughter of Edward, Earl of Lincoln. By the first wife he had one daughter Elizabeth, and a son Richard Bulkeley of Cheadle, Esq. who died before him, leaving by Catharine, daughter of George Needham of Thorniet in the county of Derby, Esq. Richard; Peter; Humphry; Francis, a captain in Virginia; Dorothy; Lucy; and Catharine.—Richard, the eldest son, who succeeded at Cheadle, married Dorothy, daughter of Sir William Hopkins, Knt. and having an only child Dorothy, who was married to Henry, third son of Sir Benjamin Ayloffe, Bart. she was mother of Sir John Ayloffe of Stanford-Rivers in Essex, who succeeded his uncle Sir Benjamin in the title, and dying 10 December 1730, unmarried, the honour devolved on his cousin Sir Joseph, who married Margaret, daughter and sole heir to Thomas Railton of Carlisle in Cumberland, Esq. and had Joseph, who died 19 December 1756, aged 21.—Sir Richard Bulkeley's issue by his second wife, the Lord Borough's daughter, were two sons and three daughters.

Sir Richard, who married Anne, daughter of Thomas Wilford of Kent, and had Richard, who died childless by his wife, the daughter of —————— Hill; Peter, who died unmarried; Robert; Margaret, married to John Bodychan of Bodychan in the Isle of Anglesey; and Anne, to Dr. Robert Lloyd. (1)

Thomas, created Viscount Bulkeley. (2)

Daughter Eleanor, married to Sir Thomas Porter of the county of Warwick. (1)

Margaret, to George Shelleto of Heath in Yorkshire, Esq. (2)

Penelope,

(3) Penelope, in 1614 to Sir Edwyn Sandys of Worſburgh, ſon and heir to Sir Samuel Sandys of Omberſley in the county of Worceſter, Knt. and died in 1680, having iſſue four ſons and three daughters, whereof Samuel, the eldeſt, was great-grandfather of Samuel, created Lord Sandys, Baron of Omberſley.

Thomas, Viſcount.¹ Thomas, the younger ſon, was ſeated at Baron-Hill near Beaumaris, and being a perſon of great merit and ſtrict loyalty to K. Charles I. was advanced by patent * under the privy ſeal, bearing date at Oxford 6 January 1643, to the dignity of Viſcount Bulkeley of Caſhel.—He married firſt Blanch, daughter of Robert Coytmore of Coytmore in the county of Caernarvon, Eſq. and ſecondly the daughter of Mr. Cheadle, who was ſome time his Lordſhip's Steward, but by her he had no iſſue, and gave way to fate by poiſon.—His children were five ſons and four daughters, viz. colonel Richard Bulkeley, (heir apparent, who was treacherouſly killed by Richard Cheadle, for which he was executed at Conway, and left no iſſue by his wife Catharine, younger daughter of Sir Roger Moſtyn of Moſtyn in the county of Flint, Knt.); Robert, who ſucceeded to the title; Thomas, (of Dinas in the county of Caernarvon, who married Jane, daughter and coheir to Griffith Jones of Caſtlemarch, Eſq.); Henry (who was maſter of the houſehold to K. Charles II. and James II. married Lady Sophia Stewart, and had James, who ſettled in France; Francis; Charlotte, married to Daniel, Viſcount Clare; Anne, to James, Duke of Berwick; Henrietta; and Laura ¹); Edwyn, died unmarried; Catharine (married to Richard Wood of Roſmore, Eſq.); Lumley, to Piers Lloyd of Liſgway, Eſq.); Mary, (ſecond wife of Sir Roger Moſtyn of Moſtyn in Flintſhire, created a Baronet 3 Auguſt 1660, and ſhe dying 16 October 1662, had iſſue five ſons and three daughters,

---

* The preamble. Cum regiæ Dignitati omnis, ſecundum Deum, univerſos et ſingulos in Regnis noſtris et Ditionibus ad Titulos & honores provehendi Poteſtas conceſſa eſt; Nos Perſonam dilectiſſimi Subditi noſtri Thomæ Bulkeley Armigeri, ex antiquiſſima Proſapia Bulkeleorum in Inſula noſtra *Mona* oriundi, plurimiſque ex Anglicana Nobilitate Familiis ſanguine immixti; necnon de Patre atque Avis de Noſtris ſemper Negotiis, et Rebus Hibernicis præſertim, optime merentibus editi, quorum ipſe Veſtigia fortiter præmit, et omni erga nos Pietate et Cultura ſuperare conatur, rite perpendentes et concedentes, eum ad Statum, Gradum, Stilum, Dignitatem, Titulum et Honorem Vicecomitis Bulkeley de Caſheli in Regno noſtro Hiberniæ provehere et promovere decrevimus. Sciatis igitur, &c. (Rot. Anno 17° Car. II. 2ª. p. f.)

¹ Collins's Supp.

daughters, of whom Sir Thomas, the eldeſt ſon, was grandfather to Sir Thomas Moſtyn, who died in 1737, whoſe ſon and heir Sir Roger, died 5 May 1739, and his ſon Sir Thomas who died 24 March 1758, was father of Sir Roger Moſtyn the preſent Baronet) ; and Penelope.

Robert, the ſecond Viſcount, in 1658 was ſheriff of the county of Angleſey, and ſerved for that ſhire in the parliament, which reſtored K. Charles II. continuing to be its repreſentative to his death, which happened 18 October 1688.—He married Sarah, daughter of Daniel Hervey of Coombe in Surry, Eſq. and had three ſons and ſix daughters; viz. Richard his ſucceſſor ; Robert, (educated at Oxford, and preſented 23 May 1683 with the degree of L. L. D. by James, Duke of York, was member of parliament for Beaumaris); Thomas, repreſentative of the county of Caernarvon ; Elizabeth, born in 1655, married to John Griffith of Glyn in Caernarvonſhire, Eſq. ; Catharine, to Philip Atkinſon, D D ; Penelope, who died unmarried ; Lumley ; Martha, to Roger Price, of Rhiwlas, Eſq. ; and Eleanor, to Sir William Smith, of Vinhall, Bart.

Robert, 2 Viſcount.

Richard, the third Viſcount Bulkeley, was born in 1658 ; repreſented the county of Angleſey in all the parliaments from *that*, which met at Oxford 21 March 1680, to his death ; and in 1701 was appointed vice-admiral of the North parts of Wales.—He married firſt Mary, eldeſt daughter of Sir Philip Egerton of Egerton and Oulton in the county of Cheſter, Knt. ſecond ſurviving ſon of Sir Rowland Egerton, Bart.) by his wife Catharine, daughter and heir to Pierce Conway of Hendre in the county of Flint, Eſq. and ſecondly Elizabeth, daughter of Henry White of Hawthlin in the county of Pembroke, Eſq. ſhe died 13 June 1752 ; and his Lordſhip deceaſing 9 Auguſt 1704, was ſucceeded by his only ſon by his firſt Lady.

Richard, 3 Viſcount.

Richard, the fourth Viſcount, who was alſo member for the county of Angleſey in ſeveral parliaments, in the reigns of Q. Anne and K. George I. ; which honour, together with thoſe of conſtable of Beaumaris-caſtle, and chamberlain of North-Wales, have been almoſt without interruption continued in this noble family from the reign of Q. Elizabeth.—On 2 September 1713 he was alſo made conſtable of Caernarvon-caſtle, but in November 1714 was ſucceeded therein by the Earl of Radnor ; and 4 June 1724 departed this life at Bath, having diſtinguiſhed himſelf by a ſteady adherence to principles of loyalty, a diſintereſted

Richard, 4 Viſcount.

terested zeal for the good of his country, and the strictest regard to all social virtues.—He married Lady Bridget Bertie, eldest daughter of James, first Earl of Abingdon, by his first wife Eleanora, eldest daughter and coheir to Sir Henry Lee of Ditchley in Oxfordshire, Bart. and by her, who died in June 1753, near Thame in the county of Oxford, left issue two sons, Richard and James, successive Viscounts; and six daughters, Bridget, who died unmarried; Eleanor-Maria, married to George Harvey of Tiddington in Oxfordshire, Esq.; Anne, to William Bertie, D. D. brother to Willoughby, third Earl of Abingdon; Elizabeth, to William Price of Rulace, Esq.; Lumley and Sarah, both died unmarried [1].

Richard, 5 Viscount. Richard, the fifth Viscount, born in 1708, was chosen 24 March 1730 member of parliament for Beaumaris; was constable of that castle, and chamberlain of North-Wales; married 12 January 1731-2 the daughter and heir of Lewis Owen of Peniarth in Merrionethshire, Esq. by his wife, the daughter of Sir William Williams, Bart. and dying 15 March 1738 without issue by her, who in May 1739 remarried with Edward, third son of John Williams of Chester, Esq. was succeeded by his brother

James, 6 Viscount. James, the sixth Viscount Bulkeley, who 19 April 1739 was chosen to supply his place in parliament; was constable of the castle of Beaumaris, and chamberlain of North-Wales.—5 August 1749 he married Emma, only daughter and heir to Thomas Rowlands of Carew in the Isle of Anglesey, Esq.; by her he had issue two daughters, Bridget, born in 1749, who died 13 July 1766; and Eleonora-Maria, born in 1750 who died the same year; and deceasing 23 April 1752 [2] æt 35, left his Lady (who remarried in 1760, with Sir Hugh Williams, Bart. died 18 August 1770, and was buried at Kanvair yn Gherney in Anglesey) encient, of a son

Thomas-James, 7 Viscount. Thomas-James, the seventh and present Viscount Bulkeley, who was born in 1752 [3] and 11 May 1784 was created a Peer of England by the title of Lord Bulkeley, Baron of Beaumaris —26 April 1777 he married Elizabeth-Harriot, only daughter of Sir George Warren, Knight of the Bath, but has no issue [4].

TITLES.] Thomas-James Bulkeley, Viscount Bulkeley, and Baron of Beaumaris.

CREATIONS.]

---

[1] Collin's Supp.   [2] Ulster's Office.   [3] Idem.
[4] Ulster's Office, and Collins's Supp.

BARNEWALL, Viscount KINGSLAND.

Creations.] V. Bulkeley of Cashel in the county of Tipperary, 19 January 1643, 19 Car. I. B. of Beaumaris in the Isle of Anglesey 11 May 1784, 24 Geo. III.

Arms.] Diamond, a cheveron between three bulls heads, cabossed and armed, pearl.

Crest.] In a ducal coronet, topaz, a bull's-head pearl, armed, gold.

Supporters.] Two bulls, pearl, armed and unguled, topaz, each gorged with a collar dancette, Ruby.

Motto.] Nec Temere, Nec Timide.

Seat.] Baron-Hill in the Isle of Anglesey, 241 miles from London.

BARNEWALL, Viscount KINGSLAND.

THE progenitor of this noble family attended the *Norman* Duke in his expedition to England; being allied, as is proved by an old chronicle, to the Dukes of Little Bretaigne, where the name still continues in great repute; after the kingdom of Ireland became subject to the English crown in the reign of Henry II, they removed hither, and upon their first arrival obtained large possessions at Beerhaven in the county of Cork, from the O Suillevans; besides which place, with the harbour and other creeks, their yearly revenues amounted to 1600l. sterling, a prodigious income in those early times.—Here they flourished, until they were all cut off by a conspiracy of the Irish, fomented by the aforesaid sept, the old proprietors of that part of the country, who suffered none of the name to escape their fury; so that the family must have been extirpated, had it not been providentially preserved by one of

the

the principal young men thereof, who at that time was studying the law in England †; whence returning soon after, he settled at Drumnagh near Dublin, where his posterity remained until the reign of James I. when that place became the estate of Sir Adam Loftus.

This preserver of the family (whose christian name is not recovered) was the father of two sons, Hugo, who died without issue 8 October 1237, 21 Hen. III. and Reginald, who becoming heir to his brother, the King by patent confirmed to him his inheritance of four carucates of land, with their appurtenances, in Drumenagh and Tyrenure: And to him succeeded another Reginald de Berneval (for so the name was then written) living in the reigns of Edward II, and III. who in 1325 held of Anna de Cogan one carucate and a half of land in Oldton, Corbally, and Haggard by fealty, homage, suit of court and ten shillings rent; and 6 Edw. III. held five carucates in Drumenagh and Tyrenure *in Capite*, by the service of one Knight's fee.—He married the daughter of ——— Molyneux of Kilbride in the county of Kildare, and had issue Sir Wulfranus (Ulpram) de Bernevall, who in the last mentioned year was of full age, then succeeding his father, and by the daughter of ——— Berford, had Sir Nicholas Bernevall of Drumenagh, whose wife was the daughter of ——— Rochfort, and his son and heir Sir Ulpram Bernevall, Knt. who seated himself at Crickstown in the county of Meath, marrying the daughter of ——— Arade, was father of Sir Nicholas Bernevall, who by the daughter of ——— Clifford had two sons, Sir Christopher, his successor at Crickstown, ancestor to the families of Crickstown and Trimleston *;
and

margin: Reginald. Reginald. Sir Ulpram. Sir Nicholas. Sir Ulpram. Sir Nicholas.

* Which Sir Christopher of Crickstown in the county of Meath, in 1445 and 1446 was Chief Justice of the King's Bench, and marrying Lady Maud Drake, widow of Sir ——— Drake of Drakerath, had issue two sons Sir Nicholas his heir, who succeeded at Crickstown; and Robert, from whom the Baron of Trimleston descends.

Sir Nicholas of Crickstown, being bred to the profession of the law, was appointed, in consideration of his good and faithful services, Chief Justice of the Court of Common Pleas for life, by patent dated

margin: Sir Christopher. Family of Crickstown, Baronets.

† Some attribute the family's preservation to the principal person's wife, who, being then big with child, escaped by flight to Dublin, where she was kindly received, and soon after delivered of a son. But this seems a little improbable; a woman with child being very incapable of preserving herself by such a flight.

and John of Frankefton (otherwife Trimlefton) from whom the Lord Vifcount Kingfland derives.

Which dated at Weftminfter 1 Auguft 1461, and fworn into that Office 14 April following. He married Ifmay, daughter and heir to Sir John, or Robert, Serjeant of Caftleknock near Dublin, and by her (who remarried with Sir Robert Bold, Baron of Ratoath) had Chriftopher his heir; and Edmund of Dunbrow in the county of Dublin, who by Catharine, daughter and heir to the faid Sir Robert Bold, by his firft wife, had Elizabeth, married to Richard Talbot of Dublin; and Robert, who fucceeded at Dunbrow, and by Ifabella, or Catharine, daughter of John Skelton Alderman of Dublin, had Mark of Dunbrow, who married Anne, daughter of Sir John Plunket of Bewley, Knt. and relict of Sir William Birmingham, Baron of Carbury, by this Lady he had Robert, born about 1557, who 24 September 1593 brought one archer on horfeback, for the county of Dublin, to the general hofting at the hill of Tarah. He married Genet, daughter of William Talbot of Malahyde, Efq. and had Edmund; he married fecondly Kinborough, daughter of James Good, M. D. of London, and by her had James, heir to his brother Edmund; Mark (of Dunbrow, who died in 1574, leaving a daughter Elizabeth, who became the wife of Thomas Fitz-Gerald of Laccagh, Efq.); Richard; Edmund; Jane, married to Peter Barnewall of Tyrenure; Kinborough, to Chriftopher Nugent, Efq.; Alice; and Mary Edward, the fon of the firft wife, fucceeded at Dunbrow after 1631, and dying without iffue, was fucceeded by his half-brother James, who 20 February 1635 had a fpecial livery of his eftate. Chriftopher Barnewall, eldeft fon of Nicholas, fucceeded at Crickftown, and marrying Ellen, daughter of Peter, Lord Dunboyne, had iffue Edward his heir; George (of Arrolfton in the county of Meath, who by Margaret, daughter of Sir Richard Euftace of Harriftown, Knt. brother to Thomas, Lord Ki'cullen, had Nicholas his heir; Edward, who by Anne, daughter of Thomas Nugent of Bracklyn, Efq. had two fons, Richard and Stadhyn; Rowland, Richard, Oliver, all died without iffue; Edmond of Cookftown in the county of Meath, who by Catharine White, was anceftor of George, living at Cookftown in 1615; Alicia, married in 1542, to Thomas Nugent of Bracklyn, Efq.; Eliz-beth, to Patrick Plunket of Gibftown; and Margaret, to John Nugent of Killaghe. Nicholas, the eldeft fon, was of Arroldfton, married Ellinor, daughter of Oliver Plunket of Gibftown, and had Chriftopher, who married Ifmay, daughter of Peter Barnewall, fon of Sir John, by his wife the daughter of Peter Nangle); Robert (of Moylagh in the county of Meath, whofe fon Thomas, by Ellen, daughter of Robert Oge Nugent of Newcaftle in the county of Weftmeath, Efq. had Robert, who was father, by a daughter

of

John. Which John was sheriff of the county of Meath in 1433 (11 Hen. VI.) and marrying Genet, daughter and heir of Robert Balfe of Galmolleston, of Edward of Moylagh, which Edward died 17 July 1632, leaving Patrick, his heir, a minor); and Barnabas, the younger son had Patrick his heir, the father of Edmund Barnewall, Gent.---Edward of Crickston, eldest son of Christopher, married Elizabeth, daughter of Sir Thomas Plunket of Dunsoghly, Knt. and by her (who remarried with William Wyfe of Waterston) had Sir Christopher his heir; Anne, married to Oliver Nugent of Drumcree in the county of Westmeath, Esq.; and Genet, to Sir Robert Dillon, ancestor to the Earls of Roscomon.---Sir Christopher the only son, of Crickston, married Catharine, younger daughter of Sir Christopher Fleming, Lord Slane, by a daughter of the house of Kildare, and had six sons and seven daughters, viz Sir Patrick his heir; Robert, John, and Nicholas, all dumb; James; Michael (of Athronan in the county of Meath, who married Anne, daughter of ------ Fitz-Lions, and widow of George Delahyde of Loughesque, Gent. and by her had Christopher; John; Thomas; Elizabeth married to Christopher, Lord Dunsany; and Maud, to Henry Warren. Christopher who succeeded at Athronan, was father of James, whose descendant Patrick brought one archer on horseback to the general hosting at the hill of Tarah, 24 September 1593); daughter Catharine, to Nicholas Hussey, Esq. Baron of Galtrim; Margaret, to Robert, son and heir to Christopher Barnewall of Rowston; Mary, to Richard, son and heir to Thomas Telling of Mataghna; Jane, and Anne dumb; Alice, to Christopher, Lord Killeen; and Maud in 1580 to Richard Nugent of Donouer, Esq.---Sir Patrick who succeeded at Crickston was living in 1578, and was knighted 28 February 1585, having sat that year in Sir John Perrot's parliament. He brought four archers on horseback for the county of Meath to the general hosting at the hill of Tarah; and having married Margaret, eldest daughter of Sir Patrick Barnewall of Fieldstown and Turvey, Knt. ancestor to Lord Viscount Kingsland, had issue five sons and three daughters, viz. Sir Richard his successor; Robert, of Stackallan, who married Alison, daughter of James Brandon of Dundalk, merchant; John; Peter; George; Catharine, married to James Everard of Randalstown; Maud, to Richard, son of James Moyle Nugent; and the youngest, to Thomas Nugent, third son of Christopher the nineteenth Baron of Delvin. Sir Richard Barnewall, Knt. eighth in descent from the first possessor of Crickstown, succeeded to that estate, married Elizabeth, daughter of Sir Oliver Plunket of Rathmore in the county of Meath, Knt. by Elizabeth, daughter of James Cusack of Portrane, and had Sir Patrick his heir; John; Thomas; Elizabeth, married to Patrick

heir to —— Netterville of Staffordston, had issue Richard Barnewall of Fieldston, Esq. which estate he acquired in marriage

trick Barnewall of Kilbrew, Esq.; Mary, to William Fitz-Gerald of Ballycorbet in the King's County, Esq. and Ellen, or Ellenor, to Randal, Lord Slane, being his first wife.---Sir Patrick Barnewall who succeeded at Crickston, was created a Baronet by privy signet, dated at Westminster 11 May, and by patent 21 February 1622, he made his will (as by inquisition taken 18 October 1624), 24 March 1615, died 21 June 1684; and having married Cicely, daughter of William, Lord Slane, had issue by her (who remarried with Patrick Barnewall of Kilbrew) four sons and three daughters, viz. Sir Richard his successor; John, (who was knighted, and 4 March 1688-9, was appointed second Justice of the Exchequer; he married Thomazine, daughter of Anthony, Viscount Tarah, and left an only daughter Mary, married to John, Lord Trimleston); George; Michael; Mary, (married to Thomas Nugent of Dunfert in the county of Kildare, Esq. and she dying in 1645, was buried in the church of Dunfert); Catharine; and Frances.---Sir Richard the second Baronet, was twenty-one years and six months old at the death of his father, and was then married to Thomazine, daughter of Edward Dowdall of Athlumey, Esq. as appears by inquisition, 15 July 1629, he had a special livery of his estate; and being engaged in the rebellion of 1641, raised and commanded about one hundred horse; he sent Christopher Barnewall of Crackenstown, and Andrew Barnewall of Kilbrew, son of Patrick Barnewall, Esq. with two hundred men under their command, to defend the town of Kilsoghlen against the English army. After the establishment of the general council at Kilkenny, he fixed his residence there, being employed as one of the provincial Council; and was excepted from pardon for life and estate by Cromwell's act of parliament, passed 12 August 1652, for the settlement of Ireland, he was after transplanted into Conaught, attainted, and deprived of all his estates until the Restoration, at which time, being one of the nominees mentioned in the act of settlement, was thereby to be restored to his mansion-house, and 2000 acres of land thereto adjoining, and died about that period [1], leaving issue two sons, viz. Sir Patrick; and John, who married a daughter of the family of Brymore, and had James, who married Margaret, daughter of Colonel Legge, brother to Lord Dartmouth, and had Barnaby (who by Jane, daughter of Kedagh Geoghegan of Westmeath, Esq. had James, who died in Hungary; George, who succeeded to the title of Baronet; two daughters; and several other children who died young); James, who married Marcella, daughter of the said Kedagh Geoghegan; and Anne, married to William Dillon of Kildare, Gent.---Sir Patrick, the third

[1] Decree in Chancery 19 February 1686 No. 8.

marriage with Elizabeth (rather Catharine) daughter and heir to John Delafeld of Fieldston, and by her had Roger his

third Baronet, who succeeded to the mansion of Crickston, with the estate assigned to his father, and K. Charles granted him an annual pension of 150l. which was continued upon the establishment, commencing 1 January 1687. He was knight for the county of Meath, in K. James's parliament, and having married Frances, daughter of Richard Butler of Kilcash, Esq. brother to James, Duke of Ormond, had issue by her (who was buried 1 February 1709, at St. James's church Dublin), Sir George his heir; Eleanor, married in 1703 to Hugh, Earl of Mount-Alexander, and died in December 1746; Mary; and Frances.---Sir George, the fourth Baronet, died 22 October 1735, leaving his said three sisters his coheirs, and the title devolved on his next heir male, George, son of Barnaby, son of John, second son of Sir Richard the second Baronet, which Sir George, fifth Baronet, came into Ireland, and procured an authentic pedigree of his family, after which, viz. 28 October 1744 he returned to the Continent ᵃ.

Robert,   We return now to Robert, second son of Sir Christopher Barnewall, of Crickston, which Robert was knighted by K. Edward IV. and in consideration of the good and faithful services done by him in Ireland for that King's father, was by letters patent, dated at Westminster 4 March 1461, pursuant to privy seal, and confirmed by the authority of parliament, created Baron of Trimleston in Ireland, which patent is enrolled amongst the records in the Tower of London, and a copy thereof is in possession of the family, attested by Lawrence Halsted, deputy keeper of the records in that tower: But we give the following copy of the said patent from the Journals of the House of Lords:---Edwardus, &c. Dei Gra. Angliæ, et Franc, et Dominus Hiberniæ, Omnibus ad quos presentes literas pervenerint, salutem. Sciatis quod nos consideratione boni et fidelis servitii quod fidelis, Legens noster Robertus Barnewall, Miles impendit tam excellentissimo Principi Patri nostro defuncto in ultimo Itinere suo in terra nostra Hiberniæ, quam nobis impendet in futuro, ordinavimus et constituimus ipsum Robertum ad essendum unum Baronum Parliamenti nostri intra terram nostram Predictam. Habendum sibi et Heredibus suis masculis de corpore Suo legitime procreatis, et advocandum per nomen domini et Baronis de Trymleston, ac unum de consilio nostro intra terram nostram prædictam pro termino vitæ suæ, cum feodis decem Librarum annuatim durante vita sua, percipiendum et recipiendum de feodi firma de Saltu Salmonum et Capella-Isold in Comitatu nostro Dubliniensi intra terram nostram predictam per manus Prioris et Fratrum Hospitalis Sti. Johannis Jerusalem in Hibernia, ad festa

ᵃ From Mr. Lodge's MS. Collect.

BARNEWALL, Viscount KINGSLAND.

his successor there,* who by Alison, daughter of Christopher, the second Lord Trimleston, had issue Sir Patrick Barnewall

festa Paschæ et Sti. Michaelis Archangeli per equales portiones. In cujus rei Testimonium has literas nostras fieri fecimus patentes. Teste meipso apud Westmonasterium 4° die Martii anno regni nostri 2°. ᵗ---He married Lady Anne Brune, or Browne, by whom he acquired a considerable estate; and he married secondly Anne, daughter of Sir Thomas Plunket, second son of Sir Alexander of Rathmore, but by her had no issue. The children by his first wife were, Sir Christopher his heir; and Thomas of Irishton, who married Elizabeth, daughter of ———— Cardiffe, and had an only daughter Elizabeth, who became the first wife of Sir Bartholomew Dillon of Riverston, Chief Justice of the King's Bench.

Sir Christopher, *the second Lord*, enjoyed that title in 1488, 4 Hen. VII. in which year he received a pardon for conspiring against the King in support of Lambert Simnell, and sat in the parliament held at Dublin in 1490, as he again did 12 September 1493, and attended the Earl of Kildare, L. D. to the battle of Knocktowe in Conaught, fought 19 August 1504. He married Elizabeth, daughter of Sir Thomas Plunket of Rathmore, and had issue two sons and three daughters, viz. Ismay, the eldest, married to William Bathe of Rathseigh; the second to John Netterville of Douth, Justice of the King's Bench; and Alison, to Christopher Barnewall, ancestor to Viscount Kingsland. The sons were

(1) Sir John, who succeeded to the honour; and
(2) Robert of Rowston in the county of Meath, of which estate he was possessed in right of his first wife Johanna, daughter and heir to ————— Rowe, and he married secondly Elizabeth, daughter of John Talbot of Dardiston, Esq. The issue of his first wife, were Christopher his heir; John (of Navan and of Kirnanston who married Margaret, daughter of John Kenly of Navan); David (of Callan, who by Catharine Preston had John; Robert; and Patrick, who married a daughter of Thomas Plunket); Ellenor, or Ellen, married to Meyler Hussey of Mulhussey; and Isabel to Richard Taylor. The issue of Elizabeth, the second wife, were, Edward; Thomas, who married Margaret Beling, and had issue; Edmond, who married Anne Edwards; William of Drogheda, who married Anne Hamlin; Alice, married

Sir Christopher.

Family of Rowston.

---

* We read in the Office of Ulster King at Arms, that the said Richard had two other sons, to the elder of which he left Staffordston; and to the youngest son Cawleston near Navan, who settling at Cawleston his posterity were thence denominated, and Sir Patrick Barnewall, in 1610, eldest son of Sir Roger, received out of the said town lands an annual rent of one marc, and one pound of pepper.

ᵗ Lord's Jour. I. 94.

Barnewall of Fieldſton, Gracedieu * and of Turvey, Knt. who 7 October 1534 was made ſerjeant at law and ſolicitor-general

married to James, or John Flatſbury of Johnſton; Anne, to John Rochfort of Keranſton, and had iſſue; Ellice; Iſmay, to Laurence Aſhe of Fornaughts, and had iſſue; Aliſon; Jane; and Cicely.---Chriſtopher, the eldeſt ſon, ſucceeded at Rowſton, married firſt, Margaret Golding; and ſecondly Genet, daughter of Oliver, Lord Louth, by whom he had Peter and Oliver. The iſſue of his firſt wife were, Robert, his heir; and Alexander of Luſton, who married Mary, daughter of James Barnewall of Brymore. Robert of Roweſton, married firſt, Margaret, daughter of Sir Chriſtopher Barnewall of Crickſton, by whom he had Chriſtopher his heir; he married ſecondly the ſiſter of William Crompe of Marchalſton. The ſaid Chriſtopher was father of Thomas of Roweſton, who had a daughter Anne, married to Thomas Everard of Randalſtown, Eſq.

Sir John. Sir John, *the third Lord*, before his acceſſion to the honour, viz. in 1509, 1 Hen. VIII. was made ſecond Juſtice of the King's Bench; 3 September 1522 appointed Vice Treaſurer, and 3 September 1524 High Treaſurer of Ireland. 1 December 1532 he received a fee-farm grant of 136 acres of arable land in Dunleer, to hold as of the manor of Trim, and 16 Auguſt 1534, he was by commiſſion dated at Weſtminſter conſtituted High Chancellor of Ireland, in the room of George Cromer, Archbiſhop of Armagh, which office he held till his deceaſe. In 1536 he was made ſteward, ſeneſchal, ſurveyor and receiver of the manors and Lordſhips of Ruſhe, Balſcadan, Woughterarde, Caſtlewarning, Clynton's-court, and Black-caſtle, together with the moiety of the manor of Portrane; in which employment he was ſucceeded by Sir Patrick Barnewall of Fieldſtown. In the ſame year he was joined with the Lord Treaſurer Brabazon, and made an incurſion into Offaley, when they obliged O Conor who was ravaging the country, to return home with all the expedition he could; and in 1537 O Neale breaking his engagement with the ſtate, and having reſolved to ſend ſome forces into Lecale, under the conduct of his ſon, to ſeize the King's caſtle of Ardglaſs, the L. D. Gray, as ſoon as he had intelligence thereof, aſſembled his forces, but before he advanced his colours into Ulſter, by the advice of the privy council, commiſſioned the Lord Chancellor Trimleſton, the Biſhop of Meath, and Chief Juſtice Aylmer, to treat with O Neile

* By patent, dated 22 July 1541. 33 Hen. VIII. he had a grant of the houſe, ſite and precinct of the priory of Gracedieu in the county of Dublin, with the appurtenances, to hold by the 20 part of a Knight's fee, and the yearly rent of 18 ſhillings and 6 pence.

tor-general of Ireland: whence he was promoted 1 October 1550 to the mastership of the rolls, on the promotion of Sir

O Neile in the borders of Ulster; who meeting them at the time appointed, and after many words passed on each side, and objected grievances, O Neile at last submitted, and both armies were a few days after disbanded. His Lordship died 25 July 1538, and having four wives had no issue by the two last; by his first wife Genet, or Jane, daughter of John Bellew of Bellewstown he had Patrick his heir; and by Margaret his second wife, daughter of Patrick Fitz-Leons, by the daughter of ――― Eustace of Newland, Esq. he had four sons and two daughters, viz. Sir Thomas (who married Ismay, daughter of Sir Bartholomew Dillon, relict of James Fleming of Stephenston and also of Richard Tath of Cookstown, Esq.); Peter, appointed 17 October 1534, the King's Serjeant at Law and Solicitor General; Andrew; James; Catharine, married to Patrick Hussey, Baron of Galtrim; and Elizabeth, first to George Plunket, Esq. son and heir to Sir John Plunket of Bewley, Knt. secondly to Christopher Eustace of Ballycotland, and thirdly to William Darcy of Platten, Esq.

Sir Patrick, *the fourth Lord*, was present 12 January 1559 in the parliament held by the L. D. Sussex, and by indenture made between Q. Elizabeth, his Lordship, and his son and heir Robert Barnewall, 27 October 1561, her Majesty demised to them the rectory, church and parsonage of Rathregan in the county of Meath, parcel of the possessions of the late priory of St. Peter's by Trim, from Michaelmas last past, for twenty-one years, at the rent of 16l. 13s. 4d. Irish.—He married Catharine, daughter of ――――― Taylor of Swords, Esq. relict of Christopher Delahyde, recorder of Drogheda, and had issue two sons, Robert, and Peter, successive Lords Trimleston.

Sir Patrick.

Robert, *the fifth Lord*, says Holingshed, " was a rare nobleman, and endowed with sundry good gifts, who having well wedded himself to the reformation of his miserable country, was resolved for the whetting of his wit, which nevertheless was pregnant and quick; by a short trade and method he took in his study to have sipt up the very sap of the common law, and upon this determination failing into England, sickened shortly after, at a worshipful matron's house at Cornbury, named Margaret Tiler, where he was to the great grief of all his country pursued with death, when the weal of the public had most need of his life." 28 August 1561 he was joined in commission with Hugh, Archbishop of Dublin, and others, for the preservation of the peace within the pale, during the absence of the L. D. Sussex in the North, against Shane O'Neile. By deed of settlement dated 27 June, 1 Eliz. his father

Robert,

Sir Thomas Cufack to the chancellorfhip 4 Auguft preceding.—He married Anne, eldeft daughter of Richard Luttrell

ther enfeoffed James Barnewall of Brymore in the manor of Rabo and other lands, to their ufe during their lives, holding to the faid Sir Patrick during his life, in Rabo, the finding of fix horfes and five boys as often as he fhould come to Dublin, and fo long as his abode fhould be there, the hay of two acres of meadow, the making and carrying thereof to Dublin, and of four loads of underwood from thence to Dublin yearly during his life, together with the hay of two acres more to Richard Fyan of Dublin, merchant, yearly, to be made and carried to his houfe in Dublin; and to ftand feized of lands in Mitchelftown to the value of 10l. a year, and of the tenements in Claterfton, and Cotterel's Farm, after his deceafe, to the ufe of the faid Robert and Anne during their lives, and of the refidue after their deceafe, to the ufe and performance of the will of Sir John Barnewall, late Lord Trimlefton, father to the faid Sir Patrick. The faid Robert, Lord Trimlefton, in 1559 married Anne, only daughter of Richard Fyan, Alderman of Dublin (by his wife Begnet, only daughter of John Stanton) and father to William Fyan, but his Lordfhip dying, as by inquifition, 17 Auguft 1573 without iffue (by his Lady who remarried with Chriftopher Sedgrave, alderman of Dublin, and died 13 April 1600) was fucceeded by his brother

Sir Peter.   Sir Peter, *the fixth Lord*, who before his acceffion to the honour, lived at Athboy, in the Barony of Deece, in the county of Meath, for which Barony he brought one archer on horfeback to the general hofting at the hill of Tarah, 24 September 1593, as he did fix others for the Barony of Navan. 21 February 1578 he was appointed one of the Commiffioners for making the limits and bounds of certain territories to be made fhire ground, and named the county of Wicklow, with the divifion of the fame into fix Baronies; he was knighted fix May 1583 in St. Patrick's church, at the creation of Sir John Bourke, Baron of Leitrim, and 26 April 1585 fat in Sir John Perrot's parliament. He was feized and poffeffed of one caftle, ten meffuages, one garden, one orchard, 200 acres of arable land, twenty of meadow, 200 of pafture, forty of wood, and a water-mill in Trimlefton; alfo of a large eftate in Gormanfton, Mountown, Cloncurry, Balfoon, Athboy, Clonifton, Dunfhaghlin, and elfewhere in the county of Meath, in all which, 20 January 1584, he enfeoffed Richard Barnewall and others, for the payment of 100l. yearly, for ten years from the feaft of Philip and Jacob next enfuing, to be applied as he fhould difpofe thereof by his laft will, and for the payment of 40l. a year, commencing after the firft ten years, if he fhould have any other iffue than he *now* had, to fuch ufes as he fhould appoint in his faid laft will, and if he

had

trell of Luttrellstown, Esq. by his wife Margaret, daughter of Patrick Fitz-Leons of Dublin, Esq. and deceasing on the

had no issue, then to such other uses as he should appoint by his said will; and the feoffees to hold the premisses to the use of himself for life, and after to the use of Robert Barnewall his son and heir, and to the heirs male of his body, saving to Genet, daughter of Thomas Talbot of Dardistown in the county of Meath, for her life 20l. sterling a year if the said Robert should take her to wife, and do so in his the said Peter's lifetime, or otherwise, before he attained the age of 21 years; also to stand seized of the castles, towns and lands of Moymondry, Irishtown, Kenock, and Clownestown to the use of himself and Dame Catharine Nugent his wife, and the survivor of them, with remainders over as before; and the lands in Rabo, the water-mill, Lutterell's-farm, and Ballyscarlet to the said Robert and his heirs male, after the death of Dame Anne Fyan sister-in-law to the said Sir Peter.—He made his will 14 February 1594, and therein directs, that his said feoffees do stand seized of the premisses to the use of his said son and heir Robert, and the heirs male of his body after his decease, remainder to his own heirs male for ever; and in default thereof to the use of Alexander Barnewall of Robertstown, and John Barnewall of Lespople in tail male; remainder to the heirs male of James Barnewall of Brymore; remainder to the heirs male of Christopher Barnewall, father of Sir John, sometime Lord of Trimleston; remainder to Sir Patrick Barnewall of Crickston, Knt. and the heirs male of his body; remainder to the uses appointed in the last will of the said Sir John Barnewall; and in default thereof to the right heirs of the said Sir Alexander Barnewall, subject to the forfeiture thereof in case of alienation or sale by him or them of any part or parcel of the premisses. Directs his debts to be paid out of the debts due to him; bequeathed his soul to Almighty God, and his body to be buried in the church of Morechurch; appointed Robert his son and heir to be sole executor; Sir Patrick Barnewall of Crickston, Sir Patrick Barnewall of Turvey, Richard Barnewall of Kilmessan, John Barnewall of Brymore, and Richard Misset of Liscartan, his overseers; directs that 160l. be raised out of his rents to the use of Genet Barnewall, his base daughter, for her preferment and marriage; to divide 10l. sterling amongst poor priests and friars, and to give forty shillings to the *bishop* Brady. He departed this life on Friday next before Easter 1598, 40 Elizabeth, at Trimleston, leaving by his wife Catharine, daughter of Sir Christopher Nugent, son and heir to Richard, Lord Delvin, an only son and successor.

Robert, *the seventh Lord*, aged 24 years at the death of his father, then married to Genet, daughter of Thomas Talbot of Dardistown,

Robert.

the ides of November (the 13) 1552, had issue Sir Christopher his heir, and three daughters, Margaret, (married to Dardistown, Esq. mentioned in the said deed of feoffment [1], and to him, his heirs and assignes for ever, Sir Patrick Barnewall of Crickstown, Knt. and Bart. by a codicil annexed to his will, and dated 26 March 1616, styling him his dear cousin, devised the manor of Stackallan, and all his estates in use, possession or reversion in the towns, hamlets and fields of Stackallan, Harmonstown, Damalston, Kilbegg, and Stahalmuck. 14 June 1609 he had livery of his estates, and in 1613 was present in parliament as he was again in 1615, and was rated 100l. to the subsidy which was granted 8 July that year. In the parliament which met [2] 14 July 1634 he was again present, and 17 same month was appointed a member of the committee for privileges, but being engaged in a dispute with the Lord Dunsany who challenged to have precedence of him in parliament by seniority of creation, the matter was demanded before the privy council, and the following decree was made:

" By the Lord Deputy and Council.
" WENTWORTH,
" The controversy depending between the Lord Baron of
" Trimleston and the Lord Baron of Dunsany for precedency,
" being this day fully heard at this board, in presence of both
" parties and their council; for as much as the said Lord of
" Trimleston did show before us at this board, letters patent
" under the great seal of England, dated 4 March, in the 2
" year of K. Edward IV. by which the honour and dignity of
" Lord Baron of Trimleston was granted to his lineal ancestor
" Robert Barnewall, and the heirs male of his body, whose heir
" the now Lord Trimleston is admitted to be, without contra-
" diction; and for as much as the Lord of Dunsany did not
" (though several days were given him for his preparation
" therein) prove before us by letters patent, writ of parliament,
" summons, or by any other record, precedent to the said let-
" ters patent of the Lord of Trimleston, that his ancestors were
" Lords Barons of Dunsany before the date of the said letters
" patent of the 2 of Edward IV. We therefore, having taken
" the premisses into mature consideration, and being required
" and authorised by his Majesty, by commission under the great
" seal of England, to hear and determine all differences of this
" kind, do order, adjudge and decree, that the said Lord of
" Trimleston, and the heirs male of his body, being Lords of
" Trimleston, shall, according to the tenour of the said letters
" patent, 2 of Edward IV. from time to time and at all times for
" ever

[1] Inq. post mortem D. Petri.   [2] Lords Jour. I. 2.

to Sir Patrick Barnewall of Crickstown, who was knighted 28 February 1585, and served that year in Sir John Perrot's

"ever hereafter, and in all places, assemblies and meetings, as
"well in parliament as elsewhere, precede and take place, and
"in commissions, Rolls of parliament, and other records, in-
"struments, evidences, muniments, writings, and escripts what-
"soever, be ranked, placed, and marshalled before the now
"Lord and all the succeeding Lords of Dunsany from hence-
"forth; provided always, that whensoever the Lord of Dun-
"sany shall produce better matter of record than now he hath
"done before us, or before any other authorised in that point
"by his Majesty, his heirs or successors, whereby the now
"Lord Baron of Dunsany, or his heirs being Lords of Dunsany
"shall sufficiently prove they ought to precede the Lord of
"Trimleston, and his said heirs in the dignity, place and de-
"gree of a Lord Baron of Parliament, that then this order and
"decree shall not bar nor impeach the said proof, and better
"matter, but the same shall stand good and valid, notwith-
"standing this our order and decree. Given at his Majesty's
"Castle of Dublin, ult. July 1634.

"Ad. Loftus, Chancellor; Ja. Armagh; Ran. Tuam; Moore; Claneboy; Conway and Kilulta; R. Canelagh; R. Dillon; Jo. Rapho; Fra. Mountnorris; Geo. Shurley; Geo. Radcliffe [1]."

In the second session of 22 November 1634, his Lordship was a member of the committee for privileges [2], but 16 March following had leave to go into the country on account of his age and known infirmities [3]. He died at Trimleston 13 October, or December, 1639, and was there buried, having had issue by his said wife, Genet Talbot, five sons and nine daughters, viz. Christopher, his heir apparent, who died before him but left issue; John; Patrick (who married first Catharine, daughter of Robert Barnewall of Brymore; and secondly Catharine, daughter of Matthew King); Richard; Matthew; daughter Mary, married to Robert Barnewall of Shankill in the county of Dublin, Esq. Catharine; Ismay; and six others whose names are not recovered.

Christopher Barnewall, Esq. the eldest son, married first Elizabeth, daughter of Sir Edward Fitz-Gerald of Tecroghan, Knt. and she dying 13 September 1619, he married secondly, in July 1621, Jane, daughter of Andrew Brereton, relict of Sir Robert Nugent, Knt. by her he had no issue, and deceased before his father 8 May 1622, leaving issue by his first wife three sons and two daughters, viz. Matthias, successor to his grandfather; Christopher; George; Bridget, married to Christopher Cusack of Ardgragh in the county of Meath, Gent.; and Jane.

Christopher.

Matthias,

[1] Lord's Jour. I. 96.   [2] Idem. 32.   [3] Idem. 59.

rot's parliament for the county of Meath, whose son Sir Richard, by Elizabeth, daughter of Sir Oliver Plunket of Rathmore,

Matthias. Matthias, *the eighth Lord*, was 25 years of age at his accession to the honour; 18 March 1639 he took his seat in parliament [1], and 12 November following was added to the committee of grievances [2]. On 2 December 1640 he had a special livery of his estate for the fine of 150l. but 17 November 1641 was outlawed in the county of Meath, whereby the honour became forfeited, and the privileges of Peerage lost to the family, according to the resolution of the House of Lords in 1695, " That such Lords " whose ancestors, or themselves, stand outlawed on record, " ought not to have a privilege of sitting in this House, or to " take upon them on any occasion any title of honour." He served against Cromwell and the English parliament, for which he was excepted from pardon for life and estate 12 August 1652, by the act then passed for the settlement of Ireland, but surviving these distracted times, he was restored as a nominee to part of his estates, viz. the principal mansion and 2000 acres of land, and also 21 May 1667, had a grant under the acts of settlement of his principal house and lands of Rabuck in the county of Dublin, and of Earlstown and others in the county of Meath.---Before 1641 he married Jane, daughter of Nicholas, the first Viscount Netterville, and by her had issue two sons, Robert, his successor; Nicholas who died of a jaundice at the age of 19 years; and a daughter Alison, married to Martin Dillon of Huntstown in the county of Dublin, Esq.

Robert. Robert, *the ninth Lord*, had also a grant of lands under the acts of settlement [3], and another under the act of grace, by K. James II. [4]; he had a pension of 100l. a year in the reign of K. Charles II. which was continued upon the establishment commencing 1 May 1687; he sat in K. James's parliament of 1689, and died in June that year. He married Margaret, daughter of Sir John Dongan. Bart. sister to William, Earl of Limerick, and by her (who died 5 November 1678, and was buried at Trimleston under a tombstone, with an inscription imparting the time of her decease) had issue two sons and five daughters, viz. Matthias and John, successive Lords of Trimleston; Jane, who died at the age of 13 years; Bridget (married to Christopher Nugent of Dardistown in the county of Westmeath, Colonel of an Irish regiment, and a Major-general in the service of France); Dymna (pursuant to articles dated 6 June 1697 with 1200l. fortune, to Richard Shee of Sheestown in the county of Kilkenny, Esq.); Catharine, to Nicholas Barnewall of Bughstown and Woodpark in the county of Meath, Esq.; and Mary, to Michael Nugent of Carlanstown in the county of Westmeath, Esq. she died at Bath in 1740.

Matthias,

[1] Lords Jour. T. 101.   [2] Idem. 142.
[3] Rot. Anno 29 Car. II. 3ª. p. f.   [4] Idem. 1 Jac. II.

Rathmore, was father of Sir Patrick Barnewall, created a Baronet by patent, dated 21 February 1622, and died 21 June

Matthias, *the tenth Lord*, was aged 16 or 17 years at the death of his father, he was a Lieutenant in the first troop of guards, under the Duke of Berwick, in the service of K. James II. in which station he lost his life in September 1692, in an action against the Germans, and dying unmarried was succeeded by his brother

John, *the eleventh Lord*, who was born in 1672, and his brother having been attainted, the estates were granted by K. William to Henry, Lord Sydney, created Earl of Romney, which estates, by due course of law, his Lordship afterwards recovered, and they are still enjoyed by the family. He married Mary, only daughter of Sir John Barnewall, second son of Sir Patrick Barnewall of Crickston, Bart, by his wife Thomazine, daughter of Anthony, Viscount Tarah, and deceased 7 April 1746 [1], having issue four daughters and six sons, viz. Thomazine (married 9 February 1729 to Jenico, Viscount Gormanston); Margaret (in January 1736, to James, Viscount Mountgarret); Bridget (to Robert Martin, Esq. son to Anthony of Dangan, in the county of Galway, and at length heir to his brother Richard Martin, she died 2 February 1764 in Britain-street Dublin); Catharine died of the small pox in 1741, æt. 16 years; Robert, the eldest son, succeeded his father; John (married in France in 1740, to Lady Waters, with a considerable fortune); Richard (who married Frances, second daughter of Nicholas, third Viscount Kingsland, and by her, who died 19 March 1735, had Nicholas, John, and Henry); Thomas, in the service of France, where he resided and married; James in the Spanish service; and Anthony, who went into Germany in his 17 year, and of whom the following account was given in a letter from a General in the Imperial service to the late Viscount Mountgarret; "Amongst all those brave men who have lost their lives at the battle of Crotzka, none is so much lamented by all as Mr. Anthony Barnewall, the Lord Trimleston's youngest son: he came into Germany in General Hamilton's regiment of cuirassiers, when his good sense, humility, good nature, and truly honest worthy principles, gained him the love and esteem of all who had the least acquaintance with him; we have had scarce any action of any note with the Turks that he was not in, and always acquitted himself with uncommon resolution; the day before the said battle he was made a Lieutenant, the next fatal day the regiment in which he had his commission was one of the first that charged the enemy; at the very first onset his captain and cornet were killed, when he took up the standard, tore off the flag, tied it round his waist, and commanded the troop; he led out twice to the charge, and was as often repulsed;

John.

[1] His will proved 11 April 1746.

June 1624); Elizabeth, (to Edward Barnewall of Drumenagh, Esq. by whom she had two sons, Marcus and Peter); and Catharine, (to James Everard of Randlestown in the county of Meath, Esq. and had issue ¹).

Sir Christopher.
Sir Christopher Barnewall of Turvey, Gracedieu and Fieldston, was also bred to the profession of the law, (in which many of the name have been very eminent) was appointed by the Earl of Ormond, 12 June in 2 and 3 years of Philip and Mary, his seneschal of the manors of *Much-Turvey*, &c. and 23 August 1560 constituted sheriff of the county of Dublin; and (as Hollinshed writes) " was the " lanthorn and light as well of his house, as of that part " of Ireland where he dwelt; who being sufficiently fur- " nished as well with the knowledge of the Latin tongue, " as of the common laws of England, was zealously bent " to the reformation of his country. A deep and a wise " gentleman, spare of speech, and therewithall pithie; " wholly

" pulsed; the third time he turned himself to his men, and said, " Come on, my brave fellows, we shall certainly now do the " work, follow me---he then set spurs to his horse and pursued " into the thickest of the enemy, where he was surrounded, de- " fending himself for a considerable time with amazing courage, " at last he fell quite covered with wounds, and dying left such " an example of true courage and bravery, as cannot fail of being " admired by all who shall hear of it." This happened in September 1739:

Robert.
Robert, *the twelfth Lord*, resided many years in France, and became very eminent for his skill in the practice of physick; after his return to Ireland he resided at Trimleston, and freely communicated his advice to all who applied for it. He married first Margaret, daughter of James Rochfort of Lorragh in the county of Kildare, Esq. and secondly Elizabeth, daughter of Mr. Colt of England, by both of whom he had issue; he had ten children by the first wife of whom three died infants, and the survivors were John and James who died unmarried; Matthias, who conformed to the established protestant religion, but died unmarried in London in February 1766; Thomas heir to his father; daughter Mary, died unmarried; Alice, who resided at Paris; and Marianne who died unmarried.

Thomas.
Thomas, *the thirteenth Lord*, and a Knight of Malta, who upon the death of his brother Matthias conformed to the established protestant religion; on the decease of his father he became possessed of the family estates, and whilst an invasion was apprehended in 1779 and 1780 he enrolled himself amongst and became a distinguished member of the Irish Volunteer army ².

¹ Ulster.   ² Extracted from Mr. Lodge's MS. Collect.

"wholly addicted to gravity; very upright in dealing, measuring all his affairs with the safety of conscience; as true as still; close and secret; fast to his friend; stout in a good quarrel; a great housholder; sparing without pinching; spending without wasting; of nature mild, rather chusing to pleasure where he might harm, than willing to harm where he might pleasure." He sickened at his seat of Turvey 23 July of a hot burning ague, and ended his life 5 (or ⁱ rather 7) August 1575, * one of his sons-in-law composing this epitaph on the occasion:

> Læta tibi, sed mæsta tuis, Mors accidit ista,
>   Regna dat alta tibi, Damna dat ampla tuis.
> Lætus es in Cœlis, ullo sine fine triumphans,
>   Mæstus at in Terris Dives inopsque jacet.
> Nam Sapiente caret Dives, qui parta gubernet,
>   Nec, qui det Misero, Munera, pauper habet.
> Te Gener ipse caret, Viduæ, Te rustica turba,
>   Atque urbana cohors, te (Socer-alme) caret.
> Non est digna Viro talis Respublica tanto,
>   Nam sanctos Sedes non nisi sancta decet.
> Mira loquor, sed vera loquor, non ficta revolvo,
>   Si Majora loquar, nil nisi vera loquar.
> Mortuus es? Nobis hoc Crimina nostra dederunt.
>   Mortuus es; Virtus hoc tibi sacra dedit.
> Vivus es in Cœlo? Dedit hoc tibi Gratia Christi.
>   Vivus ut in Mundo sis, tibi Fama dabit.

He lies buried near the upper end of the North aile of the church of Luske, under a large monument, adorned with the effigies of himself and Lady, and these inscriptions:

> On the Pillow at the West end,
> Soli Laudes Deo.
> Si. Deus. Nobiscum. quis. contra. Nos.
> On the East End of the Tomb,
> This Monument is made for the Right
> Worshipfull Sr. Christopher Barnewall of
> Turvey, Knight, by the Right Worshipfull
> Sr. Luckas Dillon of Moymet, Knight, and

Deam

---

* As appears from a testimonial produced by Sir Patrick his son, to prove the time of his father's death. (Rot. Anno 29 Eliz. D. R. 2.)

ⁱ Holingshed's Chronicle.

Deam Marion Sharl his wife, who married
Herr three years after the Deathe of the
faid Sr. Chriftopher, herr firft and loving
Hoofbande, who had Iffu 5 Sonnes and
15 Dacthers by hem.
 Wifh well to Dillon, 1589.

On the North fide are the names of the children; and
at the Weft end;

 Chriftopher Barnewall.
 Marion Sharl.

She was daughter of Patrick Cherlis, otherwife Sherle of
Shallon in Meath, Efq. and fifter and heir to John Serle,
Efq.*, and died 8 January 1607, having the faid iffue,
who were

(1) Sir Patrick, his heir.
(2) Laurence, who died without iffue.
(3) James, died young.
(4) John, of Flemingfton, and of Monkftown in Meath, where he made his will 10 October 1598, and died 10 May 1599, leaving by Cicely, daughter of Henry Cufack, Alderman of Dublin, and widow of Chriftopher, Lord Howth, an only fon Patrick, whom he committed to the care of his brother-in-law John Draicot, and his coufin Richard Barnewall; the value of whofe marriage was granted 29 May 1629 to Sir Philip Perceval, for the fine of 60l. Irifh.
(1) Daughter Catharine, married to Thomas Finglas of Weftpalfton, Efq.
(2) Margaret, the firft wife of Nicholas, Lord Howth.
(3) Genet, to Richard Stanihurft of Court Duffe, Efq. hiftoriographer of Ireland, (fon of James Stanihurft, Efq. Recorder of Dublin) who died at Bruffels in 1618.
(4) Alifon, firft to John, fon of George, and grandfon to Sir John Plunket of Beaulieu, and by him, who died before his father, had no iffue; and fecondly to Sir Edward Fitz-Gerald of Tecroghan in Meath, Knt. whofe fon by her, Sir Luke, married Mary, daughter of Nicholas, Vifcount Netterville.

 Elizabeth,

---

* The wardfhip of her body and lands had been granted upon her brother's death to Patrick Barnewall, father of the faid Sir Chriftopher, then of Gracedieu, and a ferjeant at law, for the fine of 20l. Irifh, 5 February 1555. (Rot. Anno 37 Hen. VIII. f.)

Elizabeth, to John Finglas of Westpalston, Esq. where (5)
she died 28 June 1607.

Anne, to Sir John Draicot of Mornington in Meath, (6)
Knt. (son to Henry Draicot of the same place, Esq.
master of the rolls) where she died 6 February 1639, having issue three sons and three daughters; of whom Henry
the eldest married Mary, second daughter of Oliver, the
fourth Lord Louth, by his first wife Frances, eldest daughter of Sir Nicholas Bagenal, Knight Mareschal of Ireland, and died 17 October 1624, leaving two sons, John
and Patrick; the elder of whom was born in 1611, married Elizabeth, daughter of Richard Talbot of Malahyde, Esq. and forfeited his estate on account of the rebellion.

Mable, first wife to Sir Richard Masterson of Fernes in (7)
the county of Wexford, Knt. died 24 June 1620, and had
issue by him, (who married secondly Joan, daughter of
Richard, Viscount Mountgarret [1] and deceased in 1627),
four daughters, viz. Catharine, married to Edward Butler
of Cayer, Esq.; Mary, to Walter Synnot, Esq.; Mable,
to Nicholas, son and heir to [2] Nicholas Devereux of Ballymagar, Esq. all in the said county; and Margaret, to
Robert Shee of Kilkenny, Esq.

Ismay, to Richard Delahyde of Moyclare, Esq. (8)

Eleanor, to James, the first Earl of Roscomon, and died (9)
11 October 1628.

Maud, married to Richard Belinge, Esq. (10)

Mary, married to Patrick, Lord Dunsany. (11)

Mary, ⎫ (12)
Alison, ⎪ (13)
Marian, and ⎬ died young. (14)
Anne. ⎭ (15)

Sir Patrick Barnewall, the eldest son, of Turvey and of Sir
Gracedieu * brought to the general hosting at the hill of Patrick.
Tarah

---

* In 1590 the Queen granted him a lease for 60 years of the lands
of Ardnesaddan, Corbally, Uranbegg, Knocknemanagh, Clonkrane, &c. parcel of the possessions of the monastery of Knockmoy,
at the rent of 31l. 7s. 9d. and also the lands and inheritance of the
house of Augustine friars of St. Dominick in Birmingham's country, at the rent of 1l. 11s. 8d. before which time having a lease for
21 years of the preceptory of Kilmaynham-begg in the county of
Meath, at the rent of 50 marcs, in reversion after the expiration of
a former lease thereof made to Sir John Rawson, Knight, prior of
the

---

[1] Ulster.   [2] Lodge.   [3] Idem.

Tarah 24 September 1593, one archer on horseback for his lands of Turvey, and four for Gracedieu, in defence of the county of Dublin.—He married Mary, daughter of Sir Nicholas Bagenal, Knight Marefchal of Ireland, by his wife Eleanor, daughter and coheir to Sir Edward Griffith of Penthern in Wales, Knt. and departing this life 11 January 1622, had iffue by her, who died 10 April 1609, and was buried with him in Lufke, Sir Nicholas his heir, and four daughters.

(1) —— married to colonel Rory (Roger) More of Ballyna in the county of Kildare, defcended from the great family of O More of Leix, and had iffue.

(2) Mable, to Lucas, fecond fon of Nicholas, the firft Vifcount Netterville.

(3) Eleanor, to Chriftopher, fon of William, Lord Slane, and dying in 1625, was mother by him, who died 9 June 1635, of William, or Thomas, Lord Slane, then 21 years old, who married the Lady Anne Mac-Donnell, daughter of Randal, Earl of Antrim.

(4) Bridget, to James, third fon of William, Lord Slane, and brother to the faid Lord Chriftopher, by whom fhe had Sir John Fleming of Stoholmuck in Meath, Knt.

Nicholas, 1 Vifcount.

Nicholas Barnewall of Turvey, Efq. was 30 years old at the time of his father's death; reprefented the county of Dublin the late hofpital of St. John of Jerufalem; John, Lord Trimlefton; and William Penteny, Vicar of Moorchurch, her Majefty was pleafed, on account, (as fhe writes) of the commendation made of him for his good difpofition and loyalty, to fend her warrant from Windfor 12 November 1582, for the L. J. to make him a new leafe, without fine, for 60 years, to commence upon the determination of the aforefaid leafe, referving the yearly ufual rents.—And K. James, 16 September 1616, granted to him by patent the rectories and tithes of Clane and Clonfhamboe, with the tithe-corn of Kilcock parifh, in the county of Kildare; the diffolved monafteries of Clontwoyfkert in O Hanley's country, and Kilmore near the Shannon; with the rectories and tithes of Clontwoyfkert, Kilglaffe, Kilkevine, Killmore, and Killetovan; the Eel-weares in the Shannon, and other hereditaments in the county of Rofcomon; the rectory and tithe-corn of Garretton in the county of Dublin: the rectory and tithes of Girly, &c. in the county of Meath, with all their appurtenances to hold by fealty. And the King likewife eftablifhed a ferry, to be kept at the town of Beallalegee in the county of Rofcomon, acrofs the Shannon to the King's fort in the county of Longford, every paffenger to pay one penny; for every beaft, every fix fheep, fwine or goats one penny, and for every barrel of corn a halfpenny: which ferry and boats he conferred on Sir Patrick and his heirs, at the yearly rent of 13s. 4d. with liberty to hold a Saturday market, and two fairs there, on Trinity-Monday and the Feaft of St. Simon and Jude, and two days after each, at the rent of 20 fhillings Irifh. (Lodge.)

Dublin in the parliament of K. Charles I. and in November 1641, after the rebellion was begun, had a commission to govern and command such forces, as should be raised by him and armed by the state, for the defence of the county of Dublin [1]; but dreading the designs of the Irish, he fled into Wales with his wife, several priests, and others, and stayed there till after the cessation of arms was concluded, returning 17 March 1643 in captain Bartlett's ship *.— And " the King being sensible of his loyalty, and taking " special notice both of his services in Ireland, and those " of his son Patrick in England, was pleased, for their further encouragement, to set some mark of his special grace and favour upon him, and to create him Baron of Turvey and Viscount Barnewall of Kingsland by privy seal, dated at Ragland 12 September 1645, [2] and by patent at Dublin 29 June 1646 [3] †.—He married Bridget, elder

---

* In the company of Susanna, wife of George Stockdale, Gent. and she being of his near kindred, asked him, why these gentlemen of the pale, that were anciently descended of the English, could for piety rob and destroy the English protestants as they did? thereunto he answered, that the poor Irish had the blame of all, but if the papists in England had but had as much power among themselves in England as the Irish had in Ireland, the English papists would have risen against the English protestants first, so as the poor Irish, as he called them, should not have been put to begin their quarrel here the first; adding, do you think, cousin, that the Irish durst begin as they did, but that they conceived themselves sure of the like rising about the same time in England, according to the plot that the papists of both kingdoms had among them, so as there could come no aid or assistance out of England to the protestants in Ireland, or to that effect. And Job. Ward, Esq. in his deposition says, that the said Mr. Barnewall gave the best and truest intelligence out of England, and was very intimately acquainted with some that were near the Queen, who assured him that none of the King's ships would appear upon these coasts until that ammunition, which the Irish expected daily out of France and Spain, should be first come to them, to which, or the like purpose, he had seen letters signed Nicholas Barnewall. (Deposition of Susanna wife of Geo. Stockdale, Gent. and Lodge.)

† The preamble. Nos serio animadvertentes bona et pergrata Officia Nobis et Coronæ nostræ, tam per fidelem atque nobis dilectum Nicholaum Barnewall de Turvy in comitatu Dublin in Regno nostro Hiberniæ Armigerum, in dicto Regno nostro Hiberniæ in propria persona sua, quam per Filium suum Patricium Barnewall Turmæ Equitum præfectum in Regno nostro Angliæ, præstita; nosque volentes præfatum Nicholaum Barnewall pro justo Merito in hoc Regno, ac etiam pro bono Merito predicti Patricii in Servitio nostro

---

[1] Temple, p. 51.   [2] Rot. Anno 19, 20, 21, 22, 23, 24. f. R. 17.
[3] Idem. D. R. 37.

elder daughter and coheir to Henry, the twelfth Earl of Kildare, widow of Rory O Donnel, Earl of Tyrconnel, and deceasing at Turvey 20 August 1663, [1] was buried 3 September, pursuant to the direction of his will, proved 11 September following [2]. "in the ancient monument of his forefathers in the church of Luske, in decent and competent order, according to his degree and calling." And after his funeral charges paid, wills all his personal estate, debts, goods, and chattles, for the payment and satisfaction of his debts, and if they failed, the remainder to be discharged out of the lands which he had already ordered for paying the same [2].—His Issue were five sons and four daughters, viz.

(1) Christopher, who died unmarried.

(2) Colonel Patrick Barnewall, whose services are mentioned in the preamble to his father's patent, died in England, unmarried.

(3) Henry, who succeeded to the honours.

(4) Francis, of Begstown and of Woodpark in the county of Meath, where he resided in 1667, who married first Jane, daughter and heir to Philip Fitz-Gerald of Alloone in the county of Kildare, Esq. by whom he had a son Nicholas; and secondly Mariana, daughter and heir to Richard Perkins of Lifford in Donegall, Esq. who died in February 1672 [4], and by her had issue Richard, Francis, Matthew, Patrick, Mary, Bridget, and Elizabeth.—He died 6 January 1697, and was buried the 7 at Luske, being succeeded by his son Nicholas, who married Catharine, fourth daughter of Robert, and sister to John, Lord Trimleston, and had several sons and daughters; several of the former went into foreign service.

(5) Matthew died unmarried 14 June 1668, and was buried the 16 at Luske [5].

(1) Daughter Mary, was married to Nicholas, the sixth Viscount Gormanston, and died in May 1642 at Alloone in the county of Kildare [6].

Mable,

nostro in Regno nostro Angliæ, Favoris nostri Charactere ornandum. Sciatis igitur, &c.——Cromwell, by his letter, dated at Whitehall 23 September 1658, directed, that his house at Turvey and 500l. a year of his estate should be sett to him, until the parliament's resolution concerning him was known; which was accordingly done 4 February 1658.

[1] Missal. penes Dom. Kingsland.   [2] Lodge.
[3] Prerog. Office.   [4] Lodge.
[5] Calendar of a Missal. penes Lord Kingsland.
[6] See title Ludlow.

Mable, married in January 1636 to Christopher, the second Earl of Fingall, died at Beggstown 1 February 1699, and was buried the 4 at Killeen [1]. (2)

Eleanor, married to Charles White of Leixlip, Esq. (3)

Frances, died unmarried, and was buried at Luske. (4)

Henry, the second Viscount Kingsland, on 17 May 1671 had a release of the quit-rents, imposed by the acts of settlement, and in 1685 a grant of lands under the act of grace.—He married to his first wife in 1661 Mary, eldest daughter of John, the second Viscount Netterville, and by her, who died 28 October 1663, and was buried at Luske, he had an only child Marian, born 26 March 1662, and married to Thomas, Lord Riverston, whose widow she died 16 September 1735 [2].—He took to his second wife 11 December 1664 the Lady Mary Nugent, eldest daughter of Richard, Earl of Westmeath [3], and dying worn out with age and sickness, 1 June 1688, was buried the 3 at Luske, having issue by her, who was born 21 February 1648 [4], deceased 25 June 1680, and was there interred, four sons and three daughters, viz. Nicholas his successor; Richard, born 7 August 1675, died at Turvey 4 June 1746, and was buried the 7 in St. Machin's church at Luske; Joseph, born 25 April 1677, was living in 1688; Christopher, born 22 February 1680; Mary, born 20 July 1670, was married 23 September 1687 to Thomas, Lord Howth, died 16 October 1715, and was buried at Howth; Bridget, born 6 June 1672, married to ——— Mac-Mahon, Esq.; and Mable, born 24 November 1673, was first married to Oliver, the eighth Lord of Louth, who dying in 1707, she after became second wife of Stephen Taaffe of Dowanstown, Esq. died 27 September 1710, and was buried at Duleeke [5]. Henry, 2 Viscount.

Nicholas, the third Viscount Kingsland, born 15 of April 1668, a little before his father's death, (who by age and sickness was grown very infirm, and unable to manage any affairs), being then under age, was placed in the care of Thomas, Lord Riverston, who 12 May 1688 concluded a treaty of marriage for him with Mary, youngest daughter of George, Count Hamilton, (by his wife Frances, elder daughter and coheir to Richard Jennings of Sandridge in Hertfordshire, Esq. then the wife of Richard Talbot, Nicholas, 3 Viscount.

---

[1] See title Dunsany. [2] Missal aforesaid.
[3] Articles 21 November 1660, and pursuant to a deed dated 29 same month. [4] Idem. Missal. [5] Idem. Missal.

Talbot, Earl of Tyrconnel) on the 15 of which month they were married at eight o'clock in the morning, her portion being 3000l.; and his Lordship who succeeded to an estate of 3500l. a year [1], soon after entering into the Irish army, was a captain in the Earl of Limerick's dragoons, and for his services in that station was outlawed; but upon the route at the Boyne, he went to Limerick, and continued there until the surrender thereof, [2] hence being comprehended within the articles of Limerick, he obtained a reversal of the said outlawry, as the Lords appointed to inspect the journals, found 2 December 1697 [3]. In K. William's first parliament he delivered his writ of summons 28 Oct. 1692, and took the oath of allegiance to his Majesty; but being demanded to take the oath, and make and subscribe the declaration according to the act made in England, he refused so to do, declaring it was not agreeable to his conscience. Whereupon the Lord Chancellor acquainted him, that he knew the consequence of his refusal was, that he could not sit in that house, on which his Lordship withdrew [4]; and in the session of 1703, joined with other Roman Catholicks in a petition (26 February) desiring to have the reasons heard by council, which they had to offer against passing the bill, entitled, *an act to prevent the further growth of popery*.—His Lordship departed this world 14 June 1725, and was buried the 16 in the church of Lusk, having issue by his said Lady, who died at Turvey, 15 February 1735, and was buried with him, two sons and four daughters, viz. Henry-Benedict his successor; George, (born 24 November 1711, who in April 1752 married Barbara, second daughter of Thomas, Viscount Falconberg, and died in June 1771, leaving an only son George, by his Lady, who died in London in October 1761 [5]); Elizabeth, born 31 May 1699, died unmarried at Kilkenny 15 November 1722, and was there buried; Frances, born 7 November 1700, was married to Richard Barnewall, Esq. third son of John, Lord Trimleston, and died 19 March 1735; Harriot, born 3 June 1702, died 3 November 1703; and Mary, born 12 July 1704, died 16 December following of the small-pox, and was buried at Lusk [6].

Henry-

---

[1] Chancery Decrees 14 October 1693, and 3 July 1695.
[2] Idem.   [3] Lord's Jour. I. 675.   [4] Idem. 466.
[5] Lodge.   [6] Idem. Missal.

BARNEWALL, Viscount KINGSLAND.

Henry-Benedict, the fourth Viscount Kingsland, born 1 February 1708; on the last day of the session of parliament viz. 31 March 1740 he delivered his writ of summons, and took the oath of fidelity¹, but his lordship professing the Roman Catholic religion, was disqualified from sitting in that most honourable house, or enjoying the privileges of parliament.——On 22 May 1735 he married on Arbour-hill, Honora, eldest daughter of Peter Daly of Quansbury in the county of Galway, Esq. counsellor at law, but by her who survived him and died in 1784 his Lordship had no issue, and he deceasing at Quansbury 11 March 1774, was succeeded in the honours by his said nephew

Henry-Benedict, 4 Viscount.

George, the fifth and present Viscount, who was born 12 August 1758, and being early initiated in the principles of the protestant religion, as by law established, took the oaths, and was admitted to his seat in the House of Peers 18 January 1787.

George, 5 Viscount.

TITLES.] George Barnewall, Viscount Barnewall of Kingsland, and Baron of Turvey, both in the county of Dublin.

CREATIONS.] So created 29 June 1646, 22 Car. I.

ARMS.] Ermine, a bordure ingrailed, ruby.

CREST.] On a wreath, a plume of five feathers, topaz, ruby, saphire, emerald and pearl, and thereon a falcon, with wings disclosed of the last.

SUPPORTERS.] The dexter, a gryphon, pearl; the sinister, a lion, ruby.

MOTTO.] MALO MORI QUAM FÆDARI.

SEAT.] Turvey, in the county of Dublin, 8 miles from the metropolis. This seat was built in 1565, as appears from the arms, and this inscription over the West gate;

The arms of Sir Christopher Barnewall and Dame Marion Sherle, alias Churly, who made this House in *Anno* 1565

¹ Lords Jour. III. 495

VOL. V. CHOLMONDELEY.

CHOLMONDELEY, Viscount KELLS.

THIS noble family is denominated from the Lordship of CHOLMONDELEY in the hundred of Broxton and county of Chester, and the name (like others of great antiquity) hath been so variously written, that some have enumerated 25 several ways.—In Domesday-book (which contains a survey of all England, made by the Conqueror's order, except the four counties of Westmoreland, Cumberland, Northumberland, and Durham) it is written Calmundelei, and was then part of the possessions of Robert Fitz-Hugh, Baron of Malpas. Which Fitz-Hugh also held in Cestrescire, as the same book testifies, 29 other manors, which are there specified.—But, the said Robert dying without issue male, the barony of Malpas, with the Lordship of Calmundelei, &c. devolved on his only daughter Lettice, married to William le Belward (son of John le Belward, who lived in the time of William Rufus) and by him, who was living 12 Hen. I. had William le Belward de Malpas, possessed in her right of half the barony of Malpas, who married Beatrix, daughter of Hugh Kivilioc, the fifth Earl of Chester, and coheir to her brother Earl Randal, and by her left three sons, David; Robert, hereafter mentioned; and Richard, who had a grant of one eighth part of Duckenton, otherwise Dochintode.

David, who was styled Dan-David, and from being clerk or secretary to the Earl of Chester, sometimes was written Le Clerc, and sometimes de Malpas, where he succeeded his father, and after the Earldom of Chester was annexed to the crown, was sheriff of Cheshire 36 Hen. III. of which county he was also justice, and held three Knight's fees in the said King's reign. He married Margaret, daughter and heir to Ralph Ap-Enyon, a person of great note and large possessions in Cheshire and Wales, by his wife Beatrix, sister to the aforesaid Hugh, Earl of Chester, and thereby became possessed of the entire barony of Malpas,

viz.

viz. one half by descent, and the other in right of his wife, by whom he left four sons, viz.

Sir William de Malpas, who died without issue. (1)

Philip, surnamed Gough (or, the Red) who obtained the (2) manor of Egerton near Malpas from Wion de Egerton, and residing there, did, according to the custom of that age, leave that surname to his posterity, the flourishing family of Egerton.

Peter, who took the name of Clerc, and his descend- (3) ants, by that name, became seated at Thornton, 'till they terminated in the reign of Edward III. in six coheirs; viz. Ellen, married to Sir Thomas Dutton of Dutton; Elizabeth, to Hamon Fitton; Maud, to Henry de Beeston; Margaret, to Sir William de Golbourne; Beatrix, to Thomas de Shamesbury; and Emma, to Hugh de Weverham.

David, was Lord of Golbourne, from whence he took (4) his name, and left posterity, of whom was Sir William, just mentioned.

Robert, the second son of William, Baron of Malpas, Robert. by the Earl of Chester's daughter, was ancestor to the Earl of Cholmondeley; for, having that Lordship by gift of his father, and fixing his residence there, he assumed that surname, which his spreading and flourishing descendants retained.—He married Mabel, daughter of Robert Fitz-Nigel, Baron of Halton, with whom he had the Lordship of Cristleton, and a release of the hospital of Cholmondeley, being father by her of Sir Hugh de Chol- Sir Hugh. mondeleigh, who had a release from Randal, Earl of Chester, for himself and his heirs, of all right of suits of court and justice, owing to the hundred of Broxtone for his lands in Cholmondeley. By Felice, natural daughter of Randal Blundville, Earl of Chester and Lincoln, he had issue Robert, Richard, and Felice; the eldest of whom, in several old deeds is written Robert, Lord of Cholmon- Robert. deley, and by charter gave two bovates of land with the appurtenances in Christleton, to the abbey of Chester, with his body to be buried in the church-yard of St. Werburgh.—He married Beatrix, daughter of Urian St.-Piere, or (as some say) of David le Clerc, Lord of half the barony of Malpas, and sister to Idona, the wife of the said Urian, by whom he had Richard his heir, who, in a deed Richard. without date, is written Lord of Cholmondeley, wherein he grants to Hugh his heir all his land in Cholmondeley, Wythall and other places.

Which

Hugh.	Which Hugh married Margery, sister and coheir to Richard de Kingsley, and daughter of Sir Richard, Lord of Kingsley, &c. great-grandson of Randal de Kingsley, who had the forestership of Delamer given him by Randal, the first Earl of Chester of that name, and by her, who survived him, had several daughters and three sons, where-
Hugh.	of Hugh the eldest is mentioned in several deeds in the reign of Edw. I; and 6 Edw. II. being in the commission of the peace, he was present at the castle of Chester, when David le Cooper was executed for burglary, committed at Cholmondeley and Burwardesley.—He married Catharine, daughter of William de Spurstow, and left issue four sons, Richard his heir; William, hereafter mentioned; Robert of Chorley; and Thomas, who writes himself son of Hugh de Cholmondeleigh in a charter, dated at Burton the Friday after the feast of St. Hillary 1325, whereby he granted to John de Burton, chaplain, all his estate in Burton near Turvyn, which he had received from Hugh, son of Richard, son of Simon de Burton.
Families of Chorley and Whitby.	Robert Cholmondeley of Chorley, the third son, by his wife Alice left two sons, William, who died childless; and John, who succeeded his brother at Chorley, Anno 4 Hen. IV. and, with his son Robert, 9 Hen. V. grants to Margaret, wife of Edmond de Munsale a moiety of the village of Wyncham. He married a daughter of Sir Robert Needham of Shenton, and was ancestor to John Cholmondeley of Chorley and of Goldeston, Esq. who by Joan, daughter and heir to Thomas Eyton of Goldeston, had two sons, Sir Richard; and Sir Roger, ancestor to the family at Whitby.

Sir Richard Cholmondeley, the elder son, distinguished for the valour and conduct he shewed on several occasions in the reigns of Henry VII. and VIII. was knighted in 1497 (12 Hen. VII.) by the Earl of Surry, for his services against the Scots, who had received and assisted Perkin Warbeck; was constituted lieutenant of Berwick, and some time after governor of Kingston upon Hull; the forces of which garrison he commanded (5 Hen. VIII.) at the battle of Floden, wherein James IV. King of Scotland was slain, and so serviceable was his conduct that day, that he was made lieutenant of the tower of London, and received a letter of thanks from the King, dated 27 November at Windsor.—26 December 1521 he made his will, and dying that Year, was buried in the church of St. Peter *ad Vincula*

CHOLMONDELEY, Viscount KELLS.

Vincula within the tower, under a monument, thus circumscribed;

> Jacent Corpora Richardi Cholmondeley Militis, et Dominæ Elisabethæ Conjugis Suæ. Qui —— Quorum Animabus Deus Propitietur. Amen.

He left no legitimate issue, but had a natural son Roger Cholmondeley of Lincoln's-Inn, who became Chief Justice of the King's Bench 21 March 1551 (6 Edw. VI.) and about the year 1564 built and endowed a free grammar school at Highgate in Middlesex, in the disposition of six governors, and not long after died, leaving two daughters his coheirs; Elizabeth, first married to Leonard Beckwith of Selbie in Yorkshire (whose son Roger married Elizabeth, daughter of Sir Richard Cholmondeley, Knt. and sold Selbie to the Earl of Derby) and secondly to Christopher Kenn, Esq.; and Frances was first wife to Sir Thomas Russel of Strentham in Worcestershire.

Sir Roger Cholmondeley, brother to Sir Richard, was buried in the South aile of St. Dunstan's church in the West, under a marble tomb, with this memorial;

> Here lyeth the Bodie of Sir Roger Cholmondeley, Knight for the Bodie to Kinge Henric the 8th. Which Sir Roger deceased the 28th. day of April Anno Dom. 1538.

His wife was Catharine, daughter of Sir Robert Constable of Flamborough in Yorkshire, and his issue were four sons and three daughters, Sir Richard; Marmaduke; Roger; Henry; Margaret, married to Henry Gascoigne of Sudbury, Esq.; Elizabeth; and Jane.—Sir Richard, the eldest son, of Thornton and of Raxby, was appointed constable of Scarborough-castle 2 Edw. VI. in whose first year, and 3 and 4 Phil. and Mary, he was sheriff of the county of York, and married to his first wife Margaret, daughter of William, Lord Conyers, by whom he had three sons; Francis of Raxby, (who married Joan, daughter and coheir to Sir Ralph Bulmer of Wilton in Cleveland, and died without issue in 1586); Roger of Bransby, (who married Jane, eldest daughter and coheir to Thomas Delaverer of Bransby, Esq. and left Marmaduke his heir; Richard; Thomas; William; Catharine, married to Leonard

nard Chamberlaine; Alice; and Elizabeth. Marmaduke, the eldest son living at Bransbie in 1584 married Ursula, daughter and heir to Ralph Aislabie of South-Dalton, Esq. and was ancestor to the family of Bransby, whereof Marmaduke, married Catharine, daughter of Sir Philip Hungate of Saxton, Bart.); and Richard, the youngest, married Thomazin, another daughter and coheir to the said Thomas Delaverer, and had two sons and three daughter, Richard, John, Catharine, Dorcas, and Elizabeth.—The second wife of Sir Richard was Catharine, eldest daughter of Henry Clifford, the first Earl of Cumberland, by Margaret, daughter of Philip Percy the fifth Earl of Northumberland; widow of John, Lord Scrope of Bolton, and by her he had Sir Henry Cholmondeley of Grandmount, in 1584, and also of Raxby in 1586; and two daughters, Margaret, married to James Strangeways of Orm and Sneton, Esq.; and Catharine, to Sir Richard Dutton of Whitby.—Sir Henry married Margaret, daughter of Sir William Babthorpe, Knt. and had Sir Richard, Henry, Catharine, and Margaret. Sir Richard the eldest son, born in 1580, was sheriff of Yorkshire in the last year of K. James I. and had Hugh his heir; and Margaret the first wife of Sir William Strickland of Boynton, Bart. by whom she had four daughters. Sir Hugh Cholmondeley of Whitby was created a Baronet 10 August 1641, and by the Lady Anne Compton, eldest daughter of Spencer, Earl of Northampton, had Sir William Cholmondeley, Bart. who married Catharine, third daughter of John Savile of Methley in Yorkshire, Esq. (by Margaret his second wife, daughter of Sir Henry Garraway, Lord Mayor of London), and by her, who re-married with Sir Nicholas Stroud of Westerham in Kent, Knt. where she died, and was buried at Chevening 11 December 1710, had only daughters his coheirs, the eldest of whom Elizabeth, was married to Sir Edward Dering of Surenden, Bart. and by him, who died in 1689, had Sir Cholmondeley Dering; William; Daniel; and Cecilia.

Richard.

Richard.

We now proceed with Richard, the eldest son of Hugh Cholmondeley by Catharine Spurstow. He lived in the reigns of Edw. II. and III. and by Mabella his wife had two sons, Richard and William, the elder of whom was living 31 Edw. III. in which year, being styled Lord of Cholmundley, he claimed the privilege of holding courts for trial of all manner of pleas within his demesnes of Cholmundley and Christleton, with view of frank-pledge,

waifs,

waifs, eftrays, &c.—By his wife Maud he left a fon Rich- *Richard.*
ard, who deceafing without iffue 35 Edw. III. was fucceeded by his great-uncle William, fecond fon of Hugh de
Cholmondeley and Catharine Spurftow.

Which William married Elizabeth, daughter of Sir *William.*
William Brereton of Brereton, and was dead 49 Ed. III.
when his faid father-in-law, in confideration of 166l. 13s.
4d. payable to the King within the term of 7 years, had
the guardianfhip of his fon and heir Richard, and his marriage without difparagement; with the reverfion of the
dowry (when it fhould happen) of Maud, widow of the
late Richard de Cholmondeley. And if the faid Richard,
his grandfon, fhould die before he attained his full age,
that then he fhould have the wardfhip and marriage of Catharine and Margery, fifters of the faid Richard.—Which
Richard married firft Anne, daughter of John Bromley of *Richard.*
Badington; and fecondly Alice, daughter and coheir to
Richard de Henhull, who died 11 Rich. II. and had William de Cholmondeley, who married Maud, daughter of
Sir John Cheney of Willafton in Werrall in Chefhire (coheir to her mother Maud, daughter and coheir to Thomas
de Capenhurft) and dying in 1409 (10 Hen. IV.) before
his father, left iffue Richard; and John of Copenhall in
Staffordfhire, anceftor to the Cholmondeleys of that place,
and others.

Richard, the elder fon, 4 Edw. IV. was one of the juf- *Richard.*
tices in the county of Chefter, before whom fines were levied, as he was 2 Hen. VII. in whofe fourth year he died,
leaving by Ellen, daughter of John Davenport of Davenport, Efq. Richard his heir, a benefactor to the church of *Richard.*
Baddily, on which account his effigies, according to the
cuftom of the times, was painted in glafs, and fixed in the
higheft window on the South-fide next the chancel, kneeling before a defk, with a book thereon, his coat-armour
and this infcription underneath;

  Orate pro bono Statu———et———Richardi
  Cholmondley ————————————

He married Eleanor, fifth and youngeft daughter of Sir
Thomas Dutton of Dutton (by Anne, daughter of James,
Lord Audley) and coheir to her brother John Dutton, who
died a minor, and deceafing 9 Hen. VII. left iffue

Richard Cholmondeley, Efq. alfo one of the juftices, *Richard.*
before whom fines were levied from 17 Hen. VII. to 24
              Hen.

Hen. VIII. in whose 30 year he departed this life, æt. 43. He repaired the chancel of Cholmondeley-church, on the screen whereof his arms are cut, with this inscription;

> Orate pro bono Statu Richardi Cholmondeley Et Elizabeth Uxoris ejus, Sacelli factores. Anno Domini Millesimo Quingentesimo quarto Decimo.

His first wife was Elizabeth, daughter of Sir Roger Corbet of Morton-Corbet in Shropshire, by whom he had an only daughter Maud, married to Sir Peter Newton of Beverley, by whom she had John, Charles, and Arthur. By his second wife Elizabeth, daughter of Sir Randal Brereton of Malpas, chamberlain of Chester, who remarried with Sir Randal Manwaring of Over-Pever, he had several children, whereof Catharine was married to Richard, Prestland of Prestland and Wardhill in Cheshire, Esq.; Agnes, (to Randal Manwaring of Carington, Esq. by whom she had Henry of Kilingham, living in 1566, ancestor by Eleanor, daughter of George Venables, Esq. to the family of that place); and Ursula, to Thomas Stanley of Wever, Esq. living 1580, great-grandson of John Stanley, brother to Thomas, the first Earl of Derby, by Elizabeth, daughter and heir to Thomas Wever of Wever, Esq. and by him had Thomas, who died without issue; Ralph, who left posterity by Margaret, daughter of John Masterson of Nantwich; Elizabeth, married to Roger Downes of Shrigley; Frances, to Henry Delves of Dodington; and Dorothy.— The sons were, Hugh his heir; and Randal (or Ranulph) Cholmondeley, who being educated in the study of the laws at Lincoln's-Inn, was elected 5 Edw. VI. autumn reader of that society, but did not read because of the pestilence; the next year he was lent-reader, and in 1553 (1 and 2 Phil. and Mary) being one of the judges of the sheriffs court of London, was made recorder of that city; also 4 and 5 Phil. and Mary was chosen double reader, and 1 Eliz. treble reader of the society, whereof he was a member, being then called by her Majesty's writ to be serjeant at law. He was also chief justice of the Common-Pleas, and in the aforesaid reigns member of parliament for the city of London. He lies buried in the church of St. Dunstan in the West, under a tomb in the South aile of the choir, with this memorial;

Ranulphus

Ranulphus Cholmely clara	Hic cum Conjuge dormit,
Binaque Connubii	Corpora juncta fide,
Hæc brevis Urna tenet,	Veros disjungere Amantes,
Nec potuit Mortis	Vis truculenta nimis
Justitiâ insignis	Nulli Pietate secundus,
Ranulphus clara	Stirpe creatus erat.
Non deerant Artes	Generoso pectore dignæ
Doctus et Anglorum	Jure peritus erat.
Ille Recordator Londini	Huic extitit Urbi,
Et Miseris semper	Mite Levamen erat.
Hujus acerba Viri	Londinum funera deflet,
Dicens, Justitiæ	Vive perennis Honor.

Obiit 25 Die Aprilis An. 1563.

Sir Hugh Cholmondeley, his elder brother, was 25 years of age at his father's death, and in 1544 (36 Hen. VIII) took share in the expedition to Scotland under the Duke of Norfolk, and for his valiant behaviour received the honour of Knighthood at Leith [1].—In 1557 he raised at his own expence 100 men, to march against the Scots, under the Earl of Derby, sent in September to oppose their invasion of England.—He was a person of great honour and virtue, prudence and temperance, liberality and hospitality; and his death was generally lamented, having for 50 years together been esteemed the father of his country, by his good offices to all, who applied for his assistance or advice, which appears from many arbitrations on record, that were left to his decision.—He was four times sheriff of Cheshire, viz. in 1 Edw. VI. 2 and 3 Phil. and Mary; 8 and 31 Eliz.; and a long time one of the two deputy-lieutenants of that county: being also for some years sheriff of the county of Flint, and vice-president of the marches of Wales, in the absence of Sir Henry Sidney, L. D. of Ireland.—He died 6 January 1596, in the 83 year of his age, and lies buried in the family-chancel in the church of Malpas [2], under a noble monument of alabaster, richly adorned with the effigies of him and his lady, and other decorations.

He married first Anne, daughter and coheir to George Dolman of Malpas, by Agnes his wife, daughter and heir to Thomas Hill of the same place, Esq. and secondly Mary,

---

[1] Fuller's Worthies of the county of Chester.
[2] Idem.

ry, daughter of Sir William Griffith of Pentherne in North-Wales, widow of Sir Randal Brereton of Malpas, by whom he had no issue; but by the first had three sons, Hugh his heir; Richard and Randal, who both died childless; and one daughter Frances, married to Thomas Wilbraham of Woodhey in Cheshire, Esq. living in 1580, by whom she had two daughters, Dorothy, married to John Done, Esq.; Mary, to Sir Thomas Delves; and one son, Sir Richard Wilbraham, Knt. created a Baronet 5 May 1621, who married Grace, daughter of Sir John Savage, Knt. and his heirs general by marriage are the Earls of Bradford and Dysart.

Sir Hugh. Sir Hugh Cholmondeley of Cholmondeley, who succeeded, was knighted in the memorable year of the Spanish invasion, 1588, and at his father's decease was upwards of 46 years old. He was heir to his virtues as well as estate, and gave many proofs of an honourable benevolence, a steady adherence to the protestant religion, and a firm attachment to the interests of his country.—Before he was 21 years of age, he headed 130 men, raised by his father's interest and expence, and marched with them to assist in suppressing the rebellion in the North, begun in 1570 (12 Eliz.) by the Earls of Westmorland and Northumberland, for restoring the Romish religion; who being put to flight, they and other conspirators were attainted by parliament.—In 33 and 41 of Eliz. he was escheator of the county of Chester, as also sheriff thereof, and in 1600 (42 Eliz.) was joined in a special commission with the Lord Chancellor Egerton, Lord Treasurer Buckhurst and others, for the suppression of schism.—He increased his estate by several purchases and his marriage of Mary, daughter and heir to Christopher Holford of Holford, Esq. by Elizabeth, daughter and coheir to Sir Randal Manwaring of Pever and Badaley, elder brother to Philip, from whom descended Sir Thomas Manwaring, Bart.; and departing this life 23 July 1601, was buried with his ancestors at Malpas, having issue by her [*], who died at Holford 15 August 1625, and

---

[*] Her said father was the son and heir of Thomas Holford by his first wife Margaret, daughter of —— Butler, of Bewsey, Esq. son and heir to Sir John Holford by Margery, daughter and heir to Ralph Brereton of Iscoit in Flintshire, second son of Randal, great-grandson and heir to Sir Randal Brereton of Malpas, living 29 Hen.

[r] Fuller. ut antea.

and was buried with him, five sons and three daughters, viz.

 Robert his heir, born 16 June 1584. (1)
 Hatton, who died unmarried in London, 1605. (2)
 Hugh, who died before his eldeſt brother Robert, and is anceſtor to the Earl of Cholmondeley. (3)
 Thomas, of whom preſently. (4)
 Francis, died in his infancy. (5)
 Daughter Mary, was married to Sir George Calverley of Ley in Cheſhire, Knt. (1)
 Lettice, the firſt wife to Sir Richard Groſvenor of Eaton-Boat, Knt. and Bart. by whom ſhe had Sir Richard, the ſecond Baronet, and three daughters. (2)
 Frances, the ſecond wife to Peter Venables, Baron of Kinderton. (3)

 Thomas, the fourth ſon, became ſeated at Vale-royal in Cheſhire, of which county he was ſheriff 14 Car. I. and married Elizabeth, daughter and heir to John Minſhul of Minſhul, Eſq. by Frances his wife, eldeſt daughter of Sir John Egerton of Egerton, Knt. and dying 3 January 1652, was buried at Minſhul, having iſſue three ſons and three daughters, Thomas; Robert, who died 4 September 1658; Francis, created A. M. at Oxford 17 July 1669, and was a burgeſs to ſerve in parliament in the reign of K. William; Mary, married to Thomas, eldeſt ſon of Sir Thomas Middleton of Chirk-caſtle in Denbighſhire; Catharine, to Charles Manwaring of Ighfield, Eſq. and Elizabeth, died unmarried.—Thomas, who ſucceeded, was appointed ſheriff of Cheſhire by K. Charles II. on his reſtoration, and ſo continued the next year; being alſo one of thoſe perſons, thought qualified to be made Knights of the royal oak in 1660, an order intended by the King to
              ſeveral

Family of Vale-Royal.

Hen. VI. by his wife Alice, daughter and heir to William de Ipſton, by Maud, heir to Sir Robert Swynerton, by Elizabeth, daughter and coheir to Sir Nicholas Beake, by Jane, only daughter of Ralph, Earl of Stafford, by his ſecond wife Catharine, daughter and coheir to Sir John de Haſting of Chebſey.—Lady Cholmondeley ſpent her widowhood chiefly at Holford, which ſhe rebuilt and enlarged; and by conducting with ſpirit the great ſuit ſhe had with her uncle George Holford of Newborough in Dutton, the next heir male, concerning the eſtate, which, after it had continued for above 40 years, was compromiſed by the mediation of friends, was uſually called by K. James I. *The bold lady of Cheſhire*; and in the partition ſhe had the manors and Lordſhips of Holford, Bulkeley, and other large poſſeſſions, and he had the demeſne of Iſcoit in Flintſhire, with other lands.

several followers of his fortune, who were to wear a silver medal, with a device of the King in the oak, appendant to a ribband about their necks; but it was thought proper to lay the order aside, left it might create animosities, and open those wounds afresh, which it were more prudent to heal. In that reign and the first year of James II. he represented the county of Chester in parliament; and attending the Duke of York to the University of Oxford, was complimented 22 May 1683 with the degree of Doctor of laws.—He married first Jane, daughter of Sir Lionel Tolmach of Helmingham in Suffolk, Bart. ancestor to the Earl of Dysart, by whom he had one son Robert; and three daughters, Elizabeth, married to Sir Thomas Vernon of Hodnet in the county of Salop, Bart.; Jane, who died unmarried; and Mary, first wife to John Egerton of Oulton, Esq.—His second wife was Anne, daughter of Sir Walter St. John, Bart. and sister to Henry, Lord Viscount St. John, and by her, who died 1 December 1742, æt. 92, he had two sons and one daughter, Charles, who succeeded to the estate; Seymour, who married Elizabeth, eldest daughter of John, Lord Ashburnham, widow of Robert Cholmondeley of Holford, Esq. and dying 26 July 1739 at Arden in Cheshire, left no issue by her, who deceased 26 January 1731. The daughter Johanna was married to Amos, son and heir to Sir William Meredyth of Henbury in Cheshire, Bart. by whom she had one son William, and four daughters.—Robert Cholmondeley, Esq. the only son by the first wife, married Elizabeth, sister of the said Sir Thomas Vernon, by whom leaving an only daughter Elizabeth, married to John Atherton of the county of Lancaster, Esq. the estate devolved on his brother Charles, who in several parliaments served for the county of Chester, and married Essex, eldest sister of Thomas Pitt, Earl of Londonderry, which title is extinct, by whom he had Thomas his heir, and four daughters, Essex, born in 1715 and married in August 1732 to the third son of Colonel William Meyrick; Jane, Mary, and Elizabeth, one of whom married 8 August 1753 to the Rev. Mr. Wannup, rector of Waldon in Hertfordshire.

Sir Robert, Viscount of Kells. We now proceed with Robert, eldest son of Sir Hugh Cholmondeley. He was created a Baronet 29 June 1611, being the 36 in order of creation; was sheriff of Cheshire in 1621, and advanced to the Peerage of Ireland in 1628, by the title of Viscount Cholmondeley of Kells. —He was also, in consideration of his special service in raising

CHOLMONDELEY, Viscount KELLS.

fing feveral companies of foot in Chefhire, and fending many others to the King then at Shrewfbury, (which ftood him in high ftead in the memorable battle of Kineton foon after) as alfo in raifing other forces for defending the city of Chefter, at the firft fiege thereof, and courageous adventure in the fight at Tilfton-Heath; together with his great fufferings, by the plunder of his goods and burning his houfes, was by letters patent, bearing date at Oxford 1 September 1645 created a Baron of England, by the title of Lord Cholmondeley of Wiche-Malbank (commonly called Nantwich) and by other letters patent, dated 5 March enfuing, was created Earl of the province of Leinfter.—When the royal power was at an end, and the kingdom under the obedience of the parliament, he was fuffered to compound for his eftate, but upon no lefs a fine than 7742l.—He was remarkable for his good government of the great affairs of the country; his liberal hofpitality, and many other virtues. He married Catharine, younger daughter and coheir to John, Lord Stanhope of Harrington, Vice-Chamberlain of the houfhold to K. James I. by his wife Margaret, eldeft daughter of Henry Mac-Williams of Stanbourne in Effex, Efq. but dying without legitimate iffue 2 October 1659, æt. 75, was buried by his Lady, who deceafed 15 June 1657, in the chancel of the family at Malpas. Whereupon Robert, fon of his brother Hugh, became heir to his eftate; but the lands of Holford (which came by his mother) he fettled on Thomas Cholmondeley, his natural fon by Mrs. Coulfon, to whom, as was thought, he was affianced, though never married.— Which Thomas Cholmondeley of Holford, Efq. died there 6 January 1667, and was buried 16 at Nether-Pever, on whom his chaplain Mr. Kent, in his funeral fermon, obferved, "That he was a loyal fubject, a good hufband, a " good father, a good mafter, a good landlord, a good " neighbour, a good friend, a good chriftian, and a good " man." He married Jane, daughter of Edward Holland of Eyton in Lancafhire, Efq. by whom he had three fons, Robert; Thomas; and Richard, who died young in 1665. Robert, the eldeft, was born in 1652, and married Elizabeth, eldeft daughter of John, the firft Lord Afhburnham, who furvived him, and remarried with Seymour Cholmondeley, Efq. as already mentioned.

Hugh Cholmondeley, Efq. younger brother to Robert, Earl of Leinfter, had a good eftate fettled on him by his mother, which fhe purchafed in Chefhire, and married Mary,

Hugh.

Mary, daughter of Sir John Bodvile of Bodvile-castle in Caernarvonshire, where he departed this life 11 September 1655, and was buried at Malpas, having had issue two sons and three daughters, Robert, Hugh, Frances, Elizabeth, and Catharine, but none of them left issue, except

Robert, Viscount. Robert, the elder son, who succeeding his uncle the Earl of Leinster, became heir to all the Cholmondeley lands; and, in respect of his own merits, and the services of his ancestors, was dignified with the title of Viscount Cholmondeley of Kells by patent, bearing date 29 March 1661, and took his seat in parliament by proxy 25 June that year [1]. —He married Elizabeth, daughter and coheir to George Cradock of Caverswell-castle in Staffordshire, Esq. (Sir Thomas Slingsby, Bart. marrying Dorothy her sister) and deceasing in May 1681, had issue by her, who was buried at Malpas the last day of February 1691, four sons and one daughter Elizabeth, who became the second wife of John Egerton of Egerton and Oulton, Esq. (son and heir to Sir Philip, second surviving son of Sir Rowland Egerton of Egerton, Bart. and of his Lady Bridget, daughter of Arthur, Lord Grey of Wilton, Knight of the garter, and L. L. of Ireland) and he died without issue 2 January 1732.—The sons were Hugh, created Earl of Cholmondeley; Robert, who died at Westminster-school, and was buried in the North-aile of the abbey-church; George, late Earl of Cholmondeley; and Richard, buried with his brother, where, between the coat-armour of John de Dreux and Henry de Hastings, is a most noble monument of white marble erected for them, with this inscription;

Hic jacent sepulti duo ex Filiis Nobilissimi
Domini Roberti Vice-Comitis Cholmondeley, quorum
Alter Robertus, natu secundus, Annorum nondum
Quatuordecim, Puer optimæ spei, virginalis Verecundiæ,
Ingenii virilis, hujusce Collegii regius Alumnus, et
Nobile Ornamentum, laudabiles in Literis
Latinis, Græcis, Hebraicis Progressus, generosa
Indole, honestavit, scires antiquâ Cholmondeleiorum
Familia ortum. Obiit 4 Non. Feb. An. Salutis 1678.
Alter, Richardus, natu quartus, Annorum duodecim,
Tanta bonæ Indolis edidit Specimina, ut facile
Agnoscas Fratrem. Obiit Non. Junii A. D. 1680.

Here

---

[1] Lords Jour. I. 253.

Here lie interred the Bodies of Robert and Richard Cholmondeley, Sons to the Right Honble. Robert, Lord Cholmondeley, 1682.

Hugh, the second Viscount, joining with those patriots, who opposed the arbitrary measures of K. James II. was created by K. William, Lord Cholmondeley of Namptwich by patent, dated 10 April 1689, with limitations of the honour to the issue male of his brother George.—27 March 1705 he was sworn of the privy council to Q. Anne, and 29 December 1706 advanced to the dignities of Viscount Malpas and Earl of Cholmondeley, with the like entail.— 22 April 1708 his Lordship was appointed comptroller of her Majesty's houshold, and 10 May following, when a new privy council was settled, according to act of parliament, upon the union of the two kingdoms, he was again sworn a member thereof; and 6 October that year made treasurer of the houshold; being also constituted L. L. and C. Rot. of the county and city of Chester; governor of the city and castle of Chester; and L. L. of North-Wales; but was removed from his employments in April 1713.— On the accession of K. George I. he was made (11 October 1714) treasurer of his houshold, and sworn the next day of his privy council; having on 9 of that month succeeded to the several honours and trusts, from which he had been removed in 1713; but dying unmarried 18 January 1724, he was succeeded by his brother

Hugh, 2 Viscount.

George, the third Viscount, who, after his education at Westminster, and in Christ-church, Oxford, embraced a military life, being in 1685 made a Cornet of horse, and on K. William's accession one of the grooms of his bedchamber; in 1689 Captain of the first troop of horse grenadier guards, of which he was made Colonel 4 October 1693, a Brigadier General 1 June 1697, and 9 March 1701 a Major-General; in which stations he served in all the wars of K. William's reign in Ireland and Flanders, commanding the said troop of horse guards at the battle of the Boyne; and 3 August 1692 at the battle of Steenkirk, when his Majesty attacked the French army in their camp, he distinguished himself in a very particular manner, and was wounded.

George, 3 Viscount.

9 July 1702 Q. Anne made him governor of the forts of Gravesend and Tilbury, and 1 January 1703 declared him Lieutenant-General of the horse. K. George I. also on his accession to the throne, continued him (21 January) in his posts,

posts, and 8 February 1714 constituted him Captain and Colonel of the third troop of horse guards; creating him by privy seal, dated at St. James's 19 February 1714, and by patent * at Dublin 12 April 1715, Baron Newborough of Newborough, being the first his Majesty advanced to the Peerage of Ireland; and taking further into consideration his great merits and services, was pleased to create him a Peer of England 2 July 1716, by the same title.—Upon his brother's death, he was appointed 20 March, and sworn 12 April 1725 L. L. of the county and city of Chester, C. Rot. of that county, and L. L. of those of Denbigh, Montgomery, Flint, Merioneth, Caernarvon and Anglesey, in which he was continued 3 September 1727. His Lordship was also constituted 19 March 1724 governor of the town and fort of Kingston upon Hull; made General of the horse 1 March 1726; and 6 October 1732 governor of the Island of Guernsey, into which he was sworn 15 February following.—He married Elizabeth, daughter of the Heer Van Baron Ruytenburgh in Germany, by his wife Anne-Elizabeth, fifth and youngest daughter of Lewis de Nassau, Lord of Beverwaert, by Elizabeth his wife, daughter of Count de Horn, and deceasing at his house, Whitehall, 7 May 1733, had issue by her, who died there 16 January 1721, two sons and three daughters, viz.

(1)   George, his successor.

James,

* The preamble. Cum Viros quosdam egregios Procerum Ordinibus adscribere ineunte jam Imperio decrevimus, qui ipsum ornent pariter ac stabiliant, Neminem, qui hoc sibi jure vindicet, fideli et prædilecto nostro Georgio Cholmondeley Priorem invenimus, seu propriam quam consequutus est famam, seu Gloriam ipsi à Majoribum derivatam contemplemur, Virtute bellica jamdudum meruit ut inter Legatos Exercitus Britannici primarius evaderet; necnon spectatissima erga nos Domumq. nostram fide se nobis adeo commendavit, ut Sacellitum, qui Custodiam Corporis nostri habent, constituatur Præfectus. Nec satis tamen eximii Viri Meritis datum existimamus, nisi is, cui tantopere confidimus, novo ornetur Dignitatis incremento, Titulos Anglicanos illustris illa Domus inde Originem duxit, ei aliquando suppeditabit, cum singularis ea Fælicitas Viro prænobili Comiti de Cholmondeley contigerit, ut in Fratre, quem primum semper habuit, Amicum eundem habiturus sit hæredem. Nos ei interea Honores isto in Regno destinavimus, in quo titulis Majores sui inclaruerunt, Rebus a se gestis ipse inclaruit, in prælio scilicet ad Boynam Flumen pugnato egregium Fortitudinis militaris in Amoris erga Patriam specimen adhuc Juvenis edidit, eaque Victoria reportanda partem habuit, qua Regnum Gulielmo tertio confirmatum est, cujus Pietati in Populos Imperio suo commissos debetur, quod ad nos Stirpemq. nostram Jus Sceptri pervenerit. Sciatis igitur, &c. (Rot. Anno 9 Geo. I. 1ª. p. f.)

James, born 18 April 1708, who 12 May 1725 was appointed Major to his father's third troop of horse-guards, and in January 1730 succeeded Brigadier Newton in the post of deputy-governor of Chester-castle; was chosen 25 March 1731 member of parliament for Bossiney in Cornwall; in April 1734 for Camelford, and in May 1741 for Montgomery. 11 June 1731 he was made second L.-Colonel of the said regiment of guards; 17 January 1740 Colonel of a new raised regiment of foot; succeeded Lord James Cavendish 25 December 1742 in his regiment; was made in July 1745 a Brigadier-General, and 23 September 1747 a Major-General of his Majesty's armies. In August 1749 he succeeded Sir John Mordaunt in his regiment of dragoons; 11 June 1754 was advanced to the rank of L. General; 30 April 1770 a General of his Majesty's armies, and 27 June same year was appointed governor of Chester-castle, in the room of Earl George, his brother, then deceased [1]. He married Penelope, only daughter of James, Earl of Barrymore, by his wife Penelope, daughter and heir to Richard, Earl Rivers, and deceased 13 October 1775, having had by her, from whom he was divorced 8 March 1736, a daughter, who died 24 April 1737.

The daughters were Lady Henrietta, born 26 November 1701, died in Burlington-Gardens 8 May 1769 unmarried; Lady Elizabeth, (born 28 May 1705 and married 23 January 1730 to Edward Warren of Poynton in Cheshire, Esq. then sheriff of that county, and had issue by him, who died 7 September 1737 a son George, made a Knight of the Bath; and other children; she died in December 1762); and Lady Mary, born 9 March 1713-14, died unmarried in April 1783 and was buried in the family vault at Chester.

George, the fourth Viscount Cholmondeley, in 1722 was member of parliament for the borough of Eastlow; and served after for New-Windsor; was elected 27 May 1725, on the revival of the order by K. George I. a Knight of the Bath; and 21 July 1726 succeeded William, Earl Cadogan in the post of master of the robes to his Majesty. —29 July 1727 he was constituted a commissioner of the admiralty, (which he resigned 14 May 1729) and continued governor of the castle and city of Chester, to which he had been appointed in April 1725.—On the establishment

(2)

George, 4 Viscount.

[1] Lodge. Collins IV. 222, 223, and Supp.

ment of the houshold of Frederick, Prince of Wales 5 December 1728, he was made master of his horse; and, succeeding his father, took his seat in the English parliament 17 May 1733, and five days after was appointed in his room, Steward of the royal manor of Sheene, L. L. and C. Rot. of the county and city of Chester, Vice-Admiral of North-Wales, &c.—Resigning his post of master of the horse to the Prince, he was constituted 15 May 1735 a commissioner of the treasury, which he surrendered the year after, and 21 May 1736 succeeded the Duke of Rutland as Chancellor of the Dutchy court of Lancaster, being at the same time sworn of the privy council; and 2 March 1735 was made chamberlain of Chester; in December 1743 Lord Privy Seal; and 29 December 1744 joint Vice-Treasurer of Ireland.—14 September 1723 his Lordship married Mary, only daughter of Sir Robert Walpole after Earl of Orford and by her, (who died at Aix in Provence in December 1731, and was buried at Malpas), had issue three sons; and a daughter who died an infant. The sons were

(1) George, Viscount Malpas, born 17 October 1724, was appointed to a company in L. General Howard's regiment of foot, and in 1745 was appointed Lieutenant-Colonel of the regiment of foot then raised by his father for the suppression of the rebellion. 19 January 1746-7 he married Hester, daughter and heir to Sir Francis Edwards of Grete, and of the college in Shrewsbury, in the county of Salop, Bart. and deceasing 15 March 1764, before his father, left issue by his said Lady, who survived him, an only son George-James, successor to his grandfather; and a daughter Hester, born in 1755 married to William Clapcott Lisle, Esq.

(2) Robert born 1 and baptized 28 November 1727 had a command in the army, but preferring an ecclesiastical to a military life, entered into holy orders and was appointed to the livings of St. Andrew in Hertford, and Hertingfordbury near that town. He married Miss Mary Woffington, and had issue George-James, born 22 February 1752; Horace born 18 February 1753, died young; Robert-Francis born 24 June 1756; Harriet born 4 April 1754, now the wife of William Bellingham, Esq. representative in the English parliament for Ryegate and secretary to the Chancellor of the Exchequer; Jane-Elizabeth born 22 October 1758, and Margaret born 8 July 1761 died young.

Frederick born 29 April 1731 died of the small-pox 25 April 1734.

George, the fifth and present Viscount Cholmondeley, was born 30 April 1749; 14 June 1782 appointed his Majesty's envoy extraordinary and plenipotentiary to the court of Berlin, is now L. L. and C. Rot. of the county of Chester; Colonel of the militia of said county and governor of Chester-castle: 12 April 1783 he was appointed Captain of the yeomen of the guard, and 14 of same month sworn of the privy council in Great Britain.

(3) George, 5 Viscount.

TITLES.] George Cholmondeley, Viscount Cholmondeley of Kells, Earl of Cholmondeley, Viscount Malpas, Baron Cholmondeley of Wich-Malbank, Baron Newborough of Newborough, and Baron of Newburgh.

CREATIONS.] V. Cholmondeley of Kells in the county of Meath 29 March 1661, 13 Car. II. B. of Wich-Malbank, otherwise Namptwich in the county of Chester 10 April 1689, 1 Will. and Mary. V. Malpas and Earl of Cholmondeley, both in the same county 27 December 1706, 5. Q. Anne. B. Newborough of Newborough in the county of Wexford 12 April 1715, 1 Geo. I. and B. of Newburgh in the Isle of Anglesey 2 July 1716, 3 of that reign.

ARMS.] Ruby, two helmets in chief, proper, garnished, gold, in base a garb, topaz.

CREST.] On a wreath, a demi-gryphon saliant diamond, with beak, wings and legs, topaz, holding between his paws an helmet, proper.

SUPPORTERS.] The dexter, a gryphon, diamond, its beak wings and fore-legs, as the crest. The sinister, a wolf, topaz, gorged with a collar perflew, vair.

MOTTO.] CASSIS TUTISSIMA VIRTUS.

SEATS.] Cholmondeley in the county of Chester, 128 miles from London; and Richmond in Surrey.

BURTON, Viscount DOWNE.

<small>19</small>

<small>John.</small>

<small>Sir Edward.</small>
<small>Sir Nicholas.</small>

SIR Paine Dawney of Dawney-castle in Normandy, from whom this family is descended, came into England with K. William the Conqueror. In former times they wrote their name, D'Anney, and were Lords of the manor of Shunock, or Shannock in the county of Cornwall. Of this family was John Dawnay, living in the reign of Edward I. who married Jane, third and youngest daughter of Peter Le Cave (by his wife, the only child of Sir Thomas Bromflete) and had Sir Edward D'Annay, the father of Sir Nicholas, who in the reign of Edw. II. obtained a charter for a weekly Wednesday and Friday market, and a yearly fair on the eve, day and morrow of St. James the Apostle, at his said manor of Shannock.—In 1 Edw. III. he had summons to parliament among the Barons of England, but not after [1], which was occasioned by his absence in the holy war against the infidels; whence he brought a very rich and curious medal, now in the family's possession: But continuing in the holy land many years, the estate, consisting of fifteen large manors in Cornwall, was conveyed into the family of Courtenay, Earls of Devon, by the marriage of Emmeline (or Emme) daughter and heir to Sir John Dawney of Madfordferry in the county of Somerset, to Edward, son and heir apparent of Hugh, the second Earl of Devon, who dying before his father, left issue by her two sons, Edward, the third Earl of Devon; and Hugh of Haccombe and Boconnock, Esq. father of Edward Courtenay, whom K. Henry VII. for his adherence to the house of Lancaster, advanced to the Earldom of Devonshire 28 October 1485, first of his reign.

Sir Nicholas Dawney aforesaid departed this life 7 Edward III. as appears by inquisition, and by Elizabeth his wife

[1] Dugdale.

wife had two sons, Thomas; and Sir John Dawney of Madfordferry beforementioned, made a knight Banneret by K. Edward III. at the battle of Creffy, on whose death an inquifition was taken 20 Edw. III. and he was found to have left only the said Emme, married to Edward Courtenay, Efq.

Thomas Dawney, the elder fon, marrying Elizabeth, daughter and heir to John Newton of Snaith in Yorkfhire, Efq. fixed his refidence at Eftrick in that part of England, where he was living 11 Rich. II. and was the direct anceftor of the Vifcount Downe, and alfo of Roger Dawney of Norton, Efq. who left only daughters, whereof Joan was married to John Churchill, Efq. by whom fhe had two daughters, coheirs, Margaret and Agnes, living in the reign of Edward III. *Thomas.*

Thomas Dawney aforefaid had iffue a daughter Margaret, married to —— Saltmarfh of Yorkfhire, and a fon Sir John, who fucceeded at Eftrick; married Ellen, daughter of John Barden, and died in 1417 (5 Hen. V.) having iffue Sir John; William of Rhodes; Alice, married to Robert Fleming; and Agnes to Peter Wefton.—Sir John, the elder fon, died in 1424 (2 Hen. VI.) and by Margaret, or Joan, daughter of Sir Alexander Lound, Knt. had Sir John his fucceffor; Joan, married to William Dallifon; and Catharine, to Thomas Awger, Efqrs.—Sir John, who fucceeded, married Agnes, daughter of Guy Rockliffe of Rockliffe in the county of York, Efq. and deceafing 20 October 1493, had Sir Guy, his heir; William; Margaret, married to Ralph, fon and heir of Richard Acclam; Agnes, to John Bechard; and Elizabeth, to John Langton, Efqrs. *Sir John; Sir John. Sir John;*

Sir Guy (Guydo) Dawney, Knt. was feated at Cowick in the county of York, where he lived in the reigns of Henry VII. and VIII. and died 17 Auguft 1522. He married Jane (or Joan) fifter and heir to Sir John Darell of Sezay, who died without iffue in 7 Hen. VII. and to Thomas Darell, who died alfo childlefs, and daughter of Sir George Darell of Sezay, who died 30 March 1466, by his wife Margaret, daughter of Sir William Plumpton, and had iffue Sir John his fucceffor; Anne, married to Robert Howdenby; and a younger daughter to —— Babthorpe of Drax, Efqrs. *Sir Guy.*

Sir John Dawney of Cowick was fheriff of Yorkfhire 35 Hen. VIII. and died 2 March 1553, having iffue by Dorothy, daughter of Richard, Lord Latimer, who died in *Sir John.*

November

November 1532, two sons and four daughters, viz. Sir Thomas; John of Herke, who in 1572 (14 Eliz.) was sheriff of Yorkshire, and married Elizabeth, fifth daughter of John Roper of Eltham in Kent, Esq. prothonotary of the Court of King's Bench, and attorney-general to K. Henry VIII. by Jane his wife, daughter of Sir John Fineux, Chief Justice of the said Court, and left a son John, born in 1561, seated at Potter-Brunton in Yorkshire, whose only daughter and heir Mary, was married to John Legard of Ganton, Esq. and was mother of Sir John Legard, created a Baronet in 1660; the four daughters were Elizabeth (married to Robert Aske of Aughton, Esq. by whom she had John, whose wife was Christian, daughter of Sir Thomas Fairfax of Denton); Dorothy (to Sir Henry Nevile of Chute, and had Gervaise Nevile, Esq. living in 1585); Joan (to Bryan Palmes of Narbourn, Esq. whose son John, living 1584, married Joan, daughter of George Dawney, Esq. and had three sons, George, John and Francis); and Anne, to Sir George Coniers, Knt.

Sir Thomas. Sir Thomas Dawney of Sezay and Cowick, Knt. married Edith, eldest daughter of George, Lord D'Arcie of Aston, and dying 3 September 1566, had Sir John his heir; Paul; and Frances, married to Sir William Babthorpe of Osgodby, to whom she was second wife, and Sir John, had two daughters, Mary and Christian.—Sir John, who succeeded, was knighted by Q. Elizabeth in 1580, and served the office of sheriff for Yorkshire in 1589. He married Elizabeth, daughter of Sir Marmaduke Tunstall of Thurland in Lancashire, Knt. by whom he had four sons and two daughters, Thomas; Marmaduke; William; D'Arcie; Mary, married to Ralph, the third Lord Eure of Witton, Lieutenant of the Principality of Wales for K. James I. and was mother of William, Lord Eure, born in 1579; and Dorothy died unmarried.

Sir Thomas. Sir Thomas, who succeeded his father at Cowick, was born in 1563, and honoured with knighthood by K. James I. in whose 8 year he was sheriff of Yorkshire, and was living in 1619.—He married Faith, daughter and heir to Sir Richard Ledgiard of Rysom, and had issue five sons and four daughters, John; Thomas, who died childless; George; Richard; Henry; Elizabeth, married to Sir William Acclam of Horeby; Frances, to Sir Henry Vaughan of Sutton; Margaret; and Anne.—John, the eldest son, married Elizabeth, daughter of Sir Richard Hutton,

Justice

BURTON, Viscount DOWNE.

Juftice of the King's Bench, and had two fons, Sir Chriftopher, who by K. Charles I. for his loyalty and fervices, was created a Baronet 19 May 1642, but dying without iffue, was fucceeded in title and eftate by his brother

Sir John Dawney of Cowick, who in 1660 reprefented the county of York in parliament, as he did the borough of Pontefract in 1661, 1678 and 1680, and being advanced to the Peerage of Ireland by patent *, dated at Weftminfter 19 February 1680, fat in K. James's Irifh parliament of 1689, and died in 1695 leaving iffue Henry his fucceffor, and two daughters; the one married to Mr. Ramfden of Yorkfhire, and died at York in June 1737; and the other to —— Orme of Charlton near Greenwich, Efq. where fhe died 15 December 1736, leaving one fon Garton Orme of Lavington in Suffex, Efq. appointed 1 May 1736 gentleman-ufher to the Princefs of Wales, and chofen 23 November 1739 member of parliament for the borough of Arundel.

Sir Henry, the fecond Vifcount, in 1689 was attainted by K. James's parliament in Ireland; reprefented the borough of Pontefract in 1690, and the county of York in the reigns of K. William, Q. Anne, and K. George I.— He married Mildred, daughter of William Godfrey of Thunick in the county of Lincoln, Efq. and by her, who died at Cowick in September 1725, had fix fons and two daughters, viz.

John, his heir apparent.

William.

Henry, D. D. educated in the univerfity of Oxford, refided at Charlton in Kent; was inftalled 22 June 1732 a prebendary in the cathedral church of Canterbury; and 13 May 1740 married Elizabeth, eldeft daughter of Sir Thomas D'Aeth of Knowlton in the faid county, Bart. fo created 16 July 1716, by his wife Elizabeth, daughter of Sir John Norborough, Knt. admiral and commiffioner of

Sir Chriftopher, 1 Baronet.

Sir John, 1 Vifcount.

Sir Henry, 2 Vifcount.

(1)
(2)
(3)

---

* The preamble. Cum nihil magis Majeftatem regiam illuftret, vel ad Virtutem generofos Hominum animos ftimulet, quam cum Viri Virtute, Generis nobilitate, et Prudentia fplendidi Honorum titulis decorentur; Nos igitur recolentes eximia merita dilecti et fidelis noftri Johannis Dawnay de Cowicke in comitatu noftro Eboraci Militis, et grata Servitia, quæ ipfe et Anteceffores fui nobis aut Patri noftro beatæ memoriæ fumma cum Affiduitate et Integritate præftiterunt, Eum in altiorem Honoris gradum evehi dignum effe cenfemus. Sciatis modo, &c. (Rot. Anno 33 Car. II. 1ˢ. p. f.)

of the navy in the reigns of Charles II. and James II. and heir to her brother Sir John of Knowlton, Bart. who was shipwrecked with his brother James, and his father-in-law Sir Cloudesley Shovel, 22 October 1707.—Doctor Dawney died at Piddleton near Dorchester in July 1754.

(4) Christopher, who 26 August 1749 married the daughter of Mr. Rundall of Marston, or Hutton, near York, and she died 3 January 1769, æt. 54, in the Minster-yard York.

(5) George, made captain of a ship of war 8 January 1741.

(6) Godfrey, married Elizabeth, daughter of Sir Thomas D'Aeth, Bart.

(1) Daughter Mildred, married to Sir William Fowlis, of Ingleby-manor in the North-riding of Yorkshire, Bart. and had issue William; Mildred; Anne; Catharine; and Mary.

(2) Dorothy, first to Robert Shaftoe of Whitworth in the Bishoprick of Durham, Esq. and secondly to Rev. Doctor Thomas Eden, fourth son of Sir Robert Eden of West-Auckland, Bart. Rector of Winston, and Prebendary in the cathedral of Durham, at which city she died 26 November 1734 without issue.

John. John Dawney, Esq. the eldest son, having his education in Christ-church Oxford, took the degree of A. M. 9 July 1706, and in 1713 was chosen burgess in parliament for Pontefract and Aldborough, for the former of which he was rechosen in 1715: And 10 August 1724 marrying Charlotte-Louisa, younger daughter of Robert Pleydell of Ampney-Crucis in the county of Gloucester, Esq. (by his wife Sarah, daughter of Philip Sheppard of Hampton in the same county, Esq.) and heir to her brother and sister, who both died unmarried, had issue by her, who died 8 April 1729, æt. 35 years, two sons, Henry-Pleydell, and John, successive Viscounts, and departing this life 31 July 1740, before his father, his elder son

Sir Henry-Pleydell, 3 Viscount. Sir Henry-Pleydell, born 8 April 1727, succeeding his grand-father, was the third Viscount Downe; he was chosen in 1749 and 1751 to parliament for the county of York; and 6 December 1750 Fellow of the Royal Society. He was first Lord of the Bedchamber to his Royal Highness George, Prince of Wales; lieutenant-colonel of 25 regiment, colonel by brevet, and commanded his regiment at the battle of Minden in 1759, *his* being one of the four regiments to whom the success of that day was owing;

owing; he also commanded the same regiment at the battle of Campen near Wesel, 16 October 1760, when being mortally wounded, he died 9 December ensuing [1], and was succeeded in the honour by his brother

Sir John, the fourth Viscount, born 9 April 1728; married Lora, only daughter and heir to William Burton of Luffenham in the county of Rutland, Esq. by his wife Elizabeth, daughter of George Pitt of Stratfield-sea in the county of Hants, Esq. and deceased 21 December 1780, leaving by his said Lady five sons and two daughters, viz. John-Christopher, his successor; William-Henry-Pleydell died an infant; William-Henry born 20 August 1772; Marmaduke, 27 July 1777; Thomas, 30 May 1779; Catharine, 23 August 1768; and Lora 17 June 1774 [2].

Sir John-Christopher, born 15 November 1764 [3]; assumed the name of Burton, and succeeding to the honour, became the fifth and present Viscount. His Lordship is unmarried.

Sir John, 4 Viscount.

Sir John-Christopher, 5 Viscount.

TITLES.] Sir John-Christopher Burton, Viscount Dawney of Downe, and Baronet.

CREATIONS.] Baronet, 19 May 1642, 18 Car. I. V. Dawney of the county of Downe, 19 February 1680, 33 Car. II.

ARMS.] Pearl, on a Bend cottised, diamond, three Annulets, of the field.

CREST.] On a wreath, a Saracen in armour, couped at the thighs, and wreath'd about the temples, proper, holding in his right hand a ring, topaz, stoned saphire, and in his left a lion's gamb erased gold, armed, ruby.

SUPPORTERS.] Two lions, topaz, collar'd with the coat, and ducally crowned, pearl.

MOTTO.] TIMET PUDOREM.

SEAT.] Cowick, near Snaith and Ditchmarsh in the county of York, 9 miles from Pontefract, and 176 from London; Dawney-lodge and Danby-castle in the same county.

[1] Lodge, and Ulster.   [2] Idem.
[3] Viscountess-Dowager's Letter 24 July 1785.

THE name of How frequently occurs in the ancient English writers, and hath been of long continuance in the counties of Nottingham, Somerset, Wilts, and Gloucester. At Flawborough in the hundred of Newark, says Dr. Thoroton, was a family called *De le Hou*, from their residence on the hill; and of them was Gerard, and after him Walter De le Hou, or Del Howe, who was witness to a grant, which William, son of Roger de Houton, made to Walter, son of Robert des Mores, of a toft and two bovates of land in Houton. And in the reigns of Henry III. and Edward I. Robert Del How (who passed some parcels of land in Flawborough and Dalyngton to Robert Morin) were of most note; and the place in some writings is still called Flawborough Del How.

Henry. But what we are principally to observe is, that his Lordship's ancestor Henry How, living in the reign of Henry VIII. had two sons, John, Thomas (whose son was named
John. Humphrey) and a daughter married to John Walsh.—John, the elder son, was possessed of the manor of Hunspell de la Heies in the county of Somerset, and of lands, &c. in the counties of Devon, Essex, and city of London; and died 27 May 1574, (16 Eliz.) leaving John his heir; Anne, married to William Hilliard; Susan; and Judith.——
John. John How, Esq. who succeeded, was 18 years old at his father's death, and marrying Jane, daughter of Nicholas Grubham of Bishop's-Lydiard in the county of Somerset, and sister to Sir Richard Grubham of Wishford in Wiltshire, Lord of the manor of Compton-Abdale in the county of Gloucester by purchase, who died without issue in 1629, by Margaret, daughter of Alderman William Whitmore of London, became seated at Bishop's-Lydiard, and had issue three sons and one daughter, viz. John and George, who both enjoyed a vast real and personal estate, by the gift of their uncle the said Sir Richard; Lawrence; and Elizabeth, married to John Bainton, Esq.

Sir

Sir George How, the second son, was seated at Cold-Berwick, otherwise Berwick St. Leonard's in Wilts; and supplying K. Charles I. with large sums of money during his troubles, was knighted, and served in parliament for the borough of Hindon. He married Dorothy, daughter of Humphrey Clarke, otherwise Woodechurch of Woodechurch in Kent, Esq. by whom he left two sons and one daughter, viz. Sir George; John of Somerton in Somersetshire, who married the daughter of —— Strode, Esq.; and Margaret, wife to John Still of Shaftsbury, Esq.—— Sir George Grubham How, the elder son, born in 1627, served in several parliaments for Hindon; was created a Baronet 20 June 1660; married in 1650 Elizabeth, younger daughter of Sir Harbottle Grimston of Bradfield-Hall in Essex, Bart. and dying 26 September 1676, had many children, who all died young, except one son Sir James, and four daughters; Dorothy, married to Henry Lee of Dungeon near Canterbury, Esq.; Anne, to John Lisle of Moyle's-Court in Hampshire, Esq.; Elizabeth, to Robert Hovenden of Frisley in Kent, Gent.; and Mary, to Sir George Rooke, Vice-Admiral of England, who died 26 January 1708.—Sir James How, the only son, member of parliament for Hindon, married first Elizabeth, daughter of Edward Nutt of Nackington in Kent, Esq. and she dying 8 September 1691, he took to his second wife Elizabeth, daughter and coheir to —— Stratford of Halling in Gloucestershire, Esq. who also dying in 1702 without issue, the title became extinct by his death on 19 January 1735, æt. 66.

We now proceed with Sir John How, eldest son of John by Jane, sister of Sir Richard Grubham. Who, by gift of his said uncle, had the manor of Compton in Gloucestershire (of which county he was sheriff in 1650) with Wishford near Salisbury and other estates in Wiltshire, and was created a Baronet 22 September 1660. He married 23 July 1620 Bridget, daughter of Thomas Rich of North-Cerney in the county of Gloucester, Esq. master in chancery, and lies buried under a handsome monument in the church of Withington, having issue by her (who died 15 June 1642, aged 46), three sons, Sir Richard Grubham How, Bart.; John Grubham How, ancestor to the Viscount How; and Sir Thomas How, who left no issue by Hesther, daughter of Sir William Manwaring.

Sir Richard, the second Baronet, of Compton and Wishford, married Anne, daughter of Doctor John King, Bishop

Bishop of London, widow of John Dutton of Sherborne in Gloucestershire, and was succeeded by his only son Sir Richard, the third Baronet, who served in divers parliaments for the county of Wilts, and 12 August 1673 married Mary, elder daughter of Sir Henry-Frederick Thynne of Kempsford in the county of Gloucester, Bart. sister of Thomas, created Viscount Weymouth, but by her, who died 5 September 1735, having no issue, and deceasing 3 July 1730, his estates and title descended to Scrope, Viscount How, heir to his uncle John Grubham How, second son of Sir John the first Baronet.

John. Which John often represented the county of Gloucester from 1661, to 1678 in parliament, and by his marriage became possessed of the manor of Langar in the county of Nottingham, where he fixed his residence; which manor, formerly the inheritance of the Tiptofts, passed from them to the family of Scrope, by the marriage of Roger, Lord Scrope of Bolton with Margaret, eldest of the three daughters and coheirs to Robert, Lord Tiptoft; whose descendant Thomas, Lord Scrope, Knight of the Garter, married in 1584 Philadelphia, second daughter of Henry Cary, the first Lord Hunsdon, by whom he had one son Emanuel, Lord Scrope of Bolton, created 19 June 1627 Earl of Sunderland; who having no issue by his wife Lady Elizabeth Manners, daughter of John, Earl of Rutland, settled his estate on his natural children by Martha Janes; of whom his only son John dying unmarried 31 July 1646, aged about 20, his three daughters became coheirs, and were Mary, married first to Henry Cary, son and heir to Henry, Earl of Monmouth, and secondly to Charles, the first Duke of Bolton; Elizabeth, to Thomas Savage, Earl Rivers; and Annabella, born in 1629, to the said John Grubham How, Esq. who, upon the division of the estate, had the manor of Langar allotted to her, and brought it to her husband: whose services being acceptable to K. Charles II. his Majesty, by his letters registered in the office of arms, bearing date 1 June 1663, did in consideration of those services, and as a mark of his especial grace and royal favour, grant and ordain, that the said Annabella his wife should be had, taken and esteemed as the legitimate daughter of an Earl of England, and during her life have, hold, use, take and enjoy the style, place, degree, precedency and privilege thereof in as full and ample manner, as if she had been the legitimate daughter of Emanuel, late Earl of Sunderland; with a precept of obedience to all his subjects;

subjects; from which time she was usually styled, *The right honourable Lady* Annabella How.—By her, who died 21 March 1703, and lies buried at Stowell, under a handsome marble monument, he had four sons and five daughters.

Sir Scrope, his successor. (1)

John Grubham How, Esq. born in 1657, Lord of the manor of Stowell in Gloucestershire, which he purchased from the Earl of Strafford, where he had a pleasant seat with a park, and was a person much beloved in his country. He made a considerable figure in the House of Commons, during the reigns of K. William and Q. Anne, as member for the county and city of Gloucester, and for the boroughs of Cirencester and Bodmyn.—In the former reign he was Vice-Chamberlain to Q. Mary; was sworn of the privy council to Q. Anne 21 April 1702; appointed 3 November 1704 one of the governors of her Majesty's bounty for the augmentation of the maintenance of the poor clergy; was sworn 15 May 1708 joint clerk with Edward Southwell, Esq. to the privy council of Great-Britain; 4 January 1702 made paymaster-general of the guards and garrisons, and 7 June following Vice-Admiral of the county of Gloucester; which preferments (Sir Robert Atkyns, in his history of Gloucestershire observes) he obtained not by flattery, but by freedom of speech in parliament; where, as a true patriot, he always shewed his love to his country, particularly in opposing a standing army; and signalized his great abilities in all his speeches, which had great force to persuade within doors, and to please without. He was a great enemy to foreigners settling in England; was indefatigable in whatever he undertook, particularly with respect to the old East India Company, whose cause he maintained till he fixed it upon as sure a foot as the new, even when they thought themselves past recovery. —He married Mary, daughter and coheir to Humfrey Baskerville of Pentryllos in Herefordshire, Esq., widow of Sir Edward Morgan of Llanternam in the county of Monmouth, Bart. and dying in 1721, had issue a daughter Mary, married to Sir Edmund Thomas of Wenvoe in Glamorganshire, Bart. who died in 1723; and a son

(2) Family of Lord Chedworth.

John How of Stowell, Esq., who on the decease of Sir Richard How of Compton and Wishford, Baronet, in 1730,

1 Collect.

1730, as before mentioned, succeeded to those estates, and was chosen to supply his place in parliament for the county of Wilts, as he was again in 1734, on the calling of a new parliament; was elected in April 1737 Recorder of Warwick; and in consideration of his great merits, was advanced to the Peerage of England 12 May 1741, by the title of Lord Chedworth, Baron of Chedworth in the county of Gloucester, and took his seat in the English House of Peers, 1 December following. He married Dorothy, eldest daughter of Henry-Frederick Thynne, Esq. grandfather of Thomas, Viscount Weymouth, and died 3 April 1742, by an inflammation in his bowels, having issue six sons and two daughters, viz. John-Thynne his successor; Henry-Frederick, a Captain in the royal navy; Thomas; Charles; James; William; Mary; and Anne.—John-Thynne, the eldest son, and second Lord Chedworth 23 September 1751 married Martha, eldest daughter and coheir to Sir Philip Parker Long of Arwarton in Suffolk, Bart. he was L. L. and Custos Rot. of the county of Gloucester, and constable of St. Breval's-castle in the Forest of Dean, and dying without issue at his house in Curzon-street, London, 10 May 1762, was succeeded in the title by his brother [1], since which period the title became extinct.

(3)   Charles of Gritworth in the county of Northampton, born in 1661, whose only daughter was the first wife of Peter Bathurst of Clarendon-Park in Wiltshire, Esq. next brother to Allen, Lord Bathurst.

(4)   Emanuel-Scrope, who was groom of the bedchamber to K. William, and received a grant from his Majesty of the Lieutenancy of Alice-Holt and Woolmer Forests in the county of Southampton in reversion, after the term of Colonel William Legge's interest, for 45 years, the remainder of which term he purchased; and 1 November 1695 was made Colonel of a regiment of foot; a Brigadier-General 9 March 1703; a Major-General, 1 March 1706; member of parliament for Morpeth in 1701; in 1702 appointed first commissioner of the Prizes; and in 1707 sent her Majesty's envoy-extraordinary to the most serene house of Brunswick-Lunenburg, now seated on the throne of these kingdoms.—His wife was Ruperta, natural daughter (by Mrs. Margaret Hughes) of Prince Rupert, Count Palatine of the Rhine, Duke of Bavaria and Cumberland, Earl of Holderness,

---

[1] Collins's Edit. 1754, V. 108.

Holderneffe, and Knight of the Garter, third son of Frederick, King of Bohemia and Elizabeth of Great-Britain, eldeſt daughter of K. James I.; and deceaſing 26 September 1709, had three ſons, William, who 11 October 1753 married Miſs Blake of Epping [1]; Emanuel; James; and a daughter Sophia, appointed in February 1714 maid of honour to Caroline, Princeſs of Wales; and died 4 April 1726.

(1) Daughter Bridget was born in 1650, and married to Sir John Bennet, Knight of the Bath, created Lord Oſſulſton, to whom ſhe was ſecond wife, and by him who died in 1688, æt. 70, and was buried in Harlington-church, Middleſex [2], was mother of Charles, created Earl of Tankerville; died in July 1703, and was buried with her Lord in Harlington church, under a monument erected to their memories [3].

(2) Annabella, born in 1654, died unmarried, and was buried in the South aile of Langar church, in a brick vault, made by her father for the repoſitory of his family.

(3) Elizabeth, married to Sir John Guiſe of Rencomb in Gloucesterſhire, Bart.

(4) Diana, born in 1659, was married to Sir Francis Molyneux of Teverſalt in Nottinghamſhire, Bart.

(5) Mary.

Sir Scrope How, the eldeſt ſon, born in November 1648, was educated in Chriſt-church, Oxford, where 8 September 1665 he commenced A. M. He repreſented the county of Nottingham in the reigns of Charles II. K. William and Q. Anne; and was one of thoſe patriots, who 26 June 1680 delivered a preſentment againſt the Duke of York to the grand jury of Middleſex, with reaſons for indicting him for not going to church; one of which was, that there had been divers letters read in both houſes of parliament, and at the ſecret committee of both houſes, from ſeveral cardinals and others at Rome; and alſo from other popiſh biſhops and agents of the Pope in other foreign parts, which apparently ſhewed the great correſpondence between the Duke and the Pope; and expreſſing, how the Pope could not chuſe but weep for joy at the reading of ſome of his letters, and what great ſatisfaction he took, to hear the Duke advanced to the catholick religion. That the Pope had granted *Breves* to the Duke; ſent him beads, ample indulgences, &c. But the court

Sir Scrope, 1 Viſcount.

[1] Lodge.   [2] Idem.   [3] Idem.

of King's Bench hearing of this prefentment, fent for the jury up, and difmiffed them.

Before the arrival of the Prince of Orange, to prevent the introduction of popery by the Duke of York, *now* K. James, and to preferve the conftitution of England, the Earl of Devonfhire concerted with Sir Scrope the means for inviting him to England, and (upon his landing in the Weft) joined the Earl at Nottingham, and united with him in a declaration, dated 22 November 1688, of their fenfe and refolution, which was unanimoufly fubfcribed on this principle. " We own it rebellion to refift a King that " governs by law ; but he was always accounted a tyrant " that made his will the law ; and to refift fuch a one, " we juftly efteem no rebellion, but a neceffary and juft " defence." And when neceffity forced the Princefs Anne from London, he accompanied the Earl with a good body of horfe, who marched fome miles from Nottingham to conduct her thither.—In the convention-parliament he was one of the Knights for the county of Nottingham, and voted for fupplying the vacancy of the throne with K. William and Q. Mary ; for which hearty concurrence in the revolution he was 7 March 1688-9 made a groom of his Majefty's bed-chamber (which he held to the King's death) and advanced to the Peerage of Ireland by privy feal, dated at Kenfington 3 April, and by patent at Dublin 16 May 1701 *, by the titles of Baron of Clenawly and Vifcount How, with the creation fee of 13l. 6s. 8d. ; and her Majefty Q. Anne in 1711 appointed him comptroller of the excife.—In 1674 he married firft the Lady Anne Manners, fixth daughter of John, the eighth Earl of Rutland, by whom he had one fon John-Scrope, born 5 October 1675, who died young, and two daughters, Annabella, married to Mr. Goulding ; and Margaret to Captain Mugg.—His fecond wife was Juliana, daughter of William, Lord Allington,

---

* The preamble. Cum nos regia mente recolentes, quam mature prædilectus et fidelis Subditus nofter Scroopeus How de Langar in Comitatu noftro Nottingham in dicto Regno noftro Angliæ, Miles, fe illuftravit in defenfione Religionis et Libertatis Patriæ fuæ, cum in imminenti periculo ab Inimicis, tam domefticis quam foris, fecum extiterunt ; ac etiam repetita illa Teftimonia Fidelitatis et Ligeantiæ fuæ, quæ perfonæ noftræ regali ac Regimini noftro continuò et manifefte indicavit : Et ut futuris temporibus dignofcatur, quam gratiofe accepimus hæc laudabilia fua Merita ac Servitia, ac Monumentum quoddam Favoris regalis noftri, ob Benemerita tanta, ipfo Scroop How Militi et Pofteris fuis exhibere volentes. Sciatis igitur, &c. (Rot. Anno 13 Gul. III. 2ª. p. D.

lington of Horseheath in the county of Cambridge, and of Killard in Ireland, by his wife Juliana, daughter of Baptist Noel, Viscount Cambden, and departing this life at Langar 26 January 1712, was there buried, having issue by her, who died 10 September 1747, Emanuel-Scrope, his successor, and three daughters.

Mary, appointed in 1720 maid of honour to Caroline, Princess of Wales, and 14 June 1725 became the third wife of Thomas, Earl of Pembroke, by whom she had no issue; in October 1735 she re-married with John Mordaunt, Esq. brother to Charles, Earl of Peterborough, and died 12 September 1749. (1)

Judith, married to Thomas Page of Battlesdon in Bedfordshire, Esq. second son of Sir Gregory Page of Greenwich in Kent, who was created a Baronet by K. George I. and had no issue, she died his widow in 1780. (2)

Anne, married 8 May 1728 to Colonel Charles Mordaunt. (3)

Sir Emanuel-Scrope, the second Viscount, in 1730 succeeded Sir Richard Grubham How in the title of Baronet; was member for the county of Nottingham in the reigns of K. George I. and II. and in May 1732 being appointed governor of Barbadoes, died there 29 March 1735, and his corpse being brought to England 30 September following, was deposited in the family vault at Langar.—On 8 April 1719 his Lordship married Mary-Sophia-Charlotte, eldest daughter to the Baron Kielmansegge, made a Count of the Empire in October 1751 *; she was a lady of the bedchamber to the Princess of Wales, and dying 13 June 1782 was buried at Langar: by this Lady his Lordship had issue six sons and four daughters, viz. *Sir Emanuel-Scrope, 2 Viscount,*

Scrope, who died an infant. (1)
Sir George-Augustus, who succeeded to the honour. (2)

Sir

---

* He was master of the horse to K. George I. as Elector of Hanover, and died 15 November 1717; and his Lady was Sophia-Charlotte, daughter to Count Platen of the Empire, who was made a free denizen of Ireland 9 September 1721, two days after created by patent (pursuant to a privy seal, bearing date at Kensington 14 August) Countess of Leinster; and 10 April 1722 Baroness of Brentford, and Countess of Darlington in England, being also Countess of Platen and Baroness Kielmansegge in Germany; and she died 20 April 1725.—Lady How brought a considerable estate to the family; and 15 April 1719 the King granted to her and his Lordship for life, the yearly pension of 75*l.* from Christmas preceding, which was renewed to her daughter Juliana 30 April 1758 for life. (Lodge and Pension List.)

(3) Sir Richard the prefent Vifcount.
(4) John, who died 1 September 1769.
(5) William, Knight of the Bath, Colonel of the Nineteenth regiment of dragoons, Lieutenant-Governor of the Ifle of Wight, made a Lieutenant-General 25 May 1772; and a member of the Britifh privy council; being appointed Commander in Chief of his Majefty's forces in North-America, he landed in that capacity at Bofton 25 May 1775, which ftation he continued to fill till 1778, when he obtained letters of recall. He married Frances, fourth daughter of the Right Hon. William Conolly of Caftletown in the county of Kildare, but has no iffue.
(6) Thomas, who died unmarried 14 November 1771, aged 41.
(1) Daughter Caroline, married to John How of Hanflop in the county of Bucks, and is deceafed.
(2) Charlotte, 12 Auguft 1752 to Robert Fettiplace of Swinbrook in the county of Oxford, and died in July 1787.
(3) Juliana, now living; and
(4) Mary, married to William-Auguftus Pitt of Heckfield in the county of Hants, brother to George, Lord Rivers, Colonel of the tenth regiment of dragoons, a Lieutenant-general, Commander in Chief of the forces in Ireland, and a member of the privy council in this kingdom.

Sir George-Auguftus, 3 Vifcount. Sir George-Auguftus, the third Vifcount, in May 1747, was returned to the parliament of England for the town of Nottingham, and entering into the army, obtained a company in the firft regiment of foot-guards 1 May 1749: he was promoted to a regiment of foot 28 September 1757, and afterwards commanded as a Brigadier-General under General Abercrombie in North-America, where he was killed in a fkirmifh with a party of French on the march towards Ticonderoga 5 July; he fell much lamented, and dying a bachelor was fucceeded in the honour by his brother

Sir Richard, 4 Vifcount. Sir Richard, the fourth and prefent Vifcount How, who at an early period manifefted a predilection for the naval life, and in that profeffion he has added new glory to the Britifh empire. He commanded the fquadron which failed from Portfmouth 1 June 1758, with the troops deftined to make a defcent upon the coaft of France under the command of the late Duke of Marlborough, when they deftroyed above 100 fail under the cannon of St. Maloes, and took and deftroyed Cherbourg. In 1759 he commanded the Magnanime, and fhared in the laurels of 20 November that year. In 1765 he he was appointed Treasurer of the Navy, which office he resigned in 1770. In 1776 he had the command of the fleet in North-America, and arrived at Hallifax with his squadron 14 July that year. In 1782 he relieved Gibraltar in the face of 50 sail of the line, and afterwards repulsed the combined fleets of France and Spain.—His Lordship is an Admiral of the White Flag, and being appointed first Lord of the Admiralty, resigned that office in July 1788.— 20 April 1782 his Majesty was pleased to create him Viscount How of Langar in the county of Nottingham, England; and in 1788 he was further advanced to the dignity of an Earl of Great-Britain, by the title of Earl How.

He married 10 March 1758 Mary, daughter of Chiverton Hartopp of Welby in the county of Leicester, Esq. and has issue three daughters, Sophia-Charlotte, born 19 February 1762, and married 21 May 1787 to John Earl of Altamont; Mary-Juliana, born 17 April 1765, married in August 1787 to Penn Ashton Curson of Cosall in the county of Leicester, Esq.; and Louisa-Catharine, born 9 December 1767 [1].

TITLES.] Sir Richard How, Earl and Viscount How, Baron of Clenawly, and Baronet.

CREATIONS.] Baronet 22 September 1660, 12 Car. II. V. How, and B. of Clenawly in the county of Fermanagh 16 May 1701, 13 Will. III. V. How of Langar in the county of Nottingham, 20 April 1782, 22 Geo. III. and E. How in 1788, 28 same King.

ARMS.] Topaz, a fess between three wolves heads couped, diamond.

CREST.] In a ducal coronet, topaz, a plume of five feathers, saphire.

SUPPORTERS.] Two Cornish choughs, proper, beaked and membered, ruby.

MOTTO.] UTCUNQUE PLACUERET DEO.

SEAT.] Langar-Castle in the county of Nottingham 90 miles from London.

---

[1] Supp. to Collins, Lodge and Collections.

HAMILTON, Viscount STRABANE.*

21   THIS illustrious and far spreading family may vye with, if not excel any other in Europe, for antiquity and dignity. The name was originally assumed from the manor of Hambleden, otherwise Hamilton in the hundred of East Goscote, the parish of Barkby and county of Leicester, the inheritance of the old Earls of Leicester, from whose grant the Hamiltons possessed those lands, and in gratitude to their benefactor, bore for their coat-armour, *gules, three cinquefoils ermine*, the single cinquefoil being the paternal coat of the Earls of Meullant (or, Mellent) in Normandy; and they are both placed together in St. Mary's church, Leicester, which city had also the arms it bears from the family of Leicester.

Bernard.   The descent is authentically deduced from Bernard, near kinsman to Rollo, the first Duke of Normandy, who, upon the decease of that Duke, was appointed Governor to his son Duke William, surnamed De Longue Espee (Long-Sword) who at baptism changed his name to Robert, and governed the Dutchy during his minority.—In the Year 912 he married a Lady named Sphreta de Burgundia, by

Turfus.   whom he had a son Turfus, (or Turlofus) a noble Dane, who gave name to the city of Turville in Normandy, and in 955 married Emerberga de Brigenberg, Lady of Pont-

Turloff.   Audemar, and was father of Turloff (or Turolfe) Lord of Pont-Audemar, in his mother's right; who took to wife Wevia, daughter of Harfust, a Danish nobleman, sister to Herfastus, and to Gunilda (or Gunnora) second wife to Richard, the first of that name, Duke of Normandy, great-grandfather to K. William the Conqueror. By her he

---

* This family history has been corrected by Douglas's Peerage of Scotland under the titles of Hamilton and Abercorn; from which many additions have been made, as also from the *Author's* Collections.

he had Humfrey, surnamed *De Vetulis*, Lord of Pont-Audemar, who by Albreda De la Haie-Auberie, had Roger de Bellamont (commonly called Beaumont) Lord of Pont-Audemar, who gave name to the town of Beaumont Le Roger in Normandy.—He was one of the council that persuaded the Norman Duke to invade England, in which expedition he accompanied him, with his two sons, and was afterwards a commander in the army, sent first against Gospatric, Earl of Northumberland, and then against Malcolm III. K. of Scotland, who was forced to submit and do homage to the Conqueror.—He finished and plentifully endowed the abbey of Preaux in Normandy (the foundation being laid by his father) and afterwards taking a farewell of the world, became a monk therein, chusing it for his place of sepulture.

He married Adelina, daughter of Walleranus, Earl of Mellent, sister and heir to Hugh, Earl of Mellent, and had two sons, Robert his successor, created Earl of Leicester; and Henry, surnamed de Newburgh, a pious and learned man, who rebuilt and fortified the castle of Warwick, of which he had the custody, and was created Earl of Warwick in 1076. He married Margaret, sister to Roderic, and daughter of Arnulph de Hesden, both Earls of Perche, and dying in 1123 (23 Hen. I.) left five sons, of whom Roger the eldest was ancestor to the Earls of Warwick of that surname, who ceased in Thomas de Newburgh, the sixth Earl, in 1242 (26 Hen. III.), who died without issue by his wife Ella, second daughter of William Longue-Espee, Earl of Salisbury, natural son of K. Henry II. by Rosamond Clifford.

Robert, the eldest son of Roger de Bellamont, Lord of Pont-Audemar and Earl of Mellent, obtained that castle and honour after the decease of his uncle Hugh, from the King of France, for a sum of money; and in the decisive battle of Hastings commanding the right wing of the Duke of Normandy's army, he valiantly broke in upon the enemy; and (as *Gul. Pictaviensis* writes) *Prælium illo die primum experiens, egit quod æternandum esset Laude cum Legione, quam in dextro Cornu duxit, viruen ac sternens magna cum Audacia.*——No wonder then, that for this great service (besides his inheritance in Normandy) he obtained large possessions in England when K. William shared the realm among his followers, and gave to Robert no less than 91 Lordships and Manors in the counties of Warwick, Leicester, Wilts, Northampton, and Gloucester.—He faithfully adhered

adhered to K. Henry I. againſt his elder brother Robert Curthoſe, Duke of Normandy, who on that account advanced him to the Earldom of Leiceſter in the year 1103, and conferred on him many conſiderable donations.—Henry of Huntingdon gives him a very large character, affirming him to have been the wiſeſt of all men between England and Jeruſalem; and by his vaſt poſſeſſions ſo powerful, that he made the Kings of England and France, friends or foes at pleaſure. His works of piety were many; among which, his rebuilding and endowing the church of St. Mary at Leiceſter, and placing ſecular Canons therein; his founding a college there for a Dean and 12 Prebendaries; an hoſpital at Brackley in the county of Northampton; and his large benefactions of the village of Arleſcote in Warwickſhire, the manor of Toſtes in Norfolk, and the church and tithes of Cherlenton to the Monks of Preaux, are none of the leaſt.——In 1096 he married Elizabeth-Iſabel, daughter of Hugh, ſurnamed *Magnus* (younger ſon of Henry I. King of France, by Anne, daughter of George, King of Ruſſia) who became Count of Vermandois, Valois, Chamont, and Amiens, by marrying Adelheld (or Alice) daughter and heir to Herbert, the fourth Count of Vermandois (deſcended in a male line from the Emperor Charlemaigne) by his wife Adelheld of Creſpie, daughter and heir to Ralph, the third Count of Creſpie and Valois, who in her own right was Counteſs of Valois and Amiens; and he dying 2 June 1118, was buried in the monaſtery of Preaux, having iſſue three ſons and ſeveral daughters, of whom Adelyne was married to Hugh de Montford; and Elizabeth (who was concubine to K. Henry I.) and marrying Gilbert de Clare, Earl of Pembroke, was mother of Richard de Clare, ſurnamed Strongbow, Earl of Pembroke, the conqueror of Ireland for K. Henry II. and alſo of a daughter Baſilia, married in 1175, to Reymond le Groſſe, anceſtor to Fitz-Maurice, Earl of Kerry. The ſons were

(1) Walleran, Earl of Mellent, who ſucceeded to the Norman Eſtate, and was created by K. Stephen in 1144, Earl of Worceſter; he married Elizabeth, daughter of Simon de Montfort, ſiſter to Simon, Earl of Eurieux, and aunt to Simon, Earl of Leiceſter, and had Robert, who enjoyed the Earldom of Mellent only; and by Maud, ſecond daughter of Reginald de Dunſtanville, Earl of Cornwall, natural ſon of K. Henry I., had Peter de Beaumont, Earl of Mellent, who quitting the Engliſh intereſt, and ſiding with

with the French King in 1203, was ancestor to a numerous race in France.

Robert, surnamed *Gibbosus, Le Bossu,* or *Crouch-Back,* a twin with his brother Walleran, succeeded in the Earldom of Leicester. (2)

Hugh, created Earl of Bedford by K. Stephen, on account of his marriage with the daughter of Simon de Beauchamp; but by fortifying his castle of Bedford against that King, he was degraded, and in the end reduced to such extreme poverty, that he was usually styled, *the Pauper.* (3)

Robert Le Bossu, on whom the Earldom of Leicester was settled by entail, enjoyed all his father's lands in England; firmly adhered to K. Henry I.; and for his loyalty to K. Stephen, obtained a grant of the whole county of Hereford, except a few Knight's fees; yet in the sixteenth year of that reign, he was one of those nobles, who met Henry, Duke of Normandy upon his arrival in England, and so effectually supported him, that thirty fortified castles, yielded to his obedience; whereby he so merited that Prince's esteem, that, after he had acquired the crown, he made him justice of the whole Kingdom.—— Among his many works of piety, may well be reckoned his gift of the manor of Dalby in the Woulds, Leicestershire, to the Knights Hospitallers of St. John of Jerusalem; with his foundation and plentiful endowment of the monastery of Nun-Eaton in Warwickshire, for Benedictine Nuns, wherein his Countess became one, and was buried. ——In 1119 he married Amicia (or Avicia) daughter of Rudolph (Ralph) de Guader, and turning a Canon Regular in St. Mary de Pratis, where in 1168 he was buried, having served God religiously there for 15 years, had issue four sons and two daughters; Robert his successor; Henry, Geffrey, John; Isabel, married to Simon St. Liz, the second Earl of Huntingdon and Northampton; and Avice, to William, the second Earl of Gloucester, son to Robert de Caen, natural son of K. Henry I. *Robert, 2 Earl..*

Robert, the third Earl of Leicester, was surnamed *De Blanche Mains* (White Hands) and at the coronation of Richard I., carried one of the swords of state, after having been imprisoned at Falaise in Normandy, for espousing the cause of Henry, the King's son, whom he had caused to be crowned in the life-time of his father, and dying at Duras, in Greece, on his return from Jerusalem in 1190, was there buried.—In 1167 he married Petronilla (Pernell) *Robert, 3 Earl.*

daughter

daughter and heir to Hugh de Grandmesnil (or Grentmaisnel) Lord of Hinckley and Great Steward of England, by whom he and his posterity enjoyed that Lordship and distinguished honour; and his issue were three sons and two daughters, viz.

(1) Robert de Bellamont, surnamed Fitz-Pernell, as heir to his mother, Earl of Leicester and great Steward of England, who had a grant from K. John of all Richmondshire, but died without issue in 1204, by his wife Loretta, daughter of William de Brechin, lord of Brechin.

(2) Roger, elected in 1189, and consecrated in 1198 Bishop of St. Andrews, was some time Chancellor of Scotland, and dying in 1202, was interred in the church of St. Rule.

(3) William, surnamed de Hamilton from the place of his birth, founder of the illustrious house of Hamilton.

(1) Daughter Amicia was married to Simon de Montfort, Earl of Eurieux, after Earl of Leicester in her right.

(2) Margaret, to Seyer de Quincy, created in 1207 Earl of Winchester, and by him, who died at Acon, on his return from Jerusalem in 1219, had Roger de Quincy, Great Constable of Scotland in right of his first wife Helen, eldest daughter and coheir to Alan, Earl of Galloway, who enjoyed that post, and aunt to John Baliol, declared King of Scotland in the year 1293.

Sir William Hamilton. Sir William de Hamilton, the third son, about the year 1215, and in the reign of Alexander II. K. of Scotland, going (as is generally asserted) into that kingdom, to visit his sister the Countess of Winchester, there married Mary, the only daughter and heir of Gilbert, Earl of Strathern; a lady of the first rank and quality in the kingdom, but the frequent wars, which had some time subsisted between England and Scotland, breaking out afresh after his arrival there, obliged him to return to his native country, the English having their estates in England confiscated on that account.—He had issue Sir Gilbert Hamilton, who was the first of the Family that settled in Scotland, the time of his removal thither being in the reign of Alexander II.; who gave him a kind reception, and to encourage his settlement there, made him a considerable grant of lands, *.—

Sir Gilbert.

He

* It is asserted by historians, that this Sir Gilbert left England about, or in the year 1323 (17 Edw. II.) who deliver the occasion of his departure to the following effect. Having one day in K. Edward's court spoken honourably and with respect of the great merit of Robert Bruce, then King of Scotland, John De la Spencer

HAMILTON, Viscount STRABANE.

He married in Scotland Isabella, daughter of Sir James Randolph of Strathdon, and sister to Thomas, created Earl of Murray in 1321, by his uncle K. Robert Bruce, Lord Chancellor of Scotland, and Governor of that kingdom in the reign of K. David II. and by her had two sons, Sir Walter his heir; and Sir John Hamilton of Ross-Aven, founder of the family of Prestoun in the county of Edinburgh * and its branches, of which in the reign of Charles II. Sir William Hamilton was created a Baronet.

Sir

(an officer in waiting, and a favourite of the King) thinking the discourse reflected on his master, gave him a blow, with many reproachful words; which he resented so highly, that the next day he fought with, and killed him.—His friends, well knowing Spencer's great interest and power, and that the King would resent his death, advised him to avoid his Majesty's displeasure by flying to Scotland; which he accordingly did, and was well received by K. Robert; who, to make him amends for what he had forfeited in England on his account, generously rewarded him with the lands mentioned in the text, then an appendage of the crown.—They add, that in his flight, being closely pursued into a wood, he and his servant changed cloaths with two wood-cutters, and taking their saw, were cutting through an oak tree, when the pursuers passed by; and that perceiving his servant to take notice of them, he hastily called to him, THROUGH; which word, with the oak and saw thro' it, he took for his *Motto* and *Crest*, in memory of that his happy deliverance.—He is also said to have been a very brave man, which he made appear on many occasions, particularly in the decisive battle of Bannockburn 25 July 1314, wherein his valour and conduct were so eminent, that he was knighted in the field, and had other lands given him.

This relation may be very true, but (we presume) cannot appertain to Sir Gilbert, for these reasons. His father Sir William in the year 1215 went into Scotland and married, from which time to Sir Gilbert's supposed flight there in 1323, is 108 years, which, generally speaking, is too long a term for a son to survive a father's marriage: But suppose he was not born 'till ten years after, which would be in 1225, he would, at the time of K. Robert's ascending the throne of Scotland in 1306, have been 81 years old, and at the time of his flight thither, 98, which will readily be allowed too great an age for a man to fight a duel, and fly from his prosecutors by a journey of about 300 miles. But what appears more conclusive is, what will be related in the text of his son and successor Sir Walter, who probably was the person that killed Spencer, and fled to Scotland (where his settlement then was) and received a grant of lands from K. Robert in 1324, the year after that event.

* This branch of the family differenced their coat-armour from the principal stock, by bearing the *cinquefoils, argent, within a bordure of the same*, as a note of cadency; and some of them gave the *bordure compony, argent and sable*: And as the family of Hamilton increased, and became seated in different parts of the kingdom, they distinguished their respective families by altering their arms.

Sir Walter. Sir Walter Hamilton, the eldest son, was a witness to several charters, granting lands to the Monastery of Paisley, about the end of K. Alexander III. reign; as also to the confirmation grant of the privilege of fishing for herrings, &c. to that fraternity, by James, great steward of Scotland in 1294. He is likewise one of the subscribers of the Ragman-Roll in 1296, where he writes himself Walter Fitz-Gilbert de Hamilton.—He was a person of distinguished eminence; had several military commands in the service of K. Robert Bruce, which he executed with success, and 9 of that reign was rewarded with a grant of the barony of Machanshire in the county of Lanerk; the King also bestowing on him in 1324 the barony of Cadzow, now called Hamilton, in the shire of Lanerk, also the lands and baronies of Kinniel, Larbor, Audcathie, and several others in the shire of Linlithgow; together with those of Kirkinder, Kirkowen, &c. in the shire of Wigton.—He married Mary, daughter of Adam Lord Gordon, and had issue two sons, David, and John, whose son (or grandson) John marrying Elizabeth, Daughter of ———— Stewart of Cruxtoun, with her had the lands of Ballincrief in West-Lothian; and the family afterwards matching with the daughter and heir to Sir Roger Digley of Innerwieck, that barony became their inheritance: And from this branch descended Sir Thomas Hamilton of Byres, whose son Sir Thomas was seated at Priestfield, and by Elizabeth, daughter of James Heriott of Trabrown, was the father of Thomas, appointed by K. James VI. a senator of the college of Justice; Lord Advocate, Lord Register, Secretary of State, Lord President of the Session, Lord Privy Seal, created Baron of Binney and Byres 30 November 1613; Earl of Haddingtoun 20 March 1619, and died 29 May 1637.

Sir David. Sir David Hamilton, the eldest son served K. David II. in his wars with England, and was one of his Majesty's brave attendants at the battle of Durham in 1346, when being taken prisoner with his master, he was delivered into the custody of William Zouch, Archbishop of York, but was soon released by paying a considerable ransom.—27 December 1368 K. David Bruce confirmed the charter of K. Robert.—In 1370 he sat in the parliament, when Robert II. nephew to K. David II. (who died childless) the son of his sister Margery, by Walter, Lord High Stewart of Scotland, was acknowledged to be the undoubted heir to the crown: Also, in 1373 (4 Rob. II.) being summoned to parliament, he appended his seal to the act, recognizing

that

that King's title to the crown, and settling the succession to it upon his legitimate children by his two Queens, viz. Elizabeth, daughter of Sir Adam Mure of Abercorn, and Euphemia, daughter of Hugh, Earl of Rofs.—He gave to the cathedral church of Glasgow an annuity of ten marcs sterling, issuing out of the barony of Kinneil, for the celebration of divine service at the altar of the Virgin Mary, for the health of the soul of the late K. Robert, the prosperity of K. David, for his own soul, and those of all his predecessors, and successors for ever.—He married Margaret, daughter of Sir Walter Leslie, Earl of Rofs, by Euphemia, Countefs of Rofs, daughter and heir to Earl William, son of Earl Hugh, and grandson of Earl William by Matilda, sister of K. Robert I. and deceasing in 1374, had issue two sons, Sir David, his successor at Hamilton; and Walter, ancestor to the families of Cambuskeneth, (commonly called Camskeith) in the shire of Air, of Sanghar, and its cadets.

Sir David Hamilton was knighted by K. Robert II. and upon his father's death summoned to parliament, having also been in the battle of Durham, and in 1377 (7 Rob. II.) had a grant of the lands of Bothwellmure in Lanerkshire; and likewife augmented his estate by his wife Janet or Johanna, daughter of Sir William Keith, in the sheriffdom of Ayr, Marefchal of Scotland, by whom he had one daughter Elizabeth, married in 1343 to Sir Alexander Frafier, Thane of Cowie and Dores, from whom defcends the Lord Salton, the fecond Baron of Scotland, and five fons, viz.

Sir David.

John, his fucceffor. (1)

Sir William, anceftor to the Hamiltons of Bathgate in the fhire of Linlithgow. (2)

Andrew, progenitor to the families of Bruntwood and Udftoun, whence branched thofe of Burncleugh, Rofchaugh, Pancatland, Bangour, and Wifhaw; the principal whereof were Sir Archibald Hamilton of Rofe-Hall, created a Baronet 10 April 1703; and Sir James Hamilton of Broomhill, whofe loyal fervices to K. Charles I. were rewarded in 1648, with the title of Baron of Bellhaven. (3)

George, who gave rife to the family of Boreland in Airfhire. (4)

David, who acquired a fair eftate by his marriage with a coheir of the family of Galbraith in the county of Stirling, (5)

he

he died before 1395, and was succeeded by his eldest son, from whom descended the Hamiltons of Bardowie.

Sir John. Sir John Hamilton, Lord of Cadzow, the eldest son lived in the reign of Robert III. he had been taken prisoner at sea by the English, but obtained an order from K. Richard, 28 October 1398, to be set at liberty, and in 1388 married Jacoba (Janet) daughter of Sir James Douglas, Lord of Dalkeith, ancestor to the Earl of Morton, by whom he had three sons, Sir James his heir; David, from whom sprang the families of Dalserf, Blackburn, Olershaw, Ladyland, Greene, and others; and Thomas, progenitor to the house of Raploch, from which issued those of Torrence, Darnagaber, Stanhouse, Woodhall, Aikenhead, Dechmont, Barnshill, and many other families in Scotland, with several flourishing branches in Ireland, of which the Earl of Clanbrassil is chief.

James,
I
Lord
Hamilton. Sir James Hamilton of Cadzow, was sent into England in 1423, as one of the hostages for the payment of 40,000 marcs, for the ransom of K. James I. (an evidence that he was then considered as one of the most considerable Barons of Scotland) which King sailing along the English coast, in his voyage to France eighteen years before, whither his father K. Robert III. was sending him, to avoid the evil designs of his uncle the Duke of Albany, who was endeavouring to settle the crown on his own posterity; and being sea-sick, was forced to land in England; which he had no sooner done, than he was arrested and carried to K. Henry IV. who committed him to the tower, which occasioned the death of his father 15 August 1406. He arrived at Edinburgh from his confinement 20 March 1423, soon after which he knighted Sir James Hamilton, and called him into his privy council.

In the eighth year of the reign of James II., 1445, (when the constitutions of parliament were new modelled into the form they subsisted in, until the union with England in 1707) he was entered among the Lords, all his lands being erected into the lordship of Hamilton.—In 1449 he was joined in commission with John, bishop of Glasgow; Andrew, Abbot of Melross; Alexander de Livingstowne of Calendar, Justiciary of Scotland; Patrick Cockburn, Provost of Edinburgh; and Peter Young, Dean of Dunkeld, to treat with the English about a peace; when a truce being concluded on 8 September, he had from that time, to the year 1454, a safe conduct to go into England every year, about affairs of the greatest importance.—In

the

the Earl of Douglas's rebellion, he and the Earl of Angus being sent to oppose him, entirely routed his forces in 1455, in consideration of which service he was rewarded with the baronies of Drumsargard and Carmonock, and with the heritable Sheriffalty of the county of Lanark, then in the crown, by the forfeiture of the said Earl of Douglas. —In 1451 he founded and endowed the collegiate church of Hamilton, and went to Rome to procure the Pope's bull of ratification, having a safe conduct from Henry VI. to pass through England: He was also a benefactor to the university of Glasgow 14 January 1459, then founded by bishop Turnbull; and having attained a good old age, died in 1460.

He married first Janet, daughter of Sir Alexander Livingston of Calendar, ancestor to the Earl of Linlithgow, by whom he had four sons; James, his successor; Andrew, first of the family of Silverton-Hill in the shire of Lanark, from whom Lord Belhaven is descended; Gawen, Provost of the collegiate church of Bothwell, and founder of the family of Orbiston, from which branched the Hamiltons of Dabhell Haigs (whereof Alexander was advanced to the degree of a baronet 11 February 1670, which is now extinct) Kilbrachmont, Dalziel, Monkland, Bothwellhaugh, Parkhead, and Barr: And John the youngest being seated at Whistleberry in Lanarkshire, his posterity still subsists there.

———His second wife was Euphemia, daughter of Patrick Graham, Earl of Strathern, sister to Malise, Earl of Monteith, great-grandchild to K. Robert II. both by father and mother, and widow of Archibald Earl of Douglas, and Duke of Turenne in France; by her he had one son, Sir John Hamilton of Shawfield in the county of Lanark; and two daughters, Mary, married to Sir William Keith, created by K. James II. Earl Marishal; and Elizabeth, to David Lindsay, the fourth Earl of Crawford, created Duke of Montrose, for life, by K. James III. being master of his household and chamberlain, by whom she had one son John, killed 9 September 1513, at the battle of Flowden-Field, without issue.

James, the second Lord Hamilton, was a person of remarkable courage and conduct, which he frequently manifested, particularly at Abercorn, and was in high esteem with K. James III. He was made a privy counsellor in 1440, and so continued till he entered into that memorable league with the Earls of Douglas, Ross, Crawfurd, and Murray, wherein they mutually swore never to desert one another;

James, 2 Lord.

another; that injuries done to one should be deemed as offered to all; and that they would spend their lives and fortunes in the vindication and defence of each other: But no sooner did he perceive their violent purposes against the King, than he quitted them and returned to his duty, whereupon ensued the ruin of Earl Douglas, who persisted in the rebellion.—In 1461 he was appointed one of the ambassadors to treat of a peace with England; and in 1471 his lordship and the other ambassadors, with 400 persons in their retinue, had a safe conduct to meet the Lord Howard and other commissioners in England, to treat of a league of amity: Also, 6 March 1472, he was commissioned with William Bishop of Aberdeen, David Earl of Crawfurd, John Lord Darnley, and Archibald Whitelaw Secretary of State, to treat about a lasting peace, which was concluded 28 September 1473, at Alnwycke in Northumberland.—In consideration of his excellent qualities, and in recompence of his eminent services, K. James III. was pleased in 1474 to give him in marriage his eldest sister Mary, then the widow of Thomas Boyde Earl of Arran (who died in exile at Antwerp in 1471) to which princess he was married by consent of parliament in 1474, and dying 6 November 1479, left one son James, and one daughter Elizabeth, married to Matthew Stewart, Earl of Lenox, great-grandmother by him of Henry, Lord Darnley, Duke of Albany, who 28 July 1564 being married to Mary Q. of Scots, had a son James, born 19 June 1565, who was the first King of the whole Island of Great-Britain, by the name of James VI. of Scotland and I. of England.

James I Earl of Arran.

James, the third Lord Hamilton, being endowed with all the great qualities suitable to his birth, early distinguished himself in the reign of James IV. by whom, when very young, he was called into the privy council, and in 1502 sent into England, to negociate a marriage between his majesty and the princess Margaret eldest daughter of Henry VII. which having concluded in 1503, he solemnized the nuptials with great magnificence; of which good service and great expence the King was so sensible, that he bestowed on him the Island of Arran, and created him Earl thereof by patent * dated 10 August 1503,

---

* The Preamble. Sciatis nos propter Propinquitatem Sanguinis inter nos et dilectum Consanguineum nostrum Jacobum, Dominum Hamilton, et pro suo gratuito Servitio nobis impenso et impendendo, ac pro

1503, with a commiſſion of Juſticiary within the ſaid iſland ——— Being a man of great prudence, and courage, he was ſent the year following commander of 3000 men in aid of Chriſtian II. King of Denmark, againſt the city and territory of Lubeck, whom with great conduct and ſucceſs, he brought to ſubmit to that King's conditions. He was afterwards made Admiral of Scotland; and in 1512 ſent into France at the head of 4000 men, to the aſſiſtance of Lewis XII. for his ſervices to whom he was rewarded with the honour of a Knight of the order of St. Michael, and an annual penſion of 12000 *livres* for life. But K. James IV. being killed in the battle of Flowden 9 September 1513, whilſt his Lordſhip was in France, he returned home, and ſtood fair to have been elected Regent, many giving their voices for him, in reſpect of his nearneſs in blood, his love for peace, and ſufficiency for ſuch a charge; but he generouſly yielded his pretenſions to his couſin-german John Stewart, Duke of Albany, ſon of Duke Alexander, and brother to K. James III. and was himſelf made captain and governor of Edinburgh caſtle. Alſo, on the ſaid Duke's voyage to France to renew the ancient league, which had inviolably ſubſiſted for ſome centuries between the two kingdoms, he was appointed in 1517 one of the ſix guardians of the realm, with the Earls of Angus, Huntley, Argyle, and the Archbiſhops of St. Andrew and Glaſgow, who were to rule alternately: And the Earl of Arran was unanimouſly choſen by them their *Primus* and Warden of the Marches; thus the whole authority devolving on his Lordſhip, he continued ſole Regent during the Duke's abſence, and in that interval concluded a peace with England; ſuppreſſed ſeveral inſurrections; preſerved regularity upon the borders; reſtored peace and quiet to the whole country; and diſcharged his high office to ſuch univerſal ſatisfaction, that upon the Duke's ſecond voyage into France, he was again conſtituted

---

ſuis magnis Laboribus et expenſis, factis et ſuſtentatis pro noſtro et Regni noſtri honore, tempore contractûs Matrimonii noſtri in facie Eccleſiæ ſolemnizati apud noſtrum Monaſterium ſanctæ Crucis prope Edinburg; ac cum Aviſamento et Conſenſu noſtri Conſilii ac trium Regni noſtri Statuum, pro tempore prædicto mature aviſatos, et ex noſtra expreſſa Scientia ac proprio motu dediſſe, conceſſiſſe, et hac præſenti Charta noſtra confirmaſſe eidem Jacobo, Domino Hamilton, totum et integrum Comitatum de Arran, jacentem in Vice-Comitatu de Bute, &c.

ed Regent, and obtained a general approbation of his faithful execution thereof.

He married first Beatrix, third daughter of John, the first Lord Drummond (by Elizabeth, daughter of David, Duke of Montrose, by Elizabeth daughter of James the first Lord Hamilton, as before-mentioned) by whom he had an only child Margaret, wife to Andrew Stewart, Lord Evandale and Ochiltree.—His second wife was Janet, (or Elizabeth) sister to Alexander the first Lord Home, Lord High Chamberlain of Scotland, but her former husband Sir Thomas Hay proving to be alive, he was, at his own special instance, in 1513 divorced from her by a court of delegates, and enabled to marry again; whereupon he took to his third wife Janet, daughter of Sir David Beaton of Creichton in the county of Fife, Comptroller of Scotland in the reign of James IV. widow of Sir Robert Livingston of Easter-Wemys, and departing this life in 1530, had issue by her two sons and two daughters, James, his successor; Sir John Hamilton of Clydsdale; Helen, who was the first wife of Archibald, the fourth Earl of Argyle; and Jane, the first wife of Alexander the fifth Earl of Glencairn.

James, 2 Earl.

James, the second Earl of Arran, a person of singular prudence and integrity, was in 1536, though very young, one of the attendants on K. James V. (by special appointment) in his voyage to France, where on 1 January he married Magdalene eldest daughter of K. Francis I. but that Queen dying 7 July following, the King 12 June 1538 married the Lady Mary of Lorrain, daughter of Rene, and sister of Francis, Duke of Guise, and relict of Lewis, Duke of Longueville; by whom having a son born the ensuing year, Lord Arran had the honour to be his godfather.————He was very forward and active in suppressing the incursions of the English upon the borders, and had the command of that body of troops, sent to defend the East-border; where he soon heard the mortifying news of the loss of the army at Solway, and not long after of the King's death, in his castle of Falkland 14 December 1542: Upon which event his Lordship, by the unanimous consent of parliament, was chosen Protector to Q. Mary, then only six days old, and Governor of Scotland, which was solemnly ratified by an act of the three estates, bearing date 13 March 1542-3, in which he was declared second person of the realm, and nearest to succeed to the crown on failure of the Queen and

her

her issue; and in that case to be rightful and undoubted King of Scotland; being further declared therein rightful tutor to the Queen, and governor of the kingdom, until she arrived to perfect age; and all the subjects were required to acknowledge and obey him, as sole regent, in all things belonging to his office.—This act was engrossed on a skin of parchment, and the great seal, with those of the Nobility, Prelates, and Burghs appended thereto, and it is now in the custody of his Grace of Hamilton.

His Lordship, soon after this appointment, entered into a treaty with England concerning a peace, and also a match between the infant Queen and Edward, Prince of Wales, son to Henry VIII. both which were agreed to, and ratified (on the part of Scotland) by a great majority in the parliament, which met at Edinburgh in August 1543. But the Earls of Huntley, Argyle, Montrose, Bothwell, Monteith, and Lord Fleming with many other worthy Scots opposed it, and entered into a most solemn association, whereby they bound and obliged themselves, with all their power, and at the hazard of their lives and fortunes, to oppose and obstruct the marriage, and the consequential union with England; after the treaty was concluded on, K. Henry VIII. refused to ratify it on the terms before agreed to, and made several additional demands, which being too exorbitant for the governor to comply with, that King caused his officers to seize several *Scots* ships, which, upon the faith of the treaty, had sailed to England with *French* and *Scots* goods; the governor highly resented this breach of articles, and in December 1543 he called a parliament, wherein (the 11) it was declared, that the King of England had broken and violated the treaty, and therefore it was not to be kept on the part of Scotland by law, equity, or just reason, but thenceforward to be null and void.

Upon this the war broke out again, and the governor not only most gallantly defeated the Lord Evers at Ancrum in Teviotdale, but being joined by Monsieur de Lerges, Count of Montgomery, with 3500 French auxiliaries, marched towards England in search of the Earl of Hertford, who, to retrieve the former loss, had entered Scotland, and laid waste a great part of the Merse and Teviotdale; but retired upon the governor's approach, who in his turn invaded England, ravaged the country, and returned with the glory of having defeated one army, and given chace to another, in one campaign: at which time K. Francis I. sent him the enfigns of the order of St. Michael.—But in 1547 the Scots being worsted by the Duke of Somerset at Pinky-Cleugh 10 September, with the loss of 8000 killed in the field, that nation had recourse to the French King, with whom the governor set on foot a treaty of marriage between the Queen and Francis the Dauphin, son of K. Henry II. In May 1549 that King created his Lordship, Duke of Chatelherault, and for the support of the honour, assigned to him and his heirs for ever lands of 30,000 livres a year, in confideration of his endeavour to accomplish the said match; which taking effect, her Majesty was sent into France, and *his* right of succession to the crown of Scotland acknowledged and recognized by the French King, the Dauphin, and the young Queen.

He continued Governor of Scotland to the year 1555, when the Queen being of sufficient age, chose her own guardians; by whose advice she named her mother to be regent during her abfence, to whom the Earl of Arran readily refigned that great post in full parliament, and laid down an employment, which he had held to the general satisfaction of the kingdom, and esteem of all foreign princes, who knew his deportment, for the space of twelve years. After he had thus divested himself of all authority, his conduct during his administration was solemnly and unanimously approved by the parliament, and he was again declared prefumptive heir to the crown, on the failure of Q. Mary and her iffue, and a very ample testimony given him of the good services he had done his country; the act fetting forth, " That he, by his great labours, vehement
" expences, and daily danger of himself, his kin and
" friends, had relieved their sovereign's most noble person
" from the cruel pursuits of the King and Council of Eng-
" land; and had left free the heal realm and dominions of
" his said sovereign Lady, without any part thereof with-
" holden by her Highness's old enemies of England, not-
" withstanding the assistance given them by several of the
" subjects of Scotland."

The Queen, on her return to Scotland in 1561, making choice of a new privy council (all, or most of whom were Protestants) he was appointed a member thereof; and in 1566 her Majesty sent him to take care of her interests in France, where he continued to do all the service he could, consistent with his honour and the Protestant cause, to the year 1569, when the Queen being compelled to refign the

the government to her son, she sent for him to head her party. He very zealously asserted her cause, and used his utmost endeavours to remove the Earl of Murray, then regent from his usurped authority, and restore her to the exercise of her regal power, in order to secure the peace of the country: And to that end having a commission from her, he raised what forces he could; but finding no hopes of assistance either from England or France, he endeavoured to accommodate all differences. The regent agreed to his proposals, and articles were entered into, by which the Duke and his friends were to meet him at Edinburgh 10 April 1569, in peace and safety, to consult and conclude on terms of accommodation; but when they were met, the regent, drawing out a paper, asked the Duke, if he would instantly subscribe an acknowledgement of the young King's authority, or not? To which he replied, " That he and his friends had laid down their arms
" conditionally, nor could he think himself or them oblig-
" ed to subscribe their allegiance to the King, unless, ac-
" cording to these conditions, the regent at the same time
" should grant what might be reasonably demanded in be-
" half of the distressed Queen; and therefore hoped he
" would not proceed to acts of force and fraud too, since
" not only he and his friends, but their hostages likewise
" were in his hands; desiring him to remember, that
" they had religiously observed every article of the late
" treaty, and had come secure and unarmed, as to a
" friend, firmly relying on his honour, and those assur-
" ances of safety he had given them, in the most solemn
" manner, under his own hand." To this remonstrance the regent made no reply; but, against all the laws of honour, and contrary to the stipulation, sent his Grace prisoner to Edinburgh-castle, where he was closely confined until the regent's death 23 January 1570, who was shot through the belly with a single ball at Linlithgow, by James Hamilton of Bothwell-Haugh, in revenge for an inhuman act of violence done to his wife, who in a cold winter's night had been stripped naked, and driven out of her house into the open fields, by which treatment she was frightened into fits, and soon after died.—His loyalty to Q. Mary in the time of her greatest distress was frequently acknowledged by her Majesty, who constantly called him, *father* (as her son did his son) and for which he underwent many sufferings during the course of the civil war. In 1571, with his sons, in a parliament called at Stirling by

Matthew

Matthew Stewart, Earl of Lenox, regent and grandfather to the young King, (who had burnt his castle and town of Hamilton) he was declared a rebel, and his estate forfeited; but by the treaty of Perth, which was confirmed by parliament at Edinburgh in 1573, they were restored to their estates and honours. After which, the Duke, who had retired to France, returned home, and being very aged, and infirm by his many fatigues, passed the remainder of his days in retirement at his Palace of Hamilton, where 22 January 1575 he bid adieu to the world.

By this account it is evident, he was a person of great justice and candour, and in all his actions consulted the publick good; which gave occasion to Archbishop Spotswood, in his history of the church of Scotland, to say, "That in his court there was nothing seen, that the severest eye could censure or reprove; in the public government such a moderation was kept, as no man was heard to complain; the governor was reverently obeyed, and held in as great respect, as any Kings of preceding times; he was a nobleman well inclined; open and plain, and without all dissimulation; and though he met with great troubles, yet, by the goodness of God, who doth always favour the innocent and honest-minded, he went through all, and died honourably and in peace."—He married Lady Margaret Douglas, eldest daughter of James, the fourth Earl of Morton (by Catharine his wife, natural daughter of K. James IV.) and had issue four sons, and four daughters, viz.

(1) James, 3 Earl.

James, the third Earl of Arran, who gave early proofs of inheriting the virtues of his ancestors in an eminent degree, and by Henry II. of France in 1555 was made Captain of his life-guard, with a pension of 2000 pistoles to support the dignity of his office. But he became defective in his understanding, and thereupon retired from the world, dying without issue in 1609.

(2) John, 1 Marquess of Hamilton.

John, the fourth Earl of Arran, born in 1532, privy counsellor to K. James VI. captain of Dumbarton-castle; in 1541 was appointed commendator of Arbroath-abbey, one of the richest benefices in Scotland (whose lands were erected into a temporal barony, in favour of his son, 5 May 1608); appointed, with full consent of the privy council, ambassador extraordinary to accomplish the marriage between the King and Princess Anne of Denmark, which he declined on account of his great age; so that the King going in person, his Majesty constituted him

lieutenant

lieutenant of the south of Scotland during his absence, and created him Marquess of Hamilton 19 April 1599, being the first in Scotland, who ever bore that dignity; and having lived to an advanced age, died 12 April 1604, in the highest favour with Prince and people, and was interred among his ancestors in the collegiate church of Hamilton.*

He married Margaret, daughter of John Lyon, the ninth Lord Glammis ancestor to the Earl of Strathmore, widow of Gilbert Kennedy, Earl of Cassilis, and had one son James, and one daughter Margaret, married to John, Lord Maxwell, ancestor to the Earl of Nithsdale.——James, the second Marquess of Hamilton, born 19 June 1589, was created 16 June 1619 Baron of Innerdale in Cumberland and Earl of Cambridge, which honours were limited to his issue male; sworn of the privy council; appointed 4 March following a gentleman of his Majesty's bedchamber and Lord Steward of his Houshold; constituted Lord High Commissioner to the parliament, which began 25 July 1621; installed a Knight of the Garter at Windsor 7 July 1623; and died on Ashwednesday (2 March) 1624-5 to the great grief of the King, who upon his death, and *that* of the Duke of Lenox 16 February before, prophetically apprehended his own, (which happened 27 March ensuing) saying, *that as the branches were now cut down, the root would quickly decay.*——His lady was Anne Cunningham, daughter of James, Earl of Glencairn, and his issue were three sons and three daughters, viz, James, and William, both Dukes of Hamilton; John, who died young; Lady Anne married to Hugh, Earl of Eglington; Lady Margaret, to John, Earl of Crawfurd; and Lady Mary, the first wife of James, Earl of Queensbury.

James, 2 Marquess.

James, the third Marquess, was born at Hamilton 19 June 1606, and when 14 years of age, sent for to court, and married to the Lady Mary Fielding, daughter of William Earl of Denbigh; was created Duke of Hamilton 12 April 1643, and was beheaded for his loyalty to K. Charles I. on 9 March 1648, having issue by his Lady, who died in 1638, three sons and three daughters; Charles, James,

James, 1 Duke.

* When sentence of death was passed upon his royal mistress in England, she pulled a ring off her finger, and ordered one of her servants to deliver it to her cousin Lord John Hamilton, as a token of the just sense she had of his constant fidelity and sufferings for her interest, which ring is still preserved in the Duke's family.—— (Douglas. p.332.)

James, and William, who all died young; as did Mary the eldest daughter; but Anne the second after the death of her uncle, became Dutchess of Hamilton; and Susanna the youngest was married to John, Earl of Cassilis.

William, 2 Duke.
William, the second Duke, who succeeded his brother, was born 4 December 1616; created Earl of Lanark, Lord Machanshire and Polmont 31 March 1639; made Secretary of State for Scotland in 1640, and receiving a shot in his leg 3 September 1651 in the battle of Worcester, died the next day, and was interred in the cathedral there. He married in 1638 the Lady Elizabeth Maxwell, eldest daughter and coheir to James, Earl of Dirleton, by whom he had five daughters, and one son James, who dying an infant, the estate and honours of the family devolved on his niece, the Lady Anne Hamilton, who being married to William Douglas, Earl of Selkirk, eldest son of William, the first Marquess of Douglass, by his second wife Mary, third daughter of George, Marquess of Huntly, it was stipulated by the marriage articles, that he and his children by her should take and use the surname of Hamilton; which was accordingly done, and by her he was ancestor to the present Duke of Hamilton; who being really and in fact a Douglas, we shall refer the reader to the *Peerages* of England and Scotland for a fuller account of his family; and observe here, that the male-line of the house of Hamilton, is, by failure of issue in the two brothers aforesaid, the Dukes James and William, represented by the Earl of Abercorn, descended from

(3) Lord Claud Hamilton, the third son of James, the second Earl of Arran.

(4) Lord David the fourth son died young.

(1) Daughter Lady Barbara was married to James, Lord Fleming, Lord High Chamberlain of Scotland, who died at Paris in 1558, leaving by her an only daughter Jane, first married to John, Lord Thirlestane, and secondly to Gilbert, Earl of Cassilis.

(2) Lady Anne, married to George Gordon, the fifth Earl of Huntly, Lord High Chancellor of Scotland, who died in 1576, and was father by her of George, created Marquess of Huntly, ancestor to the Duke of Gordon.

(3) Lady Margaret, to Alexander, Lord Gordon, son and heir to George, Earl of Huntly, and had no issue.

(4) Lady Jean, to Hugh, the third Earl of Eglington, and died childless.

Lord Claud, the third son, was appointed to the commendatorship of the abbey of Paisley in 1553, on the resignation of John, Archbishop of St. Andrews, which promotion was ratified by Pope Julius III.—On the breaking out of the civil war in 1567, he adhered to the interest of Q. Mary, who appointed him one of the principal commanders of her army at the battle of Langside, fought in 1568, where he performed the part of a valiant officer; but that battle being lost, the Earl of Murray (Regent) called a parliament in July at Edinburgh, where Lord Claud and other partizans of the Queen were summoned to appear; instead of obeying the summons, he persisted resolutely in the Queen's service, for which he was outlawed, and had his estate forfeited.—In 1572 the Lord Semple having possession of his estate, (by gift of the Earl of Mar, then Regent) kept a strong garrison in the abbey of Paisley, and so harrassed the tenants, that they entreated Lord Claud to relieve them; promising at the hazard of their lives, to assist him in the recovery of his estate; whereupon he so closely besieged the abbey with a strong party, that Lord Semple was forced to surrender at discretion.

In 1579 the Earl of Morton (Regent) endeavoured all he could the ruin of the house of Hamilton, both out of fear of their power, and in hope of obtaining a good share of their large estates, when forfeited; with this view, he prevailed on the old Countess of Mar, and the Earl her grandson, who were in great favour with the King, to insinuate to him, that the Hamiltons having often been declared heirs to the Crown, had in that hearty manner espoused his mother's cause, only to destroy him, who stood in their way; to prevent which, it would be adviseable for his Majesty, to use means to lessen their power. The King being thus prepared and prepossessed with an ill opinion of the family, in steps the Earl of Morton and seconds them; telling the King, it would be easy for him to put in execution the sentences of forfeiture against the family, which had never yet been repealed, nor could be but by act of parliament. A gross misrepresentation this! their forfeitures having been repealed, in all the forms, in 1573 by the act of parliament, confirming the treaty of Perth. In pursuance of this advice, the King in council resolved to apprehend the lords John and Claud Hamilton, who were then at Edinburgh, under sanction of the articles of agreement and pacification, ratified on all sides

the

Claud,
1
Lord
Paisley.

the year before: But they having received intimation of his purpose, made their escape; Lord John flying on foot in a seaman's dress to England, and thence to France, where he was kindly received and entertained by James Beaton, bishop of Glasgow, Q. Mary's ambassador at that court; and Lord Claud, after lurking some time in the borders of Scotland, being taken notice of, fled into England, and lived privately with a friend.

In 1585, after the King came to manage by his own councils, they returned to Scotland; and joining forces with several other proscribed and exiled Lords, advanced towards Edinburgh; when the King sending to know their intentions by this new rising and rebellion, they answered, " That as their enemies had contrived to get
" them banished, and had deprived them of all other
" means of sending their petitions to his Majesty, they
" were reduced to the necessity of coming in that man-
" ner, to endeavour to obtain admittance to his royal
" person, whose mercy and favour they would supplicate
" on their knees." The King hereupon was pacified, and 1 November 1585 admitted them to his presence, when falling on their knees, Lord John, in the name of them all, said, " They were come to implore in the most hum-
" ble manner his Majesty's mercy, favour, and pardon
" for coming in arms, which nothing should have com-
" pelled them to, but the want of other means to secure
" their lives from their enemies, who had taken such
" pains to misrepresent them to his Majesty; where-
" as they were loyal to him, and resolved to serve and
" obey him, as became dutiful and faithful subjects."
To this the King answered, " that though their enter-
" prize was in effect treasonable, yet in consideration
" of their being driven to it by necessity, and in hope
" of their future good behaviour, he pardoned them."
They then arose, and kissed his Majesty's hand, who addressing himself to Lord John, said, " My Lord, I never
" did see you before, and must confess that (I believe) of
" all this company you have been most wronged: Your
" family have been faithful servants to the Queen my
" mother in my minority, and (when I understood not,
" as I do now, the state of things) hardly used." Two days after, their pardon was confirmed by an act of council; proclaimed by sound of trumpet at the market-cross, and soon after a parliament being called, the acts of forfeitures were repealed, and the family restored to their ti-

tles and estates. And in 1585 the Barony and Lordship of Paisley, with the pertinents belonging to the abbey, were bestowed upon Lord Claud, and he was created Baron of Paisley.

He married Margaret, daughter of George, Lord Seton, (by Isabel, daughter of Sir William Hamilton of Sanquhar) sister to Robert, created Earl of Wintoun, and to Alexander, Earl of Dumferling, Lord High Chancellor of Scotland for 18 years; and departing this life in 1621, in a very advanced age, had issue one daughter Margaret, married to William, the first Marquess of Douglas, by whom she was great-grandmother of Archibald, created Duke of Douglas by Q. Anne, and four sons, viz.

James, created Earl of Abercorn. (1)

Sir Claud Hamilton, a gentleman of the King's privy (2) chamber, and by privy seal, dated at Westminster 6 October 1618 made constable, or commander of the castle or fort of Toome in the county of Antrim for life, with six warders, on the surrender of Sir Thomas Phillips.——As an undertaker in the plantation of the county of Longford, he had 400 acres of land granted to him there; together with the small proportions of Killeny and Teadan, containing 2000 acres, in the barony of Strabane and county of Tyrone, on which he built a strong and beautiful castle; which, with other lands mentioned in the patent, descended to his son and heir William; but K. James I. being informed, that it was the purpose and intention of Sir Claud, to confer the said proportions on his second son Alexander, did on 20 October 1618 direct his judges to admit the said William, then about 14 years old, to suffer a common recovery against him and his heirs, of the same, which was accordingly done, and the lands afterwards confirmed to Alexander by patent.——Sir Claud married the daughter and heir of Sir Robert Hamilton of Manor-Eliefton in the county of Tyrone, and had six sons and two daughters, Sir William, Alexander, Robert, George, Claud, and James, which five last died unmarried [1]; and the daughters were the Ladies of Lamington, and Gorgonoch-Stewart.——Sir William Hamilton of Manor-Eliefton, the eldest son, by his will, dated 1 May 1662, and proved 12 February 1664, ordered his body to be buried in the church of Badonie, or of Gortin, as he should afterwards appoint, having issue by his first wife, James his heir,

[1] Chancery Pleadings.

heir [1], William, Sarah, and Margaret; and by his second wife Beatrix, daughter of —— Campbell, two sons, Claud and Archibald.

(3) Sir George Hamilton of Greenlaw, and Roscrea, in the county of Tipperary, Knt. married first Isabella of the family of Civico of Bruges in Flanders, by whom he had one daughter Margaret, who became the first wife of Sir Archibald Acheson of Gosford, Bart. ancestor to Sir Archibald, Viscount Gosford.

(4) Sir Frederick Hamilton, ancestor to the Viscount Boyne.

James, [1] Earl of Abercorn. James, the eldest son of Claud, Lord Paisley, commonly designed master of Paisley, being a man of great parts and abilities, was much taken notice of at court, where he was a Lord of the King's bedchamber; who, by reason of his especial merit, advanced him in 1604 to the dignity of Baron of Abercorn; in which year he was appointed one of the commissioners on the part of Scotland, to treat of an union with England; his Majesty being also further pleased by patent, bearing date 10 July 1606, to create him Earl of Abercorn, and Baron of Hamilton, Mount-castle and Kilpatrick. And the King purposing to hold a parliament in Ireland, made choice of some few eminent persons, capable of that honour and trust, for the nobility of their birth, and their estates and possessions in this kingdom, to be assistant with the Upper House, and to have place and voice as Peers of the realm; and therefore by his letter from Westminster 31 March 1613, authorized the L. D. to call to the next parliament, by writ of summons, his right trusty and right well-beloved cousin the Earl of Abercorn, directing that he should hold the same place and precedency of an Earl in parliament, as he did at the council-table, and in all other places [2].—On 20 May 1615 he was appointed of the council for the province of Munster; and had a large grant of lands in the Barony of Strabane *; upon which he built a very strong and fair castle;

---

* His Lordship, by his last will, having an intention to confer the small proportion and manor of Strabane, and the middle proportion of Shean (the latter of which he possessed by conveyance from Sir Thomas Boyde) on his second son Claud and his heirs; and the great proportion and manor of Donalong on his third son George and his heirs, and after his decease his eldest son James being desirous to obey his father's will, did, with his guardians, convey the same to them and their heirs respectively; by which deed his mother was to have a third part thereof for her dower, and the sum of 2555l. 11s. 1d.

was

[1] Chancery Pleadings.
[2] Rot. Canc. 1c°. 11°. f. R. 35.

HAMILTON, Viscount STRABANE.

castle; a school-house and church; and about the castle was built a town, consisting of eighty houses, many of lime and stone, very well and strongly built, and the rest good timber houses, in which were 120 families, able to make 200 men, every one having arms for his defence; and there were also built three water-mills for grinding of corn [1].

He married Mariana, daughter of Thomas, Lord Boyde, (ancestor to the Earl of Kilmarnock, by Mariana his wife, daughter of Sir Matthew Campbell of Loudon in the shire of Air, by Isabel his wife, daughter of Sir John Drummond of Innpeffery, by Jenet his wife, natural daughter of K. James IV. of Scotland) and deceasing 16 March 1617, before his father, had issue by her, (who, with Sir Claud Hamilton, Knt. was made a free denizen of Ireland 12 May 1620 [2], and died in, or about the year 1633) five sons and three daughters, viz.

(1) James his successor, created Baron of Strabane.

(2) Claud, to whom his brother, by permission of K. Charles I. resigned the honour of Strabane.

(3) Sir William Hamilton, Knt. who was long resident at Rome from Henrietta-Maria, Queen Dowager of England, and in his old age married Jane, daughter of Alexander Colquhoon, Laird of Luss, and widow of Alan, Lord Cathcart, but left no issue.

(4) Sir George Hamilton, Baronet of Nova-Scotia, ancestor to the present Earl of Abercorn.

Sir

was appointed to be raised thereout, to the use of his Lordship, and his brothers William and Alexander. But by the laws of the realm, the lands descended upon and remained in his Lordship, notwithstanding his father's will and his own deed, (he being in his nonage) neither could the Countess, not being a denizen, be endowed of the said lands, nor the said sum be raised out of them for the aforesaid uses. To remedy which inconveniencies, the King, in consideration of the manifold acceptable services of the said first Earl of Abercorn, (who was a faithful servant of his crown) directed the L. D. 12 February 1619 [3], to permit the Earl, being about the age of 16 years, to suffer a common recovery and levy a fine of the premisses to the aforesaid uses. Accordingly, 12 May 1620 the countess was made a free denizen, and by patent, dated 9 May 1621, the lands were granted to Sir Claud Hamilton of Cochonogh, Matthew Craifford and James Elphingston, Esqrs. in trust for the said uses.

[1] Pynnar's Survey of Ulster.
[2] Rot. Anno 18 Jac. I. 1ˢ. p. f.
[3] Privy Seal of that date at Newmarket.

(5) Sir Alexander Hamilton of Holborn, London, Knt. who married Elizabeth, a daughter of the family of Bedingfield of Oxburgh, and had one son and three daughters. He settled first at the Court of Philip-William, Elector-Palatine, who sent him envoy extraordinary to K. James II. of England.——He accompanied to Vienna that Elector's daughter Eleanora-Magdalena, who was married to the Emperor Leopold, and being in favour with the Empress, was created a Count of the Empire, with a grant of the county of Newburg near Paſſaw, and other eſtates in Moravia and Hungary.—One of his daughters was maid of honour to the Empreſs Emilia, conſort of the Emperor Joſeph; and his ſon Count Julius, was one of the chamberlains to the Emperor, married Maria-Erneſtina, born Counteſs of Staremberg, of the family of the famous Count Staremberg, who died in 1724, and had iſſue three ſons and ſeveral daughters.

(1) Daughter Lady Anne, was married to Hugh, Lord Semple.

(2) Lady Margaret, to Sir William Cunynghame of Caprington.

(3) Lady Lucy, contracted by her father, when very young, to the Marqueſs of Antrim, who not abiding by the contract, ſhe never married, and by letters from Whitehall 28 October 1627, the Earl of Antrim was ordered to pay 3000l. to James Earl of Abercorn, for his ſon's not marrying his ſaid daughter Lucy, according to contract [1].

James, 2 Earl. James, the ſecond Earl of Abercorn, in regard of his father's ſervices; of his noble blood and lineage, being deſcended of one of the moſt ancient houſes in the realm of Scotland (as the King expreſſeth himſelf) and becauſe his Majeſty was deſirous to encourage him and his poſterity to make their reſidence in the kingdom of Ireland, for the good of his ſervice there, not doubting but that he would tread in the ſteps of his anceſtors, and apply himſelf with his beſt endeavours to deſerve that favour, when his Majeſty ſhould have occaſion to employ him in his affairs, was advanced to the Peerage of Ireland, by the title of Lord Hamilton, Baron of Strabane, with limitation of the honour to the heirs male of the body of his father the Earl of Abercorn for ever, by privy ſeal, dated at Weſtminſter 18 October 1616, and by patent * at Dublin 8 May 1617, which

---

* The preamble. Cum Jacobus Hamilton, filius prænobilis et chariſſimi Conſanguinei noſtri Jacobi Comitis de Abercorn primogenitus,

[1] Rot. Anno 3 Car. I. 3ª. p. d. R. 52.

which honour, upon his petition to K. Charles I. was conferred * on his next brother Claud, with precedency of the former creation, by patent †, bearing date 14 August 1634. He mogenitus, de antiquissima et nobilissima Familia Comitum de Arran et Marchionum de Hamilton in dicto Regno Scotiæ, et Ducum Castelli-Eraldi in Regno Galliæ oriundus, tam præclari Ingenii ac Indolis existat, ut clarissimos Antecessores suos eximiis Virtutibus se æquaturum promittat. Cumque etiam præfatus Consanguineus noster Comes de Abercorne, Pater dicti Jacobi, optime de nobis et universa Republica dicti Regni Hiberniæ meritus sit, pro eo, viz. quod optimam Coloniam de Viris fortibus et sinceram Religionem profitentibus consistentem, in Baroniam de *Strabane*, in comitatu de *Tyrone*, in provincia *Ultoniæ* deduxerit, ac ibidem diversa Castella, bene munita pro defensione dictæ Provinciæ ædificaverit, ac plurima alia servitia nobis et Coronæ nostræ præstiterit; pro quibus dictum Comitem ejusque posteros pluribus honorum titulis dignos censemus. Sciatis igitur, &c.

* At his Lordship's humble suit, the King was pleased, in consideration of his long and faithful service, by privy seal¹, dated at Westminster 7 May 1633, to authorize the L. D. Wentworth, to issue a commission under the great seal of Ireland, directed to Sir William Jones and Sir Robert Barkeley, two of the Justices of the King's Bench in England, empowering them or either of them to take the acknowledgement of a fine, according to the statute of 4 Henry VII. from his Lordship of the said state, degree, dignity, style, title, name, and honour of Lord Hamilton, Baron of Strabane, to his Majesty; and upon return of the said commission, recording of the fine in Ireland, as in such cases was usual, cancelling the patent, and making a *Vacat* upon the inrollment thereof, to grant unto the said Claud the said honour of Lord Hamilton, Baron of Strabane, and for want of his issue male, remainder to the heirs male of the body of his father, with precedency of the former patent.—On 11 November following James, Earl of Abercorn surrendered his patent of Strabane, which was ordered to be cancelled 3 February, a *Vacat* entered upon the inrollment 14 August 1634, and a new patent of that date inrolled. On 2 of which month of August the L. D. upon his throne of state, mentioned to the House of Peers the case of this surrender and transfer of the honour, with the clause of precedency, which, he said, the King referred to him, but that thinking it might give offence to the nobility, he had advised his Majesty, that *that* clause which concerned precedency might be forborn; for which the King gave him thanks, and ordered it according to his opinion. " Yet " (added his Lordship) within these six days a warrant was brought " unto me for passing of the same otherwise, which I have certified. " And with the favour of your Lordships, I give my opinion, that " if any man find himself aggrieved, he may complain to me, who " have a commission to right him, or else transmit his complaint to " the King; but it becomes not the house, when the L. D. has " passed judgment, to intermeddle; and so long as I have the ho- " nour to sit here and represent my master, will not suffer any innova- " tion in prejudice of the interest of the crown." (Lords Jour. i. 22.)

† The preamble recites the creation of James, Earl of Abercorn, to the honour of Strabane by K. James I; his surrender thereof to K. Charles

¹ Rot. A°. 9 Car. I. 1. p. d. and enrolled 16 July 1633, R. 8.

He married Catharine, daughter and heir to Gervais Clifton, Lord Clifton of Leighton-Bromfwold, widow of Efme Stewart, Duke of Richmond and Lenox, by whom he had three fons, viz.

(1) James, Lord Paifley, who died before him, and by the daughter of William Lenthal, Efq. Speaker of the Houfe of Commons in the Long Parliament, left an only daughter Catharine, firft married to her coufin William Lenthal, Efq. (who died at Burford 6 September 1686, leaving two fons, John and James), and fecondly to Charles, Earl of Abercorn, as hereafter.

(2) William, Colonel of a regiment, and killed in the wars of Germany, without iffue.

(3) George, who fucceeding to the title, was the third Earl
George, of Abercorn; but dying unmarried at Padua in his journey
3 to Rome, the male line failed in the eldeft branch; fo
Earl. that we return to

Claud, Claud, the second son of James the firft Earl; who being dignified with the title of Strabane by his brother's
2 gift, as already obferved, was prefent as fuch, by proxy,
Lord in the parliament of this kingdom 21 March 1634 [1], and
Strabane. dying 14 June 1638, was buried in the church of Leak-Patrick in the county of Tyrone.—In 1630 he married the Lady Jean Gordon [*], youngeft daughter of George, the firft Marquefs of Huntly, and had iffue two fons and two daughters; James; George; Catharine (firft married to James, eldeft fon of Sir Frederick Hamilton, youngeft fon of Claud the firft Lord Paifley, fecondly to Owen Wynne of Lurganboy in the county of Leitrim, and thirdly to John Bingham

K. Charles I. with intention to confer it upon his brother, and the King's compliance therewith, on account of the undoubted teftimonies, by which the faid Claud had approved himfelf to be worthy of that mark of his Majefty's favour and munificence. (Rot. 10. Car. I. 2ª. p. f. R. 30, 31.)

[*] She expended above 1000l. in building the caftle, court-yard and garden-walls, about the caftle of Strabane, which in the beginning of the rebellion of 1641 were all demolifhed; all the furniture burnt and deftroyed; and in December that year fhe was taken prifoner by Sir Phelim O Neile (who then was paying his addreffes to her) and by him carried from Strabane, which he burned, to his own houfe of Kinard; where he kept her two or three days, and then fent her to Sir George Hamilton, telling her, with great oftentation, *That he would never leave off the work he had begun, until Mafs fhould be fung or faid in every church in Ireland, and that a Proteftant fhould not live in Ireland, be he of what nation he would.* She afterwards became his wife, and was reduced to fo indigent and deplorable a condition, as, in 1656, to accept of the fum of 5l. from the ftate towards her relief. (Lodge, Bill in Chancery, and depofition of Captain John Perkins of Dungannon, taken 8 March 1643.)

[1] Lords Jour. 1. 62.

Bingham of Castlebar in the county of Mayo, Esqrs.); and Mariana, to Richard Perkins of Lifford in the county of Donegall, Esq.

James, the eldest son and third Baron of Strabane, was seized in fee of the manor and small proportion of Strabane, the middle proportion of Shean, and many other lands in the county of Tyrone, which (as appears by inquisition [1]) he forfeited by entering into rebellion against the Commonwealth of England, at Charlemount in the county of Armagh 20 July 1650; where he joined with Sir Phelim O Neile, one of the chief heads of the rebels, who then held out that fort against Sir Charles Coote, commander in chief of the parliament forces in Ulster, who besieged it 25 of that month; about two or three days before which, his Lordship fled with his arms to an adjoining island, then under the command of a garrison of Sir Phelim's, in which lay two companies, whom he assisted by sending three horses into the fort; which being taken 6 August, he fled to the woods and bogs of Mounterling in the county of Tyrone, where that day he was taken prisoner by a party of the Commonwealth's army. On the 13 he took a protection from Sir Charles Coote; which he forfeited 31 December ensuing, by joining again with Sir Phelim O Neile in the Island of Drumurragh; and 1 July 1649 he accepted a commission, to raise and arm a troop of horse in behalf of the Irish, with whom he afterwards acted in concert; frequently joined counsels with them, and died a Roman Catholick recusant 16 June 1655 at Ballyfatty near Strabane; leaving no issue he was succeeded by his brother

James, 3 Lord.

George the fourth Lord Strabane, who married Elizabeth, daughter of Christopher Fagan of Feltrim in the county of Dublin, Esq.*, and by his nuncupative will, made

George, 4 Lord.

---

* In the court of claims for executing the act of settlement, the said Christopher Fagan claimed his estate, and by the decree of that court 20 March 1663 was adjudged an innocent papist, and had his estate restored to him and his heirs male: And leaving two sons, Richard and Peter, and the said Elizabeth, Lady Strabane, she, on the death of her brothers without issue, could not become heir to her father under that decree, which vested the reversion in the crown. Whereupon, K. Charles II. by privy seal, dated 29 March 1684, granted the reversion to her son Claud, Lord Abercorn, his heirs and

[1] Taken at Strabane 9 August 1658, by virtue of a commission dated 7 July preceding, to enquire what estate, right and title O. Cromwell then had, or ought to have, by any act of parliament, or act of him and his council, to any hereditaments within the county of Tyrone.

made at his house of Kinure in the same county 9 April 1668 *, desired to be buried in the chapel of Kinure, but was interred in the remains of St. Mechlin's church in a field near Rush, under a large tomb on the North side, adorned with his coat-armour and this inscription:

> Here under lieth the affabell,
> Obliginge, examplar, wife, humble,
> Noble, pious, devot, most charitable,
> Most virtuous and religious the
> Right Honourable George, Lord
> Hamilton, Baron of Strabane,
> Who died the 14th of April
> Anno Domini 1668.
> This monument was erected by
> Elizabeth Strabane, alias Fagan,
> Relict of the said Lord Strabane.

His issue were two sons and two daughters; Claud and Charles, successive Earls of Abercorn; Anne, married to John, son of George Browne of *the Neale* in the county of Mayo, Esq. and died 14 August 1680; and Mary, born after her father's death, was married to Gerald Dillon, Esq. Recorder of Dublin, appointed in 1685 one of the council at law to K. James II. and 15 February 1686 his prime-serjeant, by whom she had several children.

Claud, 4 Earl of Abercorn.

Claud, the fifth Lord Strabane, succeeding also to the title of Abercorn, was the fourth Earl, and 9 January 1670, had an abatement of the quit-rents imposed on his estate by the acts of settlement; being an attendant on K. James II. from France was sworn of his privy council on his arrival in Dublin, and made Colonel of a regiment in his army, but was attainted 1 March 1688 ¹.—He attended the King into the North, in order to reduce Londonderry,

and assignes for 1000 years, to commence from the determination of the said estate tail, with a condition to be inserted in the patent, for granting to him the fee of the premisses.

* By which will he desired that all his debts should be paid, and that Elizabeth his wife should enjoy one-third of his estate then in his hands for life, or a third of his rents as they were paid, at her choice, as also a third of the estate his mother then enjoyed after his death, and to have the management of the other two-third parts for the use and maintenance of his children; but that she should have no power to dispose of any of them, or of any part of his estate, save what should belong to herself, without the consent and approbation of Sir George Hamilton, Christopher Fagan, Esq., and John Murphy, Gent. whom he appointed his special friends in trust in this matter, and he appointed his wife executrix. (Proved 26 May 1668 in the Court of Prerogative.)

¹ Inq. taken at Strabane 6 August 1692.

donderry, and, when near the city, was sent with a party from the army, to persuade the citizens to surrender the place, which they utterly refused; and making a sally some time after, his Lordship's horse was killed under him, and he very narrowly escaped, leaving his cloak and furniture behind him. After the defeat at the Boyne he embarked for France in which voyage he was killed (1690); 11 May 1691 he was outlawed and forfeited his estate and title of Strabane: But the Earldom of Abercorn devolved on his brother

Charles, the fifth Earl, who obtaining a reversal of his brother's attainder, succeeded also to the title of Strabane and the estate, to both which he was restored by their Majesties letters, dated at Whitehall 24 May 1692, and by patent at Dublin 1 July 1693 [1]. On 31 August 1695 he took his seat in the House of Peers [2]; and 2 December 1697 signed the declaration and association in defence of the person and government of K. William, and the succession of the crown according to act of parliament. He married (as already observed) Catharine, only daughter of James, Lord Paisley, eldest son of James, the second Earl of Abercorn, relict of William Lenthal, Esq. and died at Strabane in June 1701 [3], having issue by her (who deceased 24 May 1713, and was buried in the Duke of Richmond's vault, Westminster-abbey) an only child Elizabeth, who died young, and was buried in the chancel of St. Michan's church 22 February 1699; so that the issue male failed also in the second branch of James, the first Earl of Abercorn, and Sir William Hamilton, the third son, dying likewise without issue, we return to

Sir George Hamilton, the fourth son, who was seated at Donalong in the county of Tyrone, and at Nenagh in Tipperary. On 16 October 1627 he succeeded Sir Roger Hope (who died 7 September) in the command of his company in the army; and in 1641 being in Scotland with the King, had a pass to return to Ireland; but the House of Commons having voted, that no Irishman should pass out of England into Ireland, without a licence from the committee for Irish affairs, the privy council, or the L. L. he was stopped, brought by order of the House to London, and confined until 6 of April following, when he was admitted to bail.—During the rebellion he performed good

Charles, 5 Earl.

Sir George, Hamilton.

---

[1] Rot. 5 Gul. III. 2ª. p. d. [2] Lords Jour. I. 486.
[3] Le Neve's Mon. Ang.

service in Ireland for K. Charles I. as he did in 1649 for Charles II. being then a captain of horse, colonel of foot, and governor of the castle of Nenagh [1]; but in 1651 he retired with his family to France, and there continued till the restoration of the King; who being sensible of his good and acceptable services, and willing to shew him all reasonable favour for the same, created him a Baronet; and in 1671 appointed him joint patentee with James Roche, Esq. for granting licences to pedlars, petty-chapmen, and grey-merchants [*]; and being to recruit his regiment of foot in the service of the French King, his Majesty sent his directions to the L. L. 12 January 1673, to give licence unto him and his officers, to raise 600 foot soldiers of his Irish subjects by beat of drum.—He married Mary, third daughter of Thomas, Viscount Thurles, eldest son of Walter eleventh Earl of Ormond, and sister to James, the first Duke of Ormond, and by her [†], who died in August 1680, had six sons and three daughters.

James,

---

[*] On 7 February 1631 he had a licence to hold a Thursday market, and a yearly fair on 25 April at Clogher, and a fair 21 October at Ballymagary, both in the county of Tyrone.—On 23 July 1639 he had a grant upon the commission of grace, of the manor of Strabane; and 25 June that year another patent of the great proportion of Donalong; and in the act of settlement it was provided, that nothing therein contained should forfeit or vest in the King any honours, manors, or estate real whatsoever, belonging to him on 23 October 1641: Also, in the act of explanation, his Majesty having taken into his consideration the many faithful and acceptable services, performed to his father and himself in the wars of Ireland, by Sir George Hamilton, in several qualities and capacities, for which there were arrears to great value accrued to him, before and after 5 June 1649, which by agreement were reduced to 5000l. it was enacted, that the same should be satisfied out of the security set apart by the acts for satisfaction of the arrears of commissioned officers, for service before or after 5 June 1649; and he had a grant under the said acts, 16 May 1668, of the lands of Ballymacshanroe in the Barony of Ballymore and county of Cork, with two other grants of divers lands.—Further, (in recompence of his many acceptable services, performed to the King whilst in foreign countries) his Majesty, 20 December 1662, granted him by privy seal 23 April, and by patent for life, all the penalties and forfeitures which should or might accrue to the crown by reason of ploughing, drawing, harrowing and working with horses by the tail, contrary to act of parliament made in Ireland 10 and 11 Car. I. or any other former acts.

[†] Their marriage articles bear date 2 June 1629; and after the reduction of Ireland by the parliament, she obtained an order 25 May

[1] Act of explanation, wherein his arrears being reduced to 5000l. was provided to be satisfied out of the security designed by the acts for satisfaction of the arrears of such commissioned officers as served the King in Ireland before 15 June 1649.

James, who died before him. (1)

Sir George Hamilton, Knt. made a Count in France, (2) and Marefchal du Camp in that fervice; who married Frances, elder daughter and coheir to Richard Jennings of Sanddridge in the county of Hertford, Efq. fifter to Sarah, Dutchefs of Marlborough, and died in 1667, having iffue by her, who re-married with Richard Talbot, Duke of Tyrconnel, and died in Dublin 7 March 1730, three daughters; all then in their infancy, who lived with their mother in France, until they came with her into Ireland, in the reign of James II. which daughters were, Elizabeth, married to Richard, Vifcount Rofs; Frances, to Henry, Vifcount Dillon; and Mary, to Nicholas, Vifcount Kingfland.

Anthony who 1 January 1687 was a Lieutenant-Colonel, with the pay of 290l. a year upon the eftablifhment, (3) and at the Revolution followed K. James into France, in which fervice he became a Lieutenant-General, and died in that kingdom. He is prefumed the author of fome pieces written in French, which bear the name of Count Hamilton.

Thomas, bred to the fea-fervice, commanded the fhip, (4) which took the Duke of Argyle's in the Weft-Indies, and died in New-England.

Richard, made Colonel of a regiment of horfe in K. (5) James's army 15 February 1686, and Brigadier-General upon the eftablifhment, with the pay of 497l. 10s. a year; in which ftation he acted for that King in the North, and fled with him into France upon K. William's victories, where he became a L. General, and died.

John, a Colonel alfo in K. James's fervice, loft his life (6) at the battle of Aghrim.

Daughter Elizabeth, married to Philibert, Count of (1) Grammont, younger brother to Anthony, created in 1663 Duke of Grammont, Peer and Marefchal of France, Knight of the King's orders, Sovereign of Bidache, Count de Guiche and Louvignier, Baron of Hagetman and Camma, &c. by whom fhe had two daughters, Claude-Charlotte, married 3 April 1694 to Henry, Earl of Stafford, by whom fhe had no iffue; and the younger was, Superiour, or Abbefs of the Chanoneffes in Lorain.

Lucia, married to Sir Donogh O Brien of Lemineagh, (2) Bart.

Margaret, May 1653 to enjoy the middle proportion of Cloghonall and other lands, fettled on her for a jointure.

(3) Margaret, in January 1688 to Matthew Ford of Coolgreny in the county of Wexford, Esq. and had several children.

James, the eldest son, being a great favourite of K. Charles II. that Prince made him a groom of his bedchamber; Colonel of a regiment in his army *; and in 1661 concluded a marriage between him and Elizabeth, eldest daughter of John, created Lord Culpeper of Thorsway 21 October 1644, Chancellor of the Exchequer, and Master of the Rolls, who died in July 1660, by his wife Judith, daughter of Sir Thomas Culpeper of Hollingbourne in Kent, Knt. but commanding a regiment of foot on board the navy with the Duke of York, in one of his sea-expeditions against the Dutch, had one of his legs taken off by a cannon ball, of which wound he died 6 June 1673, and was buried in Westminster-Abbey under a monument, erected to his memory by his uncle James, Duke of Ormond.—By his Lady, who was maid of honour to Mary, Princess of Orange, mother of K. William, and died in 1709, he had six sons, of whom three only survived their infancy †, viz. James, who became Earl of Abercorn; George, a Colonel in the foot-guards, who lost his life in the battle of Steinkirk in 1692, commanding a regiment of foot; and William Hamilton, Esq. one of the five Kentish petitioners to the House of Commons, who 8 May 1701 desired, the parliament would turn their loyal addresses into bills of supply, that his Majesty might be enabled powerfully to assist his Allies against the growing power of France, which then caused a general consternation by the death of the King of Spain, and the alteration made in the affairs of Europe by the settlement of his dominions.—The house voted the petition scandalous, insolent and seditious, tending to destroy the constitution of parliament, and to subvert the established government; and ordered the five petitioners to be taken into the custody of the serjeant at arms; where they continued till 13 of May, when that officer

---

* By the act of explanation he had a grant of the estate of Sir Nicholas Plunket of Balrath in the county of Meath; and in consideration of his marriage, the King gave him Hyde-Park (for his own and his children's lives) but refusable at any time by the crown, on giving an equivalent for it. Accordingly, K. Charles gave him afterwards, in lieu of it, 900l. a year out of the first fruits and tenths of the dioceses of St. David's, Hereford, Oxford, and Worcester.

† Decree in Chancery.

officer (contrary to the *Habeas Corpus* act) by order of the house, and a warrant from the speaker, delivered them prisoners at the *Gate-House*, where they remained to the end of the session.—He resided at Chilston, or Boston-Place, near Lenham in Kent (an estate his mother purchased and settled on his family) of which county he was a Deputy-Lieutenant, Justice of the peace, and Colonel of the regiment of militia for the *Lath of Scray*, a division thereof; and was always very strenuous for the Protestant succession in the illustrious house now on the Throne.

He married Margaret, second daughter of Sir Thomas Culpeper of Hollingbourne, Knt. sister to Frances, wife of John, the last Lord Culpeper, and had issue four sons and one daughter, viz. John, (Sheriff of the county of Kent in 1719, who much improved his seat of Chilston; married Mary, daughter of John Wright, Esq. M. D. and had many sons and daughters, of whom the eldest son William, was page of honour to the Prince and Princess of Wales); George, (married the daughter of Monsieur Vasserot, merchant of Amsterdam, who got vast riches in the Missisippi and South-Sea schemes, after which he retired into Swisserland, his native country, where he purchased a great estate. By this Lady he had several sons and daughters, and for the sake of being near her relations, for some years resided at Geneva); Thomas, who had a command in the army, and died at his quarters in Ireland; William died when very young; and the daughter Elizabeth, was married to Edwin Steed of Steedhill in Kent, Esq. who left her a widow without issue.

Sir James, Viscount.

Sir James, the eldest son of James of the bedchamber, and grandson of Sir George Hamilton, Bart. succeeded his father in the post of groom of the bedchamber to K. Charles II. at the early age of 17 years, and was of the privy council to his brother and successor K. James, in whose army he commanded a regiment of horse; but no sooner did he perceive that King's intentions to introduce Popery, than he quitted his service; became an officer under K. William at the revolution, and carried arms and ammunition to the relief of Londonderry, when besieged by K. James's army, in which his uncle Richard Hamilton was a L.-General, and did all he could to distress the besieged; but by the means of this supply, the city was enabled to hold out, till Major-General Kirke sent in further relief from England, which occasioned the siege to be raised.— After his grandfather's death, he declined to use the title of
Baronet,

Baronet, being usually called Captain Hamilton, but in the year 1700 was obliged to bear a superior title by the Earldom of Abercorn devolving on him, as next heir to Earl Charles, the last male of the branch of Claud, the first Lord Strabane, who was second son of James, the first Earl of Abercorn. He was the sixth that enjoyed this honour, to preserve which he went to Scotland in 1706, and sat in that parliament, which concluded the union between the two kingdoms, now called Great-Britain.

K. William, in recompence of his services, called him into his privy council, and by privy seal, dated at Hampton-Court 9 November, and by patent * at Dublin 2 December 1701, created him Baron of Mountcastle and Viscount of Strabane, with the annual fee of 13l. 6s. 8d. by which titles he sat first in the parliament of Ireland 21 September 1703 [1], the first summoned to meet by Q. Anne, of whose privy council he was a member, as he was to their Majesties George I. and II.—On 14 February 1703, his Lordship was of the committee appointed to prepare an address to Q. Anne, on occasion of the evil practices lately carried on in Scotland by emissaries in France; and 3 March, to thank her Majesty for her great kindness to Ireland; also 10 February 1704-5 to congratulate her success by her victorious arms; and 6 May 1709, to draw up an address of condolence, on the death of her late Royal Consort Prince George of Denmark; and of congratulation for her great successes abroad in conjunction with her allies. On 14 November 1715 he was one of the committee to prepare an address of congratulation to K. George I. on his most happy accession; and 6 February ensuing presented to the house, heads of a bill, for the further security of his Majesty's person and government, and for extinguishing the hopes of the pretended Prince of Wales, and his open and secret abbettors [2].

In 1686 his Lordship married Elizabeth, daughter and heir to Sir Robert Reading of Dublin, Bart. so created 27 August

---

* The preamble. Regia nostra mente recolentes plurima illa et gratissima servitia prædilecti subditi nostri Jacobi, Comitis de Abercorn in Regno nostro Scotiæ, antehac præstita; et volentes insuper quod ille et posteri ejus regii favoris nostri insigne aliquod gerant, eum et posteros ejus titulo et gradu Baronis et Vicecomitis dicti Regni nostri Hiberniæ, tanquam perpetuum nostri meritorum ejus æstimationis monumentum, ornare decrevimus. Sciatis igitur, &c. (Rot. Anno 13 Gul. III. 1ª. p. d.)

[1] Lords Jour. II. 2. [2] Idem. 460.

August 1675 (by his wife Jane, relict of Charles, the first Earl of Mountrath) and dying in London 28 November 1734, had issue by her who died in Sackville-street, London 19 March 1754, nine sons and five daughters, viz.

Robert, baptized 12 July 1687, died soon after his birth. (1)
James, his successor. (2)
Robert, who died very young. (3)
John, educated in Trinity-college Dublin, who died in 1714, æt. 20, unmarried. (4)
George, died in his infancy. (5)
George, was a Cornet of horse, and in October 1742 made deputy cofferer of the Prince of Wales's houshold. He was member of parliament for St. Johnstown in Ireland, as he was in 1734 and 1747, for Wells in England, and enjoyed a good estate, as heir to his brother John. In October 1719 he married Bridget, daughter and heir to Colonel William Coward of Wells in the county of Somerset, sometime a Virginia merchant, with whom he received a large fortune, and had issue six sons and six daughters. (6)

Francis, born at Toulouse in Languedoc, took Holy Orders, and 30 January 1737 was presented to the rectories and Vicarages of Dunleer, Capocke, Disert, Moylare, Monasterboys and Drumcarre in the diocess of Armagh; in the room of Rev. John Singleton, who died suddenly in Dublin 2 March 1736-7. On 20 October 1733 he married Dorothy, second daughter and coheir to James Forth of Redwood in the King's County, Esq. secretary to the commissioners of his Majesty's revenue, and by her who died suddenly 3 June 1731, left issue. He died 20 May 1746. (7)

William, baptized 29 October [1] 1703, went a volunteer to sea, and was unfortunately cast away in the Royal Anne Galley, 10 November 1721, with Lord Belhaven, then going to his Government of Barbadoes. (8)

Charles, baptized 13 November [2] 1704, was appointed 22 April 1738 comptroller of the green-cloth to the Prince of Wales; represented the borough of Strabane in parliament, as he did in 1741 and 1743 *that* of Truro in Great Britain, when (26 May 1742) he was chosen first of the seven commissioners for examining and stating the public accompts; and in December 1743 appointed receiver-general of his Majesty's revenues in the Island of Minorca. He married and left issue, of which his eldest daughter Jane, (9)

[1] St. Peter's registry. [2] Idem.

Jane, was married 17 May 1750 to Mr. Moore author of fables for the female sex; and his youngest daughter 23 June same year became the wife of Kanton Cowse, Esq. of the board of works [1].

(1) Daughter, Lady Elizabeth, first married 2 January 1711 [2] to William Brownlow of Lurgan, Esq. member of parliament for the county of Armagh, and by him, who died 27 August 1739, had issue, William, heir to his father; Jane, baptized 30 June 1716 died before her father; Elizabeth, who married John, Lord Knapton, father of Thomas, Viscount De Vesci; Anne, baptized 25 March 1719, died at Lurgan 23 September 1736; Mary, baptized 18 December 1719, married 28 May 1743, to John, son and heir to Southwell Pigott of Cappard in the Queen's County, Esq.; and Isabella, who married first George Matthew of Thurles and Thomastown in Tipperary, Esq. and secondly in September 1761, ———— Ford, Esq. a Major in the army. William Brownlow, Esq. the only son was baptized 25 April, 1726, elected to parliament in November 1753 for Armagh, which county he continues to represent, and hath been sworn a Lord of the privy council in Ireland. 26 May 1754 he married first the eldest daughter of Rev. Charles Meredyth of Newtown, county of Meath, Dean of Ardfert, by whom he had issue, and she dying at Lyons in France in October 1763, he married secondly 23 November 1765 the third daughter of Roger Hall of Mount-Hall in the county of Down, Esq.—Lady Elizabeth, married secondly in France, Martin, Count de Kearnie [3].

(2) Lady Jane died in her infancy.

(3) Lady Mary, married to Henry Colley of Castle-Carbery in the county of Kildare, Esq. member of parliament for Strabane, elder brother to Richard, the first Lord Mornington.

(4) Lady Philippa, first married to Benjamin Pratt, D. D. Chaplain to the House of Commons, Provost of the University of Dublin, Dean of Cork, and afterwards of Down, but by him, who died 6 December 1721, and was buried at St. Mary's, Dublin, having no issue, she remarried with Michael Connell of London, Esq. and died at Paris 27 January 1767 leaving by him [4] one son.

(5) Lady Jane, 26 September 1719 became the second wife of Lord Archibald Hamilton, brother to James, Duke of Hamilton, who was killed in a duel by the Lord Mohun,

---

[1] Collect. [2] St. Peter's Registry. Idem. Collect. and Registry. [4] Lodge.

hun, 5 November 1712 and by him who died 5 April 1754 æt. 80, in Pall-Mall London [1], had four sons and two daughters, the elder of whom Elizabeth was married 16 May 1742 to Francis, Earl Brooke; and the younger 24 July 1753 to Charles, Lord Cathcart, she died 13 November 1770. Lady Jane was first Lady of the bedchamber, mistress of the robes, and privy purse to her Royal Highness Augusta, Princess of Wales.

Sir James, the second Viscount Strabane and seventh Earl of Abercorn, was sworn of the privy council in England 20 July 1738, and coming into Ireland the year following, was sworn of the privy council here 26 September, having been so appointed in July 1737. He took his seat in the House of Peers 9 October 1739 [2], was Fellow of the Royal Society; died 13 January 1743-4, and was interred the 17 in the Duke of Ormond's vault, Westminster-Abbey.—In 1711 his Lordship married Anne, eldest daughter of John Plummer of Blaxware in the county of Hertford, Esq. and had issue by her who died 16 March 1754, two daughters, the elder Lady Anne, married 16 August 1746 to Sir Henry Mackworth, Bart. another daughter born after his decease 27 February 1736; and six sons, viz.

James, his successor.

John, who being bred to the sea-service, was made Lieutenant of the ship Louisa, and in that station, in December 1736, attended his Majesty in his return from Hanover to England; when a violent storm arising, wherein all the fleet narrowly escaped being lost, his ship was wreck'd; and boats being sent to their relief, he bravely refused to go into them before the sailors, saying, *In that common calamity he would claim no precedency*; and was the last that quitted the ship. Upon his going ashore he was presented to the King, who graciously received him; and his father was complimented by the Queen on the gallant behaviour of his son.—On 12 February following he was made Lieutenant of the Diamond of 40 guns, and 14 October 1741 first Lieutenant of the Russel of 70 guns, whence (19 February) he was appointed commander of the Kingsale, from that ship preferred 10 February 1742 to the Augusta, a 60 gun ship newly launch'd; in April 1748 to the Vanguard of 60 guns, and 18 December 1755 was unfortunately drowned, being overset in his boat as he was going from his ship to Portsmouth. In November 1749 he married the widow of Richard Elliot of Port-Elliot in Cornwall,

Sir James, 3 Viscount.

(1)
(2)

[1] Lodge. [2] Lords Jour. III. 440.

wall, Esq. by whom he had issue John-James who 20 June 1779 married Catharine, daughter of Sir Joseph Copley, Bart. and has issue.

(3) William, died young.

(4) George, educated in Exeter-College, Oxford, entered into holy orders, was presented by his brother in September 1753 to the rectories of Tagheyon and Donaghadee in the diocess of Raphoe; and married Elizabeth, daughter of Richard Onslow, uncle to the present Lord.

(5) Plummer, died young.

(6) William, appointed 16 August 1742 Lieutenant of a man of war, and in 1755 Captain of the Lancaster; he married and had issue.

James, 3 Viscount. James, the third and present Viscount Strabane, and eighth Earl of Abercorn, was summoned by writ to the House of Peers in Ireland 23 March 1735-6, by his father's Barony of Mountcastle, and took his seat the same day¹: 8 August 1786 he was created a Peer of Great Britain by the title of Viscount Hamilton of Hamilton in the county of Leicester, with remainder to John-James Hamilton, son of the Honourable John Hamilton deceased, next brother to his Lordship.

TITLES.] Sir James Hamilton, Viscount Strabane, Earl and Baron of Abercorn, Baron of Strabane, Paisley, Mountcastle, and Killpatrick, Viscount Hamilton, and Baronet.

CREATIONS.] Baronet, by K. Charles II. B. of Paisley in the shire of Renfrew, Anno 1591; B. of Abercorn in the county of Lanark, Anno 1604, 2 Jac. I. E. of the same place; B. of Hamilton, Mountcastle, and Killpatrick, 10 July 1606, 4 Jac. I. B. of Strabane, 8 May 1618, 16 Jac. I. V. of Strabane and B. Mountcastle in the county of Tyrone, 2 December 1701, 13 Will. III. and V. Hamilton of Hamilton in the county of Leicester, 8 August 1786, 26 Geo. III.

ARMS.] Ruby, three cinquefoils pierced, ermine.

CREST.] In a ducal coronet, topaz, an oak-tree fructed and penetrated transversely through the main stem by a saw, proper, the frame gold.

SUPPORTERS.] Two Antilopes, pearl, their horns, ducal collars, chains and hoofs, topaz.

MOTTO.] SOLA NOBILITAT VIRTUS.

SEATS.] Paisley in the shire of Renfrew; and Witham in the county of Essex, 32 miles from London.

¹ Lord's Jour. III. 552.

MOLESWORTH.

MOLESWORTH, Viscount MOLESWORTH.

THE family of Molefworth, anciently had their refidence in the counties of Northampton and Bedford, where they flourifhed for many ages, and particularly in the reigns of Edward I. and II. in the perfon of Sir Walter de Moldefworth, or Molefworth; contemporary with whom was John de Molefworth, who, 12 Edward I. was prefented to the Rectory of North-Luffenham in the county of Rutland, by Edmond, Earl of Cornwall, fon of Richard Plantagenet, King of the Romans, youngeft fon of K. John.

The aforefaid Sir Walter de Molefworth, attended K. Edward I. in his expedition to the Holy-Land againft the infidels, (to which his coat-armour alludes) and 26 of that reign, was conftituted Sheriff of the counties of Bedford and Bucks for the fpace of ten years [1] (an office in thofe early times of great truft and authority).—In 1306, when the King on a grand Whitfuntide Feftival, to adorn his court with great fplendour, and augment the glory of his intended expedition into Scotland, knighted Edward, Earl of Caernarvon his eldeft fon; the young prince, immediately after that ceremony, at the altar in Weftminfter-Abbey, conferred the fame honour on near 300 gentlemen, the fons of Earls, Barons, and Knights, of which number was Sir Walter de Molefworth: And that prince fucceeding to the throne, 7 July 1307, directed a charter of fummons * to Sir Walter and his lady, to attend at his coronation;

---

* The Charter runs thus. Rex dilecto et fideli fuo Waltero de Mollefworth, et Conforti, Salutem. Quia hac inftanti die dominica poft feftum fancti Valentini apud Wefmonafterium proponimus coronari, vobis mandamus, quatenus vos et Confors veftra hujufmodi Coronationis noftræ folemniis, dictis die et loco celebrandis, ad Cometivam nobis et cariffimæ Conforti noftræ Ifabellæ Reginæ Angliæ, ob noftri

[1] Fuller's Worthies, co. Bedford.

coronation; appointing him that year, with Gilbert de Holme, Sheriff of the aforesaid counties, and in 1313 sole Sheriff of the same.¹—He was returned Knight for the county of Bedford to the first parliament of that King, which met at Westminster 5 of his reign, and (as was then the custom) had, with Gerard de Braybroke his colleague, writs of their expences issued, for their attendance and service; and three years after, he represented that connty again; but not long surviving, was succeeded by his son

Hugh. Hugh, who the same year, with Henry de Tilly, was Knight of the county of Huntington, in the parliament held at York, having the like writ for defraying his ex-

Sir Walter. pences; and to him succeeded his son and heir Sir Walter de Molesworth, whose son Richard is mentioned in

Richard, the pipe rolls of Northamptonshire, 13 Edward III. (1339) in relation to a fine of 20l. for a pardon to him Sir Simon Drayton, Knt., John, his son, William, son of Thomas Seymour, and Simon Squire of Drayton, and others, at the King's suit, for an infringement of the peace belonging to the royal cognizance, on the death of John de Sutton Lungeville.—He married Eleanor, daughter and heir to Sir Thomas Mortimer of the county of Lincoln, (a descendant of the noble house of Mortimer, Barons of England in the reigns of Henry III. and Edward I. whose coat-armour Lord Molesworth bears in the second quarter)

Sir Roger. John. and by her was ancestor to Sir Roger Molesworth of the county of Huntington, Knt. whose son John, of the same county, became also seated at Helpeston in Northamptonshire; served the office of Escheator for the county of Rutland, and died 14 May 1542,² leaving John his heir, then 26 years of age, who married Margaret, daughter and heir to William Westcot of Hansacre in Staffordshire, Esq. and had five sons, Anthony his heir, ancestor to the Viscount Molesworth; Robert; Bevil; John; and Wingfield.

Family of Pencarrow, Baronets. ³ John, the fourth son, settled at Pencarrow in the county of Cornwall, and made a good addition to his fortune by marriage with two wives; by the latter Philippa, daughter

tri et ipsius Consortis nostræ honorem faciendum personaliter, modis omnibus interfitis, et hoc, ficut nos deligeris, nullatinus omittatis. Teste, &c. 8vo. Februarii.

¹ Fuller's Worthies, co. Bedford.
² Inq. post mortem. ³ Baronetage of England, Edit. 1741.

daughter of Henry Rolle of Heanton in Devonshire, Esq. he had only two daughters; but by the former Catharine, eldest daughter and coheir to John Hender of Botreaux-Castle in Cornwall, Esq. he had two sons and two daughters; Hender; John, killed in the expedition to the Isle of Rhee, under the Duke of Buckingham; Jane, married to William Risdon of Vileston in Devonshire, Esq.; and Elizabeth, to John Tredenham of Philly in Cornwall, and was mother to Sir Joseph Tredenham of Tregonan, Knt. who married Elizabeth, daughter of Sir Edward Seymour of Berry-Pomroy, Baronet, and had issue, Joseph, who died an infant; John; and Seymour, who married Margaret, daughter of Thomas Lewis, Esq. relict of Sir Richard Tufton, Knt. and died in 1696, leaving her a widow [1].

Hender Molesworth, Esq. the elder son, born in 1597, married Mary, eldest daughter of John Sparke, of the Friary in Plymouth, Esq. and had issue three sons, John; Hender; and Richard, who died young.—Sir Hender of Spring-Garden, the second son, was bred a Merchant, and settling in Jamaica, lived at St. Catharine's; was president of the council of that Island in the reign of Charles II. and upon the death of Sir Thomas Lynch, chosen to act as Governor by the constitution of the Island, till a commission should arrive from England appointing a successor; in which station he continued, until K. James II. 15 September 1687, conferred the Government on Christopher, Duke of Albemarle [2]: Upon whose death, there, in the beginning of 1689 [3], he succeeded by commission from the King; and favouring the revolution, was created a Baronet, 19 July 1689, (the first advanced to that dignity by K. William [4]) with limitation of the honour to his elder brother and his heirs male.—He married first the daughter of Mr. Mangey, Goldsmith of London, widow of Mr. Thomas Tottle, Merchant, of Jamaica; and secondly, Mary, daughter of Thomas Temple of Frankton in Warwickshire, Esq. widow of the aforesaid Sir Thomas Lynch, but by neither having issue, his elder brother

Sir John Molesworth of Pencarrow, Knt. succeeded to the title. He was knighted by K. Charles II. who constituted him Vice-Admiral of the North parts of Cornwall, in which he was continued by their majesties James, William,

---

[1] Chauncy's Herefordshire.
[2] Gazette in that year. [3] Idem.
[4] Heylin's Catalogue of Baronets.

liam, and Anne; was member in K. William's laſt parliament for Boſſiney, and in the firſt of Q. Anne, for Leſtwithiel.—His firſt wife was Margery, eldeſt daughter of Thomas Wiſe of Sydenham in Devonſhire, Eſq. ſon of Sir Thomas Wiſe, Knight of the Bath in the reign of James I. and ſiſter to Sir Edward Wiſe, alſo Knight of the Bath, by whom he had three ſons, Sir John; Hender; and Sparke; and three daughters, Mary, Margery and Prudence.—His ſecond lady was Margaret, eldeſt daughter of Sir Nicholas Slaning of Moriſtow in Devonſhire, Knt. (a commander of great diſtinction in the civil wars, who loſt his life at the ſiege of Briſtol in the ſervice of K. Charles I.) but by her had no iſſue.

Sir John, the third Baronet, married the daughter of John Arſcott of Tetcott in Devonſhire, Eſq. and by her, who died of the ſmall-pox, at Blandford, in Dorſetſhire, had three ſons and four daughters; Sir John, his ſucceſſor; Hender, who died at Newington 6 February 1732, unmarried; Sparke, educated at Trinity-Hall, Cambridge, being a fellow commoner, and died at Naples 9 June 1739; Prudence, Margaret, and Mary, all died unmarried; and Prudence, married to Hugh Gregor of Eſſex-ſtreet, London, Eſq. died of the ſmall-pox at Bath 2 May 1742, æt. 23, leaving an only daughter Jane.

Sir John Moleſworth of Pencarrow, the fourth Baronet was choſen to parliament for Newport in April 1734, and in the parliaments which met in December 1744, May 1747, and May 1754 for the county of Cornwall. In 1728 he married Barbara, ſecond daughter of Sir Nicholas Morrice of Werrington in Devonſhire, Bart. and died 4 April 1766, having had iſſue by her, who died of the ſmall-pox 17 May 1735, æt. 24 and was buried in Egloſhale Church, Cornwall, two ſons; John, who ſucceeded; and William of Wenbury, in Devon, who died at Bath 9 February 1762.—Sir John, the fifth and preſent Baronet, is Colonel of the Militia and Knight of the ſhire for Cornwall; 28 September 1755, he married Frances, daughter and coheir to James Smyth of St Andries in Somerſet, Eſq. and by her, who is deceaſed, had one ſon, William; he married ſecondly, 22 June 1762, Barbara, daughter of Sir John St. Aubyn, of Clowance in Cornwall, Bart. and had iſſue John, Hender, and Barbara [1].

Anthony.
We now proceed with Anthony, the eldeſt ſon of John Moleſworth and Margaret Weſtcot.—By his marriage with Cicely, daughter and heir to Thomas Hurland of Fotheringay

[1] Baronetage II. 504. 505.

gay in the county of Northampton, Efq. he became poffeffed of that inheritance, and made it his principal place of refidence; but being a man of great generofity and hofpitality, and profufely entertaining Q. Elizabeth, at *that* his feat feveral days, at different times, he fo far involved himfelf in debt, that (to fhew he was as juft as he was generous) he fold the beft part of his eftate, and difpofed of Helpefton to an anceftor of Earl Fitz-William.— He left two fons, William; and Nathaniel, who accompanied Sir Walter Raleigh in his voyage to *Guinea*, and after his return, perifhed by fhipwreck on his paffage to Ireland.

William Molefworth, Efq. the elder fon, took fhare with the Duke of Buckingham in his unfortunate expedition to the Ifle of Rhee, in aid of the Rochellers, and by his fon-in-law, Gervais Holles, Efq. (a worthy and authentic Antiquary) is ftyled, *Protribunus Militum fub Regimine Peregrini Bertie Militis*.—He married Mary, daughter of Sir Francis Palmes, of Afhwell in the county of Rutland, and left iffue three fons, Guy, Edward, and Robert, who all bore arms in the fervice of K. Charles I. and a daughter married to the faid Gervais Holles, Efq.—Guy, the eldeft fon, going early into foreign parts, ferved under Bernard, Duke of Saxe-Weifmar many years, and returned home, by that Duke's leave, in 1639; foon after which the civil wars breaking out, he engaged in behalf of his Sovereign; was Captain-Lieutenant of the General's company (the Earl of Northumberland) and in 1642 Lieutenant-Colonel to Prince Maurice's Regiment of horfe, to the command of which he afterwards fucceeded [*]. —Edward, the fecond fon, was Captain-Lieutenant to Sir Charles Vavafor in 1640; Captain in 1642 of a foot company in Ireland; afterwards colonel of foot, and Major-General. He married the daughter of —— Hatbean, and by her, who was buried in St. John's church, Dublin 11 April 1654, had three daughters, Mary, Jane, and Frances [¹].

William.

Robert,

---

[*] He is faid by fome, to die without iffue; but it appears from an infcription on a fmall marble Monument in the church of Swords, that a daughter of Colonel Guy Molefworth of London was the firft wife of Henry Scardevile, Dean of Cloyne, Archdeacon of Roffe, Prebendary and Vicar of Swords, who died 3 February 1703, and was buried under the faid Monument. She died in childbirth, and left no iffue. (Lodge.)

[¹] St. John's Regiftry and Dr. Dudley Loftus's MSS. in St. Sepulchre's Lib.

Robert.   Robert, the youngeſt ſon of William, ſerved under his brother Guy throughout the civil war, in the ſtation of a Captain; and after this kingdom of Ireland was delivered up by the Marqueſs of Ormond to the parliament of England, he became an adventurer for carrying on the war, in order to reduce it to their obedience, by making three ſeveral ſubſcriptions, two of 600l. each, and one of 300l. for which he had allotted 2500 acres of land, Iriſh meaſure, in the Baronies of Moghergallin and Lune in the county of Meath [1]. He afterwards became a very eminent merchant of Dublin, and in high confidence with the government, then preſiding in Ireland; by whom 25 May, 1653, he was appointed with others, to take ſubſcriptions within the city and diviſion of Dublin, for the relief of the poor thereof [2], and having a difference with Mr. Vanhoohan touching the ſum of 1152l. due to him for the victualling and tranſporting of 512 men into Spain, at the rate of 45s. for each man, it was referred by the government 22 June 1753, to Alderman Daniel Hutchinſon, Alderman Thomas Hooke, Mr. Peter Wybrant, and Mr. Samuel Weſton, or any three of them, who were to call the parties before them, and ſettle their difference if they could before the 27 of that month, and if not, to certify their proceedings and opinions upon the whole matter to the commiſſioners of the commonwealth [3]; and 7 December that year, the Surveyors of the revenue and ſtores were ordered to contract with him for ſo much cloth, as ſhould be ſufficient for a thouſand tents, with the other materials neceſſary for making up the ſame, after the uſual proportions.—Alſo, the inconveniencies attending the publick, and the many ſufferings and loſſes of the merchants, by the want of ſtationed ſhips to ſerve all public occaſions on the coaſt, being very great, the commiſſioners ſought to redreſs them, and to that end, in 1654, agreed with Mr. Moleſworth for the victualling, from time to time, ſuch ſhips at Dublin, as ſhould be deſigned for that ſervice, with proviſions of all ſorts, both for quality and price, as the victuallers did the Protector's ſhips in England; the commiſſioners having often experienced the greateſt want of ſhips of force here to ariſe from their frequent retiring to Cheſter, Liverpoole, or elſewhere, to victual, where they generally lay for a long time, pretending the want of wind to come from thence: To prevent which,

---

[1] St. John's Regiſtry and Dr. Dudley Loftus's MSS.
[2] Book of orders of privy council, No. 1, p. 175.   [3] Idem, 244.

which, they took that courfe for their prefent victual on any emergent occafions, and he contracted with them to fupply 200 men, aboard the *Wren* Pink, the *Greyhound*, and other frigates, appointed for guard of the Irish coaft [1]; but not long after he preferred a petition to the commiffioners of parliament, fetting forth, that in purfuance of his faid contract, he had victualled the *Wren* Pink for two months, the charge whereof amounted to 87l. 10s. and made feveral further provifions for the winter quarter; but the money contracted for on the State's part, not being paid, he was defirous to relinquifh his contract, his difburfements being fatisfied, and his provifions being taken off his hands and put into the ftores. Upon confideration whereof, it was referred 26 January 1654 to the commiffioners general of the revenue and ftores, to enquire what victuals he had to fpare, that the fame might be taken off his hands for the fpeedy victualling the faid fhips, at reafonable prices, and therein to proceed for the good of the commonwealth's intereft, and to report the particulars of the whole charge of victualling thofe fhips with fuch provifions as were fo made, that order might be given for payment thereof [2].

On 15 Auguft 1656 he made his will, and devifed all his lands in the baronies of Screene and Lune in the county of Meath, to his loving wife Judith, and the heirs of their bodies, remainder to her and her heirs for ever; and (except a few legacies,) viz. to his fifter Holles 40l. a year for life; to his brother Edward 20l. to his own wife all her jewels, all his plate, and 2000l. Englifh, in fatisfaction of what he was obliged to perform by their marriage articles and in lieu of dower [3]; the reft of his eftate, real and perfonal, to his loving father and mother-in-law, John and Margaret Byffe, whom he appointed executors; out of which they were to give to the child or children, which his wife then went withal, or fhould thereafter have by him, fuch portion as they fhould think fit, and have the tutelage, guardianfhip, education and difpofal of it, or them, as if their own [*].

He

---

[*] K. Charles II. by patent, dated 12 May 1668, confirmed the faid lands to his wife and child, viz. to her for life; remainder to her fon and the heirs of his body; remainder to her and her heirs for ever, at the yearly rent of 7l. 15s. 10d. 1-4th.

[1] Book of Entries in Council Office. [2] Idem.
[3] Prerog. Off.

He departed this life 3 September that year, and was buried 9 in St. Audoen's church, Dublin [1]. He married 10 October 1654 Judith, elder daughter and coheir (that survived of twenty-one children) to John Byſſe, Eſq. * and by her, who re-married with Sir William Titchburne, Knt. and was mother of Henry, Lord Ferrard, had

Robert,
Viſcount.

Robert Moleſworth, Eſq. his only child, created Lord Viſcount Moleſworth, who was born at Dublin in September four days after his father's death [2], where he received Univerſity education, and by his great merit and ſervices to the crown, raiſed himſelf and family to the honours they now enjoy. In 1688, when the Prince of Orange entered England, to reſtore its violated liberties and laws, he diſtinguiſhed himſelf by an early and zealous appearance in defence of the true religion and liberty of his country, of which he continued a ſteady aſſerter to his death, at the hazard of his perſon and fortune; being attainted by K. James's parliament 7 May 1689, and having his eſtate of 2825l. a year ſequeſtered. But when K. William was ſettled on the throne, he called Mr. Moleſworth, for whom he had a particular eſteem, into his privy council, and in 1692 ſent him envoy extraordinary to the court of Denmark, where, in that honourable ſtation, he reſided ſeveral years and made thoſe uſeful remarks on tyrannical government, with which, after his return, he obliged the publick in an account of that country, † which is generally eſteemed, and hath been tranſlated into ſeveral languages.

He

---

* He deſcended from the ancient family of Byſſe in the county of Somerſet; was recorder of Dublin during the uſurpation; and 29 March 1660 appointed Chief Baron of the exchequer; having 9 July 1667 a grant of the fort of Philipſtown. His wife was Margaret, ſiſter to Sir Gerard Lowther, Knt. Baron of the exchequer, and Lord Chief Juſtice of the court of common pleas, (which Sir Gerard mentions her in his will as wife to John Byſſe, Eſq. recorder of Dublin) and dying 28 January 1679, he was buried 3 February in St. Audoen's church.

† Beſides his hiſtory of Denmark, he wrote an addreſs to the houſe of commons, for the encouragement of agriculture; tranſlated *Franco Gallia*, a latin treatiſe, written by the civilian *Hottoman*, giving an account of the free ſtate of France and other parts of Europe, before the encroachments made on their liberties; and

is

---

[1] Ulſter Office.   [2] Idem.

He served his country in the house of commons in both kingdoms, being chosen for the borough of Swords in Ireland, and for those of St. Michael, Bodmyn, and East-Retford in England; his conduct in the senate being firm and intrepid in the support of liberty, and the constitution of his country, which though sometimes disagreeable to particular persons and parties, when his maxims happened to clash with their private interest, yet it has been applauded by all parties, in their turns, as soon as the warm fit was over, and the humours of the nation had settled.—He was a member of the privy council to Q. Anne, until the latter end of her reign, when party running high, he was removed from the board, in January 1713, upon a complaint against him from the lower house of convocation [1], presented 22 December by the prolocutor, to the House of Peers, charging him with speaking these words, the day before in the presence chamber, publickly, in the hearing of a great many persons; *They that have turned the world upside down, are come hither also*: And for affronting the clergy in convocation, when they presented their address in favour of the Lord Chancellor Phipps.

Having constantly asserted and strenuously maintained the serene house of Hanover's right of succession to the throne; and being adorned with all the endowments of nature, profitable to the publick, K. George I. on the forming of his privy-council in Ireland, made him a member thereof 9 October 1714, and the next month a commissioner of trade and plantations; advancing him also to the Peerage by privy seal, dated at St. James's 21 June, and by patent * 16 July 1716, by the titles of Baron of Philipstown,

is reputed the author of several pieces, written with great force of reason and masculine eloquence, in defence of liberty, the constitution of his country, and the common rights of mankind. And certain it is, that few men of his fortune and quality, have been more learned, or more highly esteemed by men of learning, as is evident from the writings of the Earl of Shaftsbury, Mr. Locke, Mr. Molyneux, and others.

* The preamble. Cum plurimis Exemplis constet Majores nostros quoties optimos Viros ad Honores provexerint, non minus bono publico consuluisse, quam Virtutem privatam remunerasse; Nobis iisdem vestigiis libenter insistentibus, æquissimum visum est dilectum et perquam fidelem Conciliarium nostrum Robertum Molesworth Procerum in Ordinem conscribere, utpote omni Honoris incremento

[1] Lord's Journ. I. 441.

Philipstown, and Viscount Molesworth of Swords, with the creation fee of 20 marcs; and 1 July 1719 he took his seat in the house of Peers[1].—His Lordship was Fellow of the Royal Society, and continued to serve his country with indefatigable industry and uncorrupted integrity, till the two last years of his life; when perceiving himself worn out with constant application to publick affairs, he passed the remainder of his days in a learned retirement.

He married Letitia, third daughter of Richard, Lord Coloony, sister to Richard, Earl of Bellamont; and making his will, 30 April 1725, devised 50l. towards building a church at Philipstown; dying at his seat 22 May following, æt. 69, he was buried at Swords, having had issue by her, who died 18 March 1729, seven sons and four daughters, viz.

(1) John, his successor.
(2) Richard, who succeeded his brother.
(3) William, a Captain in the wars with Spain, who 11 December 1714, was appointed supervisor and valuer of his Majesty's honours, manors, messuages, &c. and surveyor of

---

mento dignissimum, sive Majorum sive ipsius respiciantur Merita, sive quid ab optima Prolis non degeneris Indole expectandum sit: Ea nempe domo Saxonica ortus, quam ab antiquissimis temporibus perillustrem reddiderunt Viri militari Laude conspicui, pluribus Virtutis et Pietatis erga Patriam Monumentis cohonestati; quæ, à Proavis sibi tradita, ad hæc usque tempora intaminata exhibuerunt Posteri. Stirpe tam clara dignum se præstitit, et illam insuper illustravit Robertus Molesworth, ornatus scilicet omnibus Naturæ et Ingenii dotibus, quibus Reipublicæ prodesse possit, et profuit, sub auspiciis invictissimi Herois Gulielmi tertii mature extitit veræ Religionis atque Libertatis Vindex acerrimus; et easdem Partes constanter sustinens, nostrum in hæc Regna succedendi Jus, difficillimis etiam Temporibus, eo animo iisque viribus asseruit, ut non minus ab Inimicis Patriæ periclitatus sit, quam de nobis et Bonis omnibus benemeritus. Quamcunque demum suscepit Provinciam, vel in Aulis exteris Orator, vel ad Senatum tam Britannicum quam Hibernicum delegatus, vel in Secretiori Regni Hiberniæ Concilio cooptatus, Fidelem, Fortem, et Perspicacem se præbuit, et de Patriæ totiusque Europæ salute impense sollicitum; quibus Rebus gerendis private ejus opes non auctæ sed imminutæ; cum Religio ei semper fuerit malis publicis crescere, mediisque in Patriæ procellis Domum suam stabilire. Viro autem tali, Genere, Moribus, tantisque Meritis insigni, illustria Virtutum præmia diutius desiderari nolentes, eos, quos Modestia sua sedulo defugerit Titulos (hoc ipso dignior) nos ultro largiri statuimus. Sciatis igitur, &c. (Rot. Anno 3 Geo. I. 3. p. f.)

[1] Lord's Jour. I. 602

of lands, which was renewed to him by K. George II. 26 October 1727. He was also 1 August 1717 made alnager, seal-master, and collector of the subsidy and alnage of all saleable and vendible cloths, kersies, cottons, ruggs, and all cloths called the old drapery, made in Ireland, and offered to sale, shipped or embarked, throughout the kingdom for the term of 31 years, at the rent of 10l. a year. And in the reign of K. George I. being chosen to parliament for the borough of Philipstown, continued many years its representative.——On 25 July 1726 he married Anne, eldest daughter of Robert Adair of Hollybrook in the county of Wicklow, Esq. member of Parliament for Philipstown, (who died 31 July 1737, and deceased at Bath 6 March 1770, having had issue by her, who died there in June 1767, three sons and six daughters viz. Robert, baptized 22 December 1729, appointed in October 1745 Cornet, and in January 1753, Lieutenant of a troop in his uncle's regiment of dragoons; John; Richard baptized 5 June 1737, entered into holy orders, and in July 1762, married the only child of James Clark of Moulsey in Surrey, Esq. Letitia, married to Captain George Johnston of Stephen's-Green, Dublin, and died 15 February 1764; Elizabeth, married 31 August 1756, to Richard Holmes Gent. Juliana, baptized 22 January 1734; Jane, Amelia, and Isabella, one of whom 20 August 1770 became the wife of Knight Mitchell of Shute-Lodge in the county of Devon, Esq.

Edward, a Captain also in the Spanish war, who in January 1725 had a company given him in Colonel Handasyd's regiment, and in July 1737 was promoted to a majority in General Moyle's. In September 1718, he married first Catharine, daughter and coheir to Thomas Middleton of Stansted-Montfitchet in the county of Essex, Esq. by her who died at Waltham in Essex in January 1731, he had a son Robert, born 16 April 1719, who died in January following; by his second wife Catharine, who died 15 February 1748, and was buried at St. Anne's church Dublin he had one daughter and a son, Nicholas, who was interred with his mother 26 June 1750; and dying 29 November 1768, left issue by his third wife Mary, two sons, John and Robert¹.

(4)

Walter,

---

¹ Chancery Bill filed 3 May 1769, and Lodge.

(5) Walter, also in the army; he married, and had two daughters, Mary who died in June 1772; and Elizabeth who died in August 1766 [1].

(6) Coote, who 25 April 1728 was honoured by his Majesty with the degree of Doctor of Physick, when he visited the University of Cambridge; was elected Fellow of the Royal Society 18 March 1730; appointed Physician to the garrison of Minorca 30 September 1735; and 13 July 1742 had the degree of M. D. conferred on him by the University of Dublin; he died 29 November 1782, aged 85.

(7) Bysse, chosen to parliament in 1726 and 1727 for the borough of Swords, and 30 April 1738 made collector of the port of Coleraine, which he exchanged in May the next year for the clerkship of the land-permits, and was thence removed to be principal clerk in the secretary's office to the commissioners of the revenue.———7 December 1731 he married Elizabeth, daughter of John Cole of Enniskillen, Esq. widow of Edward Archdall of Casle-Archdall in the county of Fermanagh, Esq. and died in 1779, having had by her who died in Dublin in January 1770, eight sons and four daughters, viz. Richard, who died 11 November 1736, and was buried at St. Peter's; Arthur, born in 1737, Major of the fourteenth regiment of dragoons, which he resigned in June 1766, and married in 1764 Catharine-Vane, daughter of Walter Fletcher of Hutton-Hall in Cumberland, Esq.; Robert, Captain in the thirty-eighth regiment, and married in 1770 to a daughter of Mr. Rose of Limerick; George; Ponsonby; Bouchier; William; John-Cole; Caroline, baptized 2 January 1734, and married 4 December 1756 to Charles Walker, Esq. a Master in Chancery; Florence, baptized 7 February 1735, married to Rev. Thomas Colclough son of Cæsar Colclough of Duffren-Hall in the county of Wexford, Esq.; Alice, and Catharine-Amelia, both deceased [2].

[(1) Daughter Margaret, baptized 9 February 1677, died 19 July 1759.

(2) Mary, * married to George Monck of Stephen's-green, Esq. and died in 1715 †.   Charlotta-

---

* She left a collection of Poems, which her father published and dedicated to Queen Caroline, when Princess of Wales.

Family of Monck. † Charles Monck of St. Stephen's-green in Dublin, Esq. with Thomas Maule, of Pitlivie, Esq. from whom the Earl of Panmure descended,

[1] Ulster's Office.   [2] Lodge Col.

Charlotta-Amelia, appointed 28 February 1714 one of (3) the bed-chamber women to the Princefs of Wales, and was

defcended, a title now extinct, was conftituted in 1627 furveyor-general of all the cuftoms in Ireland; he married the eldeft daughter of Sir John Blenerhaffett, Knt. baron of the exchequer, in the reign of K. James I. and had iffue a daughter Elizabeth, and a fon Henry Monck, Efq. who 1 May 1673 married Sarah, daughter and heir to Sir Thomas Stanley of Grange-Gorman near Dublin, Knt. and had feven fons and three daughters, viz. George, his heir; and Charles of whom hereafter; William of the Middle Temple, (baptized 27 October 1692, married Dorothy, fourth daughter of Thomas Bligh of Rathmore in the county of Meath, Efq. and fifter to John, created Earl Darnley); George, buried at St. Michan's 27 July 1726; Chriftopher and Henry who died infants; Thomas, baptized 22 June 1676, who died without iffue; daughter Jane, baptized 8 February 1673, died an infant; Rebecca, (married to John Forfter, Efq. chief juftice of the court of common pleas, and by him, who married fecondly Dorothy, youngeft fifter to George the firft Lord Carbury, had iffue two daughters, and a fon Richard, who in 1721 married Elizabeth, fecond daughter of Richard Geering, one of the fix clerks in chancery, and dying 27 February 1737 left three co-heirs, viz. Anne, married to John Hill-Forfter, fon of Edward Hill, Efq. Lieutenant of the Ordnance in Ireland; Elizabeth, married to George Tuffenell, Efq. of Middlefex; and Rebecca, to Sir Francis Lumm of Lummville in the King's County, Bart. fo created 24 February 1775.—Sarah, or Anne, elder daughter of Chief Juftice Forfter, married 1 Auguft 1728 George Berkeley, D. D. the celebrated Bifhop of Cloyne, and deceafed in 1786, having had by him, who died at Oxford 14 January 1753, feveral children, of whom the fecond fon George Berkeley, prebendary of Canterbury, chancellor of Brecknock, vicar of Cookham in Berks, and of Eaft Peckham in Kent, took the degree of LL. D. 12 February 1768; in 1760 he married a daughter of Rev. Mr. Frenfham, rector of White-Waltham in Berks, and has iffue one fon George Berkeley, Efq.—Elizabeth the younger daughter married John Rofe, Efq. of Scotland, by whom fhe had one fon now in holy orders); Elizabeth (baptized 11 June 1684, married in June 1707 Jofeph Kelly of Kelly-mount in the county of Kilkenny, Efq. fhe died 20 February 1743-4, leaving iffue by him, who died 21 May 1713);—Charles Monck of Grange-Gorman, fecond fon of Henry by Sarah Stanley, was baptized 19 May 1678, and admitted at the Irifh bar; 23 October 1705 he married Agneta Hitchcock, and died in 1752, having had by his faid wife, who died 4 May 1753, eight fons and fix daughters, of whom John, Charles, George-Stanley, William, Charles, Elizabeth, Jane, Sarah, Agneta, and Anne died young; the fecond fon was drowned 23 June 1738, as he was bathing in the fea at Clontarfe; thofe who furvived were Henry, Thomas, and Anne, who married Henry Quin, Efq. profeffor of phyfick, and died 4 November 1788. Henry, the eldeft fon, married 8 November 1739, the Lady Ifabella Bentinck, fecond daughter of Henry, Duke of Portland, by whom he had a fon William-Stanley, who died at Charleville in the county of Wicklow 13 November

was married in December 1712 to Captain William Titchburne, only surviving son of Henry, Lord Ferrard, (by his wife Arabella, sister to Sir Thomas Taylor, Bart.) and by him, who died before his father, had one son that died young; and three daughters, two of whom were living in 1754, viz. Arabella, married in May 1744 to Francis Wyat of Shakelford in Middlesex, Esq.; and Willielmina. Letitia,

vember 1746, æt. 6 years; and two daughters, Elizabeth, baptized 12 February 1742, who became the wife of George De la Poer Beresford, Earl of Tyrone, to whom, on her father's demise, she brought a personal fortune of 100,000l.; Anne, the second daughter baptized 5 March 1747, died 11 September 1762: He deceased in 1787, and was succeeded in his estates of Grange-Gorman, &c. by his nephew Charles-Stanley, son of his brother Thomas Monck, counsellor at law, who died in 1772, leaving issue by Judith, eldest daughter of Robert Mason of Mason-Brook in the county of Galway, Esq. whom he married 15 October 1753; Anne-Isabella, married in 1777 to Sir Cornwallis Maud, Bart. created Lord de Montalt; and four sons, viz. Charles-Stanley aforesaid, who in 1785 married Anne, second daughter of Henry Quin of Dublin, M. D. and has issue Henry and Anne; Henry-Stanley a Lieutenant in the thirteenth regiment of foot; Thomas-Stanley, in holy orders; and William-Domville-Stanley, a Student in the Temple. We return now to George Monck, Esq. eldest son of Henry by Sarah Stanley, he married first, as in text, Mary, second daughter of Robert the first Viscount Molesworth, she dying in 1715, he married secondly Anne, fifth daughter of Henry Ponsonby of Crotto in the county of Kerry, Esq. widow of George Brabazon, and of Alderman David Colfart of Dublin, but by her who died in 1734 had no issue. He left issue by his first wife one son Henry-Stanley; and two daughters, viz. Sarah (the authoress of some elegant poetical pieces, which, after her decease, were published by Lord Molesworth her grandfather, under the title of Poems by Miranda, she married Robert Mason of Mason-Brook in the county of Galway, Esq. and by him who died in 1739 had issue); and Margaret married first, 4 April 1730, to Henry Butler of Rossroe, in the county of Clare, Esq. and secondly to —— Brownjohn, Esq. Henry Stanley Monck of St. Stephen's-green, Esq. surveyor-general of the customs, married Jane, daughter and coheir to Henry Percy, Esq. and died 28 February 1745, having had issue by his Lady, who died 12 June 1742, two daughters, viz. Letitia, baptized 12 June 1735; and Jane who died in May 1754; and two sons, George-Paul, his heir; and Henry-Percy, baptized 31 July 1736, who married 24 December 1757 Rose, daughter of —— M'Donnell of Castlebar, Esq. and died in 1778 or 1779, leaving issue, George-Paul Monck of St. Stephen's-green, Esq. who rebuilt the mansion-house there, served in parliament for the borough of Coleraine in the county of Derry, and 24 April 1755 married Lady Aramintha Beresford, sixth daughter of Marcus, Earl of Tyrone, and hath issue. (Registries of the parishes of St. Peter, St. Anne, and St. Michan; Pedigree of Blenerhasset; Prerogative Office; Information of Rt. Hon. J. M. Mason; and Lodge.)

Letitia, married to Edward Bolton of Brazeel in the county of Dublin, Efq. member of parliament for Swords *. (4)

John, the fecond Vifcount Molefworth, was baptized 4 December 1679. In May 1710 he was appointed a commiffioner of the ftamp office, and the fame month fent envoy

John, 2 Vifcount.

* Sir Edward Bolton of the county of Lancafter, Knt. was father of Sir Richard Bolton, recorder of the city of Dublin in 1607, who received the honour of Knighthood, and was fucceffively appointed Chief Baron of the Exchequer, and Lord Chancellor of Ireland; he married Frances, daughter of Richard Walter of Stafford, Efq. and died in November 1648, leaving Edward, his heir, and feveral daughters, of whom Anne, born in 1603, married Arthur Hill of Hillfborough, Efq. and was interred at St. Bride's Dublin 7 January 1636.—Sir Edward, the fon, was folicitor-general, and appointed chief baron of the Exchequer, from whence he was removed by the ufurping powers, and had his houfe of *the Bectiffe* pillaged in the war; in 1651 he was a commiffioner for adminiftration of juftice at Dublin, with a falary of 200l. a year on the eftablifhment; he was feated at Brazeel in the county of Dublin, and left iffue a fon Nicholas, and a daughter Anne, married firft to Thomas Adderly, and fecondly to Alexander Pigott of Inifhonan in the county of Cork, Efqrs.—Nicholas of Brazeel, Efq. 1 May 1649 married Anne, fecond daughter of Nicholas Loftus of Fethard in the county of Wexford, Efq. and dying 1 Auguft 1692 was buried at St. Bride's, having iffue by her, who died 2 January 1690, three fons and four daughters, viz. Edward, his heir; Richard, heir to his brothers; Nicholas who died young; Magdalen who died young; Ifabella (born 22 December 1657, married 16 May 1695 to Sir Mark Rainsford, Knt. Alderman of Dublin, died 9 September 1709, and was buried at St. James's Dublin, having iffue by him, who died 10 November following, and was buried with her at St. James's); Francis; and Margaret, married to Theophilus Jones, of Ballymore, in the county of Leitrim, Efq.—Edward, the eldeft fon, was born at Fethard 17 October 1652, and in 1696 married Elinor eldeft daughter of Maurice Keating of Narraghmore in the county of Kildare, Efq. but dying in London in October 1705 without iffue, was fucceeded by his brother Richard, the father of Edward of Brazeel, Efq. who married Letitia, youngeft daughter of Robert Vifcount Molefworth, as in text, and dying 5 Auguft 1758 was interred at Swords, having had four fons and five daughters, viz. Richard and Edward who died young; Robert, his fucceffor; Theophilus, appointed a commiffioner for managing and directing the ftate lottery in Ireland; Elizabeth; Letitia, married to Rev. Guftavus Hamilton; Anna-Catharina, born 11 July 1721; Anna-Maria, baptized 6 May 1724, married Captain John Grant, and had iffue; and Charlotte.—Robert of Brazeel, Efq. 13 July 1754, married Elizabeth, daughter of John Blenerhaffet, Efq. and had iffue. (St. Anne's Regiftry; MS. Pedig. penes J. L. Decree in Chancery in 1673, Council Office, Black Book of the Society of King's Inns, and Peerage, Edit. 1754, III. 212.)

voy extraordinary to the Duke of Tuscany, who 23 April 1711 N. S. received him with particular marks of honour and distinction——18 December 1715 he succeeded his father as one of the commissioners of trade and plantations, being then his Majesty's Plenipotentiary to the King of Sardinia, to whom, in June 1720, he was sent envoy extraordinary; and was also his Majesty's minister at Florence, Venice, and Switzerland, which he held, till his father's death called him to Ireland, where he arrived from his embassy at Turin 8 July 1725, and took his seat in the House of Peers 7 September following [1].

He married Mary, one of the five daughters and co-heirs of Thomas Middleton of Stansted-Montfitchet in Essex, Esq. member of parliament for that county, by his wife Elizabeth, eldest daughter of Richard, Lord Onslow, but his Lordship dying in London 17 February 1725, leaving his Lady with [*] child, which proved a daughter, born 8 May 1726, named Mary, and after married in 1751 to Frederick Gore, Esq. clerk of the quit rents, and member of parliament for the borough of Tulsk, the honours and estate devolved on his next brother

Richard, 3 Viscount. Richard, the third Viscount Molesworth, who being designed by his father for the profession of the law, was sent to finish his studies at the Temple; but his genius leading him to a more active life, he disposed of his books, and, attended by a faithful servant, went into Flanders, presented himself to his father's intimate friend George, Earl of Orkney, and served a volunteer in the army, until that Nobleman in 1702 gave him a pair of colours. His merit during the course of the war raised him to the post of Captain of horse, and Aid du Camp to the Duke of Marlborough, in which station he distinguished himself in a particular manner at the battle of Ramillies, when, at the manifest hazard of his own life, he certainly (under God) preserved *that* of the General [†]. And he not only continued

---

[*] Lady Molesworth died in Hill-street London, 12 August 1766, and was buried in the family vault in Yorkshire.

[†] The truth of this signal transaction has hitherto been suppressed or very obscurely related, the fullest accounts given of it, amounting to no more than; that " At the battle of Ramillies, fought on " Whitsunday 23 May 1706, the Duke of Marlborough being ap- " prehensive of the danger, to which the Dutch troops were exposed, " galloped from the right to the left, and in the way ordered the in-
" fantry

[1] Lords Jour. II. 805.

nued to serve his country during the whole war in Flanders, wherein he exposed himself to the greatest dangers, and was

"fantry in the centre to engage, which was the grand attack. In
"his passage to succour the Dutch horse, he twice narrowly missed
"losing his life, for in attempting to leap a ditch, his horse threw
"him, where he was immediately surrounded by the enemies dra-
"goons, but an English squadron disengaged him; and as his Aid-
"de-camp Colonel Bringfield held his stirup for him to mount ano-
"ther horse, the colonel had his head shot off by a cannon-ball, which
"at the same time stunned his Grace."——Mr. Brodrick, in his compleat history of that war, differs from this account, and says,
"That while the Duke was rallying some, and giving his orders to
"others to charge, he was in very great danger; for, being singled
"out by several of the resolutest of the enemy, and having the mis-
"fortune of falling from his horse, he had either been killed or ta-
"ken prisoner, if some of the confederate foot, that were near at
"hand, had not come very seasonably to his assistance." And Mr. Lediard, in his Life of John, Duke of Marlborough, Vol. I. Page 358, after relating the substance of what is mentioned above, leaves the matter in suspence, with this remark, "Thus the relation,
"printed by authority in England, has it: But it has been said by
"some officers, who were in the engagement, that the Duke was
"borne down by some of the disordered Dutch horse. It is not im-
"possible but both might be true."

But the real and genuine account of that transaction, we shall present to our readers (drawn up for the *Author* by Richard, Lord Molesworth, by way of extract of a letter from A. B. to his friend in London) as follows,——"As for the particular account you so
"earnestly desire of me, I here send it you, word for word, as re-
"lated to me by Lord Molesworth himself, having carefully taken
"it down from a conversation that lately passed between us.

"He introduced his story by observing, that this remarkable fact
"(however evident in all its circumstances) was very industriously
"hushed up in the army; which, he said, was the easier done, be-
"cause he himself was quite silent upon it.

"He then proceeded to a short description of one particular cir-
"cumstance of the field of battle, as necessary to my understanding
"the following relation, and informed me, that from the river *Me-*
"*haigne* (which covered the right flank of the French army and
"the left of our's) to the village of Ramillies, which was about the
"centre of the two lines, the ground was firm, plain and open, in
"short, fit for cavalry to act upon: That from Ramillies to the
"enemies left and our right, the ground, on the contrary, was low,
"marshy, and cut through by many ditches and streams, not easily
"passable by either army in the face of the other. That the enemy,
"who had long been acquainted with this ground, and well saw
"the advantage to be made of its situation, had extreamly strength-
"ened their right wing of horse, not only with numbers, but with
"their choicest troops; with which having attacked our cavalry of
"the left, whom they greatly out-numbered, they soon obliged
"them to give ground in great confusion, *their* line following in
"great order. He said, that the Duke of Marlborough perceiving
 "this,

was blown up by the springing of a mine; but when the Scots and English, under the Earl of Mar and General Forster,

"this, and apprehending the consequence of the disorder, if not timely remedied, commanded some battalions of foot to advance, and properly post themselves for stopping the enemy; dispatched an Aid-de-Camp to our right wing, with orders for a considerable re-inforcement of English and other Cavalry, to be sent from thence to the left; and in the mean time, judging it necessary to keep the enemy at *bay*, after he had with great trouble and fatigue, rallied the disordered squadrons, he put himself at the head of them, and led them to the enemy; and here it was that our advanced squadrons, being repulsed and in great confusion, some of the run-aways, quite blinded by their fear, rode against the Duke, who was leading up other squadrons to sustain them, jostled him off his horse, and rode over him; at which time the remaining body of horse likewise fled, and left the Duke lying on the field, with none near him but Captain Molesworth then one of his Aid-de-Camps; who perceiving not only the Enemies line to advance upon him, but besides, a small body that had detached itself from the line, as for a pursuit, saw the Duke must inevitably fall into their hands, unless he could find the means of getting him off, in which not a moment was to be lost. The Duke's horse, when he was thrust off him, had run away beyond the line; nothing therefore remained for Captain Molesworth to do, but the mounting him, if possible, on his; which he at last effected; but with difficulty; for, when the Duke was rode over, some horse had trod on his stomach; so that he lay on the ground almost senseless, and could very little help himself.

"The Captain, however, got his Grace in the saddle, put the rein in his hand, and turning the horse's head to our line, entreated his Grace to push him that way with his utmost speed, as he accordingly did; but had not cleared the ground above three minutes, before the above-mentioned detachment came at full speed over the spot, so eager in pursuit of the Duke (whom they had certainly singled out) that the Captain then had the good fortune to escape their notice.

"By this time, the Duke had got within some of our battalions of foot, and the pursuers pressing pretty close upon the most advanced among them, which was the regiment of Albemarle Swiss, that regiment gave them their platoons very handsomely, and soon sent them back the same way, somewhat faster than they had come on; however, they now thought fit to pay the Captain a little more respect than they had done before, and honoured him as they went by, with a few strokes of their broad swords; but so luckily, that he came off with only carrying their black marks about his shoulders for some time after.

"The regiment of Albemarle, he said, continued firing to the front, as long as they thought they might do any damage to the enemy, of whom they dropt a good number to the right and left of him; but upon the first suspension of fire and smoke, he made them all the signals he could of his being a friend, and then went in to that battalion, where he was received with great friendship

"and

Forster, had entered England in favour of *the Pretender*, he was an officer of Dragoons under General Carpenter, who was dispatched to suppress them, and coming to an engagement with the enemy, at Preston in Lancashire, behaved with great bravery, and was wounded in the action.

On 11 December 1714 he was appointed lieutenant of the ordnance; was returned member for the borough of Swords to the first parliament of K. ?   and 19 March 1724, succeeded Major-General Thomas Wyndham in the command of his regiment of foot.—5 October 1731 he sat first in the House of Lords, on the death of his brother [1]; and 31 May 1732, succeeded General Crofts in his regiment of Dragoons, was sworn 26 October 1733, of his Majesty's privy council; made a Major General, 12 December 1735, and in February following a Brigadier-General on the establishment.—19 September 1736 he was constituted (and sworn the next day) with John, Archbishop of Dublin, and Arthur, Bishop of Meath, keepers of the Great Seal of Ireland, during the Lord Chancellor's absence, which commission ceased 2 February following by his return.—27 June 1737 he succeeded Lieutenant-General Owen Wynne who died 28 February 1736, in the command

" and some surprise by Colonel *Constant*, who said, *He equally re-*
" *joiced and wondered at his escape, and that he doubted not, but he*
" *should soon see him at the head of a regiment.*
" He then told him, that the Duke had got between the lines, and
" was gone towards the centre; to which, while the Captain was
" making his way as well as he could on foot, he, by chance, met
" with a foreign soldier holding the Duke's horse by the bridle;
" who, upon his claiming the horse, and giving him *a patacoon*,
" immediately resigned him, and then the Captain mounting that
" horse, pursued his way in quest of his Grace.
" He found him upon a rising ground fronting the village of Ra-
" millies, with a number of general officers and others about him,
" to whom he was distributing his orders, and when he saw the Cap-
" tain, he said, he hoped he was not hurt.
" The Captain, soon after, observing that his horse (which the
" Duke still mounted) was a little unquiet, shewed him his own, and
" said, *that* might probably prove less troublesome to him, upon
" which his Grace, shifting back to his own horse, and Colonel
" *Bringfield* (his first *Esquyer*) holding his stirrup, the enemy just at
" that time discharged a battery from the village of Ramilles which
" came among the groupe of us, and one of the balls, after grazing,
" rose under the horse's belly, and took Mr. Bringfield in the
" head."

[1] Lord's Jour. III. 149.

command of the Royal Irish Dragoons; was promoted 17 July 1739 to the rank of Lieutenant-General of his Majesty's armies; as he was, 1 January following, to the post of Master-General of the Ordnance in the room of Francis, Marquess of Montander, who died 8 August 1739 *¹*; being also, in July 1742, appointed Lieutenant-General on the establishment, with the fee of 972l. a year; a General of horse 24 March 1746; and in September 1751, Lieutenant-General and Commander in Chief of his Majesty's forces in Ireland; was Fellow of the Royal Society; a Trustee for the Barracks; a Governor of the Royal Hospital near Kilmainham; and Field-Marshal of his Majesty's forces.

His Lordship married first Jane, daughter to Mr. Lucas of Dublin; and by her, who died 1 April 1742, and was buried at Swords, had one son, who died an infant, and three daughters, viz. Mary, married 8 August 1736 to Robert, created Earl of Belvidere; Letitia, married in October 1753, to Lieutenant-Colonel James Molesworth, and died 16 June 1787; and Amelia, who died unmarried 30 January 1758.

On 7 February 1743 he married secondly Mary *, daughter of Rev. William Usher, Archdeacon of Clonfert (who died 17 of the same month) and deceased 12 October 1758, aged 78, having had issue by his lady who died 6 May 1763 †, one son Richard Nassau, and seven daughters,

* By privy seal dated at St. James's 3 December 1755, and by patent 15 January 1756, the King granted several pensions to Mary Lady Viscountess Molesworth, and his Lordship's children, viz. to her Ladyship 500l. a year; to Amelia, his daughter by his first wife, Harriet, Melesina, Mary, Louisa, Elizabeth, and Charlotte, 70l. each yearly, from the day of his Lordship's demise. (Rot. 29 Geo. II. 3. p. D,

† Extract of a letter, dated London, 7 May, 1763.———It is with the utmost horror that I relate to you the dismal catastrophe which befel poor Lady Molesworth and her family yesterday morning about 5 o'clock, when a fire suddenly broke forth in her house, by the carelessness of a servant in the nursery; in which she herself, two of her daughters, her brother who was Captain of a man of war, the children's governess, and two other maid servants perished. The other three daughters are indeed not consumed, but scarce in a condition preferable, the eldest jumping out of a second floor window, was caught upon the iron palisades, which tore her thigh so miserably, that the surgeons were obliged to cut it off directly four inches above the knee; another has her thigh bone broke close to the hip;

¹ Collect.

ters, viz. Mary, born 24 September 1744, died soon after its birth; Henrietta, born in July 1745; Melesina, born 27 December 1746, and Mary, born 30 November 1747, perished with their mother; Louisa, born 23 October 1749, married to William Brabazon Ponsonby, Esq.; Elizabeth, born 17 September 1751; and Charlotte, born 2 October 1755, in Henrietta-street, Dublin.

Richard-Nassau, the fourth and present Viscount Molesworth, was born 4 November 1748.

Richard-Nassau, 4 Viscount.

TITLES.] Richard-Nassau Molesworth, Viscount Molesworth of Swords in the county of Dublin, and Baron of Philipstown in the King's County.

CREATION.] So created 16 July 1716, 2 Geo. I.

ARMS.] Vair, on a Bordure Ruby, 8 Croslets, Topaz.

CREST.] On a Wreath, an armed Arm embowed at the Elbow, Proper, holding a Croslet, Topaz.

SUPPORTERS.] Two Pegasus's; the Dexter, Pearl, crined, winged and unguled, Topaz. The sinister, Ruby, alike crined, winged and unguled, and seme of Croslets, Gold.

MOTTO.] VINCIT AMOR PATRIÆ.

SEAT.] Breckdenstown in the county of Dublin, 6 miles from the metropolis.

hip; a third bruised from head to foot, and both much scorched.—The Hon. Coote Molesworth and his wife, who, unluckily for them, happened to be her guests, have escaped. He had the presence of mind to throw his bedding out of the back windows, upon which his wife and two children fell, otherwise they must have been dashed to pieces, for the children came from the garret down to the back area, no less than four stories high. Mr. Molesworth hung by an iron on the outside of the two pair of stairs windows, till a neighbouring carpenter brought him a ladder.——List of saved: Lord Molesworth fortunately at school; Miss Harriet, thigh cut off, and the other leg much torn with spikes; Miss Louisa, thigh broke near the hip, but set, and hopes of cure without amputation; head cut but not fractured; Mr. and Mrs. Molesworth; Miss Betty, much bruised and scorched.——Perished: Lady Molesworth; Miss Melesina: Miss Molly; Capt. Usher; Mrs. Morelle, governess to the children; Mrs. Patterson, Lady Molesworth's woman: the young ladies maid; Capt. Usher's man, who got out, but perished by returning to save his master; and two black footmen.——From Faulkner's Dublin Journal.

CHETWYND, Viscount CHETWYND.

23

Adam.

Sir John.

THE family of Chetwynd assumed a surname from the place of their residence in the county of Salop, whereof Adam de Chetwynd was of such distinction in those early times, as to marry Agnes, daughter of John, Lord Luvel, Baron of Dockinges, and Lord of Minster-Luvel in Oxfordshire; and by her was father of Sir John de Chetwynd of Chetwynd, Knt. to whom K. Henry III. in 37 of his reign, granted a charter of free-warren throughout all his demesne lands in the counties of Stafford, Salop, and Warwick; and about the beginning of Edward I. reign he received a grant of the manor of Baxterly in the last mentioned county from John, son of William Luvel, his kinsman, rendering to him and his heirs, or to Richard de Harecourt, Chief Lord of the fee, a pound of pepper yearly, at Easter, as the deed sets forth. After which, viz. in 1280 (9 Edw. I.) it was found by inquisition, that he had certain customary tenants there, who paid him one hundred shillings annual rent, and did suit twice a year at his leet; the extent of his possessions here being certified at four *yard-lands* (a quantity of different computation in different places; *vergata terræ*, or a *yard-land* containing in some countries 10, in some 20, in some 24, and in some 30 acres) but it appears, that 17 Edw. III. he had 16 messuages, 6 yard-lands, 6 acres of pasture, and two of wood in Baxterley, where the family however did not long continue. He married Isabel, daughter and heir to Philip de Mitton, with whom he had the Lordships of Ingestre, Salte, and Gretwyche, in the county of Stafford; and had issue,

William.

William de Chetwynd, whose residence was some time at Oddeston in the county of Leicester, and who had two sons, Roger, and Philip, both Knights; and Sir Ralph de Grendon, of Grendon in the county of Warwick (descended from Roger de Grendon, living in the time of K. Stephen)

Stephen) having three daughters by his second wife Anne de Clinton; Joan, the eldest, was married to this Sir Roger de Chetwynd; and, in 1343, by their joint deed, they released and quit claim to Robert de Grendon, all their right in the manors of Grendon, and Sheneston.—And, Sir Philip, his brother, marrying Alice, the next daughter of the said Sir Ralph de Grendon, became possessed, in her right, of that Lordship, where William, his son and heir, seated himself, was knighted; and 16 Rich. II. obtained a licence from the Bishop of Litchfield and Coventry, to have divine service within a private chapel for his house.—Towards the latter end of the reign of Edward III. he was retained, by indenture, with John of Gaunt, Duke of Lancaster, that King's fourth son, to serve him, as well in time of peace as war, for the allowance of ten marcs a year; which indenture, being lost, was renewed by the Duke, 50 Edw. III. with an increase of the fee to 10l. and, 10 Rich. II. that Duke, recounting his many faithful services, gave him 10l. a year more, to be received out of the issues of his honour of Tutburie.—The year after he was Sheriff of the county of Stafford, and the learned *Dugdale* is of opinion, that a great part of Grendon church was new built by him; for (says he) "it "is evident, that the pictures in glass of many of this fa- "mily, in their surcoats of arms, were set up there about "that time." [margin: Sir Philip, Sir William.]

By his wife Aliva, or Alicia, who was a widow in 1404, (4 Hen. IV.) he had two sons, Richard, and John; and a daughter, Margaret, married to William Purefoy of Shireford in Warwickshire, Esq. by whom she was mother of William Purefoy, of the same place, who died 6 Edw. IV.—John, the younger son, resided at Alspath (now called Meriden) near Coventry, in Warwickshire, of which county he was one of the chief subscribers of the articles, concluded in the parliament of 12 Hen. VI. 15 of that reign, served as one of its representatives; and, from 17 to 20 Hen. VI. inclusive, was in commission for preservation of the peace. He married Margaret, sister to the said William Purefoy, and (probably) died without issue, the estate of Meriden descending to the family at Ingestre, who sold it, in the reign of Edward VI. to John Hales of Coventry.

Richard Chetwynd, the elder son, in 1406, married Thomasine, daughter of William Frodsham, and was father of [margin: Richard.]

Sir

Sir Philip. Sir Philip Chetwynd, who, 7 and 15 Hen. IV. was Sheriff for the county of Stafford, being then a Knight; and, 12 of that reign, was returned, by the King's commissioners, one of the gentry of that county, being the tenth upon the roll.—In 17 Hen. VI. he was employed, on the King's service, in the Dutchy of *Guien*; and, three years after, constituted Governor of the city of *Baion*, in Normandy, being allowed 940 marcs to retain as many archers, for the safe custody thereof, as might be hired therewith, for three months.——Two years after this, he was retained with Humphrey Stafford, Earl of Buckingham Hereford Stafford Northampton and Perche, by indenture, dated, at London, 13 February, to do him service, during life, according to his degree, both in times of peace and war; namely, in peace, with as many men and horses as he should appoint out of his (the Earl's) Lordship of Holdernesse, in Yorkshire, taking *Bouche* of Court, and *livery* for them in his houshold, during such his continuance with him, and allowance of reasonable costs for his journey: And, in case the Earl should be commanded in any service of war, on this side, or beyond the sea, upon reasonable warning, to attend him with such number of men at arms and archers, well and sufficiently armed, horsed and arrayed, as he should assign; and receive the like wages and reward, as the Earl took of the King, or any other his captains in such expedition, with *Skippeson*, and *Reskippeson*, reasonable for himself, his men and horses; the Earl to have the thirds of all prisoners and prizes taken by him, and the thirds of the thirds of those taken by his men.—By another indenture, of the same date, he was retained with the Earl as his lieutenant of the town and castle of Calais for one year, with twenty-nine men at arms, on foot, and 20 archers; whereof two men at arms, and four archers, to be of Sir Philip's own retinue, taking for himself 16 pence a day, for his men at arms 8 pence, and his archers 6 pence, at the hands of the Earl's treasurer at war; and, moreover, for himself, and his lady, a gentleman and two yeomen, and a gentlewoman of their retinue, *Bouche* of Court, and 20l. a year of special reward; or else allowance for their *Bouche* of Court, as other soldiers of their degree used to have, as also for their *skippeson* and *r skippeson*.

He married Elene, widow of Edmond, Lord Ferrers of Chartley, daughter, and at length heir, to Thomas de la Roche, and cousin and heir to John de Birmingham, her

mother

CHETWYND, Viscount CHETWYND.

mother Elizabeth being the only child of Thomas de Birmingham, brother and heir of the said John; whose coat-armour he impaled on the dexter side of his own (probably) for the dignity of her person, being a Baroness, and a great heiress.—He died in 24 Hen. VI. having a son William, who, deceasing in his life-time, left a son William to succeed him; who was a gentleman-usher of the chamber to K. Hen. VII. but being envied by Sir Humphry Stanley, of Pipe in Staffordshire, Knight of the body to that King, he sent him a counterfeit letter, in the name of Randolph Brereton, Esq. delivered the Friday night before the feast of St. John Baptist's Nativity, 9 Hen. VII. requesting, that he would meet him, at Stafford, the next morning by five o'clock. Being thus allured out of his house, at Ingestre, and going thither, with no other attendants than his son, and two servants, he was way-laid on Tixhall-Heath, by twenty men, seven of whom were of Sir Humphry's own family, all completely armed; who, issuing out of a sheep-cot and a deep dry pit, furiously assaulted him, saying, that he should die, and accordingly slew him; Sir Humphry, in the instant, passing by, with at least 24 persons on horseback, under the pretence of hunting a deer. This tragedy is set forth in the petition of Alice, his widow, to the King; wherein she craves, that Sir Humphry, and his servants, might answer for it; but what proceedings were had therein do not appear.

William, his son, succeeded at Ingestre; and, in 6 and 27 years of Henry VIII. was Sheriff of the county of Stafford; he was father of Thomas Chetwynd, Esq. who married Jane, daughter and heir to Sir John Salter, of Salter's-Hall near Newport in Shropshire, and dying 30 September 1556, had issue John, his heir, and a daughter Dorothy, the second wife of Sir Walter Smith, to whom she was married in the reign of Edward VI. her fortune being 500l.; but he being an aged man, and she very young, she detested him to such a degree, as to prevail on herself to murder him, for which she suffered death, by being burnt at a stake, 15 May 3 Q. Mary, or (as some say) in the first year of that reign.

John Chetwynd of Ingestre, Esq. was Sheriff of Staffordshire 20 Elizabeth, and died in 1592, having married to his first wife Mary, daughter and heir to Lewis Meverell, of Bold-Hall in Staffordshire, Esq. by whom he had Sir William Chetwynd of Grendon, Sheriff of the said county

county 42 Eliz. who lies buried under a marble monument in a little chapel, on the South side of Grendon-church, with this memorial;

H.   S.   E.

WILLIELMUS CHETWYND, Eques Aur.
JOH. CHETWYND de Ingeſtre, in Agro Staff. Arm.
è MARIA ſola LUDOVICI MEVERELL de Bold,
Armigeri filia et hærede, unigenitus,
Qui ATALANTAM
ROB. HUICK de Stilleſted in Com. Cantii
Filiam et Cohæredem,
Matrimonio primitus copulavit;
Poſtea vero CATHERINAM
WALTERI ASTON de Tixhall Eq. Aurati
Filiam, STEPHANI SLANEY que reliſtam
Diem obiit XIIII. Junii A°. D. M. D. CXII°.
Ætatis ſuæ LXIII. ſine Prole.
Hoc in perennem Propatrui ſui Memoriam
WALTERUS CHETWYND Conſanguineus et
Hæres
Poſuit A°. 1676.

The ſaid Catharine, his ſecond wife, ſurviving him, re-married with Sir Edward Cope of Çannon's-Aſhby in Northamptonſhire, and died 15 January 1646, æt. 80, having burial in the church of St. Giles in the Fields, London, to which ſhe had been a benefactreſs, and her arms, impaled with thoſe of her huſband, were painted in the windows, before that church was rebuilt.

The ſecond wife of John Chetwynd, Eſq. was Margery, daughter of Robert Middlemore of Edgbaſton in Warwick-ſhire, Eſq. and he lies buried under a monument, fixed to the North-Wall of the chancel of Grendon church, with this inſcription;

Here lieth buried the bodies of John Chetwind of Ingiſtrent within the county of Stafford Eſquyer, and Margerie his ſecond wife, which John did take to His firſt Wife Marie Meverell of the Bolde in the Said Countie Eſq. and had Yſſue by the ſaid Marie One Sonne named William; and after the Deceaſe of Marie, the ſame John tooke to Wife the ſaid Margerie, Which was the eldeſt Daughter of Robarte Middlemore Of Edgbaſton in the Countie of Warwicke, Eſq. and had
Yſſue

CHETWYND, Viscount CHETWYND.

Yssue by the same Margerie five Sonnes, vid: Walter, Robte. Thomas, Edward, and Philip. Who died A°. Dni 1592, Aprilis 15. And Margerie the 20. of Decemb. 1602.

Sir Walter, the eldest son, was his successor at Ingestre; and of the others, one was ancestor to the family seated at Grendon, whose descendant, Walter Chetwynd, Esq. represented the city of Litchfield in three several parliaments of K. George I. and II. and in 1731 was made Governor of Barbadoes; married the daughter of John Goring of Kingston, and of Callowhill, in the county of Stafford, Esq. and dying, in London 5 February 1731, left issue by her, who died there 11 March following.—And Edward, the fourth son, was born about the year 1577; after his education in Exeter-college, Oxford, he took orders, and became a frequent preacher in and near that city; was chosen Lecturer of Abingdon and Bristol, in 1613, chaplain to the Queen of K. James I.; commenced Doctor of Divinity 15 July 1616; and was preferred 16 June 1617 to the Deanery of Bristol, to the great satisfaction of that city, having several other preferments. He married Helena, daughter of Sir John Harrington (an eminent poet) of Kelston in the county of Somerset, and dying 13 May 1639, was buried in the choir of his cathedral, near her, who died in Childbirth 9 November 1628, in the 39 year of her age.

Sir Walter Chetwynd of Ingestre, was Sheriff of the county of Stafford in 1607, married first Mary, daughter and heir to John Molyns, of the county of Somerset, (who died 22 May 1591) secondly the Lady Catharine Hastings, eldest daughter of George, the fourth Earl of Huntingdon, widow of Sir Edward Unton, of Wadley in Berkshire, Knt. and had issue two sons; Walter, his heir; and John, father of the first Viscount Chetwynd.

Sir Walter.

Walter Chetwynd, Esq. the elder son, married Frances, daughter of Edward, and sister and heir to Bertin Haselrig, Esqrs. which Lady lies buried at Grendon, with this inscription on her monument;

H. S. E.

Francesca unica Filia
Edvardi Haselrig de Arthingworth
In Agro Northampt. Arm.
Ac Francescæ Uxoris suæ, filiæ et Cohæredis
Will. Brocas de Thedingworth

In Agro Leic. Arm.
Tandemque hæres BERTINI HASELRIG Fratris fui,
Primo
WALT. CHETWYND Arm. hujus Manerii Domino enupta,
Cui unicum Filium
WALTERUM nomine peperit,
Poſtea vero
WOLSTANO DIXEY de Boſworth
In dicto Leic. Com. Baronetto.
Diem obiit
Nov. XVI.
A°. ab Incarn. Dni M. D. CLXXXVI.
Ætat. ſuæ LXXXI.

Walter Chetwynd, Eſq. the only ſon, very much improved his ſeat of Ingeſtre, and being patron of the church, he conſidered, that it not only ſtood very incommodiouſly, but was ſo ruinous, that it would be better to rebuild, than repair it; and by an inſtrument, bearing date, at Lambeth, 12 April 1673, having obtained a faculty from the Archbiſhop of Canterbury, to rebuild it in a more commodious place, adjoining to his houſe, the foundation was laid the ſame year, and in 1676 the building entirely finiſhed in a uniform and elegant manner, the windows and cielings being embelliſhed with the arms of the family, alſo of thoſe they had married into, as the walls were with their funeral monuments of curious white marble, and the whole vaulted for their dormitory, whither all the bodies, which had been interred in the old church, were removed and decently depoſited. Over the entrance, under the tower, on a ſmall table of white marble, is this modeſt inſcription:

Deo Opt. Max.
Templum hoc
A Fundamentis extructum
Walterus Chetwynd
(Walt. Fil. Walt. Equ. Aur. Nepos)
L. M.
D. D. D.
Anno Æræ Chriſtianæ
1676.

The church was solemnly consecrated in August 1677 by Thomas, Bishop of Coventry and Lichfield; the Dean of Litchfield preaching the sermon, and others of the clergy reading prayers, baptizing a child, churching a woman, marrying a couple, and burying a corpse, all which offices were performed the same day; the founder and patron offering upon the altar the tythes of Hopton, an adjoining village, to the value of 50l. a year, as an addition to the rectory for ever. A work this, worthy of his name and family, and more to be esteemed than all his gentility and learning, though both were very great.

In 1680 he was sheriff of the county of Stafford, and departing this life 21 March 1692, was buried in the vault of his new church, leaving no issue by his wife Anne, eldest daughter of Sir Edward Bagot of Blithfield, Bart. (which Lady was born 14 March 1642, married in 1658, and died 6 December 1671) but he had a daughter Frances, who dying before him, was buried at Grendon, under a marble monument, thus inscribed:

M. S.
Francescæ
Unicæ Prolis
Walteri Chetwynd Arm.
Ac Annæ
Filiæ Edvardi Bagot de Blithfield
In Agro Staff. Baronetti
Conjugis suæ Chariss.
Diem obiit
Vicessimo mense ætatis suæ
Ao. ab Incarn. Dni. M.D.CLXXIII.

So that he was succeeded by Walter, his cousin and godson, son of his uncle John.

Which John Chetwynd, Esq. had his education in Exeter college, Oxford, where he took the degree of A. B. 18 January 1641, and *that* of A. M. 17 October 1648. He resided at Ridge near Bloreheath in Staffordshire, was member of parliament in the reigns of Charles II. and James II. and by his Lady, who died 28 February 1738, æt. 80, he had one daughter Lucy, married to Edward Yonge, Esq. *Bath* King of Arms; and three sons, Walter, created Viscount Chetwynd; John, and William-Richard who both succeeded to that title.

Walter, the eldest son, who succeeded to the estate of his cousin, served for the boroughs of Stafford and Litchfield held in all the parliaments, from the year 1703 to his death. In the reign of Q. Anne he was master of the buck-hounds, in which post being succeeded by Sir William Wyndham 12 July 1711, he was appointed 18 January 1714 Chief Ranger of St. James's Park, and Keeper of the *Mall* there, which he also resigned in June 1727.— His Majesty K. George I. was pleased to advance him to the Peerage of Ireland, by the titles of Baron of Rathdowne, and Viscount Chetwynd of Bearhaven, by privy seal, dated at St. James's 27 May, and by patent * 29 June 1717, with limitation of the honours to the heirs male of the body of his father, and 20 marcs creation fee, payable out of the Exchequer.—On 18 January 1717 he was elected high steward of the borough of Stafford; and his Lordship marrying Mary, daughter and coheir to John Berkeley, Viscount Fitz-Harding, and Baron of Rathdowne, Treasurer of the Chamber, and Teller of the

---

* The preamble. Quoniam ad nostram dignitatem atque Amplitudinem spectat, ut viri erga nos fide, erga patriam amore præcellentes, honoribus augeantur, visum est nobilem nobisque perdilectum Gualterum Chetwynd de Ingestry Armigerum, filium dilecti et perquam fidelis Johannis Chetwynd nuper de Ingestrey Armigeri, in comitatu nostro de Stafford, in regno nostro Magnæ Britanniæ, in Procerum nostrorum Ordinem conscribere. Optimo id Merito suo, sive amicissimum ejus erga Serenissimam nostram familiam animum respiciamus, sive fidem intemeratam et egregiam operam, quam in Comitiis publicis per multos retro annos posthabitis, omnium tum temporis maleseria fervore illecebris strenue et constanter navavit, ut Sceptra Britanna, Domui nostræ auguste Legibus Patriis jam decreta, sarta nobis et tecta conservarentur; sive postquam Imperio feliciter potiti essemus, tot ac tanta ejusdem contemplemur eximii erga nos studii edita Indicia eâ in Provinciâ, quæ omnium Regni nostri non ita pridem impotentibus Partium adversarum Conatibus maxime periclitabatur, cum plurimos ibi nobis jam Hostes vel sua præsentia deterruerit, vel vacillantes in fide sustinuerit, vel in apertam perduellionem prorumpere paratos ad Officium revocarit; sive Mores ejus spectemus, ad omnia denique humanæ et generosæ Indolis munera compositos; ad quas quidem Dotes sibi proprias et congenitas, Prosapiæ quoque decus et Majorum imagines jure adjungendæ sunt, cum præsertim eorum alii foris virtute militari aut Trophæa ab Hostibus præpepta, aut summa belli Munia in Gallia, Belgio, et Hispania consecuti sint: Alii vero Domi, omnibus Pacis artibus ornati, Regio Antecessorum nostrorum rescripto in Procerum Domum vocati, omnia ibi Laudis documenta exhibuerunt; cujus itaque inclyti Stemmatis memoriam ut ab oblivione vindicemus, et recentibus prædicti Gualteri Chetwynd Meritis intertextam ævo presenti posterisque commendatiorem faciamus, ipsum Stylo ac titulo Baronis de Rathdowne et Vicecomitis Chetwynd de Bearhaven condecorare placuit. Sciatis igitur, &c. (Rot. Anno 1 Geo. I. 1. p. f.

the Exchequer in the reign of Q. Anne; by her, who was maid of honour to that Queen, and died 3 June 1741, above 70 years of age, he had no issue; and deceasing 21 February 1735 at Ingestre, after a tedious sickness, was buried in the family vault, being succeeded by his brother

John, the second Viscount Chetwynd, who from the year 1702 served in parliament for Stockbridge, St. Maws and Stafford; was Receiver General of the Dutchy of Lancaster in the reign of Q. Anne; and 8 November 1714 was made one of the Commissioners of Trade and Plantations; being also appointed 14 May 1717 his Majesty's Envoy Extraordinary to the court of Spain; and 9 March 1735 chosen to supply his brother's place as Recorder of Stafford, of which borough he was High Steward. —His Lordship had several children, of whom his eldest son died at Ingestre 30 May 1741, about 21 years of age; William-Richard, heir apparent and only son, was chosen to parliament in 1754 for the borough of Stafford, and died in February 1765 in the South of France, leaving no issue by the eldest daughter of —— Wollaston of London, Esq. whom he married 13 March 1753; and his Lordship's eldest daughter in August 1748 was married to John Talbot, Esq. brother of William, Lord Talbot, to whom she was second wife, and by him had, besides other children, John-Chetwynd Talbot, Esq. born in December 1749, married 7 May 1776, the Lady Charlotte Hill, daughter of Wills, Earl of Hillsborough; on the death of his uncle William, Earl Talbot, he succeeded him as Lord Talbot, and was created Viscount and Earl Talbot, 3 July 1784 [1]. His Lordship deceasing 21 June 1767 was succeeded in the title by his brother

John, 2 Viscount.

William-Richard, the third Viscount, who before his accession to the honour, resided at Haseler near Litchfield. In June 1708 he was appointed by Q. Anne, her Majesty's resident at the court of Genoa, whence he was recalled in 1712, and from the year 1714 was a member of the British parliament; 16 April 1717 he was made a Commissioner of the Admiralty, which he resigned in June 1727, and being appointed master-worker of his Majesty's mint, resigned that employment 3 June 1769; he succeeded to the title 21 June 1767, and deceased 3 April 1770

William-Richard, 3 Viscount,

[1] Collins's Supp. 159. 375.

1770 in his 83 year.—He married a daughter of —— Baker, Efq. and by her who died in childbirth 5 September 1726 had three fons and three daughters, viz. William, heir apparent; Richard; Grenville-Anfon (who 25 July 1783 married the daughter and heir of the late Henry Stapylton of Wighill in the county of York, Efq. and by his Majefty's permiffion affumed the name of Stapylton); daughter Deborah died in November 1784; Efther; and Louifa.

William. William Chetwynd, the eldeft fon, ferved in the Britifh parliament for the borough of Stockbridge; 19 November 1751 he married the youngeft daughter of Sir Jonathan Cope, Bart. and dying before his father left iffue two fons ¹, and three daughters, of whom the eldeft fon fucceeded his grandfather, viz.

William, 4 Vifcount. William, the fourth and prefent Vifcount Chetwynd, who was born 26 January 1753, fat firft in parliament 14 October 1773 ², and 25 June 1782 his prefent Majefty was pleafed to grant him an annual penfion of 400l. ³. His Lordfhip is married and has iffue ⁴.

TITLES.] William Chetwynd, Vifcount Chetwynd of Bearhaven in the county of Kerry, and Baron of Rathdowne in the county of Dublin.

CREATIONS.] So created 29 June 1717, 3 Geo. I.

ARMS.] Saphire, a cheveron between three mullets, topaz.

CREST.] On a wreath, a Goat's head erafed, pearl, attired, gold.

SUPPORTERS.] Two Unicorns, pearl, each gorged with a chaplet of red rofes, having a chain of the fame reexing over their backs.

MOTTO.] PROBITAS VERUS HONOS.

---

¹ Lodge.   ² Lords Jour. IV. 688.   ³ Penfion Lift.
⁴ Fielding's Peerage.

HIS Lordship's family came from Normandy to England, so early as the reign of K. William II. in the person of George de Brodrick, son of Sir Richard, descended from Rodolphus, Count of Hapsburg, second brother to Henry, Duke of Germany. Which George was lineal ancestor to Sir Thomas Brodrick, some time of Richmond in the county of York, and of Wandesworth in Surry, who married Catharine, daughter of Sir Oliver Nicholas of Aubrey in Wiltshire, and dying in 1641, in the 46 year of his age, had issue three daughters and five sons; Alan; Thomas; St.-John; Oliver; and William; of whom the two youngest died unmarried; and Alan the eldest succeeding his father at Wandesworth, became an intimate friend of the famous Earl of Clarendon, when Lord Chancellor of England; and being a man of great abilities, was knighted in 1660 *, by K. Charles II. and by letters patent dated at Westminster 2 August 1660, appointed to succeed Sir Adam Loftus in the office of surveyor, estimator and extensor-general of Ireland [1] for life, who by the King's writ dated at Westminster 26 July 1660 was superseded and directed to intermeddle no longer in the execution of that office [2]; who refusing to make a surrender thereof, his Majesty wrote from Whitehall, 26 November, to George, Duke of Albemarle, L. L. to confirm him therein; letting him know, that whereas his council,

---

* It appears that he was knighted between 2 August and 18 September, being styled a Knight in the privy seal of that date, giving him a licence of absence, the King having present use of his attendance and service in England. (Rolls Office, and Lodge,)

[1] Rot. Hib. Anno 12 Car. II. 1, p. f. M. 1,
[2] Idem. M. 2.

council, learned in the laws, had declared under their hands, that Sir Adam Loftus, by non-attendance, had forfeited his office of surveyor-general of Ireland, and by accepting a patent of the vice-treasurership of that kingdom, his former patent became void in law; and whereas his Majesty under the great seal of England, had discharged him from execution of the same, who, contrary to law, presumed to officiate, being never sworn, and had granted the same to Sir Alan Brodrick, who was sworn by the Lord Chancellor Eustace, he therefore required him to admit his deputy, John Petty, to the peaceable execution of the office according to the tenour of a warrant under the privy signet dated 18 September, which letter was followed by his Majesty's supersedeas.

19 March 1660, he was appointed one of the commissioners for settling the affairs of Ireland. In the parliament, which met 9 May 1661, he was member for Dungarvan; in which year (9 September) he was created A. M. by the University of Oxford; and in consideration that he had suffered very much in the time of his Majesty's absence beyond the sea, and was particularly employed and entrusted by him in the late great and happy work of his restoration, wherein he was instrumental, and still continued indefatigably, to render faithful and acceptable services to the crown, "for which," says the King, "he hath not "as hitherto received those real marks of our grace and "favour, which we intend, and are resolved to confer up- "on him, for the advantage of him and his posterity;" his Majesty was therefore pleased by privy seal, dated at Whitehall, 25 February 1660, to grant him the estates of Colonel John Hueson some time of Dublin, and Colonel Daniel Axtell some time of Kilkenny, attainted of high treason, ordering him to be put into quiet possession thereof, and effectual grants to be made to him of the same [1].— But the King afterwards granting those estates to his brother James, Duke of York, and Sir Alan submitting thereto; his Majesty in recompence of his ready compliance, did 22 January 1662, order a grant to be passed to him, his heirs and assignes, out of other forfeited lands, of the full moiety in value, worth, and purchase of what the said estates amounted to, which being 10,759 Acres, 3 Roods, and 20 perches, English measure, he passed patent 20 May 1663 for so much forfeited lands, as amounted to a moiety thereof,

[1] Rot. 13 Car. II. 3. p. D. R. I.

thereof, and which should or might accrue to the crown, by reason that the same was unduly obtained by bribery, forgery, perjury, subornation of witnesses, concealments, false or undue admeasurements, or by any overt act to the King's restoration or government [1].

In 1663 he came into Ireland one of the commissioners for executing the acts of settlement, being well learned in the laws, and clear in his reputation for virtue and integrity; and the act of explanation passing into a law 23 December 1665, he was 1 January ensuing, with Sir Edward Smith, Chief Justice of the Common Pleas, Sir Edward Dering Bart. Sir Winston Churchill, Knt. and Edward Cooke, Esq. appointed the five commissioners for putting it in execution.——He was endowed with a poetical wit, of which several specimens are extant; and departing this life at Wandsworth 25 November 1680, was buried there 3 December.

His brother Sir St. John Brodrick came into Ireland during the troubles of 1641, and was rewarded for his services in suppressing them, 25 November 1653, with the lands of Ballyanin (where he was then seated) Garryduffe, East and West Ballyvodicke, West-Ballintobride, and Coolemore, in the barony of Barrymore and county of Cork; of which being in possession when the acts of settlement passed, they were thereby vested in him and his heirs for ever.——He afterwards became seated at Midleton (a great part of which town, with the church, he built) was honoured with knighthood, and in the first parliament after the restoration was member for the town of Kingsale. By privy seal dated at Whitehall 21 January 1660, the King wrote, that being satisfied by an instrument, under the hand of Francis Peasley, bearing date 1 February 1649, that he then surrendered all his right, title, and interest, of and in the office of Provost Marshal General of the province of Munster, to a person that was not capable of executing the same by the laws of Ireland, and consequently the disposal of that office devolved to the King; his Majesty therefore directed a patent to issue for granting the same to St. John Brodrick, Esq. during his natural life, and in case it should be found that any patent or grant of that office was in force, that the same should be granted to him in reversion, immediately after the determination of the said patent [2].——Accordingly 2 February following,

Sir St. John.

[1] Rot. 15°, 2. p. f. R. 24.   [2] Idem. A°. 12 Car. II. 1. p. f.

following, he had a grant of the said office by patent for life, with the standing fee of 4s. 2d. ¾. per diem, and a stipend or entertainment for ten horsemen of 12d. sterling a piece per diem, with all other fees belonging to the said office, which were lawfully used and enjoyed by Sir Thomas Wenman, or Francis Peasley [1]. And upon his humble supplication to have the said office conferred upon him for life, the King by privy signet dated at Whitehall 2 May 1661, directed the same to be done in consideration of his services done to the King and for his interest in Ireland, for which he merited much to be employed by his Majesty in that kingdom [2].—On 14 March 1660 [3], he was made Captain of a foot company, pursuant to privy signet from Whitehall 28 February preceding, wherein the King writes, " By orders formerly given by George, Duke of " Albemarle, L. L. four companies were to be suspended, " which the King had confirmed; but upon the suit of " St. John Brodrick, Esq. to be gratified with a command " in Ireland, his Majesty for his many loyal services, " was pleased to supersede his former resolutions so far as " to appoint him to one of the said four companies [4]": And 30 July following he received a free pardon for all things, acted or spoken against his Majesty, before 29 December preceding *.——He married Alice, daughter of Sir Randal Clayton of Thelwell in the county of Chester, Knt. and had six sons, and as many daughters, five of whom died young, and Catharine, the survivor, married Doctor William Whitfield, and died in London 3 May 1731.   The sons were

(1) Thomas Brodrick, Esq. one of the privy council to K. William, in whose reign he was a member of parliament, and

* He had six grants of lands in virtue of the acts of settlement; and by patent, dated 2 January 1670, pursuant to privy signet dated at Whitehall 10 June, the castles, towns, and lands of Castleredmond, Corrabby, and divers others in the baronies of Barrymore, Fermoy, and Orrery, were erected into the manor of Midleton, with power to set apart 800 acres for demesne; to impark 800 more; with the privileges of courts, waifs, estrays, &c. Castleredmond and Corrabby being made a free borough and corporation, to extend every way from the middle of the town 100 acres in the whole; to be named the borough and town of Midleton; to consist of a sovereign, two bailiffs, and twelve burgesses, to be first named by him; with power to send two burgesses to parliament; to have two maces borne before the sovereign; he and his heirs to appoint a recorder, town clerk, and other officers. (Lodge.)

[1] Rot. 13⁹, 1. p. f.   [2] Idem. 2. p, D. R. 20.
[3] Idem. 3. p. f. R. 20.   [4] Idem.

and in 1703 was chosen to represent the county of Cork; in the English parliament he served for the borough of Stockbridge, as he also did in 1713; being appointed Comptroller of the Salt Duties; and 1 May 1708 joint Comptroller of the accompts of the army, with Sir Philip Meddows, which he resigned in June 1711.——On 9 October 1714 he was made a member of the privy council to K. George I. being chosen to parliament in that year for Stockbridge, as he was in the following year for Guildford * ; in 1720 was chosen (by ballot) chairman of the committee of secrecy, appointed for the detection of frauds and villainies, acted in the spring and summer preceding; and in 1722 was elected to parliament for Guildford in Surry, having served for that borough before, and so continued to his death, which happened 3 October 1730, in the 77 year of his age.——He married Anne, daughter of Alexander Pigott of Inishannon in the county of Cork, Esq. by Anne, daughter of Sir Edward Bolton of Brazeel in the county of Dublin, Knt. and left issue Laurence Brodrick, Esq. who 20 January¹ 1735 was appointed joint Register of all deeds and conveyances in Ireland, which he resigned to his colleague Arthur Hill, Esq. in September following.

Alan, created Lord Midleton. (2)

St. John Brodrick, Esq. serjeant at law, who died at Wandsworth 12 June 1707, unmarried. (3)

Randal died also unmarried. (4)

William, appointed in October 1692, Attorney-General of the island of Jamaica, to which office he was again assigned by Q. Anne in March 1710, and continued in May 1715 by K. George I. who 23 December 1718 made him his second serjeant at law, and in 1733 he was living at St. Jago de la Vega. (5)

Rev. Doctor Laurence Brodrick, who was chaplain to the House of Commons in England; was made Prebendary of Westminster 17 July 1710, and died at Kensington 19 July 1740, leaving an only daughter, who in March 1741-2, became second wife to Benjamin Bathurst, Esq. brother to Allen Lord Bathurst; and a son Laurence of Birchfield, near Kilkenny; presented 15 July 1745 to the rectory and vicarage of Callan in the diocess of Ossory; and 16 August (6)

---

* On 3 April 1718 he passed patent, for holding two fairs, on 24 June and 26 March, at Midleton, at the rent of 6s. 3d.

¹ Lodge.

August ensuing, made treasurer of Lismore, and Vicar of Tubrid, Derragrath and Ballybeacon; who married Jane, daughter of St. John Brodrick, Esq. as hereafter, and had a son born 23 April 1750.

Alan, 1 Viscount.

Alan Brodrick, Esq. the second son, was attainted with his brother James, by K. James's parliament; being brought up to the profession of the law, he became so eminent therein, that 19 February 1690 (immediately after the reduction of Ireland by K. William) his Majesty made him his serjeant at law, at the same time granting him a licence to be of council for the Mayors of the city of Cork; and 6 June 1695 appointed him solicitor-general of Ireland, in which post he was continued by Q. Anne 4 June 1702; and being returned to her first parliament, which met 20 September 1703, member for the city of Cork, he was the day following unanimously chosen Speaker of the House of Commons, and on the 24 presented to the Duke of Ormond, L. L. for his approbation *.

His conduct, however, being disagreeable to the L. L. by the opposition he gave his Grace in passing some bills, which he intended for the benefit of Ireland, and which were thereby frustrated, he was removed in April 1704, from his post of her Majesty's solicitor-general, and so

continued

---

* In his speech to his Grace on this occasion, he said, "The commons in parliament assembled, have, in obedience to your Grace's command, proceeded to the choice of a Speaker, and their choice hath terminated in me. If steady loyalty to the crown, sincere wishes and an hearty inclination, with the utmost deligence to promote the prosperity of her Majesty and this kingdom, were sufficient to qualify me for the due discharge of that great trust, I should not think it modest in me, but its opposite vice, to disable myself. For it is in the power, as it is the duty, of every man, to be a loyal subject, and a lover of his country; and I hope, I may, without the least imputation of vanity, be permitted (upon this occasion) to affirm, that I must forget my present sentiments, and be much altered from what I am, when I cease to be either."

Whereupon the Lord Chancellor thus acquainted the house, and addressed himself to their Speaker.

"Mr. Solicitor,

"The knowledge his Grace my L. L. has of you, and the character you have in the world, do fully satisfy his Grace, that you are a person fitly qualified for the great trust reposed in you; and therefore his Grace hath readily approved of the choice, which the commons have made of you to be their Speaker——It is a circumstance of great satisfaction to his Grace, that your election was unanimous, for his Grace cannot look upon this good agreement in the beginning, but as a certain presage of a happy conclusion of this session of parliament."

continued till the year 1707, when the Queen (12 June) appointed him her Attorney-General, into which he was sworn the 30 of that month.—On 17 December 1709, Sir Richard Pyne, Chief Justice of the King's Bench, dying at Ashley in England, he was appointed his successor 4 January; and the writer of Thomas, Earl of Wharton's life, then L. L. observes, " That he p.ocured that high post " for one of the most worthy patriots of that kingdom, as " an instance of the care he took of the security of religi- " on and liberty."—By this promotion, being called up to the House of Peers, he took his seat on the Woolsack 19 May 1710, and received the thanks of the commons for the faithful and eminent services, performed to that house in the chair, during the time of his being Speaker *.

The Queen, about this time, making a change in her ministry, his Lordship, among others, was removed from his employment, 4 July 1711, being succeeded by Sir Richard Cox; and the parliament of this kingdom being dissolved by proclamation 6 May 1713, and a new one ordered to meet, he was chosen representative of the county of Cork; and 25 November, the Duke of Shrewsbury opening the session, he was the next day presented to his Excellency by the House of Commons, as their Speaker †.

His constant, faithful attachment to the established religion and laws of his country, and to the succession of the crown in the illustrious House of Hanover, were so eminent and conspicuous, that no sooner had K. George I. ascended

---

* To which he replied, " I am extremely sensible of this great
" honour done me, as I always have been of the goodness of the
" House of Commons, in supporting me in the discharge of the
" trust, they were pleased to repose in me, and can't sufficiently ac-
" knowledge their favour, or express the satisfaction I take, that
" the witnesses of my behaviour during so many sessions of parlia-
" ment, have unanimously approved it, and given an uncontroula-
" ble testimony of my having, in all instances, to the best of my
" power, done my duty to the crown, the House of Commons,
" and the kingdom in general."

† When the Lord Chancellor thus addressed him:
" Mr. Brodrick,
" I am commanded by my L. L. to acquaint you, that his
" Grace, not doubting your abilities, and expecting that you will
" endeavour to keep this session quiet and easy, and to give such
" dispatch to the public business as matters of so great consequence
" and her Majesty's affairs necessarily require; does approve the
" choice the Commons have made of you to be their Speaker." ‡

‡ Lords Jour. II. 421.

ascended the throne, than he preferred him by privy seal dated 30 September, and by patent 1 October 1714, to the office of Lord High Chancellor of Ireland, into which he was sworn 14 October, and he continued in that great trust to 25 June 1725 [1].—On 9 October 1714 he was sworn of the privy council (as he had been to K. William, and Q. Anne); and, by privy seal, dated at St. James's 22 February 1714, and by patent * 13 April 1715, was advanced to the dignity of Baron Brodrick of Midleton; and, 12 November, (the first day of the first parliament after his Majesty's accession) he took his seat in the House of Peers [2].

On

* The preamble. Quandoquidem nihil habeamus in regia nostra dignitate magnificentius, quam quod ab eâ, quasi fonte unico, tituli et honores in subditos nostros deriventur; nihil apud nos sanctius habebitur, quam eos a nobis et republica bene merentibus decernere. Horum in numero, jure optimo, perquam fidelem et prædilectum conciliarium nostrum Alannm Brodrick recensemus, quem amplissimis honoribus illustrando dudum princeps populusque, tanquam emuli, contendisse videantur. Dum propria egregii Viri Merita intuemur, stemmatis sui claritudinem, quasi supervacaneum silentio præterimus, quamvis hac etiam in parte singulari splendore emineat, ab illo scilicet Gulielmi Normanni commilitone prognatus, qui jam tum domus suæ gloriam (quod Insignibus gentilitiis familiæ vel in eo sæculo propriis satis constat) a proavis militia inclytis deductam ostentarit; tantis ortus majoribus ad famam consequendam novi hominis labore ac patientia hic noster usus est, non ad eam quam jam agendus est dignitatem raptim transiliit, ac in cursu honorum per officia amplissima gradatim provectus, sollicitatoris ac deinde Attornati Generalis Muniis maxima cum Laude perfunctus, tandem principis in banco regio Justiciarii sedem occupavit, unde majori Gloria amotus est quam qua alii ad eandem dignitatem evecti sunt, nempe ob fidem in domum nostram ac religionem reformatam, isto munere istis temporibus spoliari meruit, fortunæ optimorum civium particeps illustris, qui vix ullum in republica authoritatem retinuerunt, quam armis, virtutibus, consiliis in summo Gloriæ fastigio collocassent. Noluit interim patria integerrimi juxta ac ornatissimi viri ope et auxilio carere, quem inde inferiori senatus curiæ præfecit, ubi antea oratoris partes, omni laude cumulatus, adimpleverat, hoc in munere obeundo tantum valuit gravissimi viri constantia et auctoritas, ut causa nostra in Britanniarum regno languescens, prorsus et in extremum discrimen adducta, in Hibernia novis viribus indies cresceret ac vigeret. Quum proinde æquum nobis visum fuerit in tanto viro ornando partem habuisse ipsum earum legum quas sæpius vindicavit custodem nomine ac potestate magni cancellarii constituimus, nunc insuper ut iis nunquam non invigilet, procerum ordinibus adscribi volumus. Sciatis igitur, &c. (Rot. 1 Geo. I. 1. p. f.)

[1] Lodge Collect.   [2] Lords Jour. II. 454.

On 20 March 1716, he was conſtituted one of the L. J. of the kingdom, as he was again 7 January 1717; a third time, 20 November 1719; a fourth time, 29 March 1723; and a fifth time, 20 May 1724; having been further advanced in the Peerage, by privy ſeal, dated at Hampton-Court, 31 July, and by patent *, 15 Auguſt 1717, by the title of Viſcount Middleton, with the creation fee of 20 Marcs, by which title he ſat firſt in parliament the 27 of that month [1]; and 7 January following, embarking for England with the Duke of Bolton, L. L. was choſen, during his ſtay in that kingdom, to ſerve in parliament for Midhurſt in Suſſex, for which, in March 1723, he was rechoſen †, which he continued to repreſent till his death; and on 6 June 1725, he was commiſſioned with Sir Ralph Gore, Sir John St. Leger, and others; to examine and inſpect all accompts of public money [2].

He

* The preamble. Cum aucta in nos et rempublicam merita auctos a nobis honores poſtulare videantur; cumque æquum ſit ut Alanum Baronem Brodrick de Midleton, Cancellarium noſtrum Regni noſtri Hiberniæ, talem tantumque virum, quem tot egregiæ et raræ virtutes in eo conſpicuæ, ad poſtremum nobilitatis gradum evexere, eædem multiplicatæ et magis illuſtratæ in altiorem dignitatis gradum promoveant; eum igitur, quem Hibernia ſemper experta eſt ſibi fidelem in periculoſiſſimis et pene perditis reipublicæ temporibus, quem perſpexit veræ fidei, reformatæ religionis, et ſalutis libertatiſque communis acrem et ſtrenuum propugnatorem, quem adeo in deliciis habuit, ut eum (vel renitente bis Palatio) propenſo erga eum amore, in oratorem publicum civium equitumque ſenatus eligerat ea dicendi facultate pollentem, quæ non ſolum clientium jura ſibi integra conſervaret, verumetiam lapſa in integrum reſtitueret, quumque illum tot præclaris ingenii dotibus inſtructum ipſa ejus patria certiſſimis teſtimoniis noſtro favori commendaverit, non dubitavimus eum Baronis honoribus et inſignibus jampridem augere, ſed eaſdem virtutes, quas fama in eo imminere prædicavit, nos ei ineſſe jamdudum perſpeximus. Ideoque ſicut ob celebrem de eo et vere diſſipatam laudem et præconium, eum in Conventu Nobilium in ipſis Regni noſtri initiis recepimus, jam ob eaſdem virtutes in eo à nobis ſatis compertas, et ab eo in imperii noſtri pacem et incolumitatem, in patriæ dignitatem et commodum, in civium omnium ſalutem, et coronæ noſtræ decus et ornamentum feliciter directas et adminiſtratas, eundem egregium virum in foro, in ſenatu, et in curia denique pari laude ſe gerentem, in magis ſublime Vicecomitum Subſellium, ſummo Bonorum omnium conſenſu, provehere dignati ſumus. Sciatis igitur, &c. (Rot. 4 Geo. I. 1. p. f.)

† On 12 January 1726 he had a licence to hold two fairs, upon 15 April and 12 October, at Killmac-Cleeny in the county of Cork.

[1] Lords Jour. II. 545. [2] Lodge.

He married three wives; to his first Catharine, second daughter of Redmond Barry, of Rathcormuck in the county of Cork, Esq. by his first wife Mary, daughter of John Boyle of Castlelyons, Esq. by whom he had one daughter, who died an infant, and one son St. John Brodrick, Esq. who in the reign of Q. Anne, was member of parliament for the borough of Midleton, and the city of Cork; and on K. George's accession, returned for the county, which he represented to his death. In 1721 and 1722, he was chosen to sit in the English parliament, for Beeralston in Devonshire, and 25 June 1724, sworn of his Majesty's privy council in Ireland. In 1709 he married Anne, sister to Trevor, Viscount Hillsborough, and dying in February 1727, had issue by her, who died 25 April 1752 [1], five daughters.

(1) Catharine, buried 2 November 1713, in the chancel of St. Michan's church, Dublin.

(2) Anne, married to James, son of Sir James Jeffereys of Blarney in the county of Cork, Knt. living in 1713, and by her who died in Cork 13 May 1763, had issue James-St. John of Blarney-castle, (who married the eldest daughter of John Fitz-Gibbon, Esq. and by her was father of Mary-Anne, Lady Viscountess Delvin); Alan, who died at Corke, 6 April 1758; and Arthur who died there 1 December 1760 unmarried.

(3) Catharine, married in 1737 to Charles O Neile of Shane's-Castle in the county of Antrim, Esq. eldest son of John, of Edenduff-Carrick, alias Shane's-Castle, and nephew of Charles, who married Lady Mary Powlet, eldest daughter of Charles, second Duke of Bolton, by his second wife, which Lady Mary, on her husband's decease in 1716, remarried with Capel Moore, son of Charles, Earl of Drogheda.—John O Neile aforesaid died in 1739, having had the said Charles his heir apparent; Clotworthy; daughter Catharine, married to Sir Richard Butler, Viscount Mountgarret, died 15 April 1739, and was buried at St. Michan's; Rachel; Elinor; Rose; Anne; and Mary, married to Robert Borrowes of Kildare, Esq.—Charles, the eldest son married as above, served in parliament for Randalstown, and dying suddenly left issue by his Lady who died 31 July 1742, and was buried at St. Michan's, two sons and one daughter, viz. John, his heir; St. John, born at his grandfather's house 6 May 1741,

---

[1] Chancery Bill filed 30 January 1764.

1741, and married to a daughter of Robert Borrowes, Esq.; and Anne, to Richard Jackson, Esq. second secretary to George, Lord Viscount Townsend, L. L.—John the eldest son, received a liberal education in the universities of Dublin and Oxford; he succeeded at Shane's-Castle, served first in parliament for Randalstown, and hath been elected to the last and present parliaments for the county of Antrim, and sworn of the privy council in Ireland; 18 December 1777 he married Henrietta Boyle, only daughter of Charles, Lord Dungarvan, heir apparent to John, the fifth Earl of Cork and Orrery, and by her has issue.

Mary, married 16 September 1739, to Sir John Freke (4) of Castle-Freke in the county of Cork, Bart. fourth of that title *; member of parliament for Baltimore, and chosen for the city of Cork in 1761; her Ladyship died at Castle-Freke 20 June 1761, and was interred at Midleton, having no issue by Sir John, who married secondly in 1765 Lady Elizabeth Gore, second daughter of Sir Arthur, first Earl of Arran, by whom he had Sir John, his heir, now of Castle-Freke, and the fifth and present Baronet, who represents the borough of Donegall in parliament; and 25 January 1783 married Lady Catharine-Charlotte Gore, third daughter of his uncle the present Earl of Arran.

Jane,

---

* Francis Freke, Esq. a person of good repute in Somerset, was father of Robert Freke, who was Auditor of the Treasury in the reigns of K. Henry VIII. and Q. Elizabeth, and died worth upwards of 100,000l. leaving issue Sir Thomas Freke, Knt. (who settled in Dorsetshire and was ancestor to the families of Hanning, Upway, and Farringdon, in that county); and William of Sareen in Hampshire, who took to wife the daughter of Arthur Swaine, Esq. and with his son Arthur removed into Ireland; which Arthur, heir to his father, lived near the city of Cork, and by Dorothy, daughter of Sir Piercy Smith of Youghall, Knt. had Piercy, his heir, who succeeded to his father's estates in Ireland, going to England he married Elizabeth, daughter of Raufe Freke, Esq. his kinsman, with whom he had a considerable fortune, and purchasing the estate of Bliney in Norfolk, left the same to his son Raufe Freke, Esq. who was created a Baronet of England 12 Q. Anne, and left issue three sons, viz. Sir Piercy his successor; Raufe who died at Richmond in Surry in 1727 unmarried; and Sir John who succeeded to the title.—Sir Piercy, the second Baronet, served in parliament for the borough of Baltimore, and dying unmarried in Dublin in April 1728, was succeeded in title and estate by his next surviving brother Sir John, the third Baronet, mentioned in the text. (Baronetage of England, Edit. 1771, III. 38—39.)

Family of Freke, Baronets.

(5) Jane, to Rev. Laurence Brodrick, minister of Callan, &c. as before mentioned, and had a daughter born 18 September 1758.

In 1695, his Lordship married secondly Alice, daughter of Sir Peter Courthorpe, of the Little-Island in the county of Cork, (by his second wife, Elizabeth Giffard) and sister to Colonel John Courthorpe, who was killed at the siege of Namure in Flanders, and by her, who was buried at St. Michan's 30 June 1703, he had two sons, and one daughter; Courthorpe, baptized 25 March 1700, and buried at St. Michan's 23 December following; Alan, his successor; and Alice, born 31 May 1697, married 3 March 1736 to Rev. John Castleman, Fellow of All-Souls College, Oxford, son to Jonathan Castleman, of Coberly in Gloucestershire, Esq.

On 1 December 1716, his Lordship married to his third wife Anne, daughter of Sir John Trevor, master of the rolls in England, who died 20 May 1717 aged 90; widow of Michael Hill of Hillsborough, Esq. and departing this life, at Ballyallan in the county of Cork, 29 August 1728, had no issue by her, who died 5 January 1747, and was succeeded by his only surviving son,

Alan, 2 Viscount.
Alan, the second Viscount Midleton, baptized 31 January 1701, who in September 1727 was appointed a commissioner of his Majesty's customs in England, which he held till 1730, being constituted, 27 August that year, joint comptroller of the accompts of the army, with Sir Philip Meddows; was member of parliament for Midhurst; and, 26 November 1733 took his seat in the House of Peers [1].—On 7 May 1729 his Lordship married the Lady Mary Capel, youngest daughter of Algernoon, Earl of Essex, and deceasing in England 8 June 1747, left issue by her, who, in October 1727, was appointed a Lady of the bedchamber to the Princess Anne of Great-Britain, and died in St. James's-street London, 12 March 1762, an only son,

George, 3 Viscount.
George, the third Viscount Midleton, born 3 October 1730, and named after his Majesty, who stood his godfather in person, 29 October 1751 he took his seat in the House of Peers [2]; and was chosen to the British parliament in 1754 for Ashburton in Devon.—On 1 May 1752, his Lordship married Albina, daughter of Thomas Townsend,

---

[1] Lords Jour. III. 242.   [2] Idem. 787.

BRODRICK, Viscount MIDLETON.

Townfend, Efq. brother to Charles, Lord Vifcount Townfend, and uncle to George, Marquefs Townfend of Reynham, fo created in 1788, and deceafing 22 September 1765, had iffue by her who in 1788 remarried with Edward Miller-Mundy of Shipley in the county of Nottingham, Efq. fix fons and three daughters, viz. George, his heir; Thomas, born 10 December 1756; Henry, a Captain and Colonel in the Coldftream regiment of guards; Charles, (married 8 December 1786, to Mary, daughter of Richard Woodward, D. D. Lord Bifhop of Cloyne); William, under fecretary to the commiffioners for managing the Eaft India affairs; John, an Enfign in the firft regiment of guards; Albina; Mary; and Harriot,[1] married 11 Auguft 1787 to Hon. Richard Lumley, brother to George-Auguftus, Earl of Scarborough.

George, the fourth and prefent Vifcount Midleton, was born 1 November 1754, ferves in the Britifh parliament for Whitchurch in Hampfhire: 5 December 1778 he married Frances, daughter of Thomas, Lord Pelham, and her Ladyfhip died 23 June 1783.

George, 4 Vifcount.

TITLES.] George Brodrick, Vifcount of Midleton and Baron Brodrick of Midleton.

CREATIONS.] B. Brodrick of Midleton in the county of Cork, 13 April 1715, 1 Geo. I. and V. of the fame place, 15 Auguft 1717.

ARMS.] Pearl, on a chief, emerald, two fpears heads erect, of the field, their points embrued, proper.

CREST.] A fpear, pearl, embrued, proper, iffuing out of a ducal coronet, topaz.

SUPPORTERS.] Two men in compleat armour, each holding a fpear, as the creft.

MOTTO.] A CUSPIDE CORONA.

SEATS.] Midleton in the county of Cork, 116 miles from Dublin; and Pepper-Harrow in the county of Surrey 33 miles from London.

[1] Ulfter's Office.

HAMILTON,

THIS noble branch of the houfe of HAMILTON derives from Sir Frederick, the fifth and youngeft fon of Claud, the firft Lord Paifley, as may be feen under the title of VISCOUNT STRABANE.

Sir Frederick.
Which Sir Frederick Hamilton, early embracing a military life, fignalized himfelf under the banner of Guftavus Adolphus, King of Sweden; after which, returning home in the latter end of the reign of James I. he came into Ireland, accompanied with his Majefty's letter to the L. D. dated at Weftminfter 8 April 1620, for his better grace and countenance, to have the command of the firft foot or horfe company, that fhould become void; and accordingly, upon the deceafe of Sir Francis Ruifh, fucceeded to his company of foot; which the King afterwards caufing him to relinquifh, that the Lord Efmond might have it for the defence of the Fort of Duncannon, in order to abate the charge of maintaining a peculiar ward therein; his Majefty, in confideration thereof, ordered by privy feal dated at Weftminfter 10 September 1623, that (notwithftanding any directions to the contrary) he fhould have the very next vacant company [1].

He was a gentleman in ordinary of the privy chamber to that King and Charles I. and poffeffed a great fhare of their Majefties efteem; the former of whom, in order to provide for and fettle him in this kingdom, made him confiderable grants of lands [*], and 6 Auguft 1623

---

[*] By patent, dated 18 March 1620, were granted to him, his heirs and affignes the quarter of land, called Carrowroffe, containing 788 acres of arable and pafture land, and 2612 of Bog and wood in the Barony of Dromahere and county of Leitrim, with other lands

in

[1] Rot. Anno 15 Car. I. 7. p. D. R. 2.

1623 sent him over with the following letter to the L. D. written from Salisbury. "We have already expressed our good respect to this bearer Sir Frederick Hamilton, Knt. one of the gentlemen of our privy chamber, by the grant of some lands, which we have bestowed upon him in that kingdom, and lately by assisting him with our favour for obtaining the interest of Sir John Ayres, in the Island of *Valentia* in that realm; and now at his going thither, we think meet to accompany him with these our letters, which are to recommend him to your especial favour in his affairs there; requiring you in all his causes, as well concerning that Island of Valentia, as any other rights and possessions he hath there, to take care that upon all occasions he may have justice and all possible expedition; and whatsoever good shall result unto him thereby, by your furtherance, will be very acceptable

in the same barony and county, amounting in the whole to 1568 acres of the former, and 4981 of the latter, to hold *in Capite* by Knight's service. Of all which premisses, to the intent they might be anew granted to him, under such rents, covenants and provisoes, as by his Majesty's instructions for the plantation of the county of Leitrim, were to be inserted in the patents of undertakers of the like proportions in that plantation, he petitioned K. Charles I. to accept of a surrender; who by his letter from Westminster 12 January 1629 (as an especial mark of his favour to him, in regard of his long and faithful services) directed the L. J. to accept a surrender of the manor of Hamilton, and to regrant the same, together with the several proportions purchased by him, namely 1500 acres from Captain Henry Fortescue, 500 from William Nesbitt, 200 from William Sidney, 107 from Owen Mac-Manney Mac-Mury, all in the Barony of Dromahere; 600 from James Rotney, 206 from Cahir Mac-Glanigh, 120 from Rory Mac-Glanigh, and about 77 from Terman O Rourk, in the barony of Roslogher, to be united into one manor; he to build a castle and a bawne, to perform the articles of plantation, and to be made a free denizen of Ireland by the said patent.—Accordingly he surrendered the premisses 17 May 1630, and had them regranted and confirmed, with the denization, the next day, to be holden by Knight's service and the rent of 64l. 2s. 5d. English, with the creation thereof (containing in the whole 4939 acres of arable and pasture, and 9943 of bogg and wood) into the manor of Manor-Hamilton, with a Thursday market, and three fairs on 28 April, 5 June, and 26 September, at Clonemullen, otherwise Hamilton; free warren; and liberty to impark 1000 acres.—Also, in virtue of the act for remedy of defective titles, he received a new confirmation of the premisses 19 December 1636, at the rent of 129l. 4s. 10d. halfpenny, with a Thursday market, and two fairs on 21 June and 22 September, at Dewelliske.—This estate he very much improved by erecting a stately house, one of the most costly edifices in Conaught, with a spacious Deer-park, and many other ornamental improvements.

"able to us, as being done to one whom we value and wish well unto."

In 1628, by petition to K. Charles I. he desired his Majesty to grant him the nomination and making of two Irish Baronets; which request (though his Majesty was resolved not to draw it into precedent for others) in regard the King was desirous to gratify so well deserving a servant, and was confident, he would nominate none but such as were of meet and fitting quality and condition for that dignity, was pleased to grant; and accordingly, 20 May 1619 he nominated John Magrath of Allevollan in the county of Tipperary, and John Wilson of Killenure in the county of Donegall, Esqrs. who were created to that dignity by letters patent.

Sir Frederick, with his sons James and Frederick, were very considerable officers in the service of the Kings Charles I. and II. during the rebellion of 1641, and for their respective services before 1649, had allotted large debentures, viz. to Sir Frederick, for 1343l. 9s. 1d; to James and Frederick, 2337l. 9s. 1d. each; but having no lands set out to them in satisfaction for the same during their lives, an allotment was made, to their administrator, William Hamilton of Caledon and his heirs, in trust for the two daughters of the said James, son of Sir Frederick [1], in April 1666, of lands on the estate of Sir Phelim O Neile in the county of Tyrone, and other forfeitures in the baronies of Ardagh and Granard in the county of Longford, at the rate of 12s. and 6d. the pound, at ten years purchase, besides reprises [2].

He [3] married Sidney, daughter and heir to Sir John Vaughan, a Captain in the Irish army, Privy Counsellor and Governor of the city and county of Londonderry, and had issue three sons and one daughter; James, his heir; Frederick, who lost his life in the wars of Ireland, and died unmarried; Gustavus, created Viscount Boyne; and Christiana, married to Sir George Monroe of Thermore, Major-General, by whom she had several children, the heads of many flourishing families in Scotland.

James Hamilton of Manor-Hamilton, Esq. the eldest son, married his first cousin Catharine, daughter of Claud, the first Lord Strabane, and by her, who remarried first with Owen Wynne, and after with John Bingham, Esqrs.

having

---

[1] Lodge. [2] Idem.
Rot. 15º Car. I. 7. p. D. R. 2.

having only two daughters, they carried the aforesaid estate into the families of their husbands, of which they came to a partition in 1668, and were, Hannah, married to Sir William Gore of Manor-Gore, Bart. who died in the year 1700, ancestor to the Earl of Ross; and Sidney, to Sir John Hume of Castle-Hume, Bart. in the county of Fermanagh, who died in 1695, and was father, by her, who died in 1688, of the late Sir Gustavus Hume, then a minor.

Gustavus, the youngest son of Sir Frederick Hamilton, in the reign of Charles II. was a Captain in the army; and attending the Duke of Ormond, Chancellor of Oxford, to that university, had the degree of Doctor of Laws conferred on him 6 August 1677.—On the accession of K. James II. he was sworn of his privy council; but being a steady asserter of the laws of his country, he quitted that King's service on his open violation of them, and was attainted by his parliament. And when the Irish army, under Major-General Richard Hamilton, and Major Dominick Sheldon, had taken the fort of Hillsborough, and plundered Lisburn, Belfast, and Antrim, and laid siege to Coleraine, they met with such a warm reception from Major Gustavus Hamilton, who commanded in the town, and spared no charge or pains to make it tenable, that they were forced to draw off with considerable loss, and their designs against Londonderry were for some weeks retarded. On K. William's landing in England, he raised four regiments of foot, and two of dragoons, in two counties of Ireland, where he was then chosen Governor. He marched to Colerain, repaired the ruined works of that place, and defended it five weeks against the whole Irish army, who twice attempted to storm the town; by which means he covered the city of Derry, until all the arms, ammunition, and provisions were thrown into it; which enabled them to make so extraordinary a defence [1]; he headed a regiment at the battle of the Boyne, where having his horse killed under him, he narrowly escaped death.—After this victory, he waded the Shannon at the head of the grenadiers, and storming the town of Athlone, he was appointed, upon its surrender, Governor thereof; and was in all the battles, fought after by General Ginkle, for the reduction of the kingdom; upon the accomplishment whereof he was sworn of the privy council to K. William;

made

---

[1] Letter from Frederick Lord Boyne, 30 September 1787.

made a Brigadier-General of his armies 30 May 1696, and had his services rewarded with a grant of forfeited lands *.

Q. Anne advanced him to the rank of a Major-General 1 January 1703, in whose first parliament he represented the county of Donegall, and so continued till created a Peer, of which he was also *C. Rotulorum,* and Vice-Admiral of the province of Ulster; he commanded a regiment at the siege of Vigo, and behaved so well, that the Queen presented him with a considerable quantity of plate ‡.—In May 1710, being of distinguished zeal for the Protestant interest, he was sworn of her Majesty's privy council, as he was 9 October 1714 to K. George I. who, in consideration of his faithful services and loyalty, advanced him to the dignity of Baron Hamilton of Stackallan by privy seal, dated at St. James's 27 September, and by patent † at Dublin

---

* Namely, the estate of Roger O Shaghnassy in *Custodiam,* but that being afterwards granted in fee to Thomas Prendergast, Esq. (after Sir Thomas) in recompence for his discovery of the assassination plot; he had a grant in lieu thereof, dated at Bieren 16 August 1698, N. S. of the lands of Rathlyan, Fiermore, Lartanmore, Carpangowlane, Ballygouie, Ballitore, &c. in the King's County, the city and county of Waterford, Navan, Athlone, and county of Galway, amounting to 500l. 8s. 6d. halfpenny a year, above all quit-rents and incumbrances whatever.

† The preamble. Regiam Majestatem non solum armis decoratam, legibusque armatam, sed et procerum etiam, non minus virtutibus quam generis nobilitate insignium, numero munitam pariter ac ornatam esse oportet. Cum igitur præhonorabilis et perquam fidelis noster consiliarius Gustavus Hamilton de Stackallan in comitatu Midensi Regnoque nostro Hiberniæ Armiger, per patrem suum Fredericum Hamilton nuper de Manor-Hamilton in eodem Regno equitem, armis pro libertate simul ac religione reformata sub auspiciis serenissimi Caroli primi tam in Germania, quam in Hibernia insignem, ab illustri viro Jacobo Arraniæ comite in Scotia, Duceque Castri-heraldi in Gallia, necnon Regni Scotici circa Annum Millesimum quingentesimum quadragesimum tertium prorege, regiæque ibidem stirpis consanguineo, originem ducat; necnon per matrem suam Dominam Sidneiam Hamilton, alias Vaughan, filiam Johannis Vaughan Equitis aurati, armis itidem pro libertate ac religione insignis sub Auspiciis serenissimæ Elizabethæ Reginæ in Germanica inferiori, et etiam Caroli primi in Hibernia, sub quo Civitatis Londinoderensis contra Perduelles Toparcha fuit: Majoribus etiam gaudeat præclarissimis, ac inter illos Gulielmo Sidney, Equite aurato, Henrici secundi Regis Camerario, alteroque ejusdem nominis Henrici octavi Regis etiam Camerario Domusque illius administratore, ob fortia sua facta contra Mauros in Hispania, et sæpius contra Regni hostes inclyto; ejusque filio Henrico Sidney, nobilissimi ordinis Periscelidis

‡ Letter ut antea.

HAMILTON, Viscount BOYNE.

Dublin 20 October 1715; and 12 November taking his feat in the House of Peers, he was two days after appointed one of the Lords, to prepare a congratulatory address to his Majesty on his most happy accession to the throne [r]. The King also granted him a military pension of 182l. 10s. a year, and was pleased to promote him to the dignity of Viscount Boyne by privy seal, dated at Hampton-Court 1 August, and by patent * 20 of that month 1717, with the creation

Periscelidis Equite, Regnique Hiberniæ, inter alios honores, sæpius Prorege, ubi omnia, tam pace quam bello, sub Elizabetha felicissimæ memoriæ Regina, perquam prudenter, nec minus fortiter, administravit. Cumque idem Gustavus Hamilton, à prænobili sua Prosapia minime degener, sub Carolo secundo Rege Capitaneus factus, et ad ulteriorem dignitatis gradum deinde evectus, Anno Millesimo sexcentesimo octogesimo octavo præfecturam se maluit abdicare, quam illicitis tunc temporis contra libertatem & religionem machinationibus vel aurem præbere. Et deinde ad Villam de Colerain accedens, ita se Hostibus opposuit, et alios bene affectos ad idem faciendum exemplo suo animavit, ut illorum arma à civitate Londinoderensi per aliquas septimanas divertens, illius Loci Civibus pro futura obsidione se præparandi, ac (Deo juvante) totum Regnum, si non et Britanniam etiam conservandi, opportunitatem dedit. Ob quæ tam fortiter simul ac feliciter facta, ad chiliarchæ honorem à sereniffimo et immortalis Memoriæ Rege Gulielmo provectus, ita animose et fideliter se contra hostes gessit, ut non tantum tribunus, sed et Major etiam Generalis a Serenissima Regina Anna, jure optimo, fieri mereretur. In prælio Boyniaco, Equo sub se occiso, parum à morte abfuit, per fluvium Senum plurimis Globulorum ictibus expositus (sed Deo favente tutus) pedester duxit milites ad impetum in fortissimum Athlonæ Munimentum, ardore non minus quam successu stupendo factum: Nec in prælio Aghrimensi aut obsidione Ballymorensi, Gallovidiensi, aut Limericensii (quibus omnibus interfuit) ab ullo unquam periculo se subduxit. Hibernia tandem redacta, aliquam sui partem ad pacis artes convertens, et miles comitatus Donegalensis unanimi consensu ad Regni comitia sæpius electus; necnon ad secretoria principis consilia admissus, pro libertate, pro religione, proque nostra ad Coronam Magnæ Britanniæ successione strenue semper contendens, adversæ ubique factioni se aperte, nec minus quam hostibus olim in bello, intrepide opposuit. Ob Generis itaque nobilitatem, singularem nobis illustrique nostræ Domui Fidelitatem, bonumque Affectum, omniaque alia illius Benemerita, eundem Gustavum Hamilton in procerum sive nobilium Regni Hiberniæ numerum, sub titulo Baronis Hamilton de Stackallan, cooptandum decrevimus. Sciatis igitur, &c. (Rot. Anno 2 Geo. I. 1. p. d.

* The preamble. Cum perfidelem et dilectum consiliarium nostrum Gustavum Hamilton, multas illius et præclaras virtutes respicientes, Baronem Hamilton de Stackallan jam creavimus; et cum regii sit Muneris, regalique munificentiæ et Majestati gratum, virtutem perseverantem et augescentem novis iterum debitiique honoribus continuò exornare, et publicis quibusdam notis palam attestari,

quam

[r] Lords Jour. II. 460.

creation fee of 20 marcs, by which title on the 27 he took his feat [1].

He married Elizabeth, second daughter of Sir Henry Brooke of Brooke's-Borough in the county of Fermanagh, Knt. (who preserved the town and castle of Donegall during the wars of 1641, and died in August 1671, by his second wife Anne, daughter of Sir George St. George, Knt. and Bart.) By his will he bequeathed a flagon, chalice, and pattin, all silver, to the church of Stackallan; 10l. to the poor of that parish, and 10l. to the poor of the parish of Nevagh in the county of Donegall; and departing this life 16 September 1723, in the 84 year of his age, had issue by her, who died at Stackallan 28 December 1721, one daughter Elizabeth, married to Charles Lambart of Painstown in the county of Meath, Esq. grandson to the first Earl of Cavan; and three sons, Frederick, his heir apparent; Gustavus, father of the present Viscount Boyne; and Henry Hamilton, Esq. who was born in February 1692, and 5 October 1727 made joint customer and collector of the port of Dublin; whence, 30 March 1738 he was removed to the collection of the port of Cork, and was member of parliament for the county of Donegall. In October 1722 [2] he married Mary, eldest daughter of Joshua Dawson of Castle-Dawson in the county of Derry, Esq. and dying at Cork 3 June 1743, left by her who died in March 1770 five sons, and two daughters; viz. Rev. Gustavus Hamilton, baptized 5 October 1723, who married first Letitia, eldest daughter of Edward Bolton of Brazeel, Esq. and secondly Alicia, daughter of Colonel Patterson; Joshua, appointed 3 March 1757, surveyor of the port of Waterford, married in March 1750 to Mary, eldest daughter of Sir Richard Cox, Bart. and she died in April 1764; Sackville, baptized 5 April 1732, principal secretary in the civil department of government,

quam bene acceptus, quam optatus pio et sapienti principi sit civis bonus et de patria benemeritus. Nos igitur multa virtutum observantia, et longa factorum serie confirmati, propter Constantiam nobis et fidelitatem nullis concussam periculis, propter pietatem erga patriam, et animum in reformata religione semper stabilem, propterque conatus contra inimicorum nostrorum contumaciam indefessos, prædictum Gustavum Baronem Hamilton de Stackallan ad ordinem Vicecomitum Regni nostri Hiberniæ promovere decrevimus. Sciatis igitur, &c. (Rot. Anno 4 Geo. I. 1. p. f.)

[1] Lords Jour. II. 545.
[2] Articles of marriage dated 27 October 1722.

vernment, and married to Arabella, daughter of Rev. Doctor Berkeley; Henry; Edward; Anne; and Mary, married 27 October 1763, to Rev. Nathaniel Preston, of Swainstown in the county of Meath.

Frederick Hamilton, Esq. the eldest son, on 1 September 1707 married Sophia, eldest sister to James, Lord Viscount Limerick, and died 10 December 1715 (before his father) having issue by her, who died in London 6 May 1748, two sons, and two daughters; Gustavus, successor to his grandfather; James, made Lieutenant of a ship of war 3 September 1741, died in November 1744, on board the fleet in the Mediterranean; Anne, baptized 6 May 1712, and Elizabeth born in 1715, both died young.

Gustavus, the second Viscount Boyne, born in 1710, was taken by his mother to London, upon his father's decease, who placed him at Westminster-school, and provided fit tutors for his instruction until his grandfather's death, whom he not only succeeded in his real estate, but by his will was left a very large fortune, provided he chose Sir Ralph Gore, and his uncle Henry Hamilton, his guardians, which he accordingly did [1]; after visiting the courts of foreign Princes, he returned from his travels in October 1731; and took his seat in the House of Peers 24 December following [2], being chosen 17 February 1735 to the English parliament for Newport in the Isle of Wight. —In August 1735 he was sworn of the privy council; and in June 1737 appointed a commissioner of the revenue; his Lordship made his will 5 April 1746, and died unmarried 18 of that month, leaving his cousin Richard Hamilton of Stackallan his heir in tail male [3], he was buried at Stackallan, with his grandfather, being succeeded by his first cousin Frederick, eldest son of his uncle

Gustavus Hamilton of Redwood in the King's County, Esq. who was Knight in parliament for the county of Donegall, in January 1717 married Dorothea, only daughter of Richard, Lord Bellew, which title is now extinct, and dying at Redhills in Westmeath, 26 February 1734-5, had issue by her who remarried with David Dickson, Esq. two sons and five daughters, viz. Frederick; Richard, made heir to his cousin Gustavus, Lord Boyne, and succeeded his brother Frederick in that title; Frances, baptized

---

[1] Bill in Chancery.   [2] Lords Jour. III. 181.
[3] Bill in Chancery filed 22 March 1759.

baptized 16 October 1719, died young; Elizabeth died unmarried 16 May 1742; Catharine, married 26 December 1744 to Edward Lovibond of Kingston in Surry, and of Hampton in the county of Middlesex, Esq.; Sophia, who died in August 1742; and Dorothea, born 30 April 1722 [1].

Frederick, 3 Viscount.

Frederick, the third Viscount Boyne, was baptized 9 November 1718, and 24 October 1747 took his seat in the House of Peers [2]. He married Elizabeth, daughter of Benjamin Hadley of Tullamore in the King's County, Esq. but dying at his house in Drumcondra, 2 January 1772, he was interred in St. Paul's church Dublin; being succeeded in the title by his brother

Richard, 4 Viscount.

Richard, the fourth and present Viscount Boyne, who was born 24 March 1724, he succeeded to the estates of his cousin Gustavus, the second Viscount, and sat first in the House of Peers as Lord Boyne 18 May 1774 [3]. He married Georgina, daughter of William Bury of Shannon-Grove in the county of Limerick, Esq. and by her had issue seven sons and ten daughters, viz. Gustavus, (born 20 December 1749, married 1 April 1773 to Martha, daughter of Sir Quaile Somerville of Brownstown in the county of Meath, Bart. and has issue Sarah, born 23 February 1775; and Georgina, born 14 February 1776); Charles, (born 6 October 1750, a Captain in the twelfth regiment of dragoons, and married in September 1785, to a daughter of Christopher Kirwan Lyster, Esq.); John, born 1 August 1752, and Richard, born 27 June 1758, died young; William, born 17 October 1763, died 18 October 1779; Richard, born 18 October 1764, died in November following; Richard, born 21 July 1774; Jane, born 7 September 1751, and Dorothy, born 22 September 1753, died young; Catharine, (born 28 August 1754, married 3 February 1773, to Hugh Montgomery Lyons, Esq. and has issue John, born 3 December 1774; Georgiana-Maria, born 3 December 1773; and Dorothea-Elizabeth, born 25 October 1775); Elizabeth, born 21 September 1755, Georgina, born 16 October 1756, and Mary-Anne, born 1 May 1760, died young; Mary, born 24 January 1762; Barbara, born 9 December 1766; Sophia, born 3 December 1769; and Anne, born 2 March 1777 [4].

TITLES.]

---

[1] Lodge. [2] Lords Jour. III 554. [3] Idem. IV. 762.
[4] Ulster's Office.

ALLEN, Viscount ALLEN.

TITLES.] Richard Hamilton, Viscount Boyne, and Baron Hamilton of Stackallan.

CREATIONS.] B. Hamilton of Stackallan in the county Meath 20 October 1715, 2 Geo. I. and V. of the river Boyne 20 August 1717, 4 of that reign.

ARMS.] Ruby, three cinquefoils pierced, ermine.

CREST.] The same as the Lord Viscount Strabane's.

SUPPORTERS.] Two mermaids, proper, with golden hair dishevelled, each holding a mirror, topaz.

MOTTO.] NEC TIMEO, NEC SPERNO.

SEAT.] Stackallan in the county of Meath, 21 miles from Dublin.

ALLEN, Viscount ALLEN.

THIS family, long resident in the kingdom of England, was transplanted into Holland about two hundred years ago, and came from that country into Ireland, in the person of John Allen, Esq. sent over as a factor for the Dutch in the latter end of Q. Elizabeth's reign; who being very handsome in his person, and of great skill in architecture, was much esteemed, and consulted by the most eminent of the nobility and gentry in their buildings; particularly by the Earl of Strafford, L. L. of Ireland, in his large intended edifice near Naas; and laid out the plan of his own house at Mullynahack near Dublin, leaving it to be executed by his son Sir Joshua, for whom he acquired a considerable fortune, and who
made

made very large additions thereto, by purchase * and an extensive trade, being a merchant of the first rank.

Sir Joshua. In 1664 he was Sheriff of the city of Dublin, and in 1673 served the office of Lord Mayor; was knighted, and appointed 8 June 1679 one of the commissioners for administering the oaths of supremacy and allegiance to such, as should be entered into the artillery garden; but was involved in the general act of attainder, passed by K. James's parliament in 1689; and had his estate of 2720l. a year in Ireland, and 200l. a year in England, sequestered.— He married Mary, daughter of Mr. Wybrow of the county of Chester, sister to Richard Wybrow, Esq. Captain of horse in Ireland, who died in 1720, and aunt to John Wybrow, son and heir to the said Richard; and departing this life 8 July 1691, he was buried the 10 in the parish church of St. Catharine, Dublin, having had issue by her, who died 4 September 1709, and was buried the 6 in St. James's church, Dublin, seven sons and eight daughters, of whom Joshua, Caleb, Joshua, Richard, Wybrow, William; Mary, Anne, Jane, Catharine; and Elizabeth, died young or unmarried: and the survivers were one son John, and three daughters, viz.

(1) Elizabeth, married to Anthony Shephard of Newcastle, Esq. member of parliament for the county of Longford; nephew and heir to Robert Choppoyne of Newcastle, who died in the reign of K. William, and dying 23 February 1732, had issue by him, who died 15 June 1738, æt. 65,

* Among which were by deeds of lease and release, dated 8 and 9 March 1670, from John Blackwell of Dublin, Esq. for the sum of 1333l. 6s. 8d. the towns and lands of Castle-Dillon and Mullahayes, with an island in the Liffey, containing 295 acres, 3 roods, and 18 perches plantation measure, in the county of Kildare.—20 and 21 March 1671 from Richard Talbot of Ballgriffin, Esq. for 2010l. the towns and lands of Priorstown and Rue, Coolefitch, Symonstown, Galbestown, Potterstown, &c. in the barony of Salt in the same county.—20 October 1675 from William Rochfort of Laraghes and James his son and heir, for 110l. their right in and to the first mentioned lands of Castle-Dillon, &c.—2 November 1675 a mortgage from Richard Butler, Earl of Arran, for 3700l. of the manor of Rathvilly in the county of Carlow, to receive 600l. a year thereout for the lives of his wife Mary, and of his sons John and Caleb, and after their deaths, to nominate any other in their stead, or in case of neglect of nomination, the said sum to be paid for seven years after all their deaths. He had also a grant of lands under the acts of settlement; and with his son John, another grant under the act of grace, in the first year of the reign of K. James II. (Lodge, and Rot. 18 Car. II. 1. p. D.)

65, and was there buried, five sons, Choppoyne, Joshua, John, Richard, who all died young; Anthony, member of parliament for the borough of Longford, who died unmarried 5 April 1737; and one daughter Elizabeth, the first wife of Arthur-Mohun, Lord Viscount Doneraile.

(2) Elinor, born in 1679, married 12 March 1700 to Henry Westenra of Dublin, Esq. and by him, who died in 1719, had four sons and six daughters, Henry, who died young; Warner; Henry, Captain-Lieutenant of dragoons, and is deceased; Peter, in Holy Orders who died in 1788; Mary; Elizabeth, married to Arthur Weldon of the Queen's County, Esq.; Elinor died young; Elinor; Jane, Lady Viscountess Galway; and Penelope.— Warner, the eldest surviving son, served in parliament for Maryborough, married 13 December 1738, Lady Hester Lambart, second daughter of Richard, Earl of Cavan, and by her who yet survives him, had a daughter Margaret, and several other children, of whom Richard, the second son entered into the army, married and has issue; and Henry the eldest married a daughter of Colonel John Murray, (by his wife Mary, Dowager of Cadwallader, Lord Blayney), and has issue William; Henry; Maria-Frances, married in 1788 to Sir John Craven Carden of Templemore in the county of Tipperary, Bart. so created 31 August 1787; and Hester-Harriot.

(3) Mary, born in 1667 married to Joshua Cooper of Marcray in the county of Sligo, Esq. and had two sons, Joshua, (representative of that county in parliament, who married Mary, second daughter of Henry Bingham of Newbrooke in the county of Mayo, Esq. and was father of the Right Hon. Joshua Cooper a member of the privy council in Ireland, and by Sarah, who was born in January 1723, daughter of Edward Synge, D. D. Lord Bishop of Elphin, hath issue); Richard; and five daughters, viz. Mary; Elizabeth; Anne, married to John Perceval of Templehouse, Esq.; Ellen; and Margaret.

John, 1 Viscount. John Allen, Esq. who succeeded his father Sir Joshua, was born 13 February 1666, and in the reign of K. William bore a Captain's commission in the army; represented in *that* and the reign of Q. Anne the county of Wicklow in parliament; as on K. George's accession he was chosen to do for the county of Dublin*; and 9 October 1714

---

* His estate of 600l. a year was sequestered by K. James's parliament, and 1 August 1714 the said John purchased from James, Duke of

1714 was sworn of his Majesty's privy council; who taking into consideration his great merits, advanced him to the dignities of Baron Allen of Stillorgan and Viscount Allen, by privy seal, dated at Hampton-Court 3 August, and by patent * the 28 of that month 1717, with the creation fee of 20 marcs, and 5 September he took his seat in the House of Peers [1].—In 1684 he married Mary, eldest daughter of Robert Fitz Gerald, Esq. sister to Robert, Earl of Kildare, by her, who died in 1692, he had issue three sons; and departing this life in London 8 November 1726, his corpse was brought into Ireland, and deposited (the 19) in the family vault at St. James's Dublin.——His sons were,

(1)   Joshua, his successor.

(2)   Robert, baptized 12 May 1687, was Knight for the county of Wicklow from the time he came of age to his death, of which county he was Sheriff in the years 1720 and 1721. On 17 September 1736 he was appointed secretary to the commissioners of his Majesty's revenue, but dying 16 December 1741, was buried at St. James's.——Pursuant to articles

of Ormond, part of the town and lands of Arklow, lying on the South side of the river, and containing 8528 acres plantation measure. (Lodge.)

* The preamble. Cum Reges ad summum Majestatis fastigium ideo sint evecti, ut ab iis, tanquam fontibus, virtutum omnium Rerumque gestarum præmia, honores, tituli deriventur: Cum etiam nobis exploratum sit, per dilectum nostrum consiliarium Johannem Allen de Majestate nostra et de patria sua sæpius præclare meritum esse, præsertim quod anno millesimo sexcentesimo octogesimo octavo religionem protestantium, leges et libertates Hiberniæ adversus tyrannidem ingruentem, summâ quâ potuit animi constantiâ, sit tutatus; quodque nobis et illustrissimæ nostræ familiæ prospiciens, Jus Successionis nostræ, cui plurimi infensi adversabantur, palam et strenue defenderit; nec destitit tamen quin opibus et Gratia, quibus plurimum inter suos pollebat, ulterius adniteretur, ut in conventibus provincialium et Municipiis ii tantum Equites et Burgenses eligerentur, qui fide spectata eandem quam ipse operam nobis præstitissent, quam autem accepta sit bonis omnibus singularis ejus in nos fidelitas, vel inde facile apparet quod, quo tempore præsens ordinum conventus indiceretur, tres comitatus *Dubliniensis, Kildarensis, Vicovii* eum cum duobus filiis natu majoribus elegerint, tertium vero et natu minimum *Athiæ* Municipes, idque factum rarissimo exemplo consentiens omnium Electorum vox comprobavit. Quibus omnibus rite perpensis, quo de regio nostro erga illum et filios ejus eorumque posteros favore, et de illius in nos meritis constet in perpetuum, statuimus prædictum Johannem Allen in numerum procerum regni nostri Hiberniæ adscribere. Sciatis igitur, &c. (Rot. Anno 4 Geo. I. 2 p. f.)

[1] Lords Jour. II. 550.

articles dated 22 and 23 December, he married 16 January 1707 Frances, daughter of Robert Johnson, Esq. Baron of the Exchequer, and had issue by her who died in June 1762 at Stephen's-green, two sons and three daughters, viz. Robert, appointed 1 May 1734 to succeed Thomas Upton, Esq. in the office of customer, collector and receiver of the ports of Londonderry, Coleraine, Ballyshannon, Portrush and Loughswilly, but died at Bath, unmarried, in May 1736, and 29 June was buried at St. James's; Francis, born in 1717, died young; Mary, baptized 7 July 1711, married in 1732 to Robert Boswell of Ballycorry in the county of Wicklow, Esq. collector of Wicklow; Margaret died unmarried; and Frances, born in 1719 married 8 April 1738 to William-Paul Warren of Grangebegg in the county of Kildare *, Esq. and had a son Richard, and a daughter Frances.

Richard, father of the present Viscount.

(3) Joshua, 2 Viscount.

Joshua, the second Viscount, was baptized 17 September 1685; represented the county of Kildare in parliament, whilst a commoner, of which he was Sheriff for the years 1720 and 1725; succeeding to the titles, he took his seat in the House of Peers 28 November 1727 [1], and was a member of his Majesty's privy council. On 18 October 1707 he married Margaret, daughter of Samuel Du-Pass of Epsom, Esq. first clerk in the secretary of state's office, † and dying at Stillorgan 5 December 1742, was

---

* His father Richard Warren of Grangebegg, Esq. died 6 February 1734-5, and his mother was Mary, eldest of the five daughters and coheirs of Henry Percy, Esq. (Lodge.)

† Her Ladyship was married in St Margaret's church, Westminster, the parish wherein she was born, viz. in the rector's house in Piccadilly, and she was baptized in the parish church of St. James's London. Her father quitted his employment on account of his religion, in the reign of James II. and went into Holland to the Prince of Orange, with whom he returned to England, after three years stay in that country; and refusing to accept of his post again, retired into the East-Indies, where he died in 1699. Her mother was Dorothy, daughter of Edward Ellis, Esq. who served K. Charles II. with his purse during his exile, to the amount of 24,000l. for which her Ladyship had debentures.—She gave 20 acres of good land in perpetuity, and 50l. for erecting a charter school at Arklow in the county of Wicklow, which being finished for the reception of 40 children, was solemnly opened on Christmas-day 1748, when 20 children of each sex were admitted; and by her will she charged her estate in the county of Dublin with 20l. a year for ever, for the use of said charter school. (Lodge.)

[1] Lords Jour. III. 2.

ALLEN, Viscount ALLEN.

was buried the 8 in his vault at St. Jame's, having had issue by her who died 4 March 1758, in Duke-street, St. James's, Westminster [1], two sons and five daughters, viz. John his successor; Joshua, baptized 1 July 1717, died at the age of six years, and was buried at St. James's, as were Mary, Margaret, and Catharine, who all died young; Elizabeth, baptized 19 July 1722, married 27 August 1750 to John Proby of Elton-Hall in the county of Huntingdon, created Lord Carysfort; and Frances, to Sir William Mayne, Bart. created Lord Newhaven.

John, 3 Viscount.
John, the third Viscount Allen, in 1732 was chosen member of parliament for Carysfort, and on his accession to the honours, took his seat in the Upper House 29 October 1743 [2]; but his Lordship having the misfortune to be insulted in the streets, on Friday 26 April 1745, by three dragoons, received a wound on his hand by one of them, with his broad sword, which threw him into a fever, and was the cause of his death 25 May following. His Lordship dying unmarried, was succeeded by his first cousin John, eldest son of his uncle

Richard Allen, Esq. who was baptized 22 July 1691; served in parliament in the reign of George I. for the borough of Athy, and in 1727 was chosen to represent the county of Kildare. He married Dorothy, one of the five daughters and coheirs of Major Green of Killaghy in the county of Tipperary, and died at Cromlin near Dublin 14 April 1745, having had issue by her who died 4 May 1757, five sons and four daughters, viz. John his heir; Richard, Samuel, Mary, and Dorothy, all deceased; Joshua, who succeeded to the title; Richard; Jane; and Elizabeth, married 18 December 1767 to Captain Browne.

John, 4 Viscount.
John, the fourth Viscount Allen, was chosen 15 January 1741 to supply his uncle Robert's seat in parliament for the county of Wicklow; was appointed in April 1742 Lieutenant of a troop in General Browne's regiment of horse, of which he was afterwards Captain; and took his seat in the House of Peers 9 October 1745 [3]. His Lordship having taken an active part against the government, found his military services not likely to be rewarded, he therefore retired from public life, and lived at his seat of Puncherstown in the county of Kildare, in a series of acts of benevolence, until 10 November 1753, when he died unmarried, and was succeded by his brother

Joshua,

[1] Lodge. [2] Lords Jour. III. 540. [3] Idem. 592.

Joshua, the fifth and present Viscount, who was born 26 April 1728, served in the army in Germany, as Captain of the 37 regiment of foot, during the campaigns of 1758, 1759, and 1760, under the command of Prince Ferdinand of Brunswick, and was wounded in the memorable battle of Minden in 1759; in 1761 he was appointed Deputy Quarter-Master-General to the British troops sent to the relief of Portugal under the command of General Lord Tyrawly, where he served until the peace; in 1762 he was chosen member of the British parliament for the borough of Eye in Suffolk, in the room of Lord Viscount Brome then called up to the House of Peers, on the demise of Earl Cornwallis his father, and he was re-elected for that borough in the ensuing parliament; in 1763 he was sent to join his regiment in the Island of Minorca, and was soon after appointed Captain of a company in the first regiment of foot guards, from which he retired in 1775; 26 April 1770 he obtained an annual pension of 600l.; and he sat first in the House of Peers 26 November 1753 [1].—5 August 1781 his Lordship married in Dublin, Frances, eldest daughter of Gaynor Barry, Esq. of Dormstown in the county of Meath, and by her hath issue Joshua-William; Frances-Elizabeth; and Letitia-Dorothea [2].

Joshua, 5 Viscount.

TITLES.] Joshua Allen, Viscount Allen, in the county of Kildare, and Baron Allen of Stillorgan in the county of Dublin.

CREATION.] So created 28 August 1717, 4 Geo. I.

ARMS.] Pearl, two bars wavy and a chief, saphire, on the latter an estoil between two escallops, topaz.

CREST.] On a wreath, a bezant, charged with a Talbot's head erased, diamond.

SUPPORTERS.] Two Talbots, diamond.

MOTTO.] TRIUMPHO MORTE TAM VITA.

SEAT.] Ladytown in the county of Kildare, 11 miles from Dublin.

[1] Pension List, and Lords Jour. IV. 10.
[2] His Lordships Letter 20 November 1787.

GRIMSTON,

GRIMSTON, Viscount GRIMSTON.

<small>27
Silvester.</small> THIS family is denominated from its possessions in the county of York, and descended from Sylvester de Grimston of Grimston, who attended William, Duke of Normandy, in his expedition to England as standard-bearer, and in that station valiantly fought at the battle of Hastings, where the kingdom proved the reward of their victory over Harold, who then possessed the throne: And the year following, on the Conqueror's settling his houshold, he was appointed his Chamberlain, and did homage for Grimston, Hoxton, Tonsted, and other lands, which he held of the Lord Roos, as of his honour of Roos in Holdernesse, Yorkshire.

<small>Daniel.
Sir Thomas.
John.
Sir William.
Sir Roger.
Walter.</small> He was succeeded at Grimston by his son Daniel, who married the daughter of Sir Adam Sprinuall, and was father of Sir Thomas Grimston, living in the reign of K. Stephen, who by the daughter of Sir John Boswell of Aldersey, Knt. had John, his successor at Grimston, whose wife was the daughter and heir to Sir John Goodmaghan, and his son by her was Sir William Grimston, living in 1231, who by the daughter and heir to Sir John Colholme of Colholme, had two sons, Sir Roger; and Alexander, whose wife was the daughter of John Frowick of Middlesex.—Sir Roger was Under-sheriff of the county of Kent to Hubert de Burgo, from 1223 to 1228; and marrying the daughter of Fulk Constable of Fulmark, had two sons, Walter; and Sir Gervaise Grimstone, who left no issue by his wife, the daughter of Sir John Baskerville.—Walter, who succeeded, married the daughter and coheir to Herbert Flinton of Flinton in Holdernesse, and had issue three sons, viz. William; John, Dean of Rochester and Abbot of Selby; and Robert, who married the daughter of —— Ashton.

William

William Grimston of Grimston, Esq. the eldest son, William, married Armatruid, daughter of Sir Rowland (rather John) Rysom of Rysom in Holderneſſe, Knt. and had three sons,

Thomas, living in 1420 (10 Hen. V.) who married Dyoniſia, daughter of the Lord Sutton, and had a son of his own name, who marrying the daughter of William Fitz-William of Aldwark, had iſſue two sons and two daughters, Walter, living in 1466; William, who died childleſs; Margaret, married to Robert Forthingham of Forthingham; and Anne, to William Vavaſour of Weſton in Yorkſhire —Walter Grimſton, the elder son, married Elizabeth, daughter and heir to Sir John Portington, (who was made Serjeant at Law to K. Henry VI. 17 April 1446, and four years after was Juſtice of the Common Pleas) and was father of Thomas Grimſton, Eſq. who by the daughter and heir of —— Newark, had ſix sons and two daughters, viz. Walter; William; Thomas; Henry; Gervaiſe; Joſias, who married the daughter and heir of —— Ever; Anne married to George Brigham; and Mary to —— Eſlerker of Lycett [1].—Walter, the eldeſt son, living in the time of Henry VIII. married the daughter of John Dakine of Brandſburton (or Brandſbury) in Holderneſſe, and had Thomas his heir, and a daughter Elizabeth, wife to Marmaduke Conſtable of Hatfield in Holderneſſe.—Thomas, who ſucceeded at Grimſton, had four sons and two daughters by Elizabeth, daughter of Nicholas Girlington of Hachford in Norfolk, viz. Thomas; Francis, who married Suſan, daughter of William Windeſley of Brandburton; John; Marmaduke, who married a daughter of —— Stirley; Anne, married to Robert Wright of Plow, in the county of Lincoln; and Magdalen, to John Thwenge of Overhelmſlie, and had Marmaduke Thwenge, aged 24 in 1584, William, Anne, and Margery [2].—Thomas, the eldeſt son, living in 1584, married Dorothy, daughter of Marmaduke Thwaites, by whom he had ſix sons and two daughters, Marmaduke; Thomas; John; Thwaites; Walter (who married Dorothy, daughter and coheir to Marmaduke Thirkeld of Eſtrop, Eſq.); Chriſtopher, who married Elizabeth, daughter of Martin Barney of Gunſton in Norfolk, and had a son Barney; Elinor, married to William Thornton of Newton; and Cicely to Robert Saltmarſh of Saltmarſh

[1] Lodge.   [2] Idem.

in Yorkshire, Esqrs.—Marmaduke, the eldest son, married Frances, daughter of George Gill of Hertford, by whom he had Thomas his heir, who left no issue; but some of the name and family yet subsist in Yorkshire.

(2)   Robert, ancestor to the Lord Grimston.
(3)   John, Dean of Windsor in 1418.

Robert. Robert, the second son, leaving Yorkshire, became seated in the county of Suffolk, in the reign of Henry V. by his marriage with the daughter of Sir Anthony Spilman,
Edward. by whom he was father of Edward Grimston, who succeeded him in lands at Risehungles and Ipswich in that county, and married first Philippa, daughter of John, Lord Tiptoft, sister and coheir to John, Earl of Worcester, and widow of Thomas, Lord Roos, by whom having no issue, he married secondly Mary, daughter of William Drury of Rougham in Suffolk, Esq. and by her had four sons and three daughters, of whom Elizabeth (was married to Henry Reepes, and had Elizabeth, married to Thomas Holt of Swanstead; Francis who married Catharine, daughter of Thomas Leman, and had John and Thomazine; and John who married Dorothy Sidner, and had a son John); John, the third son, was ancestor to the Grimstons of Nor-
Edward. folk and Essex; and Edward, the eldest, marrying Mar-
Edward. garet, eldest daughter of Thomas Hervey, Esq. left Edward his heir, who by Anne, daughter of John Garnish
Sir of Kenton in Suffolk, Esq. was father of another Edward,
Edward. who in the reign of Q. Elizabeth served in several parliaments for the borough of Ipswich; was knighted by her Majesty; called into her privy council; and continued by her, comptroller of Calais, having been so appointed 30 August 1552 by K. Edward VI.

In the beginning of 1558 that place being taken by the Duke of *Guise*, Sir Edward, the comptroller, was among the principal prisoners. Having, according to the duty of his post, frequently given advice of the ill condition of the garrison, but whether they, to whom he wrote, were corrupted by the French, or that the low estate of the treasury occasioned the want of supply, it was resolved he should not return to England to discover the reason, and therefore was suffered to lie a prisoner in the *Bastile*, without any care taken of him or his fellow-captives; and the ransom set on him was so high, that having lost a great estate, which he had purchased about Calais, he determined

mined to prejudice his family no further by redeeming his liberty at so high a rate, intending either to remain a prisoner, or make his escape, the latter of which he thus effected.

After about two years confinement, being lodged in the top of the *Bastile*, he chanced to procure a file, with which cutting out one of the window bars, and having a rope conveyed to him, he changed cloaths with his servant, and descended by the rope, which proving a great deal too short, he was obliged to take a long leap, which he did without hurt, and, before the outer gates were shut, made his escape undiscovered. But his beard, which was long, made him apprehend that he should be known by it; yet by a happy providence, finding in his servant's pocket a pair of scissars, he so disfigured it, as to render such a discovery very difficult, and having learned the art of war in company with the *Scots guard de Mauche*, he spoke that dialect, and so passed for a *Scots* pilgrim; by which means he escaped to England, and offering to take his trial, made his innocence so evident, that the jury were ready to acquit him without leaving the court.

He lived to a great age, deceasing in his 98 year, and having been twice married, left issue by his first wife [1] a son and successor Edward Grimston, Esq. who was seated at Bradfield in Essex, and 31 Eliz. served in parliament for the borough of *Eye* in Suffolk, his father then living. He married Joan, daughter and coheir to Thomas Risby of Lavenham in Suffolk, Esq. (whose mother was daughter and coheir to John Harbottle of Crosfield in the same county, Esq.) by which marriage he considerably enlarged his estate; and departing this life 15 August 1610, left two sons, Harbottle and Henry, who were both knighted, and married two sisters, Sir Henry having issue a son Edward, who lies buried in Beaconsfield church, Bucks, with this memorial;

Edward.

    Here lyeth the Body of
    Edward Grimstone, Esq;,
    Son of Henry Grimstone
    Knt. who died the 17th of
     March 1656 [2].

              Sir

---

[1] Lodge.   [2] Le Neve's Monument. Angl.

Sir Harbottle, 1 Baronet.

Sir Harbottle Grimston of Bradfield, the elder son, was advanced to the dignity of a Baronet 25 November 1612; and being a gentleman well esteemed in his country, was Sheriff of Essex in 1614 [1], and chosen its representative in three parliaments during the reign of Charles I.——He married Elizabeth, daughter of Ralph Coppenger of Stoke in Kent, Esq. and dying about the year 1640, had issue five sons; Edward, who married Elizabeth, daughter of Thomas Massam, Esq. and died before his father without issue; Harbottle, who succeeded; Henry, Thomas, and William.——Henry died young, and was buried in the chancel of Islington church under a fair stone, with this inscription;

> Hinc
> Sperat Resurrectionem
> (Filius Harbotelli Grimeston
> Militis et Baronetti
> Natu tertius).
> HENRICUS GRIMESTON.
> Anagramma,
> En Christi Regno sum.
> Qui moritur vivit, Christo huic,
> Mors semita, Ductor
> Angelus, ad Vitam janua
> Christus erit.
> Hac Iter ad Superos, calcans
> Vestigia Lethi,
> Intrabam Christi regia
> Templa Dei.
> 12. die Mensis Julii, An. Dom. 1627.

Sir Harbottle, 2 Baronet.

Sir Harbottle Grimston, the second Baronet, having his education in the Inns of Court, was well versed in the laws, and the ancient customs and usage of parliaments; and behaved with a steady zeal to the true interest of his country, in the distracted time of the civil war. He well knew and observed the bounds between arbitrary power and legal duty, which disposition caused him to oppose and refuse the payment of illegal taxes (on which account his father had been imprisoned in the Fleet) and in the parliament, which met 3 April 1640, being member for Colchester, for which he served to his death, he was one of the

[1] Fuller's Worthies.

the first that insisted on the calling those persons to account, who had advised the levying ship-money, and in an excellent speech on that subject, said, *He was persuaded that they, who gave their opinions for the legality of it, did it against the dictamen of their own conscience.*—But as he only intended the reform of such invasions on the liberty and property of the subject; so did he endeavour, with all his interest, to pacify the minds of those, who were set upon extorting extravagant demands from their sovereign; for he rather continued to sit, than concur with the long parliament, till after the treaty with the King in the Isle of Wight, of which he was one of the commissioners; and, as Lord Clarendon observes, behaved himself so, that his Majesty was well satisfied with him; and pressing the acceptance of the King's concessions, was, after his return, excluded by force, with others, from sitting in the House of Commons. He was, besides, the more obnoxious, for having been instrumental in procuring part of the army to be disbanded, for performing which at the several places of rendezvous he was appointed, 29 May 1647, one of the commissioners. And when the King was brought to his trial, the persons in power had such apprehensions of his duty to his Majesty, and his interest with the army and people, that they put him under confinement, and did not release him till after the King's death, as appears by this warrant.

" You are, on sight hereof, to set at liberty Sir Har-
" bottle Grimston, he having engaged himself not to act,
" or do any thing to the disservice of the parliament or
" army. Given under my hand the 30th day of January
" 1648.   FAIRFAX."
" To the Marshal-General, or his Deputy."

When he had signed a protestation, declaring all acts to be void, which from the time of his expulsion, had been done in the House of Commons, he contented himself with waiting the return of the people to their allegiance, and lived retired, until General Monck paved the way for the King's restoration; about which time the excluded members returning to the House, * all who meant well to

the

---

* The corporation of Colchester sent him the following letter:
  " Honourable Sir,
  " As we cannot but with thankfulness acknowledge the mercy of
  " God to the nation in general, so more particularly to this town,
                                                          " that

the King, contrived his election for Speaker, to which he was chosen 25 April 1660, and the before-mentioned noble author tells us, *that he submitted to it, out of a hope and confidence, that the designs it was laid for would succeed.* And so just a sense had the King of his merits, and endeavours to promote the restoration, that he called him into his privy council, and 3 November 1660 made him master of the rolls; which honourable post he very judiciously executed, to the satisfaction of all concerned in the law *.—
He

" that after the many changes and alterations we have been tossed
" in that now there is (as we are credibly informed and do believe)
" a free admission of the members of the late parliament, so long
" interrupted by force, we cannot but with much earnestness (in
" the behalf of ourselves and the free burgesses of the town) make
" our humble request, that you will be pleased to return to that
" trust, to which you were so freely and unanimously elected in the
" year 1640, which we do the rather request out of the former ex-
" perience, that not only this town but the nation in general hath
" had of your faithfulness and ability, and the many miseries and
" calamities we have groaned under since your absence; and as we
" formerly had the honour of sending so eminent and worthy a
" member, so we shall hope (by the blessing of God upon your en-
" deavours) that not only ourselves but the whole nation in general
" shall have cause to bless God for your return, and in his due time
" reap the benefit of your councils and labour in that great assem-
" bly. Sir, we shall not farther trouble you at present, than to
" assure you, we are, as by many former favours bound to be,
                                    " Your faithful and humble servants,
                                    " Thomas Peeke, Mayor.
Colchester, 23 February 1659.   " John Shaw, Recorder.
                                    " John Radhams,
                                    " John Gaell,
                                    " Thomas Reynolds ⎫
                                    " John Milbanks,   ⎬ Aldermen.
                                    " Peter Johnson,   ⎭
                                    " Andrew Fomental.

    " Sir,
    " The rest of the Aldermen, viz. Mr. Reynolds at Eastgates,
" Captain Rayner, and Mr. Jeremy Daniel, are not in town."
(Collections.)
* He compiled and published the Reports of Law Cases of Sir George Crooke, Justice of the Common Pleas. He was well read in the ancient fathers of the church, and wrote in Latin, for the use of his son, a small manual, containing the Duty of a Christian. He also left in manuscript a journal of the several debates in the treaty with K. Charles I. at the Isle of Wight, among which are many weighty arguments concerning the liberty of the subject, and the authority of church government.—His views and designs being directed to the good of the public, which he had always at heart, he was the less solicitous in the reign of Charles II. to be great at court, though he held a friendship and correspondence with many leading men, especially

He was made recorder of the corporation of Harwich for life, being the second who bore that office [1], and 24 April 1665 obtained a confirmation of the franchises and immunities of that town; being also by patent, dated at Westminster 27 July 1664, made High Steward of St. Albans for life, but died in January 1683, in the 82 year of his age.

His first wife was Mary, daughter of Sir George Crooke, Knt. who 11 February 1623 was made Justice of the Common-Pleas, by whom he had six sons and two daughters, of which sons five died before him, and George, the eldest, dying in the 23 year of his age, was interred under a monument in St. Michael's church, St. Albans, leaving no issue by his wife Sarah, younger daughter and coheir to Sir Edward Alston, Knt. M. D.; who re-married first with John, Duke of Somerset, and after with Henry Hare, Lord Coleraine.—The daughters were, Mary, married to Sir Capel Luckyn, Knt. and Bart.; and Elizabeth, in 1650 to Sir George Grubham How, of Cold-Berwick in Wiltshire, Bart.—His second wife was Anne, elder daughter and at length heir to Sir Nathaniel Bacon of Culford-Hall in Suffolk, Knight of the Bath, widow of Sir Thomas-Meautys, by her he had an only daughter Anne, who died young; and his Lady having the manors of Gorhambury and Kingsbury near St. Albans settled on her for life, he purchased the reversion thereof from Mr. Hercules Meautys, nephew of Sir Thomas, the heir at law, the former of which, Sir Samuel Grimston, his only surviving son, made the principal place of his residence.

Which Sir Samuel was born 7 January 1643, and having all the advantages of education, was an accomplished gentleman, and well esteemed in his country; served in 6 several parliaments for the borough of St. Albans, during the reigns of K. Charles II. and K. William; but was so obnoxious to K. James II. that he excepted him out of his

Sir Samuel, 3 Baronet.

manifesto

pecially the Earl of Clarendon, as appears by their letters. He was an honourable friend, a kind indulgent father and master, and finished his course like a pious, charitable and good christian, with a full assurance of happiness in another world. See the character of him and his second Lady in Bishop Burnet's History of his own Times, in the opinion of which prelate he stood so fair, that he *very judiciously observes*, he thought his only fault was, *that he was too rich.*

[1] Dale's Hist. of Harwich.

manifesto in 1692, when he had formed a design of landing in England.—He married first Elizabeth, eldest daughter of Heneage Finch, Earl of Nottingham, Chancellor of England, and by her had an only daughter Elizabeth, the first wife to William Savile the second Marquess of Hallifax, who by her had an only surviving daughter Anne, the first wife of Thomas, Lord Bruce, son of Thomas, Earl of Aylesbury, which Lady died 18 July 1717, in the 27 year of her age.—His second wife was the Lady Anne Tufton, sixth and youngest daughter of John, the second Earl of Thanet, and by her, (who lies buried in the East part of the church-yard of Tewing in Hertfordshire, under a tomb enclosed by iron rails, thus inscribed,

> Here lieth interred the Body of the Right Honourable Lady Anne Grimston, Wife to Sir Samuel Grimston, Bart. of Gorhambury in Hertfordshire, Daughter to the late Right Honourable Earl of Thanet. She departed this Life Nov. 22. 1713. in the 60th Year of her age.)

he had a son Edward, born 22 July 1674, and a daughter Mary, born the year after; but they both dying young, the dignity of Baronet expired with him, who deceased in October 1700, in the 52 year of his age, leaving a great estate, under certain limitations, to William Luckyn, Esq. second son of Sir William Luckyn of Messing-Hall in Essex, Knt. and Bart. who was son and heir to Sir Capel Luckyn, by Mary, elder sister of the said Sir Samuel Grimston.

Sir William, 1 Baronet.

Which family of Luckyn (his Lordship's paternal ancestors) were of good antiquity in Essex, of which county Robert Luckyn, Esq. was Sheriff 16 Jac. I. as in 13 of Charles I. was Sir William Luckyn of Little-Waltham, Knt.[1], who 2 March 1628 was created a Baronet; and in 1637 was Sheriff of the said county. He married Mildred, third daughter of Sir Gamaliel Capel of Rookwood-Hall in Essex, Knt. by whom he had two daughters, Jane and Elizabeth; and two sons, Sir Capel, his heir; and Sir William, also created a Baronet 13 November 1661, but he leaving by Winifred his wife, third and youngest daughter of Sir Richard Everard of Much-Waltham in Essex, Bart. an only daughter Anne, (married to Sir Henry

ry

---

[1] Fuller's Worthies.

ry Palmer of Wingham in Kent, Bart. who died without issue by her in 1706) the title became extinct.

Sir Capel Luckyn, the second Baronet, born in 1621, was member of parliament for Harwich in 1661, and married (as already observed) Mary, elder daughter of Sir Harbottle Grimston, by her, who died 18 March 1718, in the 86 year of her age, he had a numerous issue, whereof William succeeded to the title and estate; and the surviving daughters were Mildred, married first to Thomas Smyth of Blackmore in Essex, Esq. and secondly to Mr. Davison Browning of London, Linen-draper; and Sarah, first to Richard Saltonstal of South Okingdon, Esq. and secondly to Dacres Barrett of Bellhouse in Avely, Essex, Esq. to whom she was third wife, and by him, who died in 1723, had a daughter Catharine, married to Sir Philip Hall of Upton in Essex. *Sir Capel, 2 Baronet.*

Sir William Luckyn, the second but eldest surviving son, marrying Mary, daughter of William Sherington, Esq. Alderman of London, had issue ten sons and five daughters, viz. Sir Harbottle, his successor, cup-bearer to Q. Anne and K. George II. who died 4 February 1736, unmarried; William, adopted heir to Sir Samuel Grimston, and advanced to the Peerage; Capel; Henry; Charles of Merton-college, Oxford, rector of Pedmersh and Messing in Essex; Edward; Samuel; George, who died at Messing-hall 5 February 1733, æt. 37; Sherington, and James; Mary, Elizabeth, Sarah, Mildred, and Martha. *Sir William, 3 Baronet.*

Sir William, the second son, being adopted by his uncle Sir Samuel Grimston, heir to his estate, in virtue of the limitation thereof assumed the name of Grimston.— In 1710, 1713, 1714, and 1727, he was member of parliament for St. Albans, and created a Peer of Ireland by privy seal, dated at St. James's 29 April, and by patent * *Sir William, Viscount Grimston.*

at

---

* The preamble. Cum nihil in bonum publicum magis cedat, quam virtutem præmiis ornare, præsertim generis splendore illustratam, virosque egregiis gestis de patria benemeritos, et illustrissimas Angliæ familias affinitate attingentes, honoribus augere: Et cum hoc titulo se nobis præcipue commendet dilectus noster Gulielmus Grimston de Gorhambury in agro Hertfordensi Armiger, non interupta Linea à Silvestro Grimston de Grimston in agro Eboracensi ortus, qui Gulielmum Conquestorem Expeditione sua in Angliam comitabatur, ejusque vexillifer fuerat in prælio insigni apud Hastings, ubi parta Victoria, totum Regnum in principis illius ditionem redactum est; a quo Silvestro ad prædictum Gulielmum

at Dublin 29 May 1719, with the creation fee of 20 marcs, and 13 July following he took his feat in parliament [1].

His Lordship married Jane, daughter of James Cooke, citizen of London, and deceased 15 October 1756, aged 73, having had issue by her, who died 12 March 1765, in the county of Hertford, nineteen children, whereof Samuel (the eldest son, born 28 December 1707, 5 November 1730 married Mary, daughter and heir to Henry Lovell of Coleman-street London, Esq. Turkey-merchant, who died in 1725, and was youngest son to Sir Salathiel Lovell, Baron of the Exchequer, by whom he had a daughter born 1 April 1736, who died an infant; and deceasing in London 14 June 1737, in the 30 year of his age, was interred in St. Nicholas's church, St. Albans, and his widow remarried with William, Viscount Barrington); James, heir apparent; Harbottle (born 2 December 1712, was appointed 1 May 1736 gentleman-usher to the Princess of Wales, which he resigned in October 1737, and 10 May 1740 succeeded Sir William Wynne as standard bearer to the gentlemen-pentioners, of which band he was appointed Lieutenant in May 1749, in 1750 changed his name to Luckyn by act of parliament, and is deceased); George, (born 12 August 1714, was made 13 October 1729 gentleman-usher to the Prince of Wales; married in April 1744 the daughter of —— Clover of Hertfordshire, Esq and had two sons of the name of Edward, both deceased); William, born 3 January 1719; Jane, born 20 December 1718, married in August 1743

mum Grimston longa progenitorum feries extitit invicto in patriam amore, et inconcussa erga Reges suos fide. Insignes inter hos eminuit Edwardus Grimston Eques auratus à secretis Regni conciliis, et rationum publicarum *Caleti* inspector, qui, urbe *Callis* redditâ, turrem propugnavit, et, non nisi fame victus, hostium se permisit fidei: Hujus Edwardi Pronepos Harbottle Grimston Eques Auratus et Baronettus, magnus ille artium liberalium et literarum humanarum Mæcenas et exemplar, in restauratione Caroli secundi in patriam et Solium Avitum magna pars fuit ope et concilio: Dein Regni comitiis in altera Senatûs domo orator, et Rotulorum Regni Præfectus. In celeberrimi hujus viri nomen, familiam et virtutes successit præfatus Gulielmus Grimston, Pronepos hæresque non degener, qui atavorum meritis hoc addidit proprium, ut in difficillimis temporibus, cum successio nostra in hæc regna periclitaretur, strenuum se juris nostri bonique publici propugnatorem præstaret. Sciatis igitur nos, in perpetuum regii nostri favoris erga illum et ejus posteros indicium, creasse, &c. (Rot. Canc. Anno 5 Geo. I, 1. p. s.)

[1] Lords Jour. II. 612.

GRIMSTON, Viscount GRIMSTON.

to Thomas Gape of St. Albans, Esq.; and Frances, born 15 September 1725 [1].

Sir James, the second Viscount, was born 9 October 1711, married Mary, daughter of John-Askell Bucknall of Oxney in the county of Hertford, Esq. and deceasing of the gout 15 December 1773 was buried in St. Michael's church St. Albans, having had issue by her who was born 28 April 1717, and died in August 1778, three sons and five daughters, viz. James-Bucknall, who succeeded to the title; William (born 23 June 1750, representative in the British parliament for the borough of St. Albans, and married 7 February 1783 to Sophia, daughter and coheir to Richard Hoare of Baram in Essex, Esq.); Harbottle, born 14 April 1752; daughter Jane, born 10 September 1748, married 6 October 1774 to Thomas Estcourt, Esq.; Mary, born 28 May 1753, married 3 April 1777 to William Hall of Walden in Hertfordshire, Esq.; Susanna-Askell, born 28 September 1754, married 15 February 1781 to John Warde of Squerries in Kent, Esq.; Frances-Cooke, born 27 March 1757; and Charlotte-Johanna, born 10 September 1759 [2]. *Sir James, 2 Viscount.*

Sir James-Bucknall, the third and present Viscount Grimston, was born 9 May 1747; his Lordship represents the county of Hertford in the British parliament.—28 July 1774, he married Harriot only daughter of Edward Walter of Stalbridge in the county of Dorset, Esq. by Harriot, daughter and coheir to George, Lord Forester, and by her Ladyship who died 7 November 1786, hath issue James-Walter, born 26 September 1775; Harriot, born 14 December 1776; and Charlotte, born 16 January 1778 [3]. *Sir James, 3 Viscount.*

TITLES.] Sir James-Bucknall Grimston, Viscount Grimston, Baron of Dunboyne, and Baronet.

CREATIONS.] Baronet, 2 March 1628, 4 Car. I. V. Grimston, and B. of Dunboyne in the county of Meath, 3 June 1719, 5 Geo. I.

ARMS.] Quarterly, 1st and 4th pearl, on a fess, diamond, three mullets of six points pierced, topaz, and in the dexter chief an ermine spot, for Grimston, 2d and 3d diamond, a fess dancette between two leopards faces, topaz, for Luckyn.

CREST.] On a wreath, a stag's head coup'd, proper, attired, topaz.

SUPPORTERS.]

[1] Ulster's Office.   [2] Idem.   [3] Idem.

SHUTE, Viscount BARRINGTON.

SUPPORTERS.] The dexter a stag, reguardant, proper, attired, as the crest. The sinister a gryphon, reguardant, topaz.

MOTTO.] MEDIOCRIA FIRMA.

SEATS.] Gorhambury in the county of Hertford, 22 miles from London, and Messing-Hall, otherwise Baynard's-Castle, near Colchester in Essex, 44 miles from London.

SHUTE, Viscount BARRINGTON.

HIS Lordship's family is of Norman extraction, in which Dutchy, whilst it continued annexed to the English crown, were to be seen the remains of a castle bearing the name of SHUTE and formerly in the family, with other monuments in several towns of that Dutchy.

The family hath been long seated in the counties of Leicester and Cambridge, in the latter of which at Hockington, or Hogginton resided Christopher Shute, Esq. (a descendant of the Norman line) whose son Robert being bred to the law, was chosen Serjeant in Michaelmas Term 1577, was recorder of Cambridge, and served in several parliaments for that town, till by patent, dated at Westminster 1 June 1579, he was constituted second Baron of the Exchequer [1], with this clause in his grant, that he should be reputed, and have the same order, degree, esteem, dignity and preheminence, to all intents and purposes, as any inferior justice of the chief or common benches enjoyed or ought

[1] Dugdale's Origines.

ought to enjoy; and in the year 1585, he removed to the court of King's Bench. He married Thomasine, daughter of Christopher Burgoyne of Long-Staunton in the county of Cambridge, Esq. by whom he had four sons, Francis, John, Christopher, Thomas; and a daughter, married to John Hatton, Esq. father by her of Sir Christopher Hatton, made Knight of the Bath at the coronation of K. James I. ancestor to William, Viscount Hatton.

Francis Shute of Upton in Leicestershire, Esq. the eldest son, married Frances, daughter of Hercules Meautys of West-Ham in Essex, Esq. by her who re-married with Robert Ratcliff, Earl of Sussex, had several children, of whom Francis Shute of Upton, county of Leicester, Esq. left three sons, viz. James, the father of James, who died without issue; Samuel; and Benjamin ancestor to Lord Barrington. Samuel, the second son in 1681 was Sheriff of London, had three sons, Francis, Joseph, and Carroll, who all died young, and two daughters his coheirs, viz. Elizabeth, who married Francis Barrington of Tofts, in the county of Essex, Esq. and had no issue; and Anne, married first to Thomas Andrews, of Langdon-Hills, in the county of Essex, Esq.; and secondly to Doctor Knightly Chetwood of Tempsford in Bedfordshire, Dean of Gloucester, by whom she had an only son John Chetwood, Esq. L. L. D. Fellow of Trinity-Hall, Cambridge, who died unmarried.

Benjamin Shute Esq. the younger son of Francis, married Elizabeth Caryl, died in 1683, and had issue three sons and as many daughters; Samuel, Lieutenant-Colonel of horse, and Governor of New-England in 1716, who died unmarried 15 April, 1742, aged eighty years; Benjamin died also a batchelor in 1714; John created Viscount Barrington; Mary, married to Henry Yeamans, Esq.; Martha, to Henry Bendysh Esq.; and Anne, first to Richard Offley of Norton-Hall in the county of Derby, Esq. and secondly, to Richard, or Gervaise Scrope of Cockrington in Lincolnshire, Esq.

John Shute of the Inner-Temple, Esq. the youngest son, in 1708, was made a commissioner of the customs, being then a Barrister of the Inner-Temple, from which he was removed 3 January 1711 by Q. Anne; in whose reign in 1710, John Wildman of Becket in the county of Berks, Esq. settled his large estate upon him, though no relation, and but of slender acquaintance, having always approved of the Roman custom of adoption, and who in his will, dated

dated four years before his death, declared, his only reason for making Mr. Shute his heir, was, that he thought that gentleman most worthy to be adopted by him, as is expressed on the monuments, which his Lordship in 1713 erected in the church of Shrivenham, to the memory of Mr. Wildman, and of his father Sir John Wildman, Knt. Postmaster-General, and Alderman of London, who died in 1693, æt. 72.

Some years after he had another considerable estate left him by Francis Barrington of Tofts, Esq. before-mentioned, who had married his first cousin (descended from Sir Gobart Barrington of Tofts in Little-Badow, Knt. younger son of Sir Thomas Barrington of Barrington-Hall, Knt. and Bart. son and heir of Sir Francis, created a Baronet 29 June 1611, at the first institution of that dignity) by whom having no issue, and having purchased the estate from his eldest brother Sir Thomas Barrington, he re-conveyed it to him, and the reversion, for want of issue, to the said John Shute, Esq. who pursuant to the deed of settlement, procured an act of parliament to assume the name, and bear the arms of Barrington.

In 1714 and 1722 he was returned member to parliament for the town of Berwick upon Tweed; but the House of Commons taking into consideration the Harbourg lottery, came at length to this resolution, that his Lordship had promoted and carried on that fraudulent undertaking; for which 15 February 1722 he was expelled the house; and again offering himself a candidate for the said town against the Lord Polwarth, he lost the election by a majority of only four votes.

On 5 July 1729 he had a reversionary grant of the office of Master of the Rolls in Ireland, which he surrendered 10 December 1731; and being a person of great judgment and learning, was the author of a book, entituled, *Miscellanea Sacra*; of an Essay on the several Dispensations of God to mankind; and of divers pamphlets in favour of such as dissent from the established church.

His majesty K. George I. was pleased by privy seal, dated at St. James's 10 June, and by patent * at Dublin 1 July 1720,

---

* The Preamble, Cum nullum sit magis idoneum Virtutis præmium, neque ulla Res qua Hominum mentes ad eam amplexandam acrius incitantur, quam Honores in eos collati, qui probitate Animi ac Morum integritate inclaruerunt, quique in illud Sedulo incumbentes, quo Principis, Patriæque Commodis maxime inservire possent; tamen

1720, to create him Baron Barrington of Newcastle, and Viscount Barrington of Ardglass, with a fee of 20 Marcs ——On 14 December 1734 his Lordship departed this life at his seat of Becket, after an illness of seven hours continuance, in the 56 year of his age, and the 27 was buried in the parish church of Shrivenham in the county of Berks, where a monument was erected to his memory with the following inscription:

> Here lies
> The Right Honourable John Barrington,
> Viscount Barrington of Ardglass, and
> Baron of Newcastle in the kingdom of Ireland.
> His father, Benjamin, was the youngest son of
> Francis Shute of Upton in the county of Leicester, Esq.
> Who was descended from Robert Shute of
> Hockington in the county of Cambridge,
> One of the twelve judges in
> The reign of Queen Elizabeth.
> John, Lord Barrington was chosen representative
> For the town of Berwick upon Tweed, in
> Both

tamen omnem Meritorum suorum jactationem eousque effugerunt, ut etiam Præmia Virtutibus suis debita diu ac sæpe recusarint, Cumque insigne se hujusce Rei Exemplum Johannes Barrington de Becket in Comitatu Berchensi, Armiger, multoties idque in Rebus maximi momenti, et ante et postquam ad hujus Regni imperium accessimos, nobis Bonisque omnibus ostenderit, Procerum numero in Regno nostro Hiberniæ eum adscribi volumus. Etinimque est firma ejus et inconcussa erga nos Animi Affectio, studiumque perpetuum ita in Senatu semper se gessit, ut saluberrima Concilia, quæque ad Imperium nostrum Gloriamque firmandum, ac Salutem Patriæ tuendum maxime spectarent, nunquam non sit secutus; et sua privata Commoda nostris Rationibus libenter postponens, haud semel publica Munera, quibus obeundis non minus Emolumenti quam Dignitatis futurum erat, ut consequeretur, ultro sibi oblata, recusavit, cum in eo scilicet Res statu essent, ut Reipublicæ privatus, quam ad Honores evectus, magis prodesse posse se speraret; quo omni tempore tam Fide et Auctoritate sua apud omnes, quam Gratia nostra, quibus utrisque maxime pollebat, in nostris aliorumque Commodis promovendis diligentissime est usus. Virum igitur tam egregia ac præstanti Indole præditum, cujus Indicia quædam jam olim eo splendore duxerunt ut duo præcellentes Viri, eximio erga Familiam nostram in hæc Regna successuram studio, magnam sibi apud populares merito Existimationem nacti, Bono publico, consulentes, eum sibi adoptaverint, debita Meritorum suorum Mercede diutius carere haud æquum duximus. Sciatis igitur, &c. (Rot. Canc. A°. 6 Geo. I. 2. p. D.)

Both parliaments of King George the first;
And died December 14, 1734,
In the fifty-sixth year of his age,
Leaving by Anne his wife, daughter and coheiress
Of Sir William Daines,
Six sons and three daughters.
He took the name of Barrington pursuant to the
Settlement of his relation Francis Barrington
Of Tofts in the county of Essex, Esq.
And inherited the estate he had in this neighbourhood
By the will of John Wildman of Becket
In the county of Berks, Esq'.

Of the sons.
(1) William, succeeded to the title.
(2) Francis, died young.
(3) John, was Colonel of a company in the guards; after serving several campaigns became colonel of the sixty-fourth regiment, with which he went to the West-Indies under Major-General Hapson in 1758, and succeeding to the command after the death of that officer, reduced the island of Guadaloupe, the first conquest of any importance made from the French in that war. He died at Paris 2 April 1764, being then a Major-General, Colonel of the eighth regiment of foot, and Governor of Berwick; leaving issue by Elizabeth, daughter of Florentius Vassal, Esq. three sons, William; Richard; Rev. George, who 12 February 1788 married Elizabeth, daughter of Robert Adair of Stratford-Place in London, Esq.; and a daughter Louisa.
(4) Daines, one of his Majesty's council at law, and the celebrated author of " Observations upon the Statutes," appointed 24 May 1751, Marshal of the High Court of Admiralty in England, which he resigned in 1753, on being made Secretary for the affairs of Greenwich Hospital; was appointed a Welch Judge in 1757; and was after second Justice of Chester, which he resigned after 1785.
(5) Samuel appointed a Post Captain in the Navy in 1747; Colonel of the Chatham division of Marines in October 1770 in the room of Lord Viscount How, who was then made an Admiral; in 1778 he was made a Rear-Admiral; was sent to the West-Indies, and repulsed the French fleet at St. Lucia in 1779, although of more than ten times his force. In 1782 he was made a Vice-Admiral, and distinguished

---

[1] Information of Lord Viscount Barrington.

guished himself at the relief of Gibraltar, being second in command under Lord How; in February 1786 he was appointed Lieutenant-General of the Marines; and in 1787 was promoted to the rank of Admiral of the blue squadron.

(6) Shute, appointed in 1761 a Canon of Christ-Church, Oxford; in 1762 he proceeded L. L. D.; in 1768 he was appointed Residentiary of St. Paul's; 2 October 1769 Bishop of Landaff, whence he was promoted in 1782 to the episcopal see of Salisbury. He married first, Lady Diana Beauclerk, daughter of Charles, Duke of St. Albans; she deceasing in 1766, he married secondly 20 June 1770, Jane, only daughter of Sir John Guise of Rendcombe in the county of Gloucester Bart [1].

(1) Daughter Sarah married in June 1746, to Robert, only son of Uvedal Price of the county of Hereford, Esq.

(2) Anne, married in January 1747, to Thomas, only son of Sir Thomas Clarges, Bart. by whom she had Frances, married in November 1784, to Christopher Barnard, Esq. And

(3) Mary, who died unmarried in 1743.

William, 2 Viscount. William, the second and present Viscount Barrington, 21 February 1737, arrived from his travels, 13 March 1739 was chosen to the British parliament for Berwick: And 8 October 1745 took his seat in the House of Peers [2], being appointed 22 February following one of the Lord's Commissioners of the Admiralty. In 1754 his Lordship was appointed master of the great wardrobe, and in the same year was chosen to the English parliament for Plymouth; in 1755 he was sworn of the Privy Council in that kingdom, and in the same year was appointed secretary at war; in March 1761 he became Chancellor of the Exchequer, which office he continued to fill till June 1762, when he was appointed treasurer of the navy; in July 1765 his Lordship was again made secretary at war, where he continued till December 1778, when he had his Majesty's permission to retire from public business, and at the same time relinquished his seat for Plymouth, which borough he had represented without interruption for 24 years.—On 16 September 1740 his Lordship married Mary, daughter and heir to Henry Lovell, Esq. and widow of Samuel Grimston, Esq. eldest son of William, Viscount Grimston, and by her Ladyship, who died 24 September

---

[1] Information of Lord Viscount Barrington, Debret's Peerage, and Lodge.   [2] Lords Jour. III. 588.

tember 1764, had issue a son, born in February 1743, and a daughter Bothesia-Anne, born 8 August 1741, both deceased.

TITLES.] William Wildman-Barrington-Shute, Viscount Barrington of Ardglass, and Baron Barrington of Newcastle.

CREATIONS.] B. Barrington of Newcastle in the county of Dublin, and V. Barrington of Ardglass in the county of Downe, 1 July 1720, 6 Geo. I.

ARMS.] Pearl, three cheveronels, ruby, a label of three points, saphire.

CREST.] On a wreath, a Capuchin Friar, proper, with black hair, a band about his neck, pearl, vested pally of six pearl and ruby, with a cap, or cowl, of the same.

SUPPORTERS.] Two Gryphons, with wings expanded topaz, and gorged with labels, as in the coat.

MOTTO.] HONESTA, QUAM SPLENDIDA.

SEATS.] Becket-House in the parish of Shrivenham and county of Berks, 60 miles from London, and Tofts near Malden in Essex, 32 miles from London.

GAGE, VISCOUNT GAGE.

THIS noble family is of Norman extraction, and derives its descent from de Gaga, or Gage, who attended K. William I. in his expedition to England, and after the conquest thereof was rewarded with large grants of lands in the forest of Dean (which contains about 30,000 acres) and county of Gloucester; adjacent to which forest he fixed ed his residence, by building a seat at Clerenvell, otherwise Clurewall, in the same place.—He also built a large house in the town of Cirencester, where he died, and was buried in the abbey; and his posterity remained in that county for many generations in credit and esteem, of whom there were Barons in parliament in the reign of K. Henry II.¹ one whereof in the reign of Edward III. was member of parliament for Tavistock; as another was for Basingstoke in the time of Henry IV.

In whose ninth year John Gage is mentioned as a witness to deeds, and was father of another John, who married Joan, daughter and coheir to John Sudgrove of Sudgrove in Gloucestershire, who in 1416 (4 Hen. V.) divided his estate in Sudgrove, Musarder, &c. between his two daughters, the said Joan, and Alice, wife of John Bovey. —By her he left a son John, who was knighted, and 32 Hen. VI. purchased the lands that were John Bovey's in Cirencester, Musarder, Sidington, and Brimsfield, and made a further addition to his estate by marriage with Eleanor, daughter and heir to Thomas St. Clere, Esq. Lord of the manors of Aston-Clinton in Bucks, and of Ospring in Kent, (who was son of Sir Philip St. Clere of Aldham-St. Clere by Margaret, daughter of Sir Nicholas de Lovayn, Lord of the Manor of Burstow and Hedgecourt in Surry 44 Edw. III. and sister and heir to Nicholas Lovayn, Lord of Penshurst in Kent). Sir John Gage departed this life 30 September 1486, and left two sons, William his heir; and John, ancestor to the family at Rushton in Northamptonshire.

William Gage, Esq. was 30 years old at his father's death; married Agnes, daughter of Thomas Bolney, Esq. and resided at Burstow in Surry, where he made his will 14 February 1496 (the probate bears date 24 October following) and therein directed, that his body should be buried in the church of the Grey-Friars, London, to which church he bequeathed, for his sepulture there to be had, and to the intent that the brethren thereof should fetch his body to the earth, and sing a trental for his soul, forty shillings. He made other pious bequests; and, after his debts were paid and costs of burial discharged, devised all his personal estate to his wife, with the manors of Heyton, St. Clere, and Torryng in Sussex, and those of Burstow and Hedgecourt in Surry for life; she to have the custody and rule

John.
John.

Sir John.

William.

¹ Collect.

rule of his son and heir John during his nonage, and on that account to receive the profits of all his other manors and lands in the counties of Surry, Bucks, and Kent, she finding him honestly and competently with meat, drink, and raiment.

Sir John. Which Sir John Gage distinguished himself in a very extraordinary manner, both in a military and civil capacity, and became one of the most famous men in the reigns of Henry VIII. and his children.

After his father's death, he was granted in ward to Walter Stafford, Duke of Buckingham, and after his marriage with Philippa, daughter of Sir Richard Guldeford, or Guilford, Knight of the Garter, was preferred by the Duke to the service of K. Henry VIII. who in 1513 sent him into France to the sieges of Therouenne and Tournay; in the former of which he so distinguished himself that he was made captain of the castle of Calais (usually called Guisnes) and whilst in that post, performed many valiant actions against the enemy. But ere long being sent for home, he was knighted, sworn a privy counsellor, made vice-chamberlain, and captain of the guards; and a few years after, for service done on the borders of Scotland, in which expedition he was principal commander, he was made comptroller of the houshold and chancellor of the Dutchy of Lancaster in one day; being also a few days after constituted constable of the tower of London for life, at the next St. George's feast elected a Knight of the most noble order of the Garter, and 22 May 1541 was installed at Windsor *.

In 1530 (22 Hen. VIII.) he was one of the Knights, deputed by the parliament, who, with the two archbishops and the principal nobility and clergy, signed that memorable letter to Pope Clement VII., desiring his holiness to comply with the King in his divorce from Queen Catharine, his brother's widow; threatening, that if he refused (considering, the two universities of England, *that* of Paris, as well as many others in France, and what almost all men

---

* His services were also rewarded with a grant (21 Hen. VIII.) of the wardship and marriage of William, son and heir to John Baynham of Clowerwall in Gloucestershire, Esq. whom he married to his youngest daughter; and the next year were given to him and his heirs the manors of Boreham, Rokeland, Felton, Heldynglee, Fritton, and Exfett in Sussex, with Stewton in Lincolnshire; and 34 Hen. VIII. the manor of Aclifton in Sussex; together with the monastery of Combwell in Kent three years after.

men of learning and knowledge and integrity, both at home and abroad, had determined to be true, and were ready to defend in their discourses and writings) they could make no other construction of it, but that the care of themselves was committed to their own hands, and that they were left to seek their remedy elsewhere.——In 29 Hen. VIII. he was summoned among those of the court, to be present at the baptism of Prince Edward at Hampton-court; and three years after was appointed chief steward of all the honours, castles, manors, &c. in Sussex, forfeited by the attainder of Thomas Cromwell, Earl of Essex, with power to substitute a deputy; having a grant at the same time, of the Stewardship of all the liberties, privileges, franchises and lands of the Archbishop of Canterbury, during the minority of Henry, Lord Abergavenny.—In 35 Hen. VIII. the King authorized him to retain in his service, from time to time, forty persons above his usual attendants; being then employed as one of the commissioners to conclude a peace with Scotland, which was finished 1 October at Newcastle; and thereupon he was soon after joined in two commissions with the Lord Chancellor Audley, the Lord Treasurer Norfolk, and others, to redeem and ransom prisoners between the two kingdoms, and to conclude a treaty of marriage between Prince Edward, and Mary, Queen of Scots.

At the siege of Bulloigne, 36 Hen. VIII. he was in joint commission with Charles, Duke of Suffolk, as Lieutenant of his Majesty's camp; and, for sundry services there, was appointed, with Sir Anthony Browne, Captain-General of the bands of horsemen, being made a Knight-Bannaret under the royal standard of England.—He was much in favour with K. Henry VIII. who expressed his esteem for him, by causing his picture (among other his warriors and favourites) to be drawn by the famous Hans Holbein, to adorn his court-gallery, which yet remains in the possession of the crown; and appointing him one of the executors of his last will (in which he left him a legacy of 2000 marcs) to aid and assist his son Prince Edward, for the good estate and prosperity of the realm. However, towards the latter end of that reign, he was discharged, by the Duke of Northumberland's interest, from his constableship of the tower, but when Q. Mary came to the crown, was restored to that employment for life, and in 1553 made Lord Chamberlain of her houshold.

Having thus served in all these stations and offices with fidelity and diligence, from the first year of Henry VIII. to the fifth of Q. Mary, untouched with any reproach, and being then in the 77 year of his age, he ended his life at his house of Firle in Sussex, and was buried (according to his desire in his will) at West-Firle 28 April 1557, where a tomb of jasper stone and marble was erected to his memory by his son Edward, having thereon his effigies in full proportion, in the habit of the garter, with his Lady in the dress of the times, and their hands elevated, with this inscription on a brass plate in the wall, under his arms in a garter;

Hic jacet Johannes Gage, præclari Ordinis Garterii Miles, quondam Constabularius Turris London, Cancellarius Ducatus Lancastriæ, Dominus Camerarius Hospicii Reginæ Mariæ, ac unus de privato Concilio Ejusdem Reginæ; et Philippa Uxor ejus, qui obierunt Anno Dni 1557, quorum Animabus propitietur Deus.

and round the verge of the tomb is the 25 verse of the 19 chapter of Job in Latin.——His issue were four sons and four daughters, viz.

(1) Sir Edward his successor.

(2) James, seated at Bentley in Sussex, whose descendants flourished likewise at Wormley in Hertfordshire; of which branch was Henry Gage of Bentley, Esq. who died unmarried in 1718, having two brothers, and one sister Anne, married to Thomas Payne of Lewes in Sussex, Esq. One of the brothers left three sons, Thomas, a Merchant abroad; Rev. John Gage of Firle; and Henry. And the Wormley branch ceased in John Gage, Esq. who died 6 January 1731, at Seville in Spain.

(3) Robert, of Healing in Surry, of whom presently.

(4) William, left no issue.

(1) Daughter Alice, married to Sir Anthony Browne, Knight of the garter, was mother of Anthony, created Viscount Montacute; of Mary, Marchioness of Dorset; and of Mabel, Countess of Kildare.

(2) Anne, to John Thatcher, the elder, of Priesthaws in Sussex, Esq.

(3) ——, to Sir John Jennings, of the King's privy chamber, and in 1544 master of the ordnance at Bulloigne.

(4) ——, to William Baynham of Clowerwall in Gloucestershire, Esq.

Robert

Robert Gage of Healing, Esq. the third son, left two **Family** sons, Robert, who died in the reign of Q. Elizabeth for **of** the cause of Mary, Queen of Scots; and John of Healing, **Healing.** who married Margaret, daughter of Sir Thomas Copley, and had three sons, Sir Henry; Thomas, a Friar at Rome, who wrote the History of the West-Indies, but reforming to the Protestant religion, married in England during the civil war; and George.

Sir Henry Gage, the eldest son, being brought up in the army, had the command of an English regiment in Flanders, and procuring leave to make an offer of his service to K. Charles I. went to Oxford; which place in June 1644, during the King's absence, being much infested by the enemy's garrison of Bostal-House, he offered to reduce it, and did so, (with a party of foot, a troop of horse, and three pieces of cannon) [1], by having it surrendered to him, with the ammunition and much good provision. He left a garrison in it, which not only defended Oxford from those mischievous incursions, but very near supported itself by the contributions it drew from Buckinghamshire.

"He was in truth (says the Earl of Clarendon) a very
"extraordinary man, of a large and very graceful person;
"of an honourable extraction, his grandfather (great-
"grandfather it should be) having been Knight of the
"Garter; besides his great experience and abilities as a
"soldier, which were very eminent, he had very great
"parts of breeding, being a very good scholar in the po-
"lite parts of learning, a great master in the Spanish and
"Italian tongues, besides the French and the Dutch, which
"he spake in great perfection, having scarce been in Eng-
"land for twenty years before he came to offer his service
"to the King at Oxford. He was likewise very conversant
"in courts, having for many years been much esteemed in
"*that* of the Archduke and Dutchess, Albert and Isabella,
"at Brussells, which was a great and very regular court at
"that time; so that he deserved to be looked upon as a
"wise and accomplished person. Of this gentleman the
"Lords of the council, during his Majesty's absence, had
"a singular esteem, and consulted frequently with him,
"whilst they looked to be besieged, and thought Oxford to
"be the more secure for his being in it."

The Marquess of Winchester being closely shut up in his house of Basing in Hampshire, and the governor of Oxford refusing

[1] Collect.

refusing to send him any relief, Colonel Gage undertook that hazardous enterprize, with the servants of the Lords and gentlemen, and some volunteers, to the number of 250 horse and 400 foot; with which small party for so great an action he happily effected it, and supplying the garrison with two months provision, returned safe to Oxford, with the loss only of eleven men, and 40 or 50 slightly wounded. This undertaking (which is more minutely described by Lord Clarendon in his History of the Rebellion), was confessed by enemies, as well as friends, to be as soldierly an action, as had been performed in the war on either side, and redounded very much to the reputation of the commander.

After this notable service, he was sent for to assist the Earl of Northampton in raising the siege of Banbury, which he punctually performed, behaving in that action with great conduct and bravery; but after his return with the King to Oxford, and being made governor thereof 24 November 1644 and knighted, in attempting to break down Culham-Bridge near Abingdon, where he intended to erect a royal fort, to keep that garrison from molesting that side of the country, he was shot through the heart with a musquet-bullet 11 January 1644. Prince Rupert was present at the action, having approved and been much pleased with the design, which was never pursued after; and in truth the King sustained a wonderful loss in his death, being a man of great wisdom and temper, and one among the very few soldiers, who made himself universally be loved and esteemed.—His body was carried to Oxford, and interred in Christ-church cathedral, with a solemnity answerable to his merits, being attended to the grave by Prince Rupert, the Duke of Richmond, the Lord Treasurer and Chamberlain, the Secretaries, Comptroller, Lords of the privy council, most of the nobility, gentry, and chief commanders, the Vice-Chancellor and Mayor, with their respective attendants, the heralds at arms, &c. having this inscription to perpetuate his memory;

P. M. S.
Hic situs est Militum Chiliarcha,
Henricus Gage Eques Auratus, filius ac
Hæres Johannis Gage de Haling in Agro
Surienfi, Armigeri, Pronepos Johannis Gage
Honoratissimi Ordinis Periscelidis Equitis.

In Belgio meruit supra Annos xx in
Omni Prælio, et Obsidione Berghæ-ad
Zomam, Bredæ, ac præcipue S. Audomari ; ex
Belgio ad M. Britt. Regem missus, attulit Armorum
vii M. missus cum Imperio Bastalii ædes
Expugnavit, mox Basingianis Præsidiariis
Commeatu interclusis, strenue, Re jam
Desperata, Suppetias tulit. Castrum Bam:
:buriense cum Northamtoniæ Comite
Liberavit. Hinc Equestri Dignitate or:
:natus, Hostes denuo Basinga fugavit.
Jamque Gubernator Oxon. creatus, cum
Ad Culhami pontem in Hostes jam tertio
Milites audaciter duceret, plumbea trajectus
Glande, occubuit die xi. Jan. 1644.
Æt. 47. Funus solemni luctu prosecuti Principes,
Proceres, Milites, Academici, Cives, Omnes Do:
:lorem testati ex Desiderio Viri, Ingenio,
Linguar. peritiâ, Gloria militari, Pietate, Fide, et
Amore in Principem et Patriam, eminentissimi.
Hanc Memoriæ Epitomen posuit illi Pietas mær.
Lug. que Fratris Georgii Gage.

On a small stone under the monument :

    Æterna   Caducis
         Præpone.

We now proceed with Sir Edward Gage, eldest son of Sir John, Knight of the garter. He was created a Knight of the Bath by Q. Mary, in whose fourth year he was Sheriff of Surry and Sussex ; and was a pious sober judicious gentleman, as appears by his will, dated at Firle 17 December 1566, above two years before his death ; by which he directed his body to be buried in the parish church of Firle ; and that two-penny dole should be distributed to such poor people, as would resort to his burial, leaving also several sums of money to poor housholders of many adjoining parishes. He further wills, that his executors provide a decent stone to lye on his good father and mother, with the pictures of them and all their children, and those holy words engraven in brass : *Credo quod Redemptor meus vivit, et in novissimo die de Terra surrecturus sum, et in Carne mea videbo Deum Salvatorem meum.* Also, that they provide a decent gravestone to lie on him and his wife,

Sir Edward.

wife, all his sons to be kneeling behind him, and all his daughters behind her, with the same holy words to be engraven in brass. To his well-beloved wife he gives her dwelling in his mansion house at Firle, so long as she remains a widow, and leaves her the charge of bringing up all her children, except his heir-apparent; and forasmuch as according to his words, that God had pleased to send him a gentle and loving wife, who had long been coupled with him, and meaning to provide for the better maintenance of her and her children, he leaves her several lands, all her jewels, and three chains of gold, which she usually wore; to his daughters, Margery, Lucy, and Margaret, 500 marcs a piece, and to Philippa, in consideration of her being the eldest, and for other reasons, 500l. with the annuity of 10l. for their maintenance, and the like to his younger sons, the payment whereof he orders out of the rents of his manors and lands in Heighton, Firles, Hosiers, Hollandale, Compton, Exfett, Tryston, Lamporte, and Egington, or elsewhere in the county of Sussex; his manor of Crabhouse in Norfolk, &c *—He died 27 December 1568, and having married Elizabeth, daughter of John Parker of Willingdon in Sussex, Esq. by his wife Joan, daughter of Sir Richard Sackville, ancestor to the Duke of Dorset, they lie buried at Firle, with this memorial on a brass tablet in the wall, over a marble altar-tomb;

  Hic jacent Edwardus Gage Miles, et
  Uxor ejus Elizabetha, qui obierunt
  Anno Dni. 1569. Quorum Animabus
    Propitietur Deus.

And round the verge, *Scio quod Redemptor meus vivit,* &c.

Their issue were nine sons and six daughters, John his heir; Anthony, born 25 June 1540, died 31 January 1567 without issue; Thomas, born 27 January 1541, of whom hereafter, his son John succeeding to the estate; George; Edward, born 19 April 1539, married Margaret, third daughter of John Shelly of Michael-Grove in Sussex, Esq. (by Mary, daughter of Sir William Fitz-William of Gainspark-Hall in the county of Essex, ancestor to the Earl Fitz-William), and had a daughter Elizabeth, married to Sir John Stradling, the first Baronet of
             that

* Lodge Collect.

that family; Richard; John; Robert; Henry, born 16 October 1553, and died 29 July 1555; Agnes, born 16 January 1547, was married 19 November 1566 to Sir Edward Stradling of St. Donat's-Castle in Glamorganshire, Knt. and died without issue; Philippa, married to Edmond Saunders, Esq.; Mary, born 18 September 1550, married to James Thatcher, Esq.; Margery, born 5 June 1552, betrothed 17 November 1569 to Anthony Kemp, Esq.; Lucy; and Margaret, born 28 June 1559, was the wife of Henry Darell, Esq.

John Gage of Firle, Esq. the eldest son, was 30 years of age at his father's death, and heir to 15 manors, with many other lands in Sussex; the manors of Buston and Hedgecourt in Surry, and *that* of Crabhouse in Norfolk; but having survived all his brothers, and leaving no issue, though twice married [1], the estate descended to his nephew John, son of his brother Thomas; and he lies buried at Firle under an altar tomb of alabaster and marble, adjoining to his father's, with his portrait in brass in armour between his two wives, in the dress of the times, with the aforesaid verse of scripture, and over them, on the wall, this inscription in Roman characters;

> Hic jacent Johannes Gage Armiger, et duæ
> Uxores ejus, Elizabetha et Margaretta, qui
> Obierunt Anno Dni Milesimo quingentesimo
> Nonagesimo quinto, quorum Animabus
>   Propitietur Deus.

Thomas Gage, Esq. his brother, married Elizabeth, daughter of Sir Thomas Guldeford or Guilford, Knt. by his wife Elizabeth, eldest daughter of John Shelly of Michael-Grove, Esq. and deceasing in 1590, was buried at Firle under a stone, having the figures in brass of himself in armour, his wife lying by him, and a son and two daughters kneeling in a praying posture, with this memorial;

Thomas.

> Hic jacent Thomas Gage Armiger et Uxor
> Ejus Elizabetha, qui obierunt Anno Domini
> Milesimo quingentesimo Nonagesimo, qui
> Habuerunt unum filium et duas filias.
>   Quorum Animabus propitietur Deus.

[1] Lodge Collect.

And

And in a niche at the front of the tomb, is

Johannes Gage, qui hic jacet, fecit hæc Monumenta Anno Dni 1595.

The two daughters were Mary, married to Sir Thomas Pordage, Knt.; and Elizabeth, to Cressacre More of More-Hall, otherwise Gubbins, or Gobions near North-Mims, in Hertfordshire, and died 15 July 1618 *.

Sir John, 1 Baronet.

John, who succeeded his uncle in estate, was advanced to the degree of a Baronet 26 March 1622, and married Penelope, widow of Sir George Trenchard of Wolverton in the county of Dorset, Knt. third of the four daughters and coheirs of Thomas Darcy, Earl Rivers, by his wife Mary, daughter and coheir to Sir Thomas Kitson of Hengrave in Suffolk, Knt. and dying 3 October 1633, was buried with his ancestors at Firle, having issue by her † four sons and five daughters, of whom Frances was first married to Sir William Tresham of Rushton in Northamptonshire, Bart. and secondly to George Gage, Esq.; Penelope, to Henry Merrey of Barton in Derbyshire, Esq; Elizabeth, to Sir Thomas Petre of Cranham in Essex, Knt. and Bart.; and

* He was the great-grandson of Sir Thomas More, Chancellor of England, beheaded by K. Henry VIII. on whose attainder the estate was forfeited to the crown, and settled on the Princess, after Q. Elizabeth, who held it to her death, after which it reverted to the family, in the person of this Cressacre More, who had issue Thomas, Hellen, and Bridget. Thomas married Mary, daughter of Sir Basil Brooke of Madeley in Salop, and had a son Basil More, Esq. who married Anne, daughter of Sir William Humble, Bart. and sustained such great losses for his loyalty to his Prince, that he was obliged to sell the manor of Gobions to Sir Edward Desbouverie of London, ancestor to the Viscount Folkstone, whose sons in 1697 conveyed it to Mr. Pitchcroft, and he to the late Sir Jeremy Sambroke, Bart.

† She after became the second wife of Sir William Hervey of Ickworth in Suffolk, Knt. grandfather to John, created Earl of Bristol. When she was first left a widow, she was only 17 years of age and a very great beauty, and became heir to a very large fortune by her mother's leaving her the whole inheritance of the Kitsons, and her share in that of the Darcys. We are told this odd circumstance concerning her marriages; that being courted by her three husbands together, who quarrelled about her, she artfully put an end to their dispute, by threatening the first aggressor with her everlasting displeasure; by which means, they not knowing whom she might chuse, laid the quarrel asleep; and she told them humorously, if they would keep the peace and have patience, she would have them all in their turns, which happened accordingly, though so very unlikely to turn out.

and Anne, to Henry Petre, Esq. sixth son of William, the second Lord Petre.—The sons were Sir Thomas his heir; John of Stoneham in Suffolk, who left no issue; Sir Edward, of whom presently; and Henry, who married Henrietta, daughter of Thomas, Lord Jermyn of Rushbrooke in Suffolk, sister and coheir to Henry, Earl of Dover, by whom he had a son John Gage of Princethorp in Norfolk, Esq. and a daughter Mary, a nun.

Sir Edward Gage, the third son, being made heir to his mother's inheritance of Hengrave in Suffolk, became seated there; was knighted, and created a Baronet 15 July 1662. He married five wives; to his first Mary, second surviving daughter of the aforesaid Sir William Hervey (by his first wife Susan, daughter of Sir Robert Jermyn of Rushbrooke, Knt. grandfather to Henry, created Earl of St. Albans) and by her, who died 13 July 1654, had Sir William, his successor; and two daughters, Penelope, married to Edward Sulyard of Hawley-Park in Suffolk, Esq.; and Mary, to William Bond, Esq.—His second wife was Frances, second daughter of Walter, the second Lord Aston of Forfar, and by her he had one son Francis, of Packington-Hall in Staffordshire, in right of his mother, who died in child-birth of him, and he marrying Elizabeth, daughter and heir to John Devereux of Mountferrat, Esq. one of the Caribbee Islands, died 6 September 1729, and left one son Devereux.—His third wife was Anne, daughter of ———— Watkins, by whom he had one son Edward, that died unmarried. His fourth the Lady Mary Fielding, daughter of George, Earl of Desmond, who bore him four sons and two daughters; John, James, George, and Henry; Catharine, who died beyond sea; and Basilia, maid of honour to Mary D'Este, Queen of K. James II.—His fifth wife was Bridget Fielding, a daughter of the same family, and widow of ———— Slaughter, Esq. by whom he had no issue, and dying 31 January 1707, in the 90 year of his age, was succeeded by his eldest son

Sir William Gage, the second Baronet, who in 1722 was elected to parliament for the borough of Seaford, and died in February 1726, having married first Mary-Charlotte, only daughter of Sir Thomas Bond of Peckham in Surry, Bart. comptroller of the houshold to the Queen-mother of K. Charles II. by whom he had seven daughters, whereof Alice was married to Henry Sorrell of St. Edmondsbury,

Family of Hengrave, Baronets.

mondſbury, M. D. and two ſons, Thomas his heir apparent; and John, who by Elizabeth, daughter of Thomas Rookwood of Coldham-Hall in Suffolk, Eſq. had two ſons, Thomas and John.—His ſecond wife was Merelina, daughter and coheir to Thomas, Lord Jermyn, being alſo coheir to Henry, Earl of St. Albans, and to Henry, Earl of Dover, and widow of Sir Thomas Springe of Pakenham in Suffolk, Bart. but by her he had no iſſue.

Thomas, his heir apparent, married Delariviere, eldeſt daughter of Sir Symonds D'Ewes of Stow-Hall in Suffolk, Bart. by his wife Delariviere, daughter and coheir to the ſaid Thomas, Lord Jermyn, and dying before his father, in the 32 year of his age, lies buried at Hengrave with this inſcription;

> Hic jacet Thomas Gage, Arm. ex Patre Gulielmo Gage Baronetto, et Matre Charolette Bond, filiæ Unicæ Thomæ Bond, Baronetti. Duxit in Uxorem Delariviere D'Ewes, primogenitam Symondſii D'Ewes Baronetti, quam trium Filiorum Matrem reliquit Immatura Morte deſolatam, 32. ætat. anno, Animam Deo reddidit, magno ſuorum damno, ſui Solatio,
> Die 1°. Martii 1716.
> R. I. P.

His ſons were Thomas; Sir William; and Edward, who left no iſſue.—Sir Thomas, who ſucceeded his grandfather, and was the third Baronet, deceaſing at Hengrave 1 September 1741, was ſucceeded by his brother Sir William, a Portugal merchant, who 14 June 1741 married the eldeſt daughter of Captain Robert Harland, and widow of Mr. Ellis of St. Edmondſbury; and dying without iſſue 23 April 1744, left the bulk of his eſtate to the ſons of the Lord Gage [1].

Sir Thomas, 2 Baronet. We now return to Sir Thomas Gage of Firle, who ſucceeding his father Sir John, was the ſecond Baronet, married Mary, elder daughter and coheir to John Chamberlain of Shirburne-Caſtle in the county of Oxford, Eſq. and died about the year 1655, having iſſue by her, (who re-married with Sir Henry Goring of Burton in Suſſex, Bart. where ſhe was buried in 1694) four ſons and three daughters, viz.

Sir

[1] Lodge Collect.

Sir Thomas, the third Baronet, who dying at Rome whilſt on his travels, 22 November 1660, was buried in the chapel of the Engliſh College there, under a marble graveſtone thus inſcribed;   (1) Sir Thomas, 3 Baronet.

    D. O. M.
   Thomæ Gagio, Equiti
  Baronetto Anglo, Suſſexienſi,
  Patre, Honoribus ac Nominibus
   Matre, Nobilitati pari
   Maria Tankervilla,
  Alias Chamberlana nato ;
   Familiæ non magis
    Generis claritate,
 Quam perpetua Fidei Catholicæ
   Conſtantia Principiis
     Illuſtris.
   Qui in ipſo ætatis flore,
Ipſoque in almam Urbem ingreſſu,
  Deo Animam, Corpus Terræ
   Inter Cives ſuos tradidit,
xxii. Novembris Anno Dni M. D. CLX.
   Johannes Gagius Eques
  Baronettus, cariſſimo Fratri
    Mærens poſuit.

Sir John Gage, the fourth Baronet.   (2)
Henry, who died without iſſue.   (3)
Joſeph, father of the Lord Viſcount Gage.   (4)
 The daughters were Frances, married to Sir Charles Yates of Buckland in Berkſhire, Bart. ; Mary, to Anthony Kemp of Slingdon in Suſſex, Eſq. ; and Catharine, became the ſecond wife of Walter, the third Lord Aſton of Forfar, whom ſhe ſurvived without iſſue.
 Sir John Gage of Firle married firſt Mary, daughter of Thomas Middlemore of Edgebaſton in the county of Warwick, Eſq. and by her, who died 28 July 1686, had three ſons and ſeven daughters, of whom only two daughters who became his coheirs ſurvived, viz. Mary, (the ſecond wife of Sir John Shelly of Michael-Grove, Bart. by whom ſhe had two ſons and three daughters, viz. Sir John, his ſucceſſor ; Richard ; Mary, married to John, eldeſt ſon of Sir Henry Lawſon, Bart. ; Elizabeth, to Edward Sheldon of Weſton, Eſq. ; and Catharine, to George Mathew of   Thomaſtown.   Sir John, 4 Baronet.

Thomastown in the county of Tipperary, Esq.); and Bridget, married to Thomas, Viscount Fauconberg, died 18 November 1732, and was grandmother of Thomas, the present Earl.—Sir John's second wife was Mary, daughter of Sir William, and sister to Sir Rowland Stanley of Hooton in Cheshire, Barts. by whom he had one daughter Mary (the second wife of Henry Roper, Lord Teynham, she died by a miscarriage in January 1716); and three sons, successive Baronets; Sir John died 27 May 1699, in the 58 year of his age, and was succeeded by his eldest son

Sir John. 5 Baronet. Sir John, the fifth Baronet, who dying in January 1699-1700, aged about eight years, was succeeded by his brother

Sir Thomas, 6 Baronet. Sir Thomas, the sixth Baronet, who died in France on his travels in October 1713, in the 20 year of his age, and was buried at Blaye in the province of Guyenne; whereupon the title and large estate devolved to his brother

Sir William, 7 Baronet. Sir William, the seventh Baronet, born in 1695, who, renouncing the errors of the church of Rome, was created a Knight of the Bath 27 May 1725, and installed 17 July; he served in several parliaments for the Cinque-Port of Seaford; but dying unmarried 23 April 1744, the title accrued to the Lord Gage, to whose sons he left the principal part of his estate.

Joseph. Joseph Gage, Esq. his Lordship's father, had his mother's estate of Shirburne-Castle; and Elizabeth her sister being married to John, Lord Abergavenny, and having no issue, he inherited the remainder of what she had not sold, whereby the castle of Sherburne became the family seat; and so continued until the year 1716, when Lord Gage disposed of it, with the estate thereto belonging, to Thomas Parker, Earl of Macclesfield.—He also acquired a great estate by his marriage with Elizabeth, daughter of George Penruddock of the county of Southampton, Esq. and heir to her brothers, who died childless; and she deceasing 5 December 1693, left him two sons and two daughters.

(1) Thomas, created Viscount Gage.

(2) Count Joseph Gage, who being concerned in the Mississippi schemes in France, acquired a prodigious fortune in the year 1719, his wealth being computed at 12 or 13 millions, sterling; which so intoxicated him, that he made an offer to the late Augustus, King of Poland, of three millions for that crown, which his Majesty refusing, he

proposed

GAGE, VISCOUNT GAGE.

proposed to purchase the Island of Sardinia, from the then King of Sardinia, a proposal that Monarch also rejected. But by the fall of that bubble the next year, being reduced to great poverty, he sought new adventures in Spain, where in February 1727 he obtained a grant from the crown, for working and draining all the gold mines in old Spain, and fishing for all wrecks on the coasts of Spain, and the Indies; and in October 1741 was presented by his Catholick Majesty with a silver mine of immense value, to him and his heirs by patent, with the title of Count, or Grandee of the third class. After which he was constituted General of his Majesty's armies in Sicily, in which station he received a complete overthrow by Count Traun, commander of the Austrian and Piedmontese troops at Campo-Santo, 8 February 1742 [1] N. S. and in March 1743 was honoured with the title of Grandee of Spain of the first class, and Commander in Chief of the army in Lombardy; being also presented by the King of Naples with the order of St. Gennaro, and a pension of 4000 ducats a year. His wife was Lady Lucy Herbert, fourth daughter of William, the first Marquess of Powis.

Daughter Elizabeth was married to John Weston of Sutton in Surry, Esq. (1)

Anne, to Richard Arundel Bealing of Langhern in Cornwall, Esq. whose two daughters by her, Frances and Mary were married, as the reader will find under the title of Viscount Mountgarret. (2)

Thomas Gage, Esq. the elder son, in consideration of his great merit, was advanced to the Peerage of Ireland, being created Viscount Gage of Castle-Island and Baron Gage of Castlebar by privy seal dated at St. James's 13 June, and by patent 14 September 1720, with the creation fee of 20 marcs [2]. — Sir Thomas, 1 Viscount.

The many shining qualities of this nobleman are displayed, in the dedication to him of the ninth volume of the Spectators, and in the following address from the Speaker of the House of Commons, when ordered, 31 March 1732, to give the thanks of that house to his Lordship, for his great expence and service, in detecting the fraudulent sale of the Earl of Derwentwater's estate, with a present of 2000l.

"My

---

[1] Lodge Collect.
[2] Rot. Anno 7 Geo. I. 1. p. D.

"My Lord Gage,

"The house have come to an unanimous resolution, that the thanks of the house be given to your Lordship, for the great service you have done the public, in detecting the fraudulent sale of certain forfeited estates of James, late Earl of Derwentwater, and of a forfeited annuity issuing out of the same, which were vested in commissioners and trustees, to be sold for the public use. And the manner of your Lordship's making this discovery, hath shewn your disinterested regard to the public service, as the effect of it may be greatly to the public benefit.

"The applying the forfeited estates to the use of the public, being one of the principal reasons for making it thereby impossible they should ever be given back to the unfortunate families they once belonged to, the House of Commons could not, without uneasiness, think of this pretended sale, which has thrown into private hands, no way allied to the estate, so large a share of the profit due to the public, with a very low, and almost the bare appearance only of a consideration for one part, and not so much as even *that* for another.

"But your Lordship's seasonable detection of this injurious transaction will, very likely, produce justice and restitution to the public; and for this service your Lordship is now receiving a reward, that, I can answer for your Lordship, you esteem the greatest and most honourable you can acquire; and which, my Lord, will not only remain with you, but will derive a lasting honour to those, who may come after you.

"An honour, my Lord, the house hath always been most tender of in the way, and for the reason they confer it upon you; and if I may use the expression, is a sort of bounty they have ever been most frugal of granting. Few are the instances of it, not that public services have not frequently been performed, but that the thanks of the House of Commons are never given for public services, but what are the most eminent, such as that, which your Lordship hath lately done the state.

"I am very conscious how imperfectly I have conveyed the sense of the house to your Lordship; but the having no time to prepare myself for it, must be my excuse. I will only add, that no one could with greater pleasure obey the order of the house on this occasion, than I
"do;

"do; which is, to give your Lordship the thanks of the house for your said service to the public, and I do give your Lordship the thanks of the house accordingly.

His Lordship's reply.

"Mr. Speaker,
"This sudden and unexpected honour hath put me into so great a confusion, that I never was more at a loss for words to express myself than now; all I can say, Sir, is to assure you and the house, that I had no other view in promoting this enquiry, than to discharge the trust my country had reposed in me, by detecting (as far as I was able) a fraud injurious to the public. And since the house hath been pleased to distinguish my poor service, in a manner so far beyond what it deserved, or I could have expected; their approbation of my behaviour in this particular instance will, I hope, so influence my future conduct in all others, as may convince them that I shall make it my constant endeavour to merit the honour they have done me on this occasion."

From the first parliament of K. George I. he served for the borough of Tewksbury in Gloucestershire, was Verdurer of the forest of Dean in that county; admitted a fellow of the Royal Society 25 November 1731, and appointed in 1747 Steward of the Houshold to Frederick, Prince of Wales.—He married first Benedicta, or Beata-Maria-Teresa, only daughter and heir to Benedict Hall of High-Meadow in the county of Gloucester, Esq. (who died in December 1714) and she dying 25 July 1749, was interred at Newland in Gloucestershire; he married secondly 26 December 1750, Jane, daughter of ———— Godfrey, and relict of Henry-Jermyn Bond of St. Edmundsbury in Suffolk, she died 8 October 1757, and his Lordship departed this life at his seat of Firle in December 1754, leaving issue by his first wife a daughter Teresa, married 6 March 1755 to George Tasbourgh of Bedney in the county of Norfolk, Esq.; and two sons, viz.

William Hall, who succeeded to the honour, and

Thomas, who was Captain of a company in General Batareau's regiment of foot in Ireland, of which 23 February

bruary 1747 he was appointed Major, and in March 1750 Lieutenant Colonel; he was fucceffively Colonel of the eightieth, fixtieth, and twenty-fecond regiments of foot, was raifed to the rank of Major-General 5 March 1761; Lieutenant-General 30 April 1770, and a General of his Majefty's armies 26 November 1782 [1].—In 1755 being then a Lieutenant-Colonel, he went to America with General Braddock, where he raifed a regiment, which being put on the eftablifhment, he was appointed Colonel, and continued in America during the whole of that war; after the ratification of the peace then enfuing, Sir Jeffery Amherft returning home, General Gage was appointed his fucceffor as Commander in Chief; and in the late commotions in North America he was again appointed Commander in Chief and Governor of the Maffachufets, but refigned the command in October 1775.——8 December 1758, he married at Mount-Kemble in America, Margaret, daughter of Peter Kemble, Efq. Prefident of the council at New-Jerfey, and deceafed 2 April 1788, having had iffue, fix fons and five daughters, viz. Henry, born at Montreal in Canada, a Major in the army and prefumptive heir to his uncle's eftates and honours; William, born at New-York, and died young; Thomas, died an infant; John, born at New-York 23 December 1767; Thomas, died young; William-Hall, born in Park-Place, St. James's, Weftminfter, 2 October 1777; Maria-Terefa, born at Montreal 4 April 1762; Louifa-Elizabeth, born at New-York 12 December 1765; Harriet, a twin with John, born at New-York 23 December 1767; Charlotte-Mary, born in Duke-Street St. James's, 19 Auguft 1773; and Emily, born at Park-Place, St. James's, 25 April 1776.

Sir William-Hall, 2 Vifcount.

Sir William-Hall Gage, the fecond and prefent Vifcount, was Equerry to Frederick, Prince of Wales in 1742; in 1744 and 1754, was chofen to the Britifh parliament for the Cinqueport of Seaford; in January 1766 was appointed Pay-Mafter of the penfions; and 17 October 1780 was created a Peer of Great-Britain by the title of Baron Gage of Firle in the county of Suffex.—3 February 1757, he married Elizabeth, fifter to Sir Sampfon Gideon of Spalding in the county of Lincoln, Bart. and by her Ladyfhip who died 1 July 1783, aged 44, has no iffue [2].

[1] Beatfon. [2] Supp. to Collins 219, 220. &c.

[TITLES.]

TEMPLE, Viscount PALMERSTON.

TITLES.] Sir William-Hall Gage, Viscount and Baron Gage, and Baronet.

CREATIONS.] Baronet, 26 March 1622, 24 Jac. I. V. Gage of Castle-Island in the county of Kerry, and B. Gage of Castlebar in the county of Mayo, 14 September 1720, 7 Geo. I. and B. Gage of Firle in the county of Sussex, 17 October 1780, 20 Geo. III.

ARMS.] Per saltire, saphire and pearl, a saltire, ruby.

CREST.] On a wreath a Ram, proper, armed and unguled, topaz.

SUPPORTERS.] Two Greyhounds, jacinth, gorged with Coronets of fleurs de lis, topaz.

MOTTO.] COURAGE SANS PEUR.

SEATS.] High-Meadow in the county of Gloucester, 96 miles from London; Firle, near Lewes in Sussex, 40 miles from London; and East-Grinsted in the same county, 25 miles from London.

TEMPLE, Viscount PALMERSTON.

LEURIC, or Leofric, Earl of Chester (by some erroneously styled Earl of Leicester) living in the time of King Ethelbald, anno 716, is said to be ancestor to this family of TEMPLE.—He was the father of Algar, whose successor, Algar II. lived in the reign of K. Etheldred, and had issue Leofric II. the father of Leofern, or Leofwin, Earl of Mercia, whose son Leofrick, is by some affirmed to be the first Earl of Leicester, in the time of Edward the Confessor, and was chiefly instrumental in raising that Prince to the throne, as he also was of his successor Harold Harefoot.

He founded the great monastery at Coventry, which he endowed with no less than 24 Lordships, and so much enriched with ornaments of gold, silver and jewels, that none in the kingdom was furnished like it. He married the famous Godina (who is said to have ridden naked through Coventry by day, to regain the citizens their privileges, which they had forfeited by offending their Lord, her husband, and to free them from the taxes with which they were oppressed); however that may be, the pictures of this Earl and Countess were set up in the south window of Trinity church in that city (about the reign of K. Richard II. upwards of 300 years as is supposed after the transaction) the Earl holding a charter in his right hand, with these words on it:

I, Lurick, for love of thee,
Do set Coventry toll free.

There is a yearly procession of a naked figure observed on Friday after Trinity Sunday, and in a window in the High-street is the effigies of a taylor, who, according to the tradition, was the only person who ventured to look at her, and was thereupon struck blind [1]. The Earl dying 31 August 1057, was buried in his monastery, leaving

Algar. Algar his son to succeed in the Earldom of Mercia, who in 1053 was Earl of the East Saxons (Essex) upon Harold's quitting that title for the Earldom of the West Saxons, after Earl Godwin's death. He died in 1059, and lies buried

Edwyn. at Coventry, leaving Edwyn his son, a valiant nobleman, who disliking the government of the Normans, was deprived of his Earldom by the *Conqueror*, and being afterwards betrayed by three of his principal officers and confidents, lost his life in defending himself with only twenty horsemen against a superior force, in 1071.—He left a son

Edwyn. Edwyn, some time styled Earl of Leicester and Coventry, who is said to assume the surname of *Temple*, from the manor of *Temple* in the hundred of Sparkenhoe, standing in Wellesborough, " which manor (says Mr. William Bur-
" ton, in his Description of Leicestershire) was given by
" the old Earls of Leicester to the Knights Templers,
" who usually gave the name of *Temple* to their lands,
" and they granted it to one whose family was called
" *Temple*, of great account and livelyhood in those parts."
However

[1] Collins, Edit. 1779, V. 247, 248.

However, this be, Henry de Temple was Lord of Temple and Little-Shepey, in the reign of William the Conqueror, and left issue Geoffry, whose son John lived in the reign of Henry I. and was father of Henry de Temple, who married Maud, daughter of Sir John Ribbesford, and had a son of his own name, Lord of the aforesaid manors in the reign of K. John, who gave some lands in the latter to the Abbey of Meraval; leaving his son Richard to succeed him, who lived 24 Edw. I. and by Catharine, daughter of Thomas Langley, had Nicholas de Temple, living 16 Edw. II. who also gave lands in Warwickshire to the said Abbey in the 14 of that reign, and marrying Margery, daughter of Sir Roger Corbet of Sibston in the county of Leicester, was father of Richard de Temple, living 20 Edw. III. who married Agnes, daughter of Sir Ralph Stanley, and having sepulture in the church of Shepey, is commemorated by his picture, drawn in a kneeling posture, in the North-East window, with his name under-written,

Henry.
Geoffry.
Henry.
Henry.
Richard.
Nicholas.
Richard.

Richardus de Temple.

His son was Nicholas, living in 1372 (46 Edw. III.) who married Maud, daughter of John Burguillon of Newton in Leicestershire; and by her, who was his widow in 51 of that reign, left Richard (or Robert) his heir, mentioned in deeds 9 Hen. V. and 3 Hen. VI. whose wife was Joan, daughter of William Shepey of Great-Shepey in the said county, who brought him that manor, with Cunston, Bilston, and Atterton, by her he left three sons, viz.

Nicholas.
Richard.
(1)

Nicholas de Temple, the eldest son, was buried in the church of Great-Shepey, under a monument, with his Coat-Armour engraven thereon, viz. *Argent, on two Bars, Sable, six Martlets, Or,* empaled with *Azure, two Bars, and a Mullet in chief, Or,* and this circumscription;

Hic jacet Corpus Nicholai Temple, Armigeri, et
Elizabethæ Uxoris ejus, qui quidem Nicholaus
Obiit 1506.

He died without lawful issue, but left three natural daughters, to one of whom, married to ——— Whitet or Whitell, he gave Little-Shepey; to another, married to ——— Bowes, he gave Cunston and Bilston; and to the third he gave Atterton.

Robert

(2) Robert Temple, the second son, was seated at Temple-Hall, near Bosworth in the county of Leicester, and by the gift of his father had lands in Burton under Needwood; and by Grace, daughter of William Turvill, had Richard Temple of Burton, who siding with Richard III. forfeited most of his estate, and died in 1507 (22 Hen. VII.) being father of Roger, whose son Richard left issue Edmund, the father of Paul Temple, aged 29 in 1619; and Peter Temple of Temple in Leicestershire, living in 1635 who had a son John [1].

(3) Thomas, the youngest son, resided at Witney in the county of Oxford, and by Mary, daughter of Thomas Gedney, Esq. left William Temple, who married Isabel, daughter and heir to Henry Everton, and was father of Thomas Temple of Witney, who by Alice, daughter and heir to John Heritage of Burton-Derset in the county of Warwick, had two sons, Robert, his successor at Witney; and Peter, who in the last year of K. Edw. VI. received a grant of the manor of Marston-Boteler in Warwickshire, being then wrote of Derset, in right of his mother, and in 1560 (2 Eliz.) purchased the interest, which Lawrence Danet had therein; being likewise Lord of the Manor of *Stow* in Bucks, his posterity fixed their residence there. He lies buried in the church of All Saints at Derset, under a marble stone, whereto the portraits of himself and his wife in brass were fixed, and this memorial:

Thomas William.

Thomas.

Peter.

> Here under this stone lyeth the body of Peter
> Temple Esquyer, who departed out of this
> World at Stow in the county of Buckingham,
> The xxviiith day of May, Anno [1577] whose
> Soule God hathe in his blessed keeping.

His wife was Millecent, daughter of William Jekyl of Newington in Middlesex, Esq. by whom he had two sons, viz. John who succeeded at Stow; and Anthony, from whom the Lord Viscount Palmerstown descends.

Family of Temple, Viscount Cobham.

John Temple, Esq. who succeeded at Stow, married Susan, daughter and heir to Thomas Spencer of Everton in the county of Northampton, Esq. and by her had six sons and six daughters, as appears by an inscription in English, on a monument in the church of Derset, where the said John and Susan lie interred, and under the same inscription are these lines;

Cur

[1] Collins. V. 249.

Cur liberos his plurimos,
Cur hic amicos plurimos,
Et plurimas pecunias,
Vis fcire cur reliquerit ?
TEMPELLUS ad plures abiit.

The iffue of the faid Sir Thomas were, Sir Thomas his heir; George, who died an infant; John, of Franckton in the county of Warwick; Sir Alexander of Longhoufe in Effex; William, who married Jane, daughter of Sir Thomas Beaumont of Stoughton, Knt.; Peter, who married a daughter of ——— Kendal; daughter Milicent, married to Edward Saunders of Brickfworth in the county of Northampton, Efq.; Dorothy, to Paul Rifley of Chetwood in the county of Buckingham, Efq.; Catharine, to Sir Nicholas Parker of Willington in Suffex, Knt.; Sufanna, to Sir Thomas Denton of Hillefden in Bucks, Knt.; Mary, to John Farmer of Cokeham in Berkfhire; and Elizabeth, to William, Lord Say and Sele.

Sir Thomas Temple, the eldeft fon, fucceeded at Stow and poffeffed the greateft part of the eftate; he was knighted by K. James I. in June 1603, at Sir John Fortefcue's in the county of Buckingham, and 22 May 1611, was created a Baronet of England, at the inftitution of that order.—He married Efther, daughter of Miles Sandys of Latimers in Bucks, Efq. and by her * had four fons and three daughters, who lived to maturity, viz. Sir Peter, his heir; Sir John, (who married Dorothy, daughter and coheir to Edmund Lee of Stanton-Barry in Bucks, Efq., and had a numerous iffue); Thomas, L. L. D. who married and had iffue; Miles, who alfo married and had iffue; daughter Sufan, married to Sir Edward Clark of Ardington in the county of Berks, Knt.; Hefther, to Sir John Rous of Rous-Linch in the county of Worcefter, Knt.; Bridget, to

Sir Thomas, 1 Bart.

---

* Thefe children fo multiplied that his lady, who furvived him, faw 700 defcended from her. This is affirmed by Dr. Fuller, in his Worthies of England, who relates that he bought the truth thereof by a wager loft on the fubject. This Efther Lady Temple, (of whom there is an original picture at Stow) far furpaffed Mrs. Honeywood of Mark's-Hall in Effex, (mentioned by Dr. Derham and by Hearne in the preface to Leland's Itinerary, Vol. V.) who lived to fee 367 defcendants of her own body, for Lady Temple faw many more; the laft of whom, viz. the daughter of Sir Henry Gibbs of Hunnington in Warwickfhire, died in December 1737, in extreme old age. (Collins. V. 252.)

to Sir John Lenthall of Creflow in the county of Oxford, Knt.; Martha, (to Sir Thomas Peniston of Leigh in Suffex, Bart. who died 14 January 1619, and is buried at Stow); Elizabeth, to Sir Henry Gibbs of Hunnington in the county of Warwick, Knt.; Catharine, to Sir William Ashcomb of Avelscot in the county of Oxford, Knt.; Anne, to Sir William Andrews of Lathbury in Bucks, Knt.; Margaret, to Sir Henry Longueville of Billing in the county of Northampton, Knt.; and Milicent, to ———— Ogle, Esq.

Sir Peter, 2 Bart. Sir Peter, the second Baronet, and successor to Sir Thomas, served for the town of Buckingham in the two last parliaments of K. Charles I. and married two wives, first Anne, daughter and coheir to Sir Arthur Throgmorton of Paulerspury in the county of Northampton, Knt.; and secondly, to Christian, sister and coheir to Sir Richard Leveson of Trentham in the county of Stafford, Knight of the Bath, and daughter of Sir John Leveson, Knt. (eldest son of Sir John Leveson by Frances, daughter and sole heir to Sir Thomas Sands of Throwley in Kent, Knt. elder brother to Sir Michael Sands, Knt.) By the first wife, who was buried at Stow 23 January 1619, he had two daughters, viz. Anne, married to Thomas Roper, Viscount Baltinglass; and Martha, to Weston Ridgeway, Earl of Londonderry, (both which titles are extinct): And by the said Christian his second wife, who was buried at Stow 3 April 1655, (where he was interred in 1653,) he had two daughters Frances and Hester; and a son and successor

Sir Richard, 3 Bart. Sir Richard, the third Baronet, who was born 28 March 1634, served in the restoration parliament for the town of Buckingham, of which and the county thereof, he was constituted L. L. 15 November 1660; on 19 November 1661 he was one of the 68 persons of distinction, created Knights of the Bath, to attend K. Charles II. 23 of that month at his coronation. He differed essentially in politics from his cousin Sir William, was returned member for the town of Buckingham to all the parliaments of Charles II. James II. and K. William; was a leading member in the House of Commons during the reign of Charles II. and distinguished himself in the prosecution of the Popish plot, and in promoting the bill for excluding James, Duke of York from succeeding to the crown; as he did also in the convention of 1688-9, by voting for the vacancy of the throne and filling it with the prince and princess of Orange. —On 30 March 1672, he was appointed first commissioner of of the cuftoms, as he was 8 January 1675, and 9 November 1677.—On the acceffion of K. James II. he was left out of this commiffion, but was replaced, and continued to fill that employment till 14 Auguft 1694, when an act of parliament which difabled all who had offices in the cuftoms &c. from fitting in the Houfe of Commons, took place, and he preferred his feat in St. Stephen's chapel, to one at that board. He married Mary, daughter of Mr. Knap of Wefton in the county of Oxford, and heirefs to her brother; and Sir Richard deceafing in May, 1697, was interred 15 of that month at Stow, having had iffue by his lady, who was interred there 25 January 1726, four fons and fix daughters, viz. Sir Richard his heir; Purbeck, buried at Stow, 5 March 1698; Henry and Arthur, buried at Stow 4 February 1701, all died without iffue; two of the daughters died young; Hefter, the fecond, was married to Richard Grenville of Wotton Efq. anceftor to George Grenville-Nugent-Temple, Earl Nugent and Marquefs of Buckingham; Chriftian, to Sir Thomas Lyttleton, Bart. whofe fon Sir William hath been created Baron Weftcote in Ireland; Maria, firft to Doctor Weft, Prebendary of Winchefter, and fecondly to Sir John Langham of Cattefbroke in the county of Northampton, Bart; and Penelope, to Mofes Berenger of the city of London, Efq.

Sir Richard Temple, the fourth Baronet, was elected to the Britifh parliament for the town of Buckingham, on the deceafe of his father; of which town and the county thereof he was conftituted L. L. 12 April 1703.—In the firft year of Q. Anne, he was appointed Colonel of a regiment of foot, and diftinguifhed himfelf at the fieges of Venlo and Ruremond when he acted as a volunteer; he afterwards ferved with his regiment in Flanders and Germany; and 1 June 1706, was declared a Brigadier General.—Having borne a confiderable part of the fervice at the fiege of Lifle in 1708, he was fent exprefs by the Duke of Marlborough to the Queen, with an account of the furrender of that fortrefs.—1 January 1708-9 he was promoted to the rank of Major General; and 1 January 1709-10 was conftituted a Lieutenant General.--In 1710 he obtained the command of the fourth regiment of Dragoons but was not in the lift of general officers nominated to ferve under the Duke of Ormond in Flanders; and in 1713 his regiment was given to General Evans.—After the acceffion of K. George I. viz. 19 October 1714, he was created Baron of Cobham in Kent,

Sir Richard, 4 Bart. and Vifcount Cobham.

TEMPLE, Viscount PALMERSTON.

Kent, and 5 days after was declared Envoy Extraordinary and Plenipotentiary to the Emperor Charles VI.—On 13 June 1715, his Lordship was made Colonel of the first regiment of dragoons, and in the following year was constituted Constable of Windsor-Castle.—23 May 1718, he was created Viscount and Baron Cobham, remainder to the heirs of his body, in default thereof, to his sister Hester Grenville and her heirs male, with a like remainder to his sister Christian Lyttelton.—In 1721 he was appointed Colonel of the first regiment of dragoon guards; and in February 1727-8, was nominated L. L. and Custos Rot. of the county of Bucks; he was likewise a Lord of the privy council in Great Britain, and Governor of the Isle of Jersey; but resigned all his places in 1733.—In 1742, we find him a Field-Marshal and L. General of the Ordnance, at which time he was appointed Colonel of the first troop of grenadier guards; and in 1744 was appointed to the command of the sixth regiment of horse. In May, 1745, his Lordship was nominated one of the Regents during his Majesty's absence beyond the seas, and was declared Colonel of the tenth regiment of dragoons.—He married Anne, only daughter of Edmund Halsey of the borough of Southwark, Esq. but by her who survived till 29 March 1760, had no issue, and deceasing at Stow 15 September 1749 [1] was there interred, where stands a lofty fluted column, on the pedestal of which are the following inscriptions;

On one side
To preserve the memory of her husband,
Anne, Viscountess *Cobham*
Caused this pillar to be erected,
In the year 1749.

On the opposite side,
Quatenus nobis denegatur diu vivere,
Relinquamus aliquid,
Quo nos vixisse testemur.

Inasmuch as the portion of life allotted to us is short,
Let us leave something behind us,
To shew that we have lived [*][2].

Anthony

---

[*] "That Lord Cobham lived," every Englishman will remember, but his fame *as a patriot* has been perpetuated by Alexander Pope.

" And

[1] Collins Edit. 1779. V. 251. 255. [2] Seeley's descript. of Stow. 31.

Anthony Temple, Efq. the younger fon of Peter, was father of Sir William Temple, Knt. who having his grammar education in Eton-School, was removed to King's College, Cambridge, of which fociety (purfuant to the ftatutes of their royal founder Henry VI.) he became a fellow when three years ftanding; took the degree of A. M. and was mafter of the free-fchool in the city of Lincoln.—— The law was intended for his profeffion, but affecting the more refined and philofophical ftudies of that age, he became a great proficient therein, and wrote two treatifes on thofe fubjects in very elegant Latin; the former of which printed in 1581, he dedicated to the learned Sir Philip Sidney, who took him into his intimate friendfhip; and who being made Governor, by Q. Elizabeth, of Flufhing and Ramekins, two cautionary towns in the Netherlands, prevailed on Mr. Temple to leave the college, and accompany him as his fecretary.——Sir Philip fighting the Spaniards near Zutphen in Guelderland, received a fhot in his thigh, 22 September 1586, of which he expired 16 October at Arnheim, in the arms of his Secretary, to whom by his laft will he bequeathed 30l. a year for life, and had taken care to recommend him to the great Earl of Effex, then in the zenith of Q. Elizabeth's favour; who employed him in the fame ftation of Secretary (as William Davifon, Efq. Secretary of State, had alfo done) till his tragical end in the year 1600: A ftroke which proved fatal to Mr. Temple, who not only fell with the Earl from the profpect he had of making his fortune, but was purfued by Secretary Cecil; from whofe refentment being obliged to retire into Ireland, he accepted of the Provoftfhip of the Univerfity of Dublin in 1609, at the importunate folicitation of Doctor Henry Ufsher, Archbifhop of Armagh, who was well acquainted with his great worth and learning. In this capacity (being the fourth Provoft from the foundation) he lived feventeen years, and in the parliament of 1613 was its reprefentative; was made a Knight 4 May 1622 by the L. D. St. John, having been appointed 31 January 1609 a Mafter in Chancery, in which he was continued 16 April 1625, by K. Charles I.

He

"And you! brave COBHAM, to the lateft breath,
"Shall feel your ruling paffion ftrong in death,
"Such in thofe moments, as in all the paft,
"O, fave my country, Heaven! fhall be your laft."

He was a person of great learning and piety, having left some monuments of the former in four Latin treatises. He married Martha, daughter of Mr. Robert Harrison of the county of Derby; and making his will 21 December 1626, directed his body to be buried in the College-chapel, under the foot of the Provost's seat, providing that his burial be performed without all funeral pomp and solemnities of Heralds; and deceasing 15 January following, in the 73 year of his age, was there privately interred on the 20, having issue by her, who was buried in St. Werburgh's church 7 December 1675, two sons and three daughters, viz.

(1) Sir John, his heir.

(2) Thomas, educated in the university of Dublin, of which he was some time a Fellow, was presented 6 March 1626, to the Rectory of Old-Ross in the Diocess of Fernes, and took his degree of A. M. 18 June 1630; as he did *that* of B. D. at Oxford, 19 January 1638, being then of Lincoln College; where he continued not long, for, upon the turn of the times in 1641, he became a forward preacher in London, and Minister of Battersea in Surrey; afterwards a frequent preacher before the members of the Long Parliament; one of the assembly of divines; and an adventurer in Ireland, by subscribing the sum of 450l. for which he had an assignment of 750 acres of land, Irish measure, in the county of Westmeath; and 10 November 1636, for the sum of 900l. sold to Thomas Hammond of Frankton in Warwickshire, Esq. the castle and lands of Colebannagher in the Queen's county *.

Daughter

---

* He was ancestor, 'tis presumed to Robert Temple of Mount-Temple in Westmeath, Esq. who married first 11 March 1693-4, Dorothea, relict of Mr. Needham, and sister to William Cock of Leatherhead in Surry, Esq. by her he had two children who died young: He married secondly 3 February 1699, Catharine, sister to John Jephson, Esq. (made his will which was proved 20 January 1741, directing his body to be buried, if he died in Dublin, in the chancel of the Round-Church, by his first wife and two children; and if in England, then to be buried in the Temple church, near his mother, sister, and two brothers) by his last wife had an only daughter and heir, Elizabeth, baptized 29 August 1701, and married in July 1725, to Gustavus Handcock of Waterstown in Westmeath, Esq. M. P. for Athlone, by him who died 5 September 1751, she had a daughter Catharine, who died 2 April 1746; and an only son Robert, who 4 July 1751, married Elizabeth, eldest daughter of Sir John Vesey Lord Knapton, whose son Sir Thomas hath been created Viscount De Vesey, and by her who remarried with Edmund Sexten Pery, created in 1786 Viscount Pery; had an only son Gustavus, who, succeeding to his grand-mother's estates, assumed the name of *Temple*, and married a daughter of William-Henry Moore, of Drumbanagher, Esq. (Prerog. Off. St Michan's Registry, and Collections.

Daughter Catharine was married first to John Archdall (1) of Castle-Archdall in the county of Fermanagh, Esq.; secondly to Sir John Veell, Knt. and dying 13 November 1642, without surviving issue, she was buried in St. Werburgh's church, Dublin.

Mary, to Job Ward of Knockragh in the county of Wick- (2) low, Esq. brother to John Ward of Kilmank in the King's county, Esq. and died 24 December 1627, having issue a son John; and a daughter Jane, married to Robert Madden of Dunore, Esq.

Martha, died unmarried.

Sir John Temple, the eldest son, born in the year 1600, Sir John. (3) received university Education under his father in Dublin, and was sent early abroad to accomplish himself by visiting foreign kingdoms; after his return from whence, he was bred in the court of K. Charles I.; and upon his father's death, received a special livery of his inheritance 5 January 1628, for the fine of 12l. Irish; after which he was knighted by the King, and 20 February 1640 constituted master of the Rolls, and sworn of the Privy Council in Ireland.

Upon the breaking out of the rebellion 23 October 1641, he was one of the council, who signed the proclamation from the castle of Dublin, advertising the kingdom of the discovery thereof, and requiring his Majesty's good and loyal subjects to betake themselves to their defence, and stand upon their guard, so to render the more safety to themselves and the whole kingdom; requiring also that no levies should be made for foreign service, nor any men suffered to march upon any pretence whatever.—And being made Commissary-General of the army, when the L. J. and Council were the next month consulting means to secure the city and castle of Dublin, which by the confusions, weaknesses and wants, were in apparent danger of a sudden surprize, one of their principal cares was to lay in provisions for the castle in such proportion, as might enable it to endure a siege, if such a thing should be attempted; to compass which seemed a matter of great difficulty, (in regard no money was to be had to perform it) and of no less importance even for the preservation of the whole kingdom.—The Master of the Rolls, upon whom the L. J. and Council were pleased to impose this service, sent for some of the best protestant merchants, and so clearly represented to them the high necessities of the state, the great danger of the town, the publick benefit, and their own private security, in laying into the castle (whither

he

he had removed the records) such of their provisions as were stored in unsafe places, that upon his undertaking to see them satisfied, in case they were made use of for the publick service, the English and Dutch merchants presently deposited within the verge of the castle above 2000 barrels of beef, as many of herrings, and a great proportion of wheat; provisions sufficient, not only to victual the castle for many months, (which by the want of money and credit could not be otherwise provided for) but which served to maintain the whole army, billetted in the city a long time after. And he made good his engagements to the merchants, by their receiving the value of their goods within a few months, by bills drawn upon *the Chamber of* London, according to an order of both houses of parliament, for present payment to be made to such, as laid in any provisions for the army in Ireland. This seasonable service was the first step to the safety of the castle and city, and gave great comfort and security to all the English and protestants [1].

He enjoyed a particular friendship and confidence with Robert Sidney, Earl of Leicester, when declared L. L. of Ireland; and in 1643 was imprisoned, with three more privy counsellors, Sir William Parsons, Sir Adam Loftus, and Sir Robert Meredyth, accused of several high crimes, and especially for opposing the cessation, which the Earl of Ormond was commissioned by the King to conclude with the Irish: His confinement ended the next year, when he was exchanged and sent for by the parliament; who, considering him as a sufferer for the republican cause, received him well, provided a seat for him in the house soon after, and entrusted him much with the managment of the Irish affairs; the state of which, on 7 May 1647, he and the Lord Lisle reported to the house, and received *their* thanks for the good service they had done in Ireland, and he was that year made one of their commissioners in Munster.—On 16 October 1648, the commons voted him and Sir William Parsons to be commissioners of the great seal in Ireland, and dissented from the lords, who voted to have a chancellor there; but that year they dismissed him their assembly, with those called the secluded members, whom he had joined in voting, that his Majesty's concessions to their propositions of peace, then treated of with the King in the Isle of *Wight*, were sufficient grounds for settling the peace of the kingdom.

During the sad scene that followed, he continued privately in London, until the Protector 21 November 1653 joined him

[1] Temple's Hist. Reb. P. 47.

him with Miles Corbet, one of the commiffioners of government and others, to meet in fome convenient room at the courts beyond the water (the King's Inns) to confider and advife, from time to time, how the titles of the Irifh and others to any eftate in Ireland, and likewife their delinquency, according to their refpective qualifications, might be put into the moft fpeedy and exact way of adjudication, confiftent with juftice, and leaft prejudice to the publick intereft.—On 27 March 1654, he received an order for 100l. in recompence of his feveral fervices to the commonwealth, and 23 June 50l. more for the pains he had taken in the publick fervice, and the duty put upon his clerks in the court of wards, for the ufe of the commiffioners for the adjudication of claims; having alfo a further allowance of 200l. from the ftate 26 December 1655, on account (as the order expreffes) of his eminent and faithful fervices, both during the rebellion and after, and of the Protector's letter in his behalf. On 28 January following he received 25l. for one quarter's additional falary, as mafter of the rolls, which he continued to hold from the ufurped government, with the fee of 204l. 10s. a year [1]. and 21 July 1656 his extraordinary good fervices, from time to time, in behalf of the Protector and the commonwealth, were further rewarded with the fum of 100l. ; from whom he likewife received more fubftantial favours *.

On the reftoration of K. Charles, he was continued mafter of the rolls, fworn of the privy council, and, with his eldeft fon William, in the parliament of 1661 reprefented the county of Carlow †. On 26 November 1673 he was conftituted

---

* Namely, by indenture, dated 6 July 1658, the Protector demifed to him for 21 years, the towns and lands of Moghill, Caftletown, Parke, Cargan alias Ballycarney, &c. in the barony and county of Carlow, containing by furvey 1489 acres, 3 roods; the three laft denominations of which were confirmed to him 18 June 1666, under the acts of fettlement.——By another indenture of the fame date, were demifed to him the lands of Nuttftown, &c. in the barony of Balrothery and county of Dublin, containing 527 acres, 10 perches, for the like term.—And, 30 March 1659 the Protector Richard demifed to him the lands of Lifpoble, and others, in the faid county, forfeited by Richard Barnewall, for the fame term of years.

† On 6 May 1661 Henrietta-Maria, Queen Mother of England, for the fine of 540l. made him a reverfionary leafe of the Park of Blandefby,

[1] Council Off. Civil Lift A°. 1656.

constituted vice-treasurer of the kingdom, and lived with great hospitality and esteem to his death on 14 November 1677, in the 77 year of his age, in which year he gave 100l. to be laid out on some additional buildings to the college of Dublin, (on account whereof, Lord Palmerston and his heirs have a right to bestow two handsome chambers upon such students as they shall think proper) where, at his request, he was buried with his father *.—He married Mary, daughter of John Hammond of Chertsey in Surry, Esq. physician to Henry, Prince of Wales, son of K. James I. and sister to the learned doctor Henry Hammond, whose writings bespeak him one of the brightest ornaments and most strenuous advocates of the church of England. By her, who died in November 1638 at Penshurst in Kent, and was there buried, he had four sons and three daughters, of whom two sons and one daughter died young; the survivors being Sir William; Sir John, father of the Lord Palmerston; Martha, married 21 April 1662 to Sir Thomas Giffard of Castlejordan in the county of Kildare, Bart. who was buried at St. Audoen's 9 May the same year; and Mary, married first to Abraham Yarner, Esq. who 21 October 1661 was joined with his father Sir Abraham,

Blandesby, otherwise Blansby, parcel of the Honour of Pickering in the county of York, for the term of 40 years, if his two sons William and John, or either of them, should live so long, at the rent of 12l. a year, and 60l. a year for the improved profits of the premisses: Which park, with the appurtenances, 13 July 1665 he purchased for 400l. from James, Duke of York, whose possession it then was by the forfeiture of Sir Henry Danvers.—By patent, dated 29 July 1666, he had a grant of the lands of Palmerstown in the county of Dublin; and 20 May 1669 of Agha and other lands in the counties of Kilkenny, Meath, Westmeath, and Dublin, with other grants of lands under the acts of settlement; being also a trustee for the (49) officers.—Also 3 May 1672 were granted to him about 144 acres, formerly belonging to the *Phœnix Park* near Dublin; and 16 November 1675 divers houses, lands, fishings, with other hereditaments in or near the town of Chapelizod, the liberty of grazing six horses yearly in the Park, with several other lands in the Queen's county, and those of Cork and Tipperary.

* He wrote and published in a quarto volume, *The History of the Irish Rebellion;* " a piece (says Doctor Borlace in his history of
" that war) of that integrity, few can equal, none exceed; he
" having (as a Privy Counsellor) opportunity to view and consider
" all dispatches, rarely obvious to others; and being singularly en-
" tire and ingenuous, adventured then into the lists, when some
" dared scarce think on the attempt; a consideration (in reference
" to what he suffered) very considerable; though more own, that
" to this day (whatever had been barked against other accounts of
" the rebellion) never any thing was objected against his."

1 Rot. A°. 29 Car. II. 3. p. f.

ham, in the office of muster-master-general for life; and secondly 19 December 1693 to Hugh Eccles, Esq. who died in October 1716.

Sir William Temple, the eldest son, 10 March 1663 had a reversionary grant, after his father's decease, of the mastership of the rolls, and by his Majesty's letter 23 November 1677, received directions to pass patent for that office, which he did 8 December, and enjoyed until his surrender thereof 29 May 1696 to William Berkeley, Esq. (after Lord Berkeley) who resigned it in favour of the Right Hon. Thomas Carter.——On 31 January 1665 he was created a Baronet; was called into the Privy Council; and by his extraordinary learning, abilities and qualifications, did great honour to his name and family. His writings on various subjects * in the most delicate style, are justly admired; and his negotiations in foreign courts, from the year 1665 to 1679, sufficiently attest him an able statesman, and an instrument of great good to England.—In the parliament which met at Westminster 21 October 1678, he was member for the town of Northampton; and in April 1679 proposing to the King a change of the privy council, his Majesty took a resolution to form a new one, consisting of a number, not exceeding thirty, whose known abilities, interest and esteem in the nation, should render them free from all suspicions of either mistaking or betraying the true interest of the kingdom: Which resolution when he imparted, by his Majesty's order, to the Lord Chancellor Finch, he replied, *It looked like a Thing from Heaven fallen into his Majesty's Breast.* And the King valued himself so much upon it, that he acquainted the parliament of his having chosen such persons, as were worthy and able to advise him; and was resolved in all weighty and important affairs, next to the advice of his great council in parliament, to be advised by his privy council. Of which Sir William was chosen a member; and 14 March 1683 appointed by patent dated at Westminster one of the commissioners for the remedy of defective titles in Ireland.

He departed this life at his seat of Moor-park in January 1698, in the 70 year of his age; and, according to the directions of his will, his body was buried in Westminster-Abbey, and his heart in a silver box under the sun-dial in his

Family of Temple, Baronets.

---

* His Life, with a catalogue of his works, was published in 8vo. 1714, London.

his garden, opposite to the window, from which he used to contemplate and admire the works of nature, with his beloved sister the ingenious Lady Giffard; who, as she shared and eased the fatigues of his travels during his publick employments, so was she the chief delight and comfort of his retirement and old age.——He married Dorothy, second daughter of Sir Peter Osborne of Chicksands in Bedfordshire, Knt. Governor of Guernsey for 28 years, in the reigns of James and Charles I. by whom he had nine Children, but only one Son John lived to maturity, who married in France a rich heiress, viz. Mary, only daughter of Mr. Du-Plessis Rambouillet, a protestant of a very good family, and left two daughters, Elizabeth, married to John Temple of Moor-park, Esq. as will follow; and Dorothy, to Nicholas Bacon of Shrubland-Hall in Suffolk, Esq.

Sir John. Sir John Temple, the younger son of Sir John, Master of the Rolls, was appointed by patent 1 February 1660 Solicitor General of Ireland, and 19 March following one of the commissioners for the settlement of the kingdom. In 1661 he was returned to parliament for the town of Carlow, when it was ordered by the House of Lords, that he should have leave (as Solicitor-General) to be absent, and sit in the House of Commons, and the sessions being adjourned from 31 July to 6 September, he was that day chosen Speaker of the House of Commons, not having then attained the Age of thirty years.——After this he was knighted *, and being esteemed one of the best lawyers

of

---

* K. Charles II. had a great esteem for him; and by letters from Whitehall 8 March 1674, ordered a patent to pass to him and his heirs of so many lands, as should amount to 500l. a year; but instead thereof, Sir John, by petition, desired the King would please to grant him a long lease of several messuages, lands, and other hereditaments in Swords, Marshalstown, Rathcoole, Greenocke, Dunboyne, Drogheda, &c. in the counties of Meath and Dublin, which had been adjudged to John and Mary Taylor in tail, to be granted unto him for the term of 500 years, after the determination of the estate tail, at the rent of 18l. 10s. 6d. 3 farthings; together with the manor, castle, town and lands of Mobarnane, Rathmore, &c. in the county of Tipperary, to hold for the same term, at the rent of 7l. 5s. 9d. halfp.; with which the King complied, and he had a grant thereof 9 July 1681.——He also passed patent 13 May 1676, for the reversion of the towns and lands of Lackanshonen, Gurteen and many others in the county of Cork, after the expiration of a 41 years lease, made 24 February 1652 to Sir John Stephens, under the rent of 40l. a year.——And there being a highway

of the kingdom, was removed 4 March 1684 to the post of Attorney-General; in which he continued till the measures of K. James II. obliged him to leave Ireland, by whose parliament he and his brother were attainted, and had their estates sequestered; his estate being valued at 1700l. a year, but after the revolution he was restored to his employment 21 March 1690; was incorporated 3 March 1691 one of the company of the royal fishery in Ireland, consisting of a Governor, Deputy-Governor, and twelve committees; and was in such high esteem for his learning, probity and humanity, that Doctor Sheldon, Archbishop of Canterbury, made him this singular compliment, *That he had the curse of the gospel, because all men spoke well of him.*————He was frequently pressed to take upon him the highest offices in the law, but declining these eminent posts, he retired to the estate he had purchased at East-Sheen in Surry, where he ended his days 10 March 1704, in the 72 year of his age, and was buried in Mortlack church adjoining.

On 4 August 1663, he married Jane, Daughter of Sir Abraham Yarner of Dublin, Knt. Muster-Master-General (who was buried on the South side of St. Michan's church 29 July 1677) and had four sons and seven daughters.

William, baptized 21 April 1671, and buried by his grandfather Yarner 11 February 1678. (1)

Henry, created Viscount Palmerston. (2)

John, baptized 28 March 1680, was seated in right of his wife at Moor-Park near Farnham in Surry, and in May 1732 (3)

way through the *Phœnix-park*, which was very inconvenient, and the deer thereby daily trespassing upon the adjoining lands, whereby many of them were every year lost and destroyed, the King resolved to exclude that road and the lands lying on the south-side thereof, and that a wall should be made of lime and stone on the north-side of the road, from the park-gate next Chapel-Izod: which designed wall containing in length 527 perches, which, at the rate of 3 shillings and 9 pence the perch, (being the lowest rate, for which any one offered to build the wall) did amount to above 800l. besides the charge of digging the foundation and making the gates. This wall Sir John Temple proposed to build, eight feet high from the foundation, from the entrance of the park next Dublin, to Chapel-Izod, and to finish it in one year's time, from the first of May last past, in consideration of having 200l. out of the treasury in one year's time towards the charge, and a grant to him and his heirs of the lands, that should be left out of the park on the north-side of the high-way to Chapel-Izod, and what else belonged to the crown within the park, that should be excluded by the wall. Which proposal being accepted, the King granted him the said lands for ever, at the rent of one shilling, by patent, dated 9 August 1682, and he built the wall according to agreement.

1732 was made Auditor of the duties on hides, coffee tea, and chocolate. He endowed a charter proteſtan working-ſchool, built in 1737 upon his eſtate at Roundwood in the county of Wicklow, with 41 acres of land for ever, and ſubſcribed ten guineas annually towards its ſupport during his life.——He married, as before obſerved, Elizabeth, grand-daughter of Sir William Temple, Bart. died in February 1752, and had eleven children, of whom ſix died young, and his only ſurviving ſon William deceaſed 13 October 1732, ſo that he left four daughters, Mary, Jane, Henrietta, and Frances.

(+) William died an Infant.

(1) Daughter Catherine, baptized 4 September 1664, was firſt married 15 December 1681 to Charles Ward of Killough in the county of Down; and ſecondly to Charles King of Dublin, Eſq. made her will 4 June, proved 20 Auguſt 1694 [1], and died in June that year, having iſſue by the latter, who died in the year 1700, one ſon William, and three daughters, Mary, Frances, and Jane-Henrietta [2].

(2) Dorothy, baptized 7 November 1665, was firſt married on the ſame day 1682, [3] to Frances, ſon and heir to Sir Robert Colvil of Mount-Colvil in the county of Antrim, Knt. who dying in a ſhort time after, ſhe became the firſt wife of Sir Baſil Dixwell of Broom-Houſe in Kent, Bart. and died about the year 1718, without iſſue.

(3) Elizabeth, baptized 31 March 1667, died unmarried, and was buried 3 July 1663 in the veſtry of St. Michan's church.

(4) Mary, baptized 30 May 1668, was married 17 January 1683 to Thomas Flower of Durrow, Eſq. and was mother of William, created Lord Caſtle-Durrow [4].

(5) Lucy, baptized 29 Auguſt 1669 [5], never married.

(6) Jane, born in 1672, was firſt married to John, Lord Berkeley of Stratton, and by him, who died 27 February 1696, had an only daughter, that died when three years old; and 16 May 1700 ſhe became the ſecond wife of William Bentinck, Earl of Portland, by whom ſhe had two ſons and four daughters, viz. William, one of the nobles of Holland; Charles-John, an officer in the army of the States-General; Lady Sophia, married 24 March 1738 to Henry de Grey Duke of Kent, and died his widow 14 June

---

[1] Prerog. Off.   [2] Bill in Chancery.   [3] Articles dated the 4.
[4] See Viſcount Aſhbrook.   [5] St. Michan's Regiſtry.

14 June 1748; Lady Elizabeth, to Dr. Henry Egerton, Bishop of Hereford; Lady Henrietta, Viscountess Limerick; and Lady Barbara, married to William Godolphin, Esq. and died 1 April 1736.——Lady Portland was appointed 12 April 1718 governess to the three Princesses, eldest daughters of K. George II. as she was in January 1737, and in June 1738, to the younger Princesses, and dying in London 26 March 1751, aged about 80 years, was buried with her father.

Frances, married to William, Lord Berkeley, of Stratton (brother and heir to the aforesaid Lord John) Master of the Rolls in Ireland, and died in childbirth 16 July 1707, leaving issue by him, who died 26 March 1741, three sons and four daughters, of whom John the eldest son succeeded to the title. (7

Henry Temple, Esq. the elder son, was appointed 21 September 1680, with Luke King, Gent. Chief Remembrancer of his Majesty's Court of Exchequer in Ireland, during their respective lives, which, on the death of Mr. King, was renewed to him, and his son Henry for life, 6 June 1716. And his Majesty K. George I. was pleased to advance him to the Peerage, creating him by Privy-Seal, dated at St. James's 4 February, and by patent * at Dublin 12 March 1722, Baron Temple of Mount-Temple, and Viscount Palmerston of Palmerston, with the creation fee of 20 marcs, entailing the honours on the issue male of his brother John.—In 1727, and 1732, he was chosen member of parliament for the borough of East-Grinsted in Sussex, in 1734 for Bossiny in Cornwal, and in 1741 for Weobly in the county of Hereford.

Henry, 1 Viscount.

His Lordship married to his first wife Anne, daughter of Abraham Houblon of London, Esq.; and by her, who died 8 December 1735, had three sons and two daughters.

Henry, his heir apparent. (1)

R 2   John,

---

* The Preamble. Cum Reipublicæ utile sit, nobis pulchrum Virtutis præmiis benemerentibus decernere, nec minus deceat Memoriam bonorum Civium quam maxime cultam efficere, Henricum Temple, preclaris ortum majoribus, novis honoribus augere statuimus; cujus Avus et pater Muneribus in Hibernia publicis, ea fide, prudentia, et abstinentia functi sunt, ut adhuc etiam grato Animo recolant illius Regni Cives. Patruus vero, periculis et Negotiis ad exteras Gentes Legatus, felicem Regi et civitati operam navavit: atque Rebus gestis juxta ac scriptis, quid vivida vis Animi possit, ostendit. Virum itaque tali Stirpe natum, prisca Fide et Moribus antiquis præditum, cui nostra Dignitas et Salus publica maxime cordi sunt, libenter Titulis infignimus. Sciatis igitur, &c. (Rot. A°. 9. Geo. I. 2 p. f.)

(2) John, died an infant.

(3) Richard, member of parliament for Downton in Wilts, who 18 May 1748, married Henrietta, daughter of Thomas Pelham of Stanner in Sussex, Esq.; he died of the small-pox 8 August 1749, having had a son born 18 February before, by his said wife, who in February 1753, remarried with George, Lord Abergavenny [1].

(1) Daughter Jane, died 23 December 1728, in the 24 year of her age.

(2) Elizabeth, also died unmarried 3 June 1737, at East-Sheen.

11 May 1738, his Lordship married to his second Lady, Isabella, daughter of Sir Francis Gerard of Harrow on the Hill in Middlesex, Bart. widow of Sir John Fryer, Bart. Lord Mayor of London in 1721, but by her, who died 11 August 1762, near Hammersmith, he had no issue, and deceasing at Chelsea 10 June 1757, aged 84, was succeeded by his grandson, the eldest son of Henry Temple his heir apparent.

Henry. Which Henry 18 June 1753, married first the eldest daughter of Colonel Lee, by the Lady Elizabeth Lee his wife, sister to George-Henry, late Earl of Litchfield, who dying at Lyons in France, in October 1736 without issue, he married secondly 12 September 1738 Jane, youngest daughter of Sir John Barnard, then Lord Mayor of London, by her who died 13 August 1762 he had one son Henry; and he dying at his father's seat, 18 August 1740, was buried at Mortlack.

Henry, 2 Viscount. Henry the second and present Viscount Palmerston was born 4 December 1739, took the oaths and his seat in the House of Peers 22 October 1761 [2], was appointed a Commissioner of the Admiralty 16 September 1766, which he resigned in 1777 [3], served first in the British parliament for the borough of Eastlow in Cornwall, and at present represents Boroughbridge in the county of York.—In October 1767, he married first Frances, daughter of Sir Francis Poole of Poole-Hall in the county of Chester, Bart. She deceased at his Lordship's house in the Admiralty 2 June 1769 without issue; and in January 1783 his Lordship married to his second and present Lady, Mary, daughter of Benjaman Mee of the city of Bath, Esq. and has issue a son Henry-John, born 20 October 1784 [4].

TITLES.]

---

[1] Debret's Peerage and Lodge.   [2] Lords Jour. IV. 205.
[3] Beatson.   [4] Information of his Lordship.

BATEMAN, Viscount BATEMAN.

TITLES.] Henry Temple, Viscount Palmerston of Palmerston in the county of Dublin, and Baron Temple of Mount-Temple in the county of Sligo.

CREATION.] So created 12 March 1722, 9 Geo. I.

ARMS.] Quarterly, the first and fourth topaz, an eagle displayed, Diamond. The second and third, pearl, two bars, Diamond, each charged with three martlets, Topaz.

CREST.] On a wreath, a talbot sejant, diamond, gorg'd with a plain golden collar.

SUPPORTERS.] The dexter, a lion reguardant, pæan, viz. black powder'd with yellow. The sinister, a horse reguardant, pearl, with mane, tail, and hoofs, topaz.

MOTTO.] FLECTI, NON FRANGI.

SEAT.] Broadlands, near Rumsey in Hampshire, 79 miles from London.

BATEMAN, Viscount BATEMAN.

THE Name of Bateman is to be met with in ancient English history; as that William Bateman, Esq. was Sheriff of the counties of Hertford and Essex in 1395 (19 Rich. II.) and so continued for three years [1], and 20 October 1422 (1 Hen. VI.) John Bateman was made Chirographer, and keeper of the writs and rolls of the common-pleas office in this kingdom of Ireland.

But the Lord Viscount Bateman's family was anciently seated at Halesbrooke, near St. Omer's in Flanders, and hereof was Gyles Bateman, Esq. whose son Joas coming to

Gyles,
Joas,

[1] Fuller's Worthies.

to England, and settling in London, became a merchant of that city; where, by his justice and fair dealing, he acquired a good fortune; and dying in April 1704, was buried the 13 in the Dutch church in the Augustine Friars, London, leaving a successor Sir James, by his wife Judith. Which Lady founded an hospital at Upper-Towting in Surry, fronting the road to Mitcham, for the benefit of six alms-women, who have each the allowance of 2s. 6d. by the week, and half a chaldron of coals yearly, and are to be nominated by the heir of his family for ever. On a marble over the door is this inscription:

> THIS BUILDING WAS ERECTED AT
> THE CHARGE OF MRS. JUDITH
> BATEMAN, WIDOW OF JOAS
> BATEMAN LATE OF LONDON, ESQ.
> JULY, ANNO 1709.

Sir James. Sir James Bateman, being free of the Fishmongers company, was Sheriff of London for the year 1701 [1], being then one of the directors of the bank, and in 1710 and 1713 was chosen member of parliament for Ilchester in Somersetshire, as in 1714 he was for Eastlow in the county of Cornwall. In 1717 he served the office of Lord Mayor of London [2], which dignity of the chief magistrate of the chief city of Europe, was never so splendidly maintained by any lord mayor before; and *Janua patet, Cor magis*, might with great propriety and justice have been inscribed on the gates of Sir James Bateman's house.

He was a considerable benefactor to many publick charitable foundations, as the London work-house, Christ's Hospital, Greenwich Hospital, &c. In 1718 he was appointed Sub-Governor of the South-Sea Company, which project he formed in Q. Anne's reign, and brought to such perfection, that, contrary even to the expectation of its most sanguine well-wishers, the proprietors a little before his death (which happened 10 November 1718) were going to be gratified with a dividend upon the capital of little less than ten millions, sterling, notwithstanding the grievances and disadvantages, they laboured under on the part of Spain; and which a few days before his decease, Sir James caused to be drawn up in so exact a manner, as shews him to have been a perfect master of all the branches

[1] Seymour's Survey of London. [2] Maitland's hist. of Lon. II. 1196

branches of trade and commerce, which he improved both to the benefit of his country and himself; and to that end, no man was or could be more indefatigable; evident proofs whereof were his forming the aforesaid project, and the share he had, all K. William's time, in planning and negotiating, at home and abroad, the publick money schemes; and to credit the government of the King of England (under whose countenance and protection the merchant flourished) he by some thousand pounds outbid all other offers for a late forfeited estate; hence it was no wonder his death was visibly perceived and felt to be a publick loss.

He married Esther, youngest daughter and co-heir to John Searle of Finchley in the county of Middlesex, merchant of London, which Lady lies buried at Towting under an uncommonly beautiful monument, on the north-side of the altar, with this memorial.

> In the Memory of that excellent Person
> Dame Esther Bateman, youngest Daughter
> Of John Searle late of Finchley, Esq; the
> Prudent, virtuous, and dearly beloved Wife
> Of Sir James Bateman, Knt. and Alderman
> Of London, after eighteen Years spent in the
> Sacred Friendship of Matrimony, she departed this Life the 30th Sept. 1709 in
> The 35th Year of her Age, leaving four Sons,
> William, James, Richard, and Henry, and
> Three Daughters, Anne, Judith, and Elizabeth.
> Her Affectionate and Sorrowful
> Consort erected this Monument, in Testimony
> Of his constant Tenderness, Esteem and
> Respect for one of the best of Wives.
> Anno 1710.

One of the sons married a daughter of Sir Robert Chaplin, Bart. and of the daughters, Judith was married 10 April 1724 to Thomas Bourchier of Christian-Melford in the county of Wilts, Esq. and died 11 March following; Anne died unmarried; Elizabeth, was first married to Mr. Western of Ravenhail in Essex, by whom she had one son and two daughters, the one married in December 1754 to Mr. Duminelle, a native of France; and the other 10 February 1735 to John Hanbury of Kelmarsh in the county of Northampton, Esq.——Mr. Western deceasing 12 August

gust 1729, she re-married in February 1735 with George Dolliffe of Bedford-Row, London, Esq.

William, 1 Viscount. William Bateman, Esq. the eldest son, had all the advantages of education, and when abroad on his travels, made a better figure than some of the foreign princes, through whose dominions he passed; and collected, or rather engrossed every thing curious in painting, statuary, &c. returning an accomplished gentleman, and possessed of a noble fortune, he was not only called into the house of commons by his country for Leominster in 1722 and 1727, but fell under the notice of K. George I who was pleased to think him worthy of a place among the Peers of his kingdom of Ireland; and accordingly by Privy Seal, dated at St. James's 2 June, and by patent at Dublin 12 July 1725, created him Viscount Bateman and Baron of Culmore [1].——On 12 January 1731, he was created a Knight Companion of the Order of the Bath, installed 30 June following, and 22 February 1732 elected a Fellow of the Royal Society.

He married the Lady Anne Spencer, only daughter of Charles, Earl of Sunderland, by his second wife the Lady Anne Churchill, second daughter and coheir to John, Duke of Marlborough, and his Lordship dying at Paris in December 1744, left issue by her who died 19 February 1769, in Cleveland-Row St. James's, two sons, John his successor; and William, appointed 27 December 1745 Captain of a ship of war, and 10 April 1752 chosen member of parliament for Gatton in Surry; 17 April 1755 he married Miss Hedges of Finchley in Middlesex, and died 19 June 1783.

John, 2 Viscount. John, the second and present Viscount Bateman, in February 1745, was chosen to parliament for Orford in Suffolk, and served for the borough of Woodstock; and in July 1747 he was constituted L. L. and *Cust. Rot.* of the county of Hereford, appointed High Steward of Leominster, and sworn of the British Privy Council. On 10 July 1748 his Lordship married the daughter and coheir of John Sambroke, Esq. niece to Sir Jeremiah Sambroke, Bart. of Gubbins in the county of Hereford.

TITLES.] John Bateman, Viscount Bateman, and Baron of Culmore.

CREATION.]

---

[1] Rot. A°. 12 Geo. I. 1. p. f.

MONCTON-ARUNDEL, Viscount GALWAY.

CREATION.] B. of Culmore in the county of Londonderry, and V. Bateman in the kingdom of Ireland, 12 July 1725, 11 Geo. I.

ARMS.] Topaz, on a Fefs, Diamond, between three Mufcovy Ducks, proper, a Rofe of the Field.

CREST.] On a Wreath, a Duck's Head and Creft between two Wings erect, proper.

SUPPORTERS.] Two Lions, Pearl, gorg'd with plain Collars, Diamond, charg'd with a Rofe between two Fleurs de lis, Topaz, and Chains, of the latter, affixed to each Collar.

MOTTO.] NEC PRECE, NEC PRETIO.

SEATS. Totteridge near Barnet in the county of Hertford, 10 miles from London. Shobden-Court in the county of Hereford, 102 miles from London and Upper-Tooting near Stretham in the county of Surry, about 6 miles from London.

MONCTON-ARUNDEL, Viscount GALWAY.

THIS Family hath been of long duration in the north of England, and derives its defcent from Simon Moncton of Moncton near Boroughbriggs in the county of York, Efq. which Lordfhip his pofterity enjoyed until it was made a Nunnery in 1326 (20 Edw. II.) and called Nun-Moncton.——He had iffue two fons, Henry; and Simon, from whom defcended Thomas Moncton, who became poffeffed of the Lordfhip of Cavil in the faid county by marriage, as follows, (which his pofterity enjoyed in 1753).

Sir John Cavil of Cavil married Amy, daughter of Sir John Hotham, by whom he had an only daughter and heir Catherine, who being married to Sir Thomas Bofvile, had

had issue Sir Anthony Bosvile, living in 1398 (22 Rich. II.) and he marrying Elizabeth, daughter of Peter, and sister and heir to Thomas Samon (or Santom) had by her an only child Janet, married to William Moston of Hunscot in the county of Warwick, Esq. living in 1433 (12 Hen. VI.) by whom she had three daughters, their coheirs, Margaret, married to John Danby; Johanna, to Robert Meyler; and Elenor, the eldest, in 1454 (33 Hen. VI.) to the aforesaid

Thomas. Thomas Moncton, Esq. who, in her right, became Lord of Cavil, and had issue a daughter Joan, and two sons, Robert his heir, and John Moncton of the county of Lincoln, Esq. living 3 Hen. VIII. the father of Anthony Moncton of West-Rising in that county, who married Helen, daughter of William Haselwood of Hayton in Yorkshire, and had Robert his heir; John of Kelsey in Lincolnshire; Anthony; and Philip. Robert, the eldest son, resided at Wharam-Grange, and by Margaret, daughter of Thomas Booth of Bishop-Norton in Lincolnshire had William his heir, born in 1579, ancestor to the family of Wharam-Grange; Philip; Anthony; Mary; and Helen.

Robert. Robert Moncton, Esq. who succeeded his father Thomas at Cavil, lived in the reigns of Edw. IV. Hen. VII. and VIII. and in 1476 marrying Janet, daughter and heir

William. to Robert Lucas, Esq. had William his heir, a Captain of foot, who by letter from the Earl of Hertford, dated 12 August 1545, was charged in the King's name, to repair with his men to Newcastle upon Tyne before the 20 of that month, the realm being threatened with an invasion from the French and Scots. He married Anne, daughter of Sir Robert Aske of Aughton in the county of York, by whom he had three sons, Christopher his successor; Thomas of Lownsborough, living in 1584, who married Margery, daughter of John St. Quintin of Gainstead in Yorkshire, Esq. by his wife Margaret, daughter and coheir to Robert Buckton of Helmswell, Esq. and Robert, who died without issue.

Christopher. Christopher, who succeeded, married Frances, daughter of George Hussey of Duffield in Yorkshire, Esq. by whom

Marmaduke. he had Marmaduke Moncton of Cavil, Esq. who marrying Elizabeth, daughter of Matthew Wentworth of West-Brastane, Breton, or Elmshall, in the said county, Esq. by his wife Maud, daughter of Sir William Middleton of Stockel, in the West-Riding of Yorkshire, had issue one daughter Frances, and two sons, Sir Philip his heir; and
John

John Monćton of Garton in Yorkſhire, and Burland in Cheſhire, who died in 1622, and by Suſanna, daughter of William Berry of Waleſby in the county of Lincoln, Eſq. had four ſons, William, who died unmarried; John of *Melton Super Montem* in Yorkſhire, who being ſtrictly loyal to K. Charles I. ſerved in his army as a Major of foot, and by Mary daughter of Samuel Oldfield of Oldfield, near Rippon in Yorkſhire, had an only daughter married to John Fountayne, Eſq. in her right of Melton, by whom ſhe was grandmother of John Viſcount Galway.——The third ſon was Edmond, and the fourth Marmaduke, who was a captain of foot in the ſervice of K. Charles I; ſeated himſelf at Hodroyd in Yorkſhire, and aſſumed the ſurname of Berry by a ſpecial covenant, made on his marriage with Mary, daughter and heir to Richard Berry of Waleſby, Eſq by the laſt will of her father, by whom he had a daughter Elizabeth.

We now proceed with Sir Philip Monćton of Cavil, elder ſon of Marmaduke by Elizabeth Wentworth. He was born in 1576, honoured with knighthood in 1617 by K. James I; and marrying Margaret, daughter and coheir to Francis Sutton, Eſq. was father of Sir Francis Monćton, who, for his loyalty to his Prince, was knighted in York by Charles I. 25 January 1641, and married Margaret, daughter and coheir to Thomas Savile of Northgatehead in Wakefield (founder of Wakefield ſchool for 63 children, and deſcended from a very ancient and numerous family in the county of York) and ſiſter to Elizabeth, wife to Sir William Wentworth of Aſhby-Puerorum in the county of Lincoln, grandfather of Thomas, Earl of Strafford; by her he had

Sir Philip Monćton, of Hotheroid in Yorkſhire, knighted at Newcaſtle in 1643, who having ſerved ſome time in parliament for Scarborough, was reputed for his loyalty to K. Charles I. a delinquent, and for his ſervices to that unfortunate King underwent two ſeveral baniſhments, with divers impriſonments during the courſe of the war; his grandfather, father, and himſelf, being all at one time ſequeſtered by Cromwell; in conſideration whereof, K. Charles II. in 1653 wrote him a letter with his own hand (which was delivered by Major Waters) promiſing, in regard to his ſervices, that if it pleaſed God to reſtore him, he ſhould ſhare with him in his proſperity, as he had been content to do in his adverſity.

He

MONCTON-ARUNDEL, Viscount GALWAY.

He married Anne, daughter and heir to Robert Eyre of Highlow in the peak and county of Derby, Esq. Sheriff of that shire in 1658,* and had two sons, Robert, his heir; and William, who being Lieutenant of a man of War, was killed in 1706 before Barcelona.—Robert, the elder son, succeeding his father, was one of those patriots, who promoted the restoration of the laws and liberties of their country, by retiring into Holland, and returning with the Prince of Orange, when he came to accomplish that great work; who, after his accession to the crown appointed him a commissioner of trade and plantations; and he served in 1695 in parliament for Pontefract; and in 1701, for Aldborough in the county of York.—He married Theodosia, daughter and coheir to John Fountayne of Melton, Esq. by the only daughter of John Monćton of that place, by Mary, daughter of Samuel Oldfield of Oldfield, Esq. as already observed, and by her having two sons, John and Robert, the younger died unmarried; and

Robert,

John, 1 Viscount. The elder succeeding to the estate, was by the privy seal, of K. George I. bearing date 25 May 1727, directed to pass patent for the honours of Baron of Killard and Viscount Galway; but his Majesty dying before the patent could pass the seals, K. George II. by privy seal, dated at Kensington 24 June, and by patent at Dublin 17 July¹ 1727, was pleased to confirm those dignities to him and his heirs male, with the creation fee of 20 marcs.——In 1722 and 1727, he served in parliament for the borough of Clitheroe in Lancashire, and in April 1734 was chosen for Pontefract, as he was again in May 1741 and 1747; on 29 May 1734 he was appointed one of the commissioners of his Majesty's revenues in Ireland (which he resigned in April 1749)

* By this marriage a very great descent in blood was derived to the family. Her father was grandson to Robert Eyre of Highlow, Esq. by Catharine, daughter and heir to Sir Humphrey Ferrers, descended from Sir Thomas Ferrers of Tamworth, who was descended from William de Ferrers, Earl Ferrers Derby and Nottingham, by Margaret his wife, eldest daughter of Roger Quincy, Earl of Winchester, hereditary Lord High Constable of Scotland, by his wife Helen, daughter of Allan, Lord of Galloway, who died in 1233, by Margaret, eldest daughter of David, Earl of Huntingdon and Garroich, who died in 1210, by Maud, daughter and coheir to Hugh Kiviliec, Earl Palatine of Chester; which David, Earl of Huntingdon, was younger brother to Malcolm IV. and William the Lion, Kings of Scotland, sons of Henry, Prince of Cumberland, who died in 1152, before his father David I. the ninety-first King of Scotland.

¹ Rot. A°. 1. Geo. II. 1. p. f.

1749) and 4 October 1737 took his feat in the Houfe of Peers¹.—In October 1748 he was made Surveyor-General of his Majefty's honours, caftles, lordfhips, lands, woods, &c. in England and Wales; and 1 July 1749 created Doctor of Laws at the inftallation of the Duke of Newcaftle, Chancellor of the Univerfity of Cambridge; and his eldeft fon William, was at the fame time created A. M.

He married firft the Lady Elizabeth Manners, youngeft daughter of John, the fecond Duke of Rutland, and by her who died of a fever 22 March 1729, æt. 21, had iffue three fons and one daughter; William, his fucceffor; Robert, (Colonel of the feventeenth regiment of foot, and Lieutenant-Governor of Annapolis-Royal; in 1761 was appointed Governor and Commander in Chief of the province of New-York and a Major-General of his Majefty's forces; he was after appointed Governor of Berwick and Holy-Ifland; and 30 April 1770 was conftituted a Lieutenant-General); John, who died 2 October 1728; and Elizabeth, who died 23 July 1732.—In November 1734 his Lordfhip married Jane, daughter of Henry Weftenra of Dublin, Efq. by his wife Elinor, daughter of Sir Jofhua Allen; by her he had iffue, Philip, born 27 July 1738; Edward-Henry, born in Auguft 1739; Henry, born in February 1742; and a daughter Mary, born 10 April 1737, and married 17 April 1786, to Edmund, Earl of Cork and Orrery.

His Lordfhip departed this life 15 July 1751, and was fucceeded by his eldeft fon

William the fecond Vifcount who in 1747 was chofen member of parliament for Pontefract; appointed in December 1748, Receiver-General of his Majefty's crown and fee-farm rents in the counties of York, Durham, Northumberland, Cumberland, Weftmorland, Lancafter, &c.; and 5 April 1749 took his feat in parliament, as member for the borough of Thirfk, in Yorkfhire, having vacated his feat for Pontefract by accepting the aforefaid employment.—— On 12 Auguft 1747 he married Elizabeth, daughter of Mr. Villa-Real, a Lady of a very large fortune; affumed the name of Arundel * agreeable to the will of Lady Frances Arundel;

William, 2 Vifcount.

---

* 22 December 1769, a licence was granted to his Lordfhip, to his eldeft fon and his heirs male, and all others in the remainders as they fhall come into poffeffion of certain real eftates, devifed to them by the will

¹ Lords Jour. IV. 363.

Arundel; and deceased 18 November 1772, having had issue by his said Lady three sons and two daughters, viz. John, who died in 1769; William-Henry, and Robert Monckton Arundel succeffive Viscounts; Elizabeth, born 20 July 1754, married 2 September 1774, to Francis Sykes, Esq. and had issue Elizabeth, born 14 August 1775; and Charlotte-Frances, married 13 February 1785 to Anthony-Purlton Bennett of the county of Dorset, Esq.

William-Henry, 3 Viscount.

William-Henry, the third Viscount was born 15 May 1749, who dying 2 March 1774, the titles devolved on his brother

Robert, 4 Viscount.

Robert Monckton-Arundel, the fourth and present Viscount, who was born 18 August 1752; serves in the British parliament for the city of York, and was appointed Comptroller of his Majesty's houshold 27 March 1784.——In March 1779, he married Elizabeth, third daughter of Daniel Mathew of Felin-Hall in Essex, Esq.; and has issue, William-George, born 6 April 1782; Elizabeth; Mary; Maria-Henrietta; and a fourth daughter born 22 November 1784 [1].

TITLES.] Robert Monêton-Arundel, Viscount of Galway, and Baron of Killard.

CREATION.] B. of Killard in the county of Clare, and V. of the town of Galway, 17 July 1727, 1 Geo. II.

ARMS.] Diamond, on a cheveron between three martlets, topaz, as many mullets, of the field.

CREST.] On a wreath, a Martlet, as in the coat.

SUPPORTERS.] Two unicorns, ermine, gorg'd with Eastern crowns, topaz.

MOTTO.]

SEAT.] Serleby, in the county of Nottingham.

will of his aunt, the Lady Frances Arundel, deceased, widow of Richard Arundel, only brother of John, late Lord Arundel of Trerice, and sister to John, Duke of Rutland, to take upon them and to use respectively the name of Arundel, and also to bear the arms of Arundel, duly exemplified to them according to the law of arms, as they shall come into possession of the said estates. (Gazette.)

[1] Ulster Office.

WINGFIELD,

WINGFIELD, Viscount POWERSCOURT.

THIS ancient noble family is denominated from the manor of WINGFIELD in the county of Suffolk, where they had a seat before the Norman conquest, called Wingfield-Castle, which, though now in ruins, denotes its ancient grandeur; and Cambden writes [1], that this manor gave both a name and seat to a large family in those parts, famous for their knighthood and ancient gentility, which brought forth an abundance of renowned knights, and among the rest, two celebrated Companions of the Order of the Garter under the reign of K. Henry VIII.[2]. The family came early to be divided into several eminent branches, which from time to time afforded knights of the shire, and sheriffs of the county of Suffolk, many of whom were likewise famous in feats of arms.

   Mr. Anstis, Garter King of Arms, in his history of that order, makes a doubt whether the castle of Wingfield was the seat of the family, till the time of Sir John Wingfield, living in 1348, since (says he) the patronage and advowson of that place was in Sir Richard Brews in 1302, 1323, and 1329; but from the family pedigree it appears, that Robert Wingfield was Lord of Wingfield-Castle, so early as the year 1087, and left the same to his son, John de Wingfield, the father of another Robert, Lord of Wingfield, who married Joan, daughter of John Falstaff of the county of Norfolk, and had Thomas Wingfield, his successor there, who by Alice, daughter of Nicholas de Weyland of the said county, was father of Sir John Wingfield, Lord of Wingfield, and of Dynington, who married Anne, daughter of Sir John Peachy, and left four sons, Roger and Giles, who both died childless; Sir John; and Richard, whose issue failed in his grandson William, the son of his son Sir William Wingfield, Knt. Lord of Dynington [3].——Sir John Wingfield,

margin: Robert, John, Robert, Thomas, Sir John, Sir John,

33

---

[1] Britann. titl. Suffolk.   [2] Idem. titl. Northampton.
[3] Pedigree communicated to J. L. by Richard, Viscount Powerscourt.

Wingfield, Knt. who succeeded, died in the latter end of Edward II. or first of Edward III. leaving three sons by the daughter and heir of —— Honeypot; viz.

(1) Sir John Wingfield, who in 1348 presented as patron, to the church of Saxmondham in Suffolk, and was living in 1360, (25 Edw. III.)[1]—He married Alianor, daughter of Sir Gilbert de Glanville*, by whom he left an only daughter and heir Catharine, married to Michael Delapole, the first of that name, created Earl of Suffolk in 1385, to whom she carried the manors of Wingfield, Stradbrook, Silham, Tresingfield, Saxmondham, Netherhall in Saxlingham, and a very large estate in the counties of Suffolk and Norfolk[2], and by him, who died 5 September 1388 (12 Rich. II. had five sons, Michael, his successor, ancestor to the family of Suffolk, long extinct; Thomas, William, Richard, and John.

(2) Richard of Dynington †, who in 1325 was beyond sea with K. Edw. II. and in 1342 presented to the church of Dynington,

* So the pedigrees have it; yet Mr. Anstis observes, "there is an appearance she was the daughter of the afore-mentioned Sir Richard de Brews, who not only presented to several churches immediately before the advowsons thereof came into this family, but this same Lady, being co-executrix of her husband's will, ordered on the foundation of the collegiate church at Wingfield in 1362, prayers for the soul of Sir Richard de Brews, there named immediately after the father and mother of her deceased husband, and the name of Glanville is not mentioned in that bead-roll; and her younger son Thomas in his will devises silver-plates with the arms of Brews. To the mastership of this college Sir Michael Delapole presented in October 1379, in right of his Lady, sole daughter and heiress of Sir John Wingfield."——This observation is far from being conclusive; for had she been the daughter of Sir Richard Brews, she would probably have mentioned him *as her father*; and the latter part is a manifest contradiction; for, how could she have a younger son Thomas to devise silver-plates by his will, when Sir Michael Delapole presents to the mastership of Wingfield college in right of her only daughter and heir? It is more likely that she was the widow of Sir Richard de Brews, by whom she had her male issue, and (as the pedigrees of the family testify) daughter of Sir Gilbert de Glanville.

† Thus Mr. Anstis places him, but doubtless his authority has deceived him; for, in the pedigree communicated by Lord Powerscourt, he is made the son of Sir John by the daughter of Peachy, brother (not son) to Sir John, who married the daughter of Honeypot, and will be found to be the same person with Richard, mentioned in the text, whose issue failed, if the reader will observe the chronology, for in 1348 his elder brother's son presents in the church of Saxmondham, and in 1349 his own son presents to the church of Dynington.

[1] Anstis order of the Garter.   [2] Idem.

WINGFIELD, Viscount POWERSCOURT.

Dynington, as did his son Sir William in 1349 and 1355. Which Sir William was returned to parliament 50 Edw. III. and represented the county of Suffolk in the 5. 6. 7. 10. 13. and 14 years of Richard II. He made his will 17 July 1397, and lies buried under a fair stone in the chancel at Letheringham, adorned with the portraiture of an armed Knight, his feet resting against a lion, and this inscription;

> Hic jacet tumulatus Dominus Willelmus Wingfield Miles, Dominus istius Villæ, et patronus Istius Ecclesiæ qui obiit 1 Junii 1398.
> Cujus Animæ propitietur Deus [1].

He had two wives, Joan and Margaret; and by the former was father of William Wingfield, Esq. who left no issue by his wife Catharine, daughter of —— Wolfe, who survived him, and by her will, dated at Cotton in Suffolk 19 May 1418, gave 10l. to the parishioners there, to keep an anniversary for her husband on the feast of St. Bartholomew; and 20l. to be kept in a chest, to be lent to her tenants upon pledges, without interest, every borrower to say five *Pater nosters*, five *Aves*, and *Credo* for her soul, &c. She lies buried in the chancel at Dynington by her husband, with this broken inscription;

> Hic jacet Willelmus Wingfield, Armiger, et Katherina Uxor ejus Dominus et patronus istius Villæ Quorum animabus * .

(3) Sir Thomas.

Sir Thomas Wingfield, who by his marriage with Margaret, daughter and heir to William Bovile [3], and widow of William Carbonel, became seized of Letheringham in Suffolk, before 38 Edward III. in which church they and several of their descendants are interred, the family continuing there till after the revolution.——He makes his will there 17 July 1378 (proved 27 September) and orders himself

---

* This pedigree of Sir John and Richard is proved by an inquisition, taken after the death of this William in 1418 (6 Hen. V.) finding that William Delapole, Earl of Suffolk, was his next heir, and that by his death, without issue, several lands descended to him, among which was Denyngton; where that family founded an hospital. (Anstis. Lodge.)

[1] Weaver 755. [2] Idem. [3] Family Pedig.

self to be buried in the choir of that priory; that the sum of 46l. 13s. 4d. should be expended on his funeral; and devises several sums for the repair thereof, and of the parish church, with his silver cross and a vestment of the arms of the Earl Warren, &c.; devises to his son John 12 of his best silver dishes, 12 silver sawcers, 12 spoons, 6 silver pieces with the coat armour of Brews, and his golden cross, upon condition that it should not be sold or alienated, but remain to his heirs for ever; and gives him all his wardrobe with cloaths, armour, &c.—He had a daughter Margaret, married to Sir Thomas Hardell, and the said son

Sir John. Sir John Wingfield, Lord of Letheringham, who in some pedigrees, is said to have served the *Black Prince* in his French wars, and to have written his acts very learnedly; but it is more probable it was his uncle Sir John; However, he had the honour of Knighthood, when he presented to the free chapel of Stradbroke in 1389. He married Margaret, daughter of Sir Hugh Hastings [1] of Elsing in Norfolk, and by her (who was buried with him in the choir of Letheringham church [2]) had Sir Robert Wingfield, whose wife was Elizabeth, daughter of Sir John Russel [3] of Strensham in Worcestershire, and dying 3 May 1409, was buried with her at Dennington, with this inscription;

Sir Robert.

Hic jacet Dominus Robertus Wingfield miles et Elizabetha, Uxor ejus qui quidem Robertus obiit tertio die Maü 1409 [4],

Having issue Robert, William, Anne, and Margaret, a nun.

Sir Robert. Robert Wingfield, the elder son, was knighted by K. Henry VI. at Hereford, on Whitsunday in his fourth year, and attended on the Duke of Norfolk in an embassy, of whose lands he was made steward, for the good service he had done to the noble Prince his father and himself. He increased his estate by marriage with Elizabeth, daughter and coheir to Sir Robert Goussell, by his wife Elizabeth, daughter and heir to John Fitz-Allan, (brother to Richard, Earl of Arundel) by Eleanor his wife, daughter and heir to John, Lord Maltavers [5], and deceasing in the year 1431, was buried at Letheringham, having issue six sons, and a daughter Elizabeth, the first wife of Sir William Brandon, Knt. whose son Sir William, was father of Charles Brandon, Duke

---

[1] Pedigree.   [2] Weaver's funeral monuments, 755.   [3] Pedig.
[4] Weaver. 759.   [5] Sidney's state papers. I. 78.

Duke of Suffolk, who married Mary, daughter of K. Henry VII.—The sons were

 Sir John, his successor at Letheringham. (1)

 Sir Robert, who in 1450 (28 Hen. VI.) with Sir Henry Barlow, were Knights in parliament for the county of Hertford [1]; and 3 Edw. IV. had licence to perform feats of arms with Lewis de Brueil of France. He was Comptroller of that King's houshold, and died before 23 November 1481, having sepulture at Rushford, or Rushworth in Norfolk, leaving no issue by his wife Anne, daughter and heir to Sir Robert de Harling, and widow of Sir William Chamberlayne of Gedding in Suffolk, with whom he obtained a plentiful estate, and in October 1492 (or 1493) she took to her third husband John, Lord Scrope of Bolton, Knight of the garter. (2)

 Richard, died also without issue before the year 1509; as did (3)

 Sir Thomas, before 12 Edw. IV. whose wife was Philippa, daughter of John, Lord Tiptoft, sister to Edward, Earl of Worcester, coheir to her nephew Edward, Earl of Worcester, and widow of Thomas, Lord Roos.—He obtained a grant 23 January 8 Edward IV. of several lands belonging to that Lord, which were forfeited 1 of that reign, upon his attainder by act of parliament [2]. (4)

 William, who made his will the last day of February, 1509, directing his body to be buried under the same stone with his brothers Richard and Thomas, in the priory of Letheringham, devising lands for the maintenance of one canon there, of the order of St. Augustin, for fourscore years; to which he also bequeathed two basons and an ewer of silver, with a plain cup and cover; and gave divers sums to several priories, for a trental to be sung, in each, for his soul and those of his friends. (5)

 Sir Henry Wingfield, seated at Orford in Suffolk, who by his will, dated 21 February 1483, desired to be buried in the *Freres* of Orford, by his first wife Alice, his second Lady being Elizabeth, daughter of Sir Robert Rook [3], and she lies buried in Westhorp-chancel, Suffolk (where the aforesaid Charles Brandon, Duke of Suffolk had a seat) with this inscription; (6) Families of Upton and Tickencote.

  Orate pro Anima Elizabethæ Wingfield,
  Uxoris Henrici Wingfield, Militis.

[1] Chauncy's Hertfordshire.   [2] Collect.   [3] Pedig.

He had two sons; Thomas, Captain of Deal-Castle, who died without issue; and Sir Robert Wingfield of Orford, who in 1520 (12 Hen. VIII.) was present at the memorable interview that King had with Francis I. of France, between Guisnes and Ardres; when, in their march, the number of the French being perceived by the Lord Abergavenny to be double the number of the English, he was appointed with that Lord, the Earl of Essex, and Edward Poynings to take an account of the French King's attendants.—In 35 Hen. VIII. he had a grant of the manors of Upton and Ailesworth in the county of Northampton, with other lands thereabouts, having as Camden relates, *a fine house with lovely walks at Upton.* He married Margery, daughter of George Quarles, of Norfolk, and was father of Sir Robert Wingfield of Upton, who married Elizabeth, daughter of Richard Cecil of Burleigh, Esq. sister to the Lord Treasurer Cecil, and by her, who re-married with Hugh Allington, Esq. had four sons and two daughters; Sir Robert, his heir, John; Richard, who died unmarried; Peregrine; Dorothy, married to Adam Claypole of Latham in Lincolnshire, Esq; and Cicely.—John Wingfield of Tickencote in the county of Rutland, the second son, married first the daughter of Paul Gresham, and secondly the daughter of ———Thorold, and was father by the former of Sir John Wingfield (called in the Cromwell pedigree Sir Richard) of Tickencote, who married Frances, daughter of Edward, Lord Cromwell of Okeham, and had Sir Richard Wingfield his heir, John, Charles, and Francis of Gray's-Inn: Sir Richard was godson to Sir Richard Wingfield, Viscount Powerscourt, who by his will left him 100l. in token of his love. He married Elizabeth, eldest daughter of Sir William Thorold of Marston in Lincolnshire, Bart. and had two sons, John, Charles, and an only daughter, Frances, married to Eusebius Buswell, otherwise Pelsant, Esq. (by whom she had Sir Eusebius Buswell of Clipston in Northamptonshire, created a Baronet 5 March 1713). John Wingfield of Tickencote, Esq. the elder son, by Dorothy, elder daughter of Sir Thomas Mackworth of Normanton in the county of Rutland, Bart. (who died in 1694, by his first wife Dorothy, daughter of Captain George Darrell of Cale-Hill in Kent) was father of John Wingfield, Esq. who married Elizabeth, daughter and coheir to Sir John Oldfield of Spalding in Lincolnshire, Bart. and by her who died 3 March 1769, had John, his successor, at Tickencote, (which after became

the

the seat of Thomas Orby-Hunter, Esq.); Anthony, who died a student at Cambridge; Richard and Oldfield, who both died young; Thomas, Rector of Market-Overton, who married the daughter of William Julien, Esq.; Oldfield, a merchant in Hull; Elizabeth, Margaret, Dorothy, and Anne [1].

Sir Robert Wingfield, who succeeded at Upton, was burgess in parliament for Stamford in the reign of James I.; married the daughter of Sir John Crooke [2], and was father of another Sir Robert, who married Elizabeth, third of the four daughters and coheirs of Sir Roger Aston, Gentleman of the Bedchamber to K. James I. by Mary, daughter of Alexander Steuart, Lord Ochiltree, and by her had Sir Mervyn Wingfield, the father of Sir Henry of Upton, who married in France, and died without issue; and a daughter [3].

We now return to the eldest son of Sir Robert by Elizabeth Gousell, viz. Sir John Wingfield, Lord of Letheringham. who had a licence in 1437 (15 Hen. VI.) to erect a chantry in Stradbroke; in 33 of which reign he was Sheriff of Norfolk and Suffolk, and had a privy seal, dated 23 November, for 60l. to defray the expences thereof. He was knighted in the tower of London 26 June 1461 (1 Edw. IV.) and in 1471 was again Sheriff of those counties, being then one of the King's privy council, for which attendance he had a privy seal, 7 October, for 40l. a year, as had been accustomed to other Knights in such cases.——In 1477 he was a commissioner to treat with the French ambassadors at Amiens; and, in all probability, the broken inscription in Letheringham-church (whose fragments are preserved in *Weaver*'s funeral monuments) relates to his death on 10 May 1481.—He married Elizabeth, daughter of Sir John Fitz-Lewis of Essex, by Anne, eldest daughter of John Montacute, Earl of Salisbury, and by her (who in her will, dated 14 July 1497, and proved 22 December 1500, directs her body to be buried near her husband's tomb in Letheringham) had issue three daughters, Anne; Elizabeth, married to —— Itchingham; and the younger to —— Brews, by whom she had issue two sons, Thomas and John.—Sir John had also twelve sons, viz.

Sir John.

Sir John Wingfield of Letheringham, sheriff of the counties of Norfolk and Suffolk in 1 Rich. III. and 8 Hen. VII. who married Anne, daughter of the Lord Audley, and had three

(1) Family of Letheringham,

[1] Pedigree.   [2] Idem.   [3] Pedig.

three sons and four daughters; of whom Sir Anthony Wingfield, the eldest son, was Esquire of the King's body, and commanded to receive the honour of a Knight of the Bath at the designed coronation of Edward V. He was of the privy council to K. Henry VII. and appointed one of the commissioners to muster the archers of Suffolk for the relief of Bretagne; was knighted by K. Henry VIII. for his conduct at Therouenne and Tournay; after which he was made comptroller of the houshold, and by that title installed 8 May 1541 a Knight of the Garter at Windsor. He was also constituted Vice-Chamberlain of the houshold, Captain of the guards, and executor of that King's last will, who left him a legacy of 200l. and assigned him of council to his son K. Edward VI [1].

He married Elizabeth, eldest daughter of Sir George Vere, sister and coheir to John, the fourteenth Earl of Oxford, and had issue, five sons, Sir Robert; Charles, and Anthony, both died childless, the former having married a daughter of —— Rich, and the latter, a daughter of —— Blenerhasset [2]; Henry, (who married a daughter of —— Bacon, and had Robert, who by his first wife, the daughter of —— Rosers, had Anthony, and by his second wife, the daughter of —— Drake, had a son Edmond); and Richard, who by the daughter and heir of —— Hardwicke, was father of Sir John Wingfield, who, with Sir Richard, and Sir Edward Wingfield, Knts. in 1596 went commanders in the fleet fitted out against Spain, consisting of 150 ships; with 6360 land forces on board, under the command of Robert Earl of Essex, and Charles, Lord Howard of Effingham, Admiral of England; Sir John was Quarter-Master-General of this army, Sir Richard a Colonel, and Sir Edward a Captain of 1000 gentlemen volunteers. In this expedition *Cales* was taken, and Sir John lost his life, being the only Englishman of note that perished, and was honourably interred with a military funeral in the principal church [3].——He married Susan, daughter of Richard Bertie, Esq. (by his wife Catharine, daughter and heir to William, Baron Willoughby of Eresby, widow of Charles Brandon, Duke of Suffolk) sister to Peregrine Bertie, Lord Willoughby of Eresby, ancestor to the late Duke of Ancaster, and widow of Reginald Grey, Earl of Kent, by whom he had a son Peregrine, born in Holland, in 1583 [4].

[1] Weaver. 756.   [2] Pedig.
[3] Camden's Annals of Q. Eliz.   [4] Pedig.

We now proceed with Sir Robert Wingfield, eldeſt ſon of Sir Anthony, Knight of the Garter, who ſucceeded to the eſtates of Letheringham, &c. and being Captain of the guard to K. Edward VI. was ſent by the Lords of the council to Windſor (in 1549) to induce the King to remove his uncle Edward Seymour, Duke of Somerſet, Lord Protector, when he ſo well perſuaded his Majeſty, both of the loyal affection of the Lords to him, and of their moderate deſires againſt the Duke (who was then preſent) that the King conſented to his removal, and a guard was ſet upon him.—He was knighted in the reign of Q. Mary; married Cicely, daughter of Thomas, Lord Wentworth of Nettleſted [1], and had three ſons; of whom Sir Anthony, the eldeſt, was ſheriff of Suffolk 39 Eliz. after which he was knighted, and leaving no iſſue by Mary, daughter of John Bird of Denſton in Suffolk, Eſq. was ſucceeded by his brother Thomas, who was alſo a Knight, and by his ſecond wife, a daughter of Sir Drue Drury of Riddleſworth in Norfolk, Knt. left one ſon Sir Anthony Wingfield, of Goodwins in Suffolk, created a Baronet 17 May, 1627, who died about the year 1638, æt. 38, and by Anne, daughter of Sir John Deane of the ſame county, Knt. was father of Sir Richard Wingfield, Bart. who (the old manſion being decayed) built and reſided at Eaſton in Suffolk, and married firſt the daughter of Sir John Jacob, Bart. and ſecondly, the daughter of Sir John Winter of Lidney in Glouceſterſhire, by each of whom he left a ſon, viz. Sir Robert, the third Baronet, who dying unmarried, his half-brother Sir Henry ſucceeded; who ſerving in the French army, had his leg ſhot off by a canon-ball at Dulward in Loraine, and was there buried in 1677, leaving iſſue by Mary, eldeſt daughter of Mervyn, Earl of Caſtlehaven, two ſons; Sir Henry, who, being a minor, was educated by his mother in the Romiſh religion, and following the fortunes of K. James II. ſold his eſtates of Letheringham, Eaſton, &c. to the Earl of Rochford in K. William's Reign, and dying without iſſue male, in 1712, was ſucceeded by his brother Sir Mervyn Wingfield, who married Mary, daughter of Theobald Dalton of Grenan in the county of Weſtmeath, Eſq. which lady died in childbirth, leaving an only daughter Mary, married in 1731 to Francis Dillon, Eſq. eldeſt ſon of William Dillon, Eſq. of Proudſton and Kilmainham in the county of Meath, and ſhe died 20 February 1765, leaving iſſue [2].

Sir

---

[1] Pedig.   [2] See title V. Dillon.

(2) Sir Edward Wingfield was the second son of Sir John of Letheringham; and to him K. Henry VII. 20 February 1492 granted an annuity of 20l. for life. He left no issue by his wife Anne, Countess of Kent.

(3) Henry, a Priest, presented by his father in 1480 to the rectory of Baconsthorp in Norfolk, and was also rector of Rendlesham in Suffolk. He died in the year 1500, and by his will, dated 5 August, and proved 22 December that year [1], orders a tomb to be made for himself in the church-yard of Letheringham, upon which the *Palmes* might be laid in passion week.

(4) Sir John Wingfield, the younger, of Dunham-Magna in Norfolk, had a grant from K. Henry VII in his second year of an annuity of 40l. for life. He married Margaret, daughter of ―― Durward, by whom he had Thomas, his heir; and William, an Augustine canon at the surrender of the monastery of Westacre in that county, who was after instituted to the rectory of Burnham-thorp, of which he was deprived in the beginning of Q. Mary's reign for being married, and was oblied to be divorced. He died in 1556, leaving two sons, Thomas of Winch in Norfolk, and Anthony.—Thomas, the eldest son of Sir John of Dunham, succeeded there; and by Elizabeth, youngest daughter of Sir Thomas Wodehouse of Kimberley in the said county, Knight of the Bath, had two sons, Roger of Dunham, who married the daughter of ―― Golding; as did John the daughter of Thomas Townshend, and they both left issue female; of whom Elizabeth (daughter of Roger) was married to Thomas, son and heir to Henry Poole of Dichling in Sussex, Esq. and by him, who died 13 February 1609, had one son and two daughters [2].

(5) William was Sewer to Henry VII. married Joan, daughter of Thomas Walgrave, and died 4 December 1491, without issue *.

(6) Sir Thomas, some time Captain of Deal-Castle, was slain in the battle of Bosworth, on the part of Henry VII. without issue.

(7) Sir Robert, bred up by his aunt the Lady Scrope, became a Knight of the Holy Sepulchre in Jerusalem, Mareschal of Calais; Lieutenant of that Castle, Deputy of the Town and the Marches, and lastly Mayor of that place. He was of

---

* Mr. Anstis, in his history of the Garter, says, he left posterity; but Lord Powerscourt's pedigree makes him die childless.

[1] Collect. [2] Pedig.

of the privy council to Henry VIII. in whose third year he went ambassador with the Bishop of Winchester, (or Worcester) to the Council of Lateran, and the next year to the Emperor; when he procured out of the archives of the city of Constance, and caused to be printed at Lovaine, *Discerptatio super Dignitate et Magnitudine Regnorum Britannici et Gallici, habita ab utriusque Oratoribus et Legatis in Concilio Constantiensi.* He was also ambassador to Pope Leo; was commissioned 21 February 1516 to treat with the Swifs, and in 1523 went in the army, sent to France under the command of the Duke of Suffolk.—By his will, dated 25 March 1538, and proved 12 November 1539, he orders himself to be buried in the north-aile of St. Nicholas's church in Calais, where he had built a place for his sepulture, if he should chance to die in that town, or the marches thereof; but if in Norfolk, within ten miles of his college of Rushforth, then to be buried in the midst of a chapel on the south-side in that college, where the body of his uncle and godfather Sir Robert Wingfield, comptroller of K. Edward the IV. house, lay; and that upon his grave be placed a marble stone, with a cross of Jerusalem thereon; and in case he should die in London, then to be buried in the church of St. Peter, in which parish his house stood. He died 18 March 1538, without issue by his lady Jane Clinton.

Sir Walter married the daughter of —— Mac-William, and died also without issue [t]. (8)

Lewis, Ancestor to the Viscount Powerscourt. (9)

Edmond, who married Margaret, the Widow of John Ashfield, and dying in, or about, 1530, left a son John, the father of Richard Wingfield, who died childless. (10)

Sir Richard Wingfield, a commander with his brother Robert, against the Cornish rebels, 12 Hen. VII. appointed by K. Henry VIII. Mareschal of the town and marches of Calais 14 November 1511; and the next year, being Knight of the King's body, and of the privy council, was one of the ambassadors to treat with the Pope and the Emperor.—On 6 August 1513 the Mareschalship of Calais was regranted to him, and Sir Robert his brother, during their lives; and that year, being Mareschal of the army, he was created a Banneret at the siege of Tourney, and joined with Sir Gilbert Talbot in the deputyship of Calais. —He was sent into Flanders ambassador to Charles, Prince of (11) Family of Kimbolton.

[t] Pedig.

of Spain; and appointed, with the Duke of Suffolk, to receive the Queen dowager of France, to settle her dowry, and conduct her into England.—On 10 October 1515 he had a licence to import 100 hogsheads of wine; 4 March 1518 a grant, in reversion, of divers manors in Suffolk, after the decease of Elizabeth, Countess of Oxford; 15 May 1519 the annuity of 50l. payable by the treasurer of the chamber, with another of 200l. for his services; and was one of the four *sad and ancient Knights* (as *Stow* expresseth it) who in 1520 were made gentlemen of the King's bedchamber; the next year he was one of Cardinal Wolsey's retinue, to meet the Emperor in Flanders.— He was also Chancellor of the dutchy of Lancaster; and 23 April 1522 having the honour to be elected Knight of the Garter in the same scrutiny with Ferdinand, afterwards Emperor, he was installed 11 May at Windsor; having obtained, in *that* and the ensuing year, a grant of the castle of Kimbolton in the county of Huntingdon (where Q. Catharine some time resided, after her divorce; it being her jointure, and upon the old foundations of which Sir Richard built new lodgings and galleries) the manors of Swynshead and Hardwicke, with the advowsons of several abbies and priories, forfeited by the Duke of Buckingham.—That year, with Sir William Sandys, Knight of the Garter, he led the rear of the army sent into France; and attended on the Emperor into Spain with the Lord Admiral; on his return from whence he was present at the burning of Morlaix; and in 1525, with Cuthbert, Bishop of London, was sent ambassador into Spain, where he died at Toledo 22 July, and was buried with great solemnity in the church of the Friars observants of St. John de Pois (where none were interred but by the special command of the Emperor) by the directions of Navera, King of Arms of Spain, and Christopher Barker, Richmond-Herald, after Garter King of Arms, and Knight of the Bath.

He married to his first wife Catharine, youngest daughter of Richard Woodville, Earl Rivers, coheir to her brothers, and widow first of Henry Stafford, Duke of Buckingham, and after of Jasper of Hatfield, Duke of Bedford, by which marriage Sir Richard became great uncle to K. Henry VIII. His second wife was Bridget, daughter and heir to Sir John Wiltshire, Comptroller of Calais, by whom Stone-castle near Gravesend came into the family, and she remarried with Sir Nicholas Hervey, grandfather

father by her to William, created Lord Hervey of Kidbroke.———His issue were four sons and four daughters; Charles, his heir; Thomas, who left posterity; Jacques; Laurence, who left issue; Catherine, Cecil, Mary, and Elizabeth.

Jacques Wingfield, the third son, was made Master of the Ordnance, and Munition in Ireland; sworn of the privy council to Q. Elizabeth; and 27 January 1560 had a commission to execute martial law in the territories of the Byrnes and Tooles, and the marches of Dublin.—He accompanied the L. D. Grey in his expedition to Glandelogh, against certain rebels under the command of Fitz-Eustace and Pheogh Mac-Hugh; as he did the L. D. Sidney, in 1569, to Cork, in order to subdue Sir Edmund Butler and his brethren; when the deputy encamping (19 August) on the further side of the castle of Ballymartyr, did, by the advice of this Jacques and Mr. Thomas Ellyott, master-gunner, remove his camp to the other side [1]. And in 1575 he was in the same deputy's army, sent to the North against Sorley-Boye and the Scots, who had assaulted the garrison of Carrickfergus *.

Charles Wingfield of Kimbolton, Esq. the eldest son, was 12 years old at his father's death, and marrying the daughter of —— Knowles, had Thomas, his successor, who by Honora, daughter of Sir Anthony Denny [2], Privy Counsellor to K. Henry VIII. had Sir Edward of Kimbolton, who about the latter end of Q. Elizabeth's reign married Mary, fifth daughter of Sir James Harrington of Exton in the county of Rutland, and had Sir James his heir, father by the daughter of William Bowden, Esq. of Sir Edward-Maria Wingfield, Knt. who sold the estate of Kimbolton to the Duke of Manchester's ancestor, which

still

---

* Mr. Anstis, Garter King of Arms, writes, that he died without issue; but it appears from his nuncupative will, registered in the Prerogative-office, Dublin, that on 31 August 1587, being very weak, he declared his said will in the parish of St Giles in the Fields, London, in the presence of Sir George Carew, Edward Darcy of the Queen's privy chamber, and others, when calling his son Thomas to him, and his said son beseeching him to discharge the love of a father towards him, for his advancement and living, according to his former promise and intention, he said, taking him by the hand, *Here, take you all, you all, I give you all, and do make you mine executor*; therewith lifting up his other hand. (Lodge.)

[1] Collect.   [2] Pedig.

still continues the seat of that noble family, and died without issue [1].

(12) Sir Humphrey Wingfield, the youngest son, educated in Gray's-Inn, where he was Lent reader 8 Hen. VIII. and four years after Sheriff of Norfolk and Suffolk; being chosen Speaker of the House of Commons 24 Hen. VIII. and 29 June 1537 (being then a Knight) had a grant of the manors of Overhall and Netherhall in Dedham, Essex, and the manor of Crepinghall in Stutton, near Brantham in Suffolk. He resided at Brantham; married a daughter of —— Wiseman, and died in 1546, having issue a daughter Anne, who married Alexander Newton; and a son Robert Wingfield, Esq. father by Bridget, daughter of Sir Henry Pargeter, of Humphrey Wingfield, who married the daughter of Sir Thomas Neville, and had issue Paul, who by Jane Turpin, had Humphry, father by a daughter of Sir Paul Breuse, Knt. of John Wingfield of Brampton or Brentham, who married a daughter of Mr. Herick [2], and dying in 1546, gave rise to that branch, and to the Wingfield's of Winston in the same county.

Lewis. We now proceed with Lodowic, or Lewis, the ninth son of Sir John Wingfield, by the daughter of Sir John Fitz-Lewis. He settled in Hampshire, and married the daughter of Henry Noon [3], by whom he had three sons, John, who died without issue; Sir Richard; and George, from whom the present Lord Powerscourt derives.

Sir Richard. Sir Richard Wingfield, the second son, was Governor of Portsmouth in the reign of Q. Elizabeth, and married Christian, only daughter of Sir William Fitz-William of Miltown, sister to Sir William, L. D. of Ireland, and by her, who after married George, fifth son of Sir Henry Delves of Dodyngton in Cheshire, had two sons, Sir Richard, and John, who 25 July 1621 was made Dean of Kilmacduagh, and died without issue.

Sir Richard, Viscount Powerscourt. Sir Richard, from his youth, was brought up in the profession of a soldier, his first setting out being in this kingdom under his uncle the Lord Deputy, where he behaved well against the Irish rebels; and afterwards by his merit advanced himself to the degree of a Captain in Flanders, whence being sent into France and Portugal, he was made Lieutenant-Colonel to Sir John Norris's regiment; in which stations having performed many services, he returned to Ireland, where, in 1595, he was wounded in the elbow

[1] Pedigree.   [2] Idem.   [3] Idem.

bow by a musquet-shot, in an expedition against Tyrone, and was so indefatigable in suppressing the insurrections and incursions of the Irish, that in recompence thereof, he was knighted in Christ-church 9 November the same year, by the L. D. Russel.——After this he was made a Colonel in the expedition to Cales, where his bravery was very conspicuous, and when that service was ended, returning to Ireland, he exposed himself to many dangers, under the said Sir John Norris, president of Munster, received many wounds, and acquired great honour; so that the Queen thinking such service and merit worthy a reward, and the office of Mareschal of Ireland having been a good time void by the death of Sir Richard Bingham, she appointed him to that office 29 March 1600, with fifty horsemen for the execution thereof, a company of foot, and admitted him into her privy council.——The next year he was sent by the L. D. into Leix, to prosecute Tyrrell, and his adherents [1], and was afterwards dispatched from Kilkenny, to draw forces out of *the pale*, to assist at the siege of Kingsale, as Sir John Berkeley, Serjeant-Major, had done from the frontiers of Leinster and Conaught [2]; with which arriving at Cork 9 October 1601 [3], they were sent the next day with some horse and foot, to view and chuse a fit ground near Kingsale, where the army might sit down to besiege that place, then in the hands of the Spaniards under Alphonso O Campo [4].——The siege being successfully carried on by the L. D. Mountjoy, Sir Richard, with the Earls of Thomond and Clanrickard, 2 January 1601 signed the articles of capitulation, made between the L. D. and Don Juan D'Aquila, Captain, Camp-Master-General, and Governor of the King of Spain's army, for the quitting of Kingsale, and all places held by him in the kingdom [5].—— The consequence of which great victory was, the retaining Ireland in obedience to the crown of England; banishing the Spaniards; driving Tyrone back to his lurking places in Ulster; forcing O Donel to fly into Spain; dispersing the rebels and establishing peace throughout the kingdom.

Q. Elizabeth deceasing not long after, and K. James succeeding to her throne, his Majesty 20 April 1603 renewed to Sir Richard the post of Mareschal of the army, and Knight-Mareschal of Ireland, calling him also into his privy

---

[1] Moryson's hist. Ireland.   [2] Pacata Hibern.   [3] Moryson.
[4] Pacata Hibern.   [5] Cox. 413. &c.   [6] Cambden's Annals.

vy council.—In 1608 Sir Cahir O Dogherty raising new commotions in Ulster, and among other outrages, burning the new city of Londonderry, Sir Richard Wingfield, and Sir Oliver Lambart were sent from Dublin (1 May) with a small body of men to suppress him; and no sooner did they enter the territory of Tyrconnel, than the traitors withdrew into their fastnesses, whom they diligently pursued and harrassed; and 14 June taking Sir Neile O Donel prisoner in the camp at Raphoe, conveyed him on board a King's ship lying in the harbour; and coming to a battle, Sir Richard slew O Dogherty; took Castledoe; and dispersed his rebellious followers *¹.

After these and many other noble services in war, he served in the parliament of 1613 for Downpatrick, and 4 March that year was joined with Thomas Jones, Archbishop of Dublin and Lord Chancellor, in the government of the kingdom, as he was again 4 May 1622, with the Lord Chancellor Elye.—In 1615 he was appointed, by his Majesty's commission of instructions of 20 May, one of the council to the Earl of Thomond, president of Munster, who were to sit and advise with him, then and whenever they should have occasion to repair into the province. He also commanded a troop of horse and company of foot with the pay of 15 shillings a day upon the establishment; and his Majesty (as himself expresseth it) taking especial notice of the most acceptable services, so valiantly performed by him in divers parts of the kingdom, but especially at the siege of Kingsale, where Q. Elizabeth's army under his conduct and command, as Marshal thereof, did give that memorable overthrow to the arch-traitor Tyrone, whereupon his hopes being frustrate, the general peace of that kingdom hath since most happily ensued; was pleased of his own

---

* This signal service was rewarded 29 June 1609, with a grant to him and his heirs of the lands of Powerscourt, with all the lands, tenements and possessions, lying within the whole province of Fercullen, containing five miles in length, and four in breadth, with all their appurtenances in the county of Wicklow, at any time reputed to belong thereunto; which 25 May 1611 were erected into a manor, at the crown-rent of 6l. Irish.——Also 3 December 1610 he had a grant of the castle and lands of Benburb, &c. in the county of Tyrone, containing 2000 acres, at the rent of 16l. a year from Easter 1614, which were created into the manor of Benburb, with many privileges: And in the plantation of the county of Wexford, many lands, erected into the manor of Wingfield, were granted to him, with 800 acres for a demesne, and a fair on 24 August at Annaghs.

¹ Cox II. 14.

own accord, in consideration thereof, and in regard of his other merits, which were many, to confer upon him the honour and dignity of Viscount of Powerscourt by privy seal, bearing date at Westminster 1 February, and by patent 19 of that month 1618 *.

On 15 July 1624 he was made one of the commissioners and keepers of the peace in the provinces of Leinster and Ulster, during the L. D. Falkland's absence to oversee the late plantations, and settle the country.—On 30 November 1631 he makes his will, and amongst other bequests, gives to Francis, second son of his loving cousin Sir Edward Wingfield, 1000l. to be put forth to interest, for his maintenance, until he came to the full age of 22 years, and if he died without issue, the same to his brothers, Lewis, Anthony, Edward, and Cromwell in like manner, remainder to their father, Sir Edward, whom he made executor, and residuary legatee, hoping that he would see all things performed according to his intent and true meaning, as

---

* The Preamble. Cum in omni republica viri virtute militari præstantes præ cæteris honorari et splendidis titulis ornari semper meruerunt, quod non solum tempore belli republicæ adjumento sed tempore pacis ornamento esse solent. Cumque dilectus & fidelis consiliarius noster Richardus Wingfield, Miles, marischallus exercitus nostri in hoc regno Hiberniæ dignissimus, ab ineunte ætate inter arma versatus primum in hoc regno Hiberniæ adolescens ac tiro contra rebelles animum fortem ac indolem bellicosam ostendit. Deinde in Belgis centurio creatus, postea in Gallia & Portugallia vice colonellus Domini Johannis Norreis clarissimi ac fortissimi ducis, & in expeditione Gaditana colonellus factus, se gentibus exteris strenuum & formidabilem militem demonstravit. Tum deinde in hoc regnum Hiberniæ reversus, sub eodem illustri duce Johanne Norreis regalem exercitum tunc imperante semper in his versatus, continuis periculis se objiciebat; in quibus cum multis vulneribus, magnam gloriam adeptus est. Deinceps vero per serenissimam sororem nostram Elizabetham Angliæ reginam, marischallus exercitus sui potentissimi in hoc regno constitutus, sub illustrissimo prorege, Carolo Domino, apud Kinsaliam nequissimi proditoris Comitis de Tyrone & aliorum rebellium copias omnes congregatas penitus fregit & fudit. Postea denique, dicta rebellione de Tyrone extincta et universa pace in hoc regno stabilita, cum audacissimus proditor O Doghertie novam civitatem de Derry incendio destruxisset, magnosque tumultus in Ultonia concitasset, prefatus marischallus noster parva manu militum dictum O Doghertie in aperto prælio occidit, cohortesque illi adhærentes subito dissipavit. Cumque etiam post multa alia præclara servitia in bello per ipsum peracta, tempore pacis in administranda republica nobis non defuit, ac postremo locum Justiciarii seu summi gubernatoris dicti regni nostri Hiberniæ una cum reverendissimo Archiepiscopo Dubliniensi in absentia Arthuri Domini Chichester deputati nostri dicti regni nostri dignissimi supplevit. Sciatis quod &c. (Rot. pat. a°. 16°. 4°. p. D.)

as his trust was in him.——His Lordship married Elizabeth, daughter and heir to Robert Meverell of Throwley in the county of Stafford, Esq. (widow of Edward, Lord Cromwell of Okeham [1], who died 24 September 1607, and was buried in Downe church abbey; whose son Thomas, Lord Cromwell, was father of Wingfield, and Vere-Essex, Earls of Ardglass) dying without issue 9 September 1634, the title became extinct; and the estate devolved to his said cousin and next heir male Sir Edward Wingfield, son of Richard, and grandson of George, the third son of Lewis Wingfield, who settled in Hampshire, as before observed.

George. Which George Wingfield, Esq. married as we presume
Richard. Ratcliffe, youngest daughter of Sir Gilbert Gerard, master of the rolls to Q. Elizabeth, and was father of the said Richard, who accompanied his cousin Sir Richard into Ireland, and married Honora, eldest daughter of Tiege O Brien of Smithstown, second son of Murrogh, the first Baron of Inchiquin, by whom he had the aforesaid Sir Edward, and several daughters, [2] of whom Honora was married to Do-
Sir nogh Mac-Connor O Brien of Lemeneith, Esq.—Sir Ed-
Edward. ward Wingfield, heir to his cousin Richard, Lord Powerscourt, was bred a soldier from his youth, and became a person of great power and command in Ireland. He attended the Earl of Essex in his expedition to Ulster against the Earl of Tyrone, when the L. D. consenting to hold a parley with him, six principal persons were appointed their attendants on each side, amongst whom was Sir Edward Wingfield; and after a short parley, commissioners being named to treat of a peace the next day, a truce, from six weeks to six weeks, was concluded, to begin from that day 'till the first of May; yet so, as it should be free on both sides to renew the war after fourteen days notice. He was also a commander at the siege of Kingsale, having landed in Munster with 1000 recruits [3], and performed divers other services to the crown.——He lived in Butter-lane, Dublin, married Anne, daughter of the afore-mentioned Edward, Lord Cromwell [4], died at Cornew in the county of Wicklow 22 April 1638, and was buried at Powerscourt (according to the directions of his will, * dated 16 of that month)

---

* Sir Edward by his will, left to his eldest son Richard, and the heirs male of his body, all the lands he possessed in England, according

[1] Pedig. and Rot. A°. Car I.¹. p. f. R. 36. [2] Idem, Pedig.
[3] Cox. hist. 451.   [4] Pedig.

month) having issue by her, who died 11 July 1636, and was interred the 19, in the church of Stagonel, a daughter Christian, to whom Richard Lord Powerscourt devised 600 pounds; and six sons, viz. Richard his heir; Francis who died childless; Lewis grandfather to the late Viscount; Anthony, citizen and woollen-draper of London, who died in 1653 *; Edward; and Cromwell of Killmurry in the county of Wicklow, living in 1676 '.

Richard Wingfield of Powerscourt, Esq. the eldest son, Richard, was left a minor, but in 1639 represented the borough of Boyle in parliament, and 24 November 1641 was appointed cording as the Lord of Powerscourt left and conveyed them unto him; also the Lordship of Benbourb in the county of Tyrone, charged with the payment of 1000l. lent thereon by Mr. Edward Smith; certain lands adjoining to the Blackwater, held from the Lord Primate; also the castle, town and lands of Powerscourt, in the county of Wicklow; the farm of Balleman, county of Dublin; the manor of Wingfield, in the county of Wexford; the town and lands of Ballecullen; the lease and mortgage of Aghoule, with all other his estate in the town and county of Wicklow; reserving all the rents of the manors of Benbourb and Powerscourt for the payment first of his debts and then of his legacies.—He bequeathed all his lands in the county of Limerick and Clare to his second son Francis, (after his own mother's decease, the said Francis to have only 50l. a year thereout during her life) and his heirs male.—To his son Lewis 1000l.; to his sons Anthony, Edward, and Cromwell 800l. a piece. —To his mother, as a testimonial of filial duty of affection, a diamond-ring, such as his executors should think fit, in value not to be under 20l.; to every of his sisters a ring worth 5l. each.—To his son Richard his house in Butter-Lane, with the furniture, utensils and appurtenances, also his plate, jewels, utensils and houshold stuff, as well in England as in Ireland.—To his honourable kinswoman the lady Esmond, whom he had ever found very careful of him, especially in that his sickness, 10l. to be bestowed on a ring by his executors, or if she liked better, to take a ring round set with diamonds, that was then at Powerscourt in one of his boxes.—Left divers other legacies to his friends and servants; and to his dear and well beloved friends Edward Blunt of Bolton and Erasmus Burrowes of Grangemellon, both in the county of Kildare, 20l. a piece, and ordained them executors.—Left as a token of his love and affection, to his brother the Lord Cromwell, 20l. to buy a Sword; to Lady Cromwell 10l. to buy a Ring; to each of Lord Cromwell's sons 5l. to buy them swords; to each of his lordship's daughters 5l. to buy them rings; to his noble friend Sir George Wentworth, as a token of his love and affection, his young black stone Horse. (Prerog. office.)

* By his will dated at London, 16 March 1653, proved 16 May following, he directed his body to be buried at Powerscourt if it might be done with conveniency, and left his estate both lands and chattels to his brother Lewis and Cromwell, to be equally divided, between them. (Lodge.)

' Chancery Pleadings.

ed a captain to assist in suppressing the rebellion, having a warrant, dated 14 of that month, to raise 60 men in the county of Wicklow, and another, to receive from the stores 38 musquets, and 20 pikes. By this rebellion he was a great sufferer, having his house of Powerscourt burnt, his goods and stock destroyed, and his life lost in the service of the crown.----On 7 May or March 1640 he married Elizabeth, eldest daughter of Sir Henry Folliott [1], created Lord Folliott, Baron of Ballyshannon 22 January 1619, and who died 10 Nov. 1622, (by his wife Anne, daughter of Sir William Stroud of Stoake under Hambden in Somersetshire) and sister of Thomas Lord Folliott, and dying in 1644 or 1645, had issue by her, (who re-married first on Sunday 12 April 1646 with Edward Trevor, Esq. brother to Marcus, Viscount Dungannon, and afterwards with Colonel Sir John Ponsonby of Besborough) Folliott his only Son, and a daughter Anne, baptized 5 February 1641, who died unmarried.

Folliott, Viscount Powerscourt.

Folliott Wingfield, Esq, was baptized in St. Michan's parish 3 November 1642, and being left very young, was put under the guardianship of Sir John Ponsonby, and of his mother by order of the high court of chancery in England, dated 4 March 1653, with all his lands and the management of his estate [2] 'till granted in ward to Roger, Earl of Orrery, by privy seal, dated at Whitehall 29 September, and by patent [3] 26 February 1660, and the next year, though under age, was returned to parliament both for the county of Wicklow, and the borough of Tallagh. And K. Charles II. not only taking into his princely consideration the signal services done and performed to his royal progenitors and predecessors by Sir Richard Wingfield, Lord Viscount Powerscourt, in France, the Netherlands, Spain, Portugal, and Ireland, by the overthrow of the Spaniards, and the rebel Tirone at Kingsale, and in all other places where Q. Elizabeth had wars, and afterwards to K. James I. in the killing and defeating the rebel O Doharty, and constantly persevering in his said services of war, and in the civil government as a Lord Justice, and always a privy counsellor of the kingdom of Ireland from his youth, 'till he died full of age, honour and merit; but also conceiving great hopes of Folliott Wingfield, Esq. his cousin, and heir to his estates in England and Ireland, the son and heir of Richard Wingfield Esq. deceased in the

---

[1] Pedig.   [2] Decree in Chancery 20 February 1655.
[3] Rot. 13 Car. II. 2. p. f.

the service of K. Charles I. son and heir of Sir Edward Wingfield Knt. deceased, whom the said Sir Edward Wingfield Knight-martial, being his near kinsman in blood, and of his sirname and family, constituted heir to succeed him in his estates in England and Ireland, which estates the said Folliott Wingfield did enjoy accordingly, by the settlement made by the said Knight-martial in his life time, was pleased, in order to continue the memory of his so deserving ancestors, and to encourage him to imitate their noble services, to renew the honour to him and his heirs male by privy seal, dated at Oxford 11 January, 1664, and by patent 22 February 1665 *
On 2 May 1671 he was made *Cust. Rot.* ¹ of the county of

---

* The Preamble. Cum nos regia mente commemorantes eminentia & acceptabilia servitia regalibus progenitoribus & predecessoribus nostris, impensa per Richardum Wingfield militem, nuper Dominum Vicecomitem de Powerscourt, marischallum regni nostri Hiberniæ, in Francia, Belgia, Hispania, Portugalia, & in dicto regno nostro Hiberniæ, tam in subversione Hispanorum archirebellis Tyrone apud Kingsale, quam in omnibus aliis locis, in quibus nuper præcharissima soror nostra Regina Elizabetha, felicissimæ memoriæ, debellata fuit, ac etiam postea persoluta ad nuper præcharissimum Avum nostrum Regem Jacobum, inclitæ memoriæ, in vincendo & occidendo rebellem O Dohertye; etiamque considerantes cum quam indefesso labore in iisdem serviciis, tam in bello quam in civili gubernatione perstetit, (viz.) bis Justiciarius dicti regni nostri Hiberniæ, & continue a juventute sua usque diem suum extremum gravidus ætate necnon meritis & honore coronoratus. Cumque etiam concepimus spem magnam de prædilecto & fideli nostro Folliot Wingfield de Powerscourt in comitatu Wicklowe in dicto regno nostro Hiberniæ, armigero, consanguineo & herede dicti nuper Domini Vicecomitis, filio & herede Richardi Wingfield armigeri, nuper defuncti in servitio patris nostri gloriossimæ memoriæ, qui fuit filius, & hæres Edwardi Wingfield, militis, quem dictus Richardus Wingfield mariscallus sibi, ut proximum consanguineum & familiæ et cognationis existentem hæredem sui successione in omnibus suis terris, tenementis & hereditamentis, tam in regno Angliæ quam Hiberniæ constituit; quæ quidem terræ, tenementa & hereditamenta prædictus Folliot Wingfield, virtute cujusdam stabilimenti facti per dictum militem mariscallum in vita sua, modo gaudet & tenet. Cumque etiam dictus Richardus Wingfield miles mariscallus & nuper Dominus Vicecomes de Powerscourt prædictus ab hac vita discesserit absque hærede masculo de corpore suo procreato, & superinde titulus & honor Domini Vicecomitis de Powerscourt modo extinctus est; Sciatis igitur quod nos regio affectu commemorantes desudata opera dicti prænobilis Vicecomitis Richardi Wingfield & ipsius memoriam futuris temporibus commendare intendentes, ac etiam ut prædictus Folliot Wingfield tot aut talia memoranda servitia imitari incitaretur, De gratia nostra speciali, &c. (Rot. pat. Canc. Anno. 18º. Car. II. 1ª p. D. R. 31.)

¹ Rot. 23 Car. II. 1. p. f.

of Wicklow; and by his laft will bequeathed to the poor of St. Bride's parifh, Dublin, 20l. for the rebuilding of which church in 1683, he had given 20l. the like fum to the poor of Powerfcourt, and 1000l. out of the refidue of his perfonal eftate, for the founding and erecting a charity fchool in the parifh of Powerfcourt, to teach poor boys to read and write Englifh, and inftruct them in the church catechifm *gratis*, until fit to be put to trades, as William, then Archbifhop of Dublin and his fucceffors, for the time being, and his executor Edward Wingfield Efq. fhould advife---He married the lady Elizabeth Boyle, eldeft daughter of the faid Earl of Orrery, but by her, who died 17 October 1709, and was buried the 20 in the Earl of Cork's tomb in St. Patrick's church, where his Lordfhip was alfo interred 17 February 1717, having no iffue, the title again became extinct, and the eftate defcended to his firft coufin Edward, fon of his uncle Lewis.

Lewis. Which Lewis Wingfield, Efq. had 400l. left him by the will of Richard, Lord Powerfcourt, and 1000l. by that of his father; he married Sidney [1], fixth daughter of Sir Paul Gore of Manor-Gore in the county of Donegall, Bart. by whom he had Edward his heir; Thomas who died without furviving iffue, and Richard, who by Anne his wife, had a fon Richard, baptized 14 March 1707,—Edward Wingfield, Efq. Counfellor at law, fucceeded to the eftate of Powerfcourt, and married firft Eleanor, fecond daughter of Sir Arthur Gore of Newtown-Gore in the county of Mayo; fecondly, the daughter of Doctor William Lloyd, Bifhop of Killala; and dying at his houfe in William-Street 7 January 1728, was buried at Powerfcourt with his laft wife, who died the 12 of the fame month and year; having iffue, by his firft wife, an only fon Richard, created Vifcount Powerfcourt, and two daughters.

Edward.

(1) Ifabella, married in April 1722 to Sir Henry King of Rockingham in the county of Rofcomon, Bart. and was mother of Edward Earl of Kingfton.

(2) Sidney, married 17 April 1723 to Achefon Moore of Ravilla or Aghnecloy in the county of Tyrone, Efq. member of parliament for Bangor, and died 10 December 1727, having an only fon James, baptized 6 Auguft 1726; and three daughters, Eleanor; Mary, married 26 June 1753 to Roger Palmer of Palmerftown in the county Mayo, Efq.;

and

[1] Prerog. Off. and Pedig.

WINGFIELD Viscount POWERSCOURT.

and Sidney, born the day of her mother's death, who was married 25 April 1751 to Hodgson Gage of Macgillegan in the county of Derry, Esq.

Richard Wingfield of Powerscourt, Esq. the only son was baptized in St. Michan's Parish 19 August 1697, served in parliament for the borough of Boyle, until his majesty was pleased to advance him to the honours of baron Wingfield of Wingfield, and Viscount Powerscourt of Powerscourt by privy seal, dated at St. James's 26 January, and by patent * 4 February 1743, and in April 1746 he was called

Richard,
Viscount.

---

* The Preamble. As honours and dignities are the proper and just reward to persons, who have eminently merited from their King and country, and as a continuance of those honours in their name and family is an incitement to their posterity to persevere in the practice of those virtues, that ennobled their ancestors. And whereas we bear in our royal mind a remembrance of the great and faithful services, performed for our royal predecessors by Richard Wingfield, Knt., late Lord Viscount of Powerscourt, who being by our late royal predecessor Elizabeth, Queen of England, appointed Mareschal of her army, in this kingdom, under the then Lord Mountjoy, did defeat and disperse at Kingsale the troops of the Earl Tyrone, and the other rebels associated with him. And when, after the suppression of the rebellion of the aforesaid Earl of Tyrone, and the establishment of a general peace through this Kingdom, the notorious rebel O Dogherty had burn'd the then new city of Derry, and raised great disturbances in the province of Ulster, he, the above-mentioned Mareschal, with a small number of forces, conquered and slew the said O Dogherty in open battle, and dispersed all his adherents; and after these services in time of war, the said Mareschal being twice appointed one of the L. J. and chief governors of our kingdom of Ireland, was no less eminent for his ability and services in the administration of the public government in times of peace. And, as upon the death of the said Richard Wingfield, late Mareschal and Lord Viscount of Powerscourt without issue male (whereby the said honour and title of Powerscourt was extinct) our late royal predecessor King Charles II. bearing in his royal remembrance the above-mentioned services of the said Mareschal and Viscount of Powerscourt, and being desirous to transmit the memory of the same to posterity, was pleased to create Folliott Wingfield, late of Powerscourt in the county of Wicklow, Esq., cousin and heir of the said Mareschal, a peer of this kingdom, by the name of Folliott Wingfield, Lord Viscount of Powerscourt; and as the said Folliott, Lord Viscount of Powerscourt is deceased without issue male, whereby the said title and honour of Lord Viscount of Powerscourt is again become extinct; and as we have the same desire with our royal predecessors, to preserve the remembrance of good and faithful services done to them and ourselves; and as we are satisfied in our princely judgment, that Richard Wingfield of Powerscourt, Esq., cousin and heir to the said Richard Wingfield, Viscount of Powerscourt, Mareschal of Ireland, and to the said Folliott Wingfield, Lord Viscount of Powerscourt, is a person, who, besides his noble descent, and his possessing the Estates of his said ancestors, hath, by his own abilities and

services

called into the privy council.—30 August 1721 he married to his first wife Anne, daughter of Christopher Usher of Usher's-Quay in Dublin, Esq. by whom he had no issue; and secondly, 13 April 1727, pursuant to articles dated 11 of that month ¹ Dorothy-Beresford, daughter of Hercules Rowley of Summer-Hill in the county of Meath, Esq. member of parliament for the county of Londonderry, who died 19 September 1742 ² and his Lordship departing this life, at Chelsea in Middlesex, 21 October 1751, was buried 17 November following at Powerscourt; leaving issue by her who died in London in July 1785 ³ two sons and two daughters viz.

(1) (2) Edward and Richard, } successive Viscounts.

(1) Daughter Frances, born 2 June 1728, to whom her father bequeathed 5000l. and was married pursuant to indenture, 26 November 1747, to John Gore, Esq. created Lord Annally, but by him who died in 1783 when that title expired, she had no issue,

(2) Isabella to whom her father also bequeathed 5000l.; 7 March 1770 she married Sir Charles Style of Wateringbury in the county of Kent, Bart. and by him who died 18 April 1774, has issue a son Sir Charles, successor to his father, and a daughter Dorothy ⁴.

Edward, 2 Viscount. Edward the second Viscount Powerscourt was born 23 October 1729; after a learned education at home, he visited the courts of many foreign princes; and on his return was chosen to parliament for Stockbridge in the county of Hants; he sat first in the house of peers, 15 February 1762 ⁵, and dying unmarried in London 6 May 1764, was succeeded by his only brother

Richard, 3 Viscount. Richard the third Viscount, who was baptized 24 December 1730, received 6000l. by the bequest of his father, and sat first in the House of Peers on the decease of his brother, 22 October 1764 ⁶.————In September 1760, he married Lady Emilia Stratford. daughter of John Earl

services in Parliament, rendered himself to be no less regarded by his country, than his constant and hearty Attachment and fidelity to ourselves and our government have made him acceptable to us, and worthy to sustain the honours, enjoyed by his illustrious ancestors. Know ye therefore, &c. (Rot. Anno. 17. Geo. II. 3. p. f.)

¹ Mentioned in his will dated 14 March 1747, and proved 5 February 1752, in court of Prerogative. ² Collect. ³ Idem ⁴ Lodge and Collect. ⁵ Lords Jour. IV. 237. ⁶ Idem. 342.

FLOWER, Viscount ASHBROOK.

Earl of Aldborough, and deceasing 8 August 1788, aged 58 was buried at Powerscourt, having had issue three sons and three daughters, viz. Richard, his heir; John; Edward, who died in April 1767; Martha; Emilia; and Harriot.

Richard the fourth and present Viscount Powerscourt, was born 29 October 1762 [1]; and 20 February 1789 he had his introduction to the House of Peers.

Richard, 4 Viscount.

TITLES.] Richard Wingfield, Viscount Powerscourt of Powerscourt, and Baron Wingfield of Wingfield.

CREATION.] B. Wingfield of Wingfield in the county of Wexford, and V. Powerscourt of Powerscourt in the county of Wicklow, 4 February 1743, 17 Geo. II.

ARMS.] Pearl, on a bend, ruby, cottised, diamond, three pair of wings conjoined, of the field.

CREST.] On a wreath, an eagle rising with wings expanded, pearl, beholding the sun in its splendor.

SUPPORTERS.] Two pegasusses, pearl, with expanded wings, manes, and hoofs, topaz.

MOTTO.] FIDELITE EST DE DIEU.

SEATS.] Powerscourt in the county of Wicklow, 10 miles from Dublin, and Powerscourt-House, in William-Street, Dublin.

FLOWER, Viscount ASHBROOK.

THE family of Flore or Flower, an ancient and eminent name in the county of Rutland, had a seat in the own of Oakham on a fair estate of freehold, namely, ten messuages, 100 acres of land, ten of meadow, with the appurtenances, held of the Lord of the manor by Fealty only; which estate, or the greatest part of it, was sold in Q. Elizabeth's reign by William Flower, a *cadet* of the family,

[1] Ulster.

William. William Flore of Oakham, Esq. was Sheriff of the county of Rutland 10 of Richard II.[2] and its representative in parliament the 6 and 8 of that King; with his wife Elena, he lies buried in the body of Oakham-church, under a stone with this circumscription;

✠ Hic jacent Willielmus Flore et Elena
Uxor ejus, qui quidem Willielmus obiit
Primo ——————— Septuagesimo nono, quor'
Animabus propitietur Deus. Amen.[3]

Roger. Roger Flower his son and successor, was Knight of the shire for the said county 20 Rich. II.; 1 and 4 Hen. IV. and 2 Hen. V. being in 4, 5 and 7 years of the last reign, and 1 Hen. VI. Speaker of the House of Commons.—He was a person of great note in the said town and county; and the charities, devised by his will, are a signal monument of his piety. He died in, or about the year 1424, appointing by his will, that he should be buried in the church of All-Saints in Oakham, and his best animal to be given to the Vicar for a mortuary, to whom also he gave ten shillings for tythes forgotten; to the Chaplain of Oakham he bequeathed 2 shillings, and to every other Chaplain inhabiting the same town one shilling; to the guilds of the Holy Trinity, the blessed Virgin, and St. Michael of Oakham 40 shillings; and to every order of Friars at Stamford, the Carthusians at Coventry, the Abbey of Westminster, and the priory of Laund, 6 marcs to pray for the souls of Catharine his late wife, William his father, Ellen his mother, Edmond Duke of York, &c. and to certain Chaplains to celebrate for his own soul, the soul of K. Henry V. and those above-named, 40l.; to the poor, and the performing of his exequies 50 marcs; to the alms-house of Oakham, towards repairing of the Chapel, and ornaments of the altar, 50 shillings, and to every poor man of the house four-pence; to the mending of the highways, bridges and causeways, at Oakham, the like sum of 50 shillings; and to 20 poor people there, each a gown of Coventry-frize, and a new shirt. Being the lessee or farmer of the parsonage tythes at Oakham, under the Abbot and

---

[1] Wright's Rutland 97. [2] Idem. 136. [3] Idem. 98.

and convent of Westminster, he gave to every Monk of that abbey, being a priest, one shilling, and no priest, 8 pence; to the great guild at Coventry, 40 shillings; to the priory of Brooke, 13s. 4d.; to the Nuns of Langley and Huntingdon, and the priory of Newstead near Stamford, each the like sum; to the master of the chantry at Manton (one of his executors) his own pair of beads, with ten *Aves* of silver, and a *Pater noster* gilt; praying him to be mindful of him, when he said over our Lady's Psalter on them. He also chiefly built the spire of the steeple of Oakham; and to his second wife, who survived him, he gave the manors of Steneby and Braceby in Lincolnshire, if she took upon her the mantle and ring, and vowed chastity.—His first wife was Catharine, daughter and heir to William Dalby of Exton in the county of Rutland, Esq.[1] by whom he had five sons and one daughter, who married Sir Henry Plessington of Burley in the said county, and she lies buried in Oakham church near the north door, where was engraven on a plain stone

> ———— Filia Rogeri Flore, quondam
> Uxor Henrici Plessington.

Thomas Flore of Oakham, the eldest son, in 1430 was sheriff of the county of Rutland; and three years after[2] returned by the King's commissioners appointed to take account of all the gentry of England, one of the gentlemen of that county, of which he was again sheriff in 1441, 1450, 1456, 1465, and 1470.—He married Agnes, daughter and heir to Richard Saltby of the county of Lincoln, Esq.[3] and dying 6 December 1473, was buried in the church of Oakham, near the north building, under a stone adorned with brass plates and sculpture, thus inscribed;

> Hic jacent Thomas Flore quondam de
> Okeham Armiger, qui quidem Thomas
> Obiit die Lunæ prima post Festum Sancti
> Nicholai Episcopi, An. Dom. Mil. CCCC. LXXIII.
> Cujus Anime propicietur Deus. Amen.

Roger,

[1] Wright's Rutland, 136.   [2] Fuller's Worthies of Rut.
[3] Wright, p. 136.

Roger.   Roger, his son and heir, succeeded at Oakham, and by Jane, daughter and coheir to Sir John Fraunces of Burley [1], was father of Sir Richard Flower, who removed to Whitwell in the same county of Rutland, where he had a good seat and estate of freehold, viz. two messuages, 40 acres of land, 20 of meadow, and a water-mill [2], which he held of the prior of St. John of Jerusalem in England, as of his manor of Whitwell, by the rent of seven shillings and suit of court there.—In 1501 (17 Hen. VII.) he was a Knight, and sheriff of the county of Berks [3], which office in 1507 he served for Rutlandshire; and dying 16 September 1523 [4] (15 Hen. VIII.) an office was taken at Ketton 7 November following, before John Molesworth, escheator, whereby it was found, that he died seized (among other things) of the manor of Little-Hambleton, with lands there and in Great-Hambleton, a fair estate in Oakham, the mediety of one messuage, 15 acres of land and 5 acres of meadow in Langham; 100 acres of wood in Burley, also a messuage, 10 acres of land, and 10 of meadow in Exton [5].—His first wife was Elizabeth, daughter and coheir to Sir John Tessington of Stamford, Knt. by whom he had Roger, his successor at Whitwell, who by the said inquisition was found to be then 30 years old and upwards, and by Dorothy, daughter of Reginald Conyers of Wakerly in the county of Northampton, Esq. (who remarried with Andrew Noel of Dalby in Leicestershire, and of Brooke in Rutlandshire, ancestor by her to Sir Verney Noel of Kirby-Mallory, created a Baronet 6 July 1660) had Richard Flower of Whitwell, Esq. who married Alice, daughter of Sir John Harrington of Exton, and had John his heir, sheriff of the county of Rutland for the years 1565, 1569, and 1577, who marrying Mary, (or Margery) only daughter of Anthony Colley of Glaiston in the said county, by his first wife Catharine, daughter of Sir William Skeffington of Skeffington, had John Flower, Esq. (ancestor by Jane, daughter of Ralph Sheldon of the county of Worcester, Esq. to the family some time after residing at Whitwell) and three daughters, Anne, married to Robert Kay of Woodsome in Yorkshire, Esq. Alice, to Charles Segrave; and Mary [6].

George.   Sir Richard Flower by his second wife Elizabeth, daughter of William Brookesby of the county of Leicester, had many children; of whom George, the sixth son, married Margaret

Sir Richard.

---

[1] Wright. p. 136.   [2] Idem.   [3] Fuller's Worthies.   [4] Wright. 136.   [5] Idem. 137.   [6] Idem. 136.

Margaret daughter of John Salisbury, Esq. and was father of Francis Flower, some time an attendant on Sir Christopher Hatton, Lord Chancellor of England, whose son George in Q. Elizabeth's reign embracing a military life, was a very active and brave officer against the rebels in Ireland, commanding a company of 100 foot in the old army. His conduct and courage were so well approved, that in April 1600 he was sent into Carbery in the county of Cork, with 1200 foot and 100 horse, to oppose Florence Mac-Carthy and others in rebellion, when he destroyed the country as far as Ross; and in his return falling into an ambush, laid for him by the said Florence, with 2000 men at Awnebuy, between Kingsale and Cork, he extricated himself with great resolution and bravery, killing Carbry O Connor and 100 rebels, and wounding as many more, without the loss of any person of note, having two horses killed under him.

Sir George.

After this he was made Serjeant-Major of her Majesty's army, and in that station sent by the president of Munster in 1601, to assist Sir John Berkeley, Governor of Conaught, with 1000 foot, to prevent the passage of the Irish over the Shannon: On 29 March he arrived at Quin in Thomond, where having intelligence that they were at no great distance, he drew towards them, and by a smart engagement put them entirely to the rout. On 21 April he returned to Limerick, and thence 28 September went to view the enemy's situation and numbers near Kingsale, who sallied out upon him, but met with so warm a reception, as obliged them to retire; and about the same time having taken Mac-Donogh-Durrow, brother to the governor of Cloghan-castle near Baltimore, he summoned the place, and sent the governor word, he would hang his brother, if he did not instantly surrender; but a priest, lately arrived from Rome, being in the castle, whom he would not give up, he suffered his brother to be executed; yet, having found means to procure the priest's escape, he sued for protection four days after, and surrendered the castle.— And the Irish being routed 24 December, he and Captain Hervey were sent to receive the castles of Downbuy, Castlehaven, and Baltimore from the Spaniards, pursuant to the articles of capitulation; after which he was knighted, and 1 August 1627 was appointed Governor and Constable of the fort, newly erected in Waterford, being also in 13 of that month joined in commission with Sir Richard Aldworth and Sir Francis Slingsby, to execute jointly and separately

parately martial law, upon all offenders among the old fleet foldiers and the new levies within the province of Munſter, according to the late orders of war, eſtabliſhed for the good conduct of his Majeſty's ſervice in Ireland. —Soon after this he died, and was ſucceeded by his ſon

Sir William. Sir William Flower, who, during the rebellion of 1641, was an officer in the army under Michael Jones, Governor of Dublin; by whom and the parliament commiſſioners he was ſeized 22 July 1648, with other officers, on ſuſpicion of their affection to the Marqueſs of Ormond, their former General, then upon his return into the kingdom, and ſent priſoners to England: But he lived to ſee the reſtoration of the King, to whoſe firſt parliament in 1661 he was returned member for Iriſhtown; was made Captain of a foot company, and afterwards Lieutenant-Colonel to his Majeſty's regiment of guards in Ireland; was ſworn of his privy council; appointed 22 May 1662 one of the truſtees for ſatisfying the arrears of the commiſſioned officers, who ſerved the King in Ireland before 5 June 1649; and his Majeſty 5 June 1663 demiſed to him, jointly with Thomas Piggott, Eſq. one of his Majeſty's privy council, all the eſtate of Charles Dunn (ſon and heir to Barnaby Dunn, Eſq.) of Ballybrittas in the Queen's county, forfeited for rebellion, to hold for 31 years, at the rent of 20l. a year, during the life of Sybilla Dunn, otherwiſe Piggott, relict of the ſaid Barnaby, and 30l. a year after her deceaſe.— He had alſo three grants of lands under the acts of ſettlement; was appointed 19 July 1669, with John Povey, Eſq. Sir Amos Meredyth, Bart. Sir William Uſſher, Knt. and Alderman Peter Wybrants, commiſſioners of Appeals, concerning the duties of exciſe and new impoſts, with the yearly fee of 120l. each; and 26 October 1675 again made a truſtee for the (49) officers, according to the intents and purpoſes of the King's declaration of 30 November 1660, for the ſettlement of the kingdom.

He married Frances, daughter of Walter Weldon of St. John's Bower in the county of Kildare, Eſq. widow of William, ſon of Sir Arthur Savage of Rheban, Knt. and by her who died 26 December 1673, and was buried the 28 at Finglas, had three ſons and one daughter; Thomas, his heir; L. Colonel Henry Flower, whoſe ſervices were rewarded with a grant of lands under the acts of ſettlement, who in 1654 married Anne Hawtrey, but died without iſſue 6 September 1678; Captain William Flower; and Alice,

Alice, married to Richard Jones, Esq. And by his second wife, Sir William had a daughter Anne, married to Robert Mercer of Dublin, merchant.

Thomas Flower of Durrow in the county of Kilkenny, Esq. the eldest son, lived also at Finglas near Dublin; was attainted 7 May 1689 by K. James's parliament, having his estate sequestered, and 700l. personal fortune taken from him, to which he was restored by K. William, whose army he supplied from his granaries with above a thousand barrels of wheat.——On 17 January 1683 he married first Mary, fourth daughter of Sir John Temple, Attorney-General of Ireland, sister of Henry, Viscount Palmerston, by her he had one son William, created Lord Castle-Durrow, and a daughter Mary, who died unmarried. By his second wife the daughter of Mr. Jeffreys of the county of Brecknock in Wales, he had a son Jeffreys, and a daughter Catharine, baptized 9 December 1694, who died young.

On 4 May 1700 he makes his will (the probate bears date 4 July following [1]) and thereby bequeaths his body to be buried at Finglas, in a vault to be made by his executors, and leaves 150l. to erect a tomb, which he was obliged to do by his uncle's will; all his real estate in Ireland, he gave to his eldest son William, to his second son Jeffreys, and to his own brother Captain William Flower, and the heirs of their bodies successively; remainder to his right heirs for ever. And whereas, upon a settlement made by his wife, he had power to charge his estate in Brecknockshire with 2000l. at his death, he left the said estate, which he had discharged from several incumbrances, to his second son Jeffreys, remainder to his eldest son William, remainder to his brother William, and their respective heirs successively, remainder to his right heirs; bequeathed to his eldest son all his chattles real and personal in Ireland, and to his second son all his personal estate in Brecknockshire, to his brother William, the annuity of 50l. a year for life, out of the Irish estate, and all his right to what was due to him from the King for 1000 and odd barrels of wheat; to his aunt Stephens of Chepstow 15l.; to his aunt Elizabeth Pitt 15l.; to his sister Mrs. Elizabeth Jeffreys 10l.; and to Francis Oakwell 6l. yearly, during their lives. To his good friend Nicholas Plunkett, Esq. his gold clock-watch and 20l. to buy a ring; to his good friend Mr. James Spooner his grey gelding and 20l. to buy mourning; to his good friend John,

---
[1] Reg. Diocefs Offory.

John, Bishop of Ossory 20l. to buy a ring and his best gelding or mare; and to Mr. John Price of Brecon 20l. to buy a ring, appointing him and William Flower his brother to be executors of such part of his will as related to his son Jeffreys, desiring that he might be continued at school in Ireland, till fit for the University, and then to be sent to the College of Dublin or Oxford, as his overseers should see fit; and appointed the said Bishop, his good friend Sir John Temple, and his said brother William, to be overseers of such part of his will as related to his son William. To the parish of Finglas he gave 30l. with 20l. more that his daughter Mary desired might be given, to be put out at interest for them, on such security, as Sir John Hely, Chief Justice of the Common Pleas, the Rector of the Church for the time being, and Mr. James Spooner should approve of, or else to be laid out on a purchase, and the profits thereof to be paid to such poor of the parish, as his heir and the Rector should direct. He also left to the parish-poor of Kanerynath in Brecknockshire and of Chepstow, 5l. each; and two acres of land near Chepstow, which he had purchased from Mr. Richard Morgan, towards keeping his great-grandmother's tomb in repair, and the *overplus* to be distributed among the poor of the parish on 25 February yearly.

William, 1 Baron.
William Flower, Esq. who succeeded at Durrow*, was baptized 11 March, 1685, and in October 1715 chosen to represent the county of Kilkenny in parliament, as he was in that month 1727 the borough of Portarlington, for which he had served in the reign of Q. Anne, and in 1731 was sheriff of the county of Kilkenny.—His Majesty thinking him, who had sat so long in the lower house of parliament, worthy a place in the upper house, was pleased by privy seal, dated at Hampton-court 4 September, and by patent †
27 October

---

* On 11 October 1676, for the sum of 1000l. a mortgage from the Earl of Arran of 100l. a year-rent, upon the lands of Durrow and Ballyspellan in the county of Kilkenny, was made to his father; and his Lordship 19 February 1708 had a release of the lands of Durrow and others from James, Duke of Ormond, to him and his heirs for ever, at the rent of 68l. 13s. 4d. with three fat beeves, or 4l. 8s. 6d. per annum in lieu thereof, at the Duke's election, &c. being the rents and duties reserved when the premises were granted by lease to his grandfather. And 15 October 1703 he had the grant of a Friday market, and three fairs to be held every second Thursday in May, August, and November, at Durrow.

† The Preamble. Cum fidelis et perquam dilectus noster Gulielmus Flower de Castle-Durrow in Regno nostro Hiberniæ Armiger
Avos

27 October 1733, to create him Baron of Castle-Durrow; and 2 November he took his seat in the House of Peers [1]; and was called into his Majesty's privy council.—He married Edith, daughter of Toby Caulfield of Clone in the county of Kilkenny, and deceasing 29 April 1746, was privately buried in the family vault at Finglas pursuant to his will [2], having had issue two sons and two daughters; Jeffrey, baptized 26 September 1717, died young; Henry; the eldest daughter died young; and Rebecca the youngest, married 6 July 1741 to James Agar Esq. member of parliament for Gowran, and had issue [3].

Henry, the second Lord Castle-Durrow, in August 1740 was made Cornet of a troop of Horse, and soon after a captain. He took his seat in the House of Peers 28 October 1747 [4], and his Majesty was pleased to advance him further in the Peerage, by creating him Viscount Ashbrook by privy seal, dated at Kensington 24 August, and by patent [5] 30 September 1751, by which title his Lordship took his seat 8 October following [6].

Henry,
1
Viscount.

In March 1740 he married Elizabeth [7], daughter of Lieutenant-General William Tatton, and his Lordship * dying at St. Stephen's-Green Dublin 27 June 1752, was buried at Finglas, having issue by her who died 10 February 1759, one son William, and two daughters.

Elizabeth,

Avos suos Gulielmum Flower et Johannem Temple, Milites, aliosque Majores, summa, in Principem suum Fidelitate, Virtutibus, bonorumque Morum similitudine imitatus, in diversis parliamenti Hibernici Sessionibus se probe, incorrupte, et honesta Moderatione gessisset; dumque in privatis Rebus agebat, tam justæ quam stabilis Amicitiæ Exempla præbuisset; hæc Veritas et Fides, hæc sinceri Animi constantia, hæc Integritas vitæ, Benignitatem regiam et Nobilitatis nomen gradumque merentur. Sciatis igitur, &c. (Rot. A°. 7 Geo. II. 1. p. f.)

* His Lordship made his will 25 June 1752, proved 31 July following, and thereby devised his estate to his only son William and his issue male and female; remainder to his daughters Elizabeth and Mary and their issue male and female. Appointed his Lady and Henry, Viscount Palmerston, executors and guardians of the person and estate of his son, and guardians of the fortunes of his daughters, being 6000l. a piece, and his wife guardian of their persons. He left to his sister Rebecca Agar 50l. and it appears by said will that his Lady had 1000l. a year jointure. (Prerog. Off.)

[1] Lords Jour. III. 235.   [2] Prerog Off.   [3] See V. Clifden.
[4] Lords Jour. III. 665.   [5] Rot. A°. 25 Geo. II. 2 p. f. R. 1.
[6] Lords Jour. III. 782.   [7] Ulster.

(1) Elizabeth, born at Castle-Durrow 26 January 1741; and
(2) Mary, born in Dublin 12 February 1747, married 1 January 1788, to the Rev. John Nichol, Rector of Remenham in Bucks.

William, 2 Viscount. William, the second Viscount, was born at Castle-Durrow 25 June 1744.—He married Elizabeth, daughter of Mr. Ridge of the county of Oxford, and deceased in August 1780, having had issue two sons and four daughters, viz. William, his heir; Henry-Jeffreys, born 16 November 1776; daughters Elizabeth, Harriot, Caroline, and Sophia [1].

William, 3 Viscount. William, the third and present Viscount Ashbrook was born 19 October 1767, and is unmarried.

TITLES.] William Flower, Viscount Ashbrook, and Baron of Castle-Durrow.

CREATION.] B. of Castle-Durrow in the county of Kilkenny 27 October 1733, 7 Geo. II.; and V. Ashbrook in the kingdom of Ireland 30 September 1751, 25 Geo. II.

ARMS.] Quarterly, the first and fourth pearl, on a cheveron voided, diamond, between three ravens, each holding an ermine spot in its beak, proper, as many pellets. The second and third ruby, three towers, pearl, both borne by the name of Flower.

CREST.] On a wreath, a raven, as in the coat.

SUPPORTERS.] Two tygers, reguardant, proper, gorg'd with ducal coronets and chains, topaz.

MOTTO.] MENS CONSCIA RECTI.

SEAT.] Castle-Durrow in the county of Kilkenny, 60 miles from Dublin.

[1] Ulster.

MORRES,

MORRES, Viscount MOUNT-MORRES.

THE family of Morres, or Morreis, defcended from the houfe of Montmorency, came into England with William the Conqueror, and having lands granted to them in the principality of Wales, foon after fettled in the Ifle of Anglefey.

Harvey de Monte-Marifcoe, who lived at Beaumaris, being nephew to Richard, Earl of Chepftow, commonly called Earl Strongbow, attended his uncle into Ireland in the reign of K. Henry II.———On the reduction of the kingdom he obtained confiderable grants of lands in the counties of Wexford, Tipperary, and Kerry; fome of which are ftill vefted in the family, but the greater part were carried by intermarriages into the houfes of Ormond and Leinfter.

The faid Harvey, in 1175, married Nefta, daughter of Maurice Fitz-Gerald, anceftor to the Dukes of Leinfter. In 1178, or 1179 he founded and largely endowed the abbey of Dunbrody in the county of Wexford; in 1179 he retired from the world and became a brother in the monaftery of the Holy Trinity in Canterbury, but he was buried at Dunbrody, where a ftately monument was erected to his memory. He left the remainder of his large eftate to his brother Geoffry de Marreis, or Marifcoe, who was chief governor of Ireland in 1215, 1226, and 1230; one of his defcendants in K. Edward II. time was created a peer by the title of de Monte Marifcoe, but he was foon after killed, with his fon, in a fea fight with pirates who then infefted the coafts of Ireland.

John, of Knockagh in the county of Tipperary, anceftor to this noble Lord, was created a Knight Baronet by patent 28 March 1632, he married a daughter of Pierce Walſh of Abingdon in the county of Limerick, and was father of Redmond, who married Ellis daughter of Garret Wale, of the ancient family of Coolnemucky, in the county of Waterford, and had iſſue John (who was father of Redmond, which Redmond had a ſon Simon); Harvey; and Edmond.

Harvey.   Harvey, the ſecond ſon carried on this line.——He ſettled at Caſtle-Morres in the county of Kilkenny, obtained a grant from K. Charles II. erecting that eſtate into the manor of Caſtle-Morres, with very ample privileges; he married Frances third daughter of Pierce Butler of Barrowmount, in the county of Tipperary, Eſq. of the houſe of Ormond; and had ſeveral ſons, but the only ſurvivor was

Francis.   Francis, who in Auguſt 1706, married Catherine daughter and heireſs to Sir William Evans of Kilkreen, in the county of Kilkenny Bart. and by her who died 6 Auguſt 1747, had iſſue three ſons.

(1)   Harvey, created Viſcount Mount-Morres.

(2)   Sir William-Evans, created a Baronet, 24 April 1758; he married firſt Margaret, daughter and heireſs to Joſiah Haydocke of the city of Kilkenny, Eſq. and of Buelick in the county of Tipperary, and by her who died 22 Auguſt 1753, had iſſue one ſon Haydocke-Evans, and two daughters Iſabella and Mary; 1 July 1755 he married ſecondly, Maria-Juliana, eldeſt daughter and coheir to William Ryves of Upper-Court in the county of Kilkenny Eſq., and by her had one ſon William-Ryves, born 7 November 1763.——Sir William was ſucceeded by his eldeſt ſon Sir Haydocke-Evans; who married the only daughter of Ralph Gore of Barrowmount in the county of Kilkenny, but dying in December 1776, without iſſue by his lady, who remarried with William Gore of St. Valori in the county of Wicklow, Eſq. by whom ſhe has iſſue; he was ſucceeded in the title of Baronet, by his only brother Sir William-Ryves Morres.

(3)   Redmond, one of his Majeſty's council at law; he repreſented the city of Dublin in parliament, and died at Bruſſels in 1784. He married 27 March 1740, Elizabeth ſole daughter and heir to Francis Lodge of the city of Dublin, Eſq., and had iſſue, two ſons and three daughters viz. Lodge-Evans, (member of parliament for the borough of Bandon-Bridge, and treaſurer to the general poſt-office;

office; in 1771 he married a daughter of Mr. Fade, she died in February 1787 without issue); Redmond in holy orders; the daughters were Eleanor, married 27 March 1762 to Robert Browne of Brownes-Hill in the county of Carlow, Esq.; Frances, to Andrew Prior of Rathdowny in the Queen's County Esq.; and Elizabeth to Ephraim Hutchinson of the city of Dublin, Esq.

Harvey, the eldest son succeeded at Castle-Morres; represented the borough of Irish-Town in parliament, and was created Baron of Mount Morres, by privy seal at Kensington, 23 April 1756 [1] and by patent 4 May [2] same year; and 7 of that month was introduced and took his seat in the upper house of parliament [3]. 19 April 1763 [4] by privy seal at St. James's, and by patent at Dublin 29 [5] June following, was further advanced to the dignity of Viscount Mount Morres, and took his seat by that title 11 October 1763 [6].

He married first 3 November 1742 Lady Letitia [7] fourth daughter of Brabazon, late Earl of Besborough, and by her who died 9 February 1754, had issue one son Harvey-Redmond; two daughters, viz. Letitia (married first to the hon. Arthur Trevor, only son of Arthur Viscount Dungannon; and secondly to Randal-William, the present Earl of Antrim); and Jane born in January 1749—50 to the Rev. Joseph Pratt. He married secondly in July 1755, Mary, eldest daughter of William Wale of Coolenemucky in the county of Waterford, Esq. niece to Brabazon Earl of Besborough, and relict of John Baldwin of Curralanty in the King's County, Esq., whom she married 15 April 1734, and he died without issue in 1754; by this lady who was born 9 January 1713, and died in September 1779, his Lordship had Francis-Harvey born 1 September 1756, and William born in 1760 [8]; his Lordship deceased 6 April 1766, and was succeeded in the title by his eldest son

Harvey-Redmond the second and present Viscount, who sat first in parliament 4 October 1777 [9], and is yet unmarried.

Harvey, 1 Viscount.

Harvey-Redmond, 2 Viscount.

TITLES.

[1] Rot. Pat. de A°. 29°. Geo. II. 4ª. p. f. R. 30.
[2] Idem. R. 31.   [3] Lords Jour. IV. 77.
[4] Rot. pat. de. A°. 3 Geo. III. 3ª. p. D. R. 10.
[5] Idem. R. 20.   [6] Journals. IV. 268.
[7] Ulster.   [8] Id.   [9] Lords Jour. V. 8.

TITLES.] Harvey-Redmond Morres Viscount and Baron Mount-Morres.

CREATIONS.] B. Mount-Morres of Castle-Morres, in the county of Kilkenny 4 May 1756, 29 Geo. II. and V. Mount-Morres of Castle-Morres, 29 June 1763, 3 Geo. III.

ARMS.] Topaz, a fess dancette, and in base a Lion rampant, Diamond.

CREST.] On a wreath, a demi Lion rampant, diamond, armed ruby.

SUPPORTERS.] Two angels proper, in loose garments, pearl, crined and winged, Topaz.

MOTTO.] SI DEUS NOBISCUM, QUIS CONTRA NOS.

SEAT.] Castle-Morres, in the county of Kilkenny, 65 miles from Dublin.

TREVOR, VISCOUNT DUNGANNON[*].

UNDER the title of EARL OF HILLSBOROUGH, the reader will observe that Michael Hill of Hillsborough in the county of Down, Esq. great-grandfather to this noble Lord, married Anne, only daughter of Sir John Trevor of Brinkenalt in the county of Denbigh, Knt. and sister to Arthur Trevor, Esq. by which Lady he had two sons; Trevor, the eldest, was created Viscount Hillsborough, and Arthur the youngest, was created Viscount Dungannon.

Which Arthur Hill, Esq. was appointed 11 June 1719, keeper of the records in Birmingham Tower, on the resignation of the Right Honourable Joseph Addison; in December 1734, he resigned that office, and 8 March following, was constituted (with Laurence Broderick Esq.
pursuant

[*] Lodge. Edit. 1574, II. 242. and M. S. Collect.

pursuant to a reversionary grant made to them 27 March 1718) register of the memorials of all deeds, conveyances, &c. in Ireland, an office, instituted by act of parliament 6 Q. Anne, and with which he was solely invested 2 October 1736, but surrendered the same in May 1749, to John Burton, Esq. who resigned in favour of the Right Honourable George Ogle.—In the parliament called in 1715, he served for the Borough of Hillsborough, in 1727 was elected Knight of the Shire for Down; and in 1736 he was Sheriff of that county.—20 August 1750, he was sworn of his Majesty's most honourable Privy Council, and by patent in 1754, was appointed Chancellor of the court of Exchequer, into which office he was sworn 25 June same year; but he resigned in 1755 on being made a commissioner of his Majesty's revenue.—He married to his first wife Anne, third daughter and coheir to Joseph Deane Esq., Chief Baron of the Exchequer [1], but she dying at Gilgorm, about a year after her marriage, in child birth (and the child deceasing with her) he married secondly, 12 January 1737, [2] Anne, daughter and heir to Edmund Francis Stafford of Brownstown in the county of Meath, and of Portglenone in the county of Antrim Esq., who died in 1722; and by her (who was born 25 December 1715, and yet survives him;) had issue three daughters, viz. Anne (born 7 April 1740, and married 6 February 1759, to Garret created Earl of Mornington;) Prudence, (born 23 June 1742, and married 22 May 1765, to Charles Powell Leslie of Glaslough in the county of Monaghan, Esq.; Jane, who died unmarried 17 February 1765, at her father's house in G. Britain Street, aged 15 years, and was buried at St. Mary's Church in Dublin); and one son

Arthur born 24 December 1738, elected to parliament for the Borough of Hillsborough; 27 February 1762, married Letitia eldest daughter of Harvey, created Viscount Mount Morres; and deceasing 19 June 1770, left issue by her (who remarried with Randal-William, Earl of Antrim,) one son Arthur, who succeeded to the title.

In 1762, Mr. Hill became possessed of a considerable landed property in Wales, (the estates of his grandfather Sir John Trevor, lying in the counties of Denbigh, Salop, and Middlesex, the same being bequeathed by his mother's brother

---

[1] See Earl of Shannon. n. [2] Articles dated 11 January 1737.

brother Arthur Trevor, Esq. son of Sir John Trevor, Knt. aforesaid, which estates were limited first to Arthur Hill and his issue male, remainder in default thereof to Wills, Earl of Hillsborough and his issue male, with this provisoe, that each person so inheriting should assume the name and arms of Trevor) on which he changed his name from Hill to Trevor, by act of parliament; and was advanced to the peerage of Ireland pursuant to privy seal at St. James's 27 December 1765 [1], and patent at Dublin 17 February 1766 [2], creating him Baron Hill of Olderfleet, and Viscount of Dungannon, by which (latter) title he took his seat in the upper house of parliament, 28 February 1766 [3], and his Lordship deceasing in Dublin 30 January 1770, was interred at Belvoir.—being succeeded in the honours by his grandson [4]

Arthur 2 Viscount.

Arthur, the second and present Viscount, born 2 October 1763 and yet unmarried.

TITLES.] Arthur Hill, Baron Hill of Olderfleet, and Viscount of Dungannon in Ireland.

CREATIONS.] So created 17 February 1766, 6 Geo. III.

ARMS.] Quarterly, 1st. and 4th. parte-per-bend, sinister, ermine, and erminois, a lion rampant, armed ruby, for Trevor. 2d. and 3d. diamond, on a fess, pearl, between three leopards, passant guardant erminois, three escallops, ruby, for Hill.

CREST.] A wyvern, diamond, armed ruby.

SUPPORTERS.] Two lions rampant, erminois, ducally gorged, proper.

MOTTO.] QUID VERUM ATQUE DECENS.

SEATS.] Belvoir, in the county of Down, 78 miles from Dublin, and Brinkenalt in the county of Denbigh.

ROWLEY,

---

[1] Signet office, and Rot. pat. A°. 6°. Geo. III. 2ª. p. f. R. 6. [2] Idem. [3] Lords Jour. III. 69. [4] Lodge Collect and Almon.

ROWLEY, Viscountess LANGFORD.

THE prefent Right Honourable Hercules Langford Rowley, derives his defcent from a family which was feated at Carmichan in the county of Chefter, where Randolfe Rowley was living in the reign of K. Edward II.——He was fucceeded by his fon Randolfe, living 19 K. Edward III. who was the father of

Randolfe.
Randolfe.

Roger de Rowley of Carmichan, living 13 K. Richard II. which Roger by Rofe his wife, had two fons, Randolfe, his heir, and Nicholas.

Roger.

Randolfe of Carmichan the elder fon, living in 2 K. Henry VI. married Margaret, daughter of John Licelor, and had Randolfe living 18 Henry VI. whofe fon Robert, had a fon Robert living 31 of that reign, who by Elizabeth his wife, had a fon, whofe name we have not recovered, but according to the pedigree he removed his refidence to Elington, in the county of Huntingdon, and was father of Robert, who fold his lands of Carmichan and other places in Chefhire to Henry Manwaring, Efq. 13 Henry VIII.

Nicholas, the fecond fon of Robert aforefaid, in 1429, 7 K. Henry VI. married Cifley, daughter and coheir to Thomas Le Wolfe of Church-Lawton, in the county of Chefter, Efq. *; in her right he became feated there, and had iffue John Rowley of Lawton, who had a fon John. living 7 Hen. VIII.; which John by Cifley his wife, had two fons, of whom Hugh, the elder dying without iffue, was fucceeded by his brother William Rowley of the fame place, who married Ellen, daughter of Hugh Brereton of Wimerfley, brother to Sir Andrew Brereton, Knt. and had iffue three fons, viz.

Nicholas.
John.
John.
William.

John, whofe only fon William, died young.

(1)

Robert,

---

* Defcended from Winthianns de Rode, fecond fon and heir to Henry de Rode of Rode in the county of Chefter, father of Randolfe de Rode, alias le Wolfe of Church-Lawton, anceftor in the 8th defcent, to the faid Thomas, father of Cicely.

(2) Robert, who married Agnes, daughter of Richard Yardley of Park, in the county of Stafford, and had a son William of Lawton, living in 1633, whose offspring remained at Lawton 24 August 1684; and

(3) Hugh, who married Mary Rowley, daughter of ———
Hugh. Rowley of Shelton, in the county of Stafford, a younger branch of the Rowleys of Hickley in that county, and by her had issue, three sons, who all settled in the county of Derry; in the reign of K. James I. and were

(1) John, of Castle-Roe;

(2) Nathaniel, of the city of Londonderry, who married, but died without issue; and

(3) William, of Tobermore in the county of Londonderry, who for some time bore arms against the rebels, but died in April 1642; he married Mary, daughter of John Dillon of Castle-Dillon in the county of Armagh, Esq. and had issue three sons and three daughters, viz. John, slain at Ballymoney in the county of Antrim, in an engagement with the Irish rebels in March 1641, as was his brother William, whose eldest son Edward was living in April 1662 and then of the age of 30 years; Hugh Rowley of Culmore, Esq. member of parliament for Newtown-Lemavady in 1692; he married 17 October 1661, Mary, eldest daughter of Edward Rowley of Castle-Roe, Esq.; Daughter Mary, born in 1629, died in 1684; Margery, died young or unmarried; and Catherine, married William Smith, Archdeacon of Armagh.

John. John, of Castle-Roe, the eldest son of Hugh, came into Ireland in the reign of K. James I. as sole agent for the building of the towns of Derry and Coleraine, for the London Society, and brought his brothers already mentioned, with him. In the parliament of 1613, he represented the county of Coleraine, so called before its erection into that of Londonderry; upon the incorporation of the city of Derry, that year, he was by the charter appointed the first mayor. Dying in 1618 he left issue by Mary[1] daughter of Robert Gage of Rands in the county of Northampton, Esq. and Dowager of the barony of Kirkcudbright, one son Edward and three daughters, viz. Anne, (married to Tristram Beresford[2] of Coleraine, Esq. ancestor to the noble family of Tyrone); Elizabeth who died young; and Mary[3], married to James Clotworthy, Esq. brother to John, created Viscount Massareene, and by him had an only

[1] Ulster Office.   [2] Idem.   [3] Idem.

only daughter Mary, married to the Hon. Robert Fitz-Gerald, by whom she was grandmother of James, first Duke of Leinster.——The Lady Baroness Kirkcudbright, married thirdly Sir George Trevilian of Nettlesome in the county of Devon; and she married lastly Robert M'Lelan, Esq. and died 7 August 1639 [1].

Edward Rowley of Castle-Roe, Esq. only son of John, was representative of the county of Londonderry, in the parliaments of 1634 and 1635.——He was the first who raised a regiment of foot against the rebels in Ulster, and died honourably in the field. He married Lettice [2], daughter of Sir Hugh Clotworthy [3] of Antrim, Knt. and sister to the above-mentioned James Clotworthy, and by her who died 12 October 1681, had issue two sons and two daughters, viz.

Edward.

John, who succeeded his father. (1)

Hugh, who married Martha, daughter and heir to Owen O Conolly, the honoured discoverer of the plot formed by the Irish for the surprisal of Dublin 23 October 1641, and the massacre of the protestants all over the kingdom. (2)

Daughter Mary, was married to Hugh Rowley of Culmore, Esq. as before observed, and (1)

Lettice, who died unmarried, 5 November 1642 [4], aged 20 years. (2)

John, the eldest son, born 22 May 1635, was knighted in February 1661 for his important services at the time of the restoration. He was member of parliament for the county of Londonderry in that year, and died 21 August 1679. He married 26 December 1671, Mary [5], eldest daughter of Sir Hercules Langford of Summer-Hill in the county of Meath, Bart. (by Mary, daughter of Henry Upton of the county of Devon, afterwards of Castle-Norton in the county of Antrim, Esq. and had issue Arthur; Henry; Theophilus; Mary, and Martha [6]; of whom Mary was the only survivor); who dying 18 June 1683 [7], was buried at St. Michan's Dublin; and the estate of Summer-Hill came to this family. Sir John Rowley had issue by her, who died at Summer-Hill in 1684 one daughter, Lettice, who married Arthur, Viscount Loftus of Ely; and a son and heir

Sir John.

Hercules,

---

[1] Ulster's Office. [2] Idem. [3] Idem. [4] Idem. [5] Idem. [6] Idem. [7] Idem.

ROWLEY, VISCOUNTESS LANGFORD.

Hercules. Hercules, who was member of parliament for the county of Londonderry, from the year 1703, to his death 19 September 1742; he left issue, by Frances daughter of Arthur Upton of Castle-Upton in the county of Antrim, Esq. whom he married in January 1705, a daughter Dorothy-Beresford, married to Richard Viscount Powerscourt; and a son and successor

Hercules-Langford. Hercules-Langford, who in 1743 was elected to parliament in the room of his father, for the county of Londonderry, and in 1761 for that of Meath, which he has continued to represent in every parliament since that time; and is one of his Majesty's most honourable Privy Council. He married, 31 August 1732, Elizabeth [1] only daughter of Clotworthy Upton Esq. (member of parliament for the borough of Newtown, in 1695, and in 1703 for the county of Antrim, which he represented to his death in June 1725) by Jane his wife, daughter of John Ormsby of Ballyvenoge in the county of Limerick, Esq. and her only brother John Ormsby dying without issue, his estates devolved upon his niece Mrs. Rowley now lady Langford, who has had issue three sons, and four daughters, viz.

(1) Hercules [2], born 29 October 1737, representative in parliament for the county of Antrim.

(2) Clotworthy, who 20 January 1775, married Elizabeth daughter of William Crosbie of the county of Kerry, Esq., and niece to Garret late Earl of Mornington; he died in 1781, leaving issue by her who died 12 March 1779, an only daughter Frances [3].

(3) Arthur, deceased.

(1) Daughter Jane [4], married to Thomas Earl of Bective;
(2) Catherine, to Edward-Michael Lord Longford;
(3) Elizabeth; and
(4) Maria [5].

His Majesty was pleased to advance Mrs. Rowley to the peerage of this kingdom, by the titles of Viscountess Langford of Langford Lodge, and Baroness of Summerhill, with limitation of the honours of Viscount and Baron to her heirs male by her husband the Right Hon. Hercules Langford Rowley, by privy seal, dated at St. James's 27 December 1765, and by patent at Dublin 19 February, 1766 [6].

TITLES.] Elizabeth-Ormsby Rowley, Viscountess Langford of Langford Lodge in the county of Antrim, and Baroness of Summerhill, in the county of Meath.

CREATION,

---

[1] Ulster's office. [2] Ibid. [3] Ibid. [4] Ibid.
[5] Ulster's office. [6] Rot. 6º. Geo. III. 2. p. f. R. 4.

ANNESLEY, Viscount GLERAWLY.

CREATION.] So created 19 February 1766, 6 Geo. III.

ARMS.] Quarterly, 1st and 4th, quarterly, viz. 1st and 4th ruby, a bend between 6 croslets, fitchee, topaz; 2d and 3 diamond, 3 chess rooks and a chief pearl. 2d and 3d diamond, a cross moline, pearl.

CREST.] As borne by Mr. Rowley, a wolf's head erased, diamond, langued, ruby.

SUPPORTERS.] The dexter, a pallas; the sinister, the representation of temperance; both proper.

MOTTO.] BEAR AND FORBEAR.

SEAT.] Summerhill, in the county of Meath, 20 miles from Dublin.

ANNESLEY, Viscount GLERAWLY [a].

FRANCIS THE FIRST VISCOUNT VALENTIA married to his second wife, Jane, sister to Philip first Earl of Chesterfield, relict of Sir Peter Courtney, Bart.; and by her had seven children, of whom the eldest son was Francis, who was born in the parish of St. Giles in the fields London, 23 January 1628. He fixed his residence in Ireland, living at Cloghmaghericatt now Castle-Wellan in the county of Down; to oppose the arbitrary measures of K. James II. he raised a body of horse and foot, but was compelled to fly, and was attainted by the Irish parliament, who sequestered his estate of 390l. a year. He married Deborah, daughter

[a] From Lodge edit. 1754. II. 284. 285. and collections.

daughter of Doctor Henry Jones, Bishop of Meath and widow of John Boudler of Dublin, Esq. and by her, who died 4 September 1672, and was buried at St. John's Dublin, had issue three sons and five daughters, viz. Francis, who succeeded his father; Arthur and Henry who died without issue; daughter Jane, married to James Bailie of Inishargie in the county of Down, Esq. and died his widow 25 January 1748, æt. 87; Deborah, to the Rev. Charles Ward; Mary died an infant; Anne married to Henry, only son of Sir Edward Wood; and Catherine the youngest, died young.

Francis. Francis, the only surviving son, was baptized 24 October 1663, was educated at the Inner-Temple, and denominated of Thorganby, Esq. By an act passed the 11 and 12 K. William, he was appointed one of the trustees for the sale of the forfeited estates in Ireland; and 9 Q. Anne was constituted one of the commissioners for stating the public accompts of the kingdom, and so continued for three years; he served from the year 1705, in several parliaments both in England and Ireland; for the boroughs of Westbury and Downpatrick, and was a leading member, and the first promoter in the House of Commons, of the scheme for building 50 new churches in the city and suburbs of London, and was one of the commissioners for that purpose. 5 July 1695, he married Elizabeth daughter of Sir Joseph Martin of London, Knt., and had issue seven sons and two daughters, viz.

(1) Francis, L. L. D. a gentleman of great honour, candour, good breeding, charity and generosity; in September 1725, he was presented by Edward, Earl of Derby to the considerable Benefice of Winwick in Lancashire, and died 1 May 1740 at Newport in the county of Salop, on his journey to Bath. Whilst a youth at the University he married Elizabeth Sutton, but she being found guilty of adultery, he delivered a petition to the House of Peers, praying to have his marriage with the said Elizabeth dissolved, and to enable him to remarry; upon reading the same, 25 April 1725 leave was given for a bill to be brought in for that purpose, which being done, it received the assent of the house 19 May following, and the royal assent 31 of that month, in the same year [1], whereupon he married secondly Anne, daughter of Robert Gayer Esq. by his wife Lady Elizabeth

Annesley

---

[1] See Ruffhead's English Statutes of that year, in table of contents.

Annesley, and by her had issue, three sons, viz. Arthur, Francis, and James. Arthur the eldest, succeeded to considerable estates in Oxfordshire and in the North of Ireland; and he died in 1775, leaving issue two sons, the elder of whom Arthur, is now in possession of the family inheritance, and married to Miss Hardy.

Henry, baptized 29 September 1700, was Captain of the Diamond ship of war a fifth rate of 40 guns; and died in 1728 in the West Indies. (2)

Martin Annesley, D. D. baptized 12 October 1701, was rector of Frilsham and vicar of Bucklebury in the county of Berks; he married 12 December 1732, Mary, daughter of William Hanbury of Little Martle, in the county of Hereford, Esq. and died in June 1749. (3)

John and } both died unmarried. (4)
James, } (5)

William created Lord Glerawly. (6)

Arthur, died unmarried in January 1786, leaving Arthur Annesley of Blechendon-Park in the county of Oxford, his heir. (7)

Daughter Elizabeth, married to William Maguire of Dublin, Esq. son of Richard Maguire also of Dublin, Banker, and by him had fourteen children, of whom the survivors were William, Arthur, and Joseph now living. (1)

Deborah the younger daughter died unmarried. (2)

Francis Annesley of Castle-Wellan, married secondly in July 1732, Elizabeth, daughter of John Cropley of Rochester, Esq. and widow of William Gomeldon of Summerfield-Hall in Kent, Esq. she dying 20 May 1736 without issue, he married thirdly 31 August 1737, Sarah, only daughter of William Sloane of Portsmouth, Esq. and relict of Sir Richard Fowler of Harnage-Grange in the county of Salop, Knt. by neither of whom he had issue, and departing this life 7 August 1750, was succeeded by his sixth, but eldest surviving son

William, barrister at law, who was chosen to parliament 19 October 1741, for the borough of Middleton in the county of Cork; and 23 November 1750 appointed High Sheriff of the county of Down for the ensuing year.—He was advanced to the peerage of Ireland by the title of Baron Annesley of Castle-Wellan in the county of Down pursuant to privy seal at Kensington 28 July [1], and by patent at Dublin 20 September 1758 [2], he took his seat in the House of Peers 29 November 1759 [3]; and 23 September 1766,

William, 1 Viscount.

---

[1] Signet office. and Rot. de. A°. 32°. Geo. II. 1ª p. D. R. 46.
[2] Idem. Rot. 47.   [3] Lords Jour. IV. 162.

1766, his Majesty was pleased by privy seal at St. James's [1], and patent 14 November following [2], to create him Viscount Glerawly in the county of Fermanagh, by which title he took his seat in parliament 27 January 1768 [3].— He died at Clontarffe 12 September 1770, in the 61 year of his age, leaving issue by Lady Anne Beresford, eldest daughter of Sir Marcus, first Earl of Tyrone, whom he married 16 August 1738, (and she died 12 May 1770) four sons and one daughter, viz.

(1) Francis-Charles, who succeeded his father.

(2) Marcus, born 17 April 1743 died unmarried.

(3) Richard, born 14 April 1745, member of parliament for the borough of St. Canice, Kilkenny, and appointed in 1785 a commissioner of his Majesty's revenue; he married a daughter of Robert Lambert of Dunleddy, in the county of Down, Esq. and has issue three sons and two daughters.

(4) William, born 3 March 1747, entered into holy orders, and in May 1787, was promoted to the Deanery of Downe.—He married the only daughter of John Digby of Landenstown in the county of Kildare, Esq. and has issue.

Catharine the only daughter was married to Sir Arthur, now Earl of Arran, and died 21 November 1770, leaving issue.

Francis-Charles, 2 Viscount. Francis-Charles, the second and present Viscount, was baptized 27 November 1740, and 1 March 1771, he took his seat in parliament on the decease of his father [4]; he married 8 February 1766, Mary, daughter and heir to Richard Grove, of Ballyhimmock in the county of Cork, Esq. but hath no issue.

TITLES.] Charles Francis Annesley, Viscount Glerawly and Baron Annesley.

CREATIONS.] B. Annesley of Castle-Wellan in the county of Down, 20 September 1758, 32 Geo. II. and V. Glerawly in the county of Fermanagh, 14 November 1766, 7 Geo. III.

ARMS.]

---

[1] Signet Office and Rot. de A°. 7. Geo. III. 1ˢ. p. f. R. 24.
[2] Idem. Rot. 25.
[3] Lords Jour. IV.. 436
[4] Idem. 552

ANNESLEY, Viscount GLERAWLY.

ARMS.] Pally of fix, pearl and faphire; over all a bend, ruby.

CREST.] On a wreath, a moor's head, pale-faced, couped, proper.

SUPPORTERS.] The dexter, a Roman Knight; the finifter, a Moorifh prince; both habited and furnifhed, proper.

MOTTO.] VIRTUTIS AMORE.

SEAT.] Caftle-Wellan in the county of Down, 63 miles from Dublin.

END OF THE FIFTH VOLUME.

THE INDEX.

A.

ABERCROMBIE, General 86
ABERCORN, Earl of 109, 110, 111, 113, 114, 115, 117, 123
Aberdeen, Bishop of 98
Abergavenny, Lord 209, 220, 224
Abingdon, Earl of 28
Acclaim, Richard 73
——— Sir William 74
Acheson, Sir Archibald 110
Adair, Robert 137, 204
Adderley, Thomas 141
Addison, Joseph 292
Aislabie, Ralph 58
Albany, Duke of 96, 98, 99
Albemarle, Duke of 129, 159, 162
Aldborough, Earl of 279
Aldworth, Sir Richard 283
Agar, James 287
Allen, Viscount 181, 184
——— John 181
——— Sir Joshua 181, 253

Allen, Anthony 183
——— Richard 180
Allington, Lord 84
——— Hugh 260
Alpraham, Matthew 15
Alston, Sir Edward 195
Altamont, Earl of 87
Amherst, Sir Jeffrey 224
Andrews, Thomas 205
——— Sir William 230
Ancaster, Duke of 262
Angus, Earl of 97, 99
Anne, Princess 84
Annesley, Sir Francis 20
——— Francis 299, 301
——— Arthur Francis 301
——— James ib.
——— Arthur ib.
——— William ib.
——— Richard 302
——— Revd. William ib.
——— Francis-Charles ib.
Annally, Lord 278
Antrim, Earl of 48, 291, 293
Antrim,

VOL. V.   X

INDEX.

Antrim, Marquess of 112
Apenyon, Ralph 54
Archer, Lord 4
——— John ib.
Archdall, Edward 138
——— John 235
Ardglass, Earl of 272
Ardern, Sir Thomas 15
——— John 19
Argyle, Earl of 99, 100, 101
——— Duke of 119
Armagh, Archbishop of 36, 233
Arran, Earl of 98, 100, 102, 104, 106, 169, 182, 286, 302
Arscott, John 130
Arundell, Lady Frances 253
——— Richard 254
——— Lord 254, 258, 260
Ashburnham, Lord 64, 65
Ashbrooke, Viscount 279, 287
Ashcombe, Sir William 230
Ashenhurst, Ralph 16
Ashe, Lawrence 36
Ashfield, John 265
Aske, Robert 74
——— Sir Robert 250
Aston, Lord 217, 219
——— Sir Roger 261
Atherton, John 64
Atkins, Sir Robert 4, 11, 81
Atkinson, Dr. Philip 27
Audley, Lord 16, 59, 261
——— Lord Chancellor 209
Aungier, Rev. Ambrose 21
Awger, Thomas 73
Aylesbury, Earl of 196
Aylmer, Chief Justice 36

Aylworth, Bray 7
Ayloffe, Sir Benjamin 25
——— Sir John ib.
——— Sir Joseph ib.
Ayres, Sir John 173
Axtell, Colonel Daniel 166

B.

Babthorpe, Sir William 58, 73, 74
Baconsal, William 18
Bacon, Sir Nathaniel 195
——— Nicholas 240
Bagenal, Sir Nicholas 47, 48
Bagott, Sir Edward 155
Bailie, James 300
Bainton, John 78
Baker, ——— 158
Baldington, Thomas 5
Baldwin, John 291
Balfe, Robert 32
Baliol, John 92
Baltinglass, Viscount 230
Bangor, Bishop of 20
Barden, John 73
Barkeley, Sir Robert 113
Barlow, Sir Henry 259
Barnard, Christopher 205
——— Sir John 244
Barnstaple, Baron 2
Barnwall, Family of Crickstown, Baronets 30
——— Peter 31
——— Sir John 31, 39, 43
——— Edmund 32
——— Christopher 32, 33, 39, 41
——— Sir Patrick 32, 33, 35, 36, 39, 40, 41, 43
——— Sir Richard 32
——— Patrick 33, 46
Barnwall,

INDEX.

Barnwall, Richard 33, 38, 39, 46, 52, 237
——— Andrew 33
——— Sir Christopher 34, 36, 46
——— Family of Rowston 35
——— Sir Roger 35
——— James 36, 38, 39
——— Robert 37, 39, 41
——— Alexander 39
——— John ib.
——— Nicholas 42, 49
——— Anthony 43
——— Edward 44
Barney, Martin 189
Bartlett, Captain 49
Barrett, Dacres 197
Barry, Redmond 168
——— Gaynor 187
Barrington, Viscount 198, 200, 203
——————— Francis 201, 202
——————— Sir Gobart 202
——————— Sir Thomas ib.
——————— Sir Francis ib.
——————— General John 204
——————— Daines ib.
——————— Admiral Samuel ib.
——————— Shute 205
Barrymore, Earl of 69
Baskerville, Humphrey 81
——————— Sir John 188
Bathe, William 35
Bathurst, Benjamin 163
——— Peter 14, 82
——— Lord 82, 163
Bateman, Viscount 245, 248
——— William 245, 248
Bateman, John 245
——— Gyles ib.
——— Joas ib.
——— Sir James 246
Battareaus, General 223
Baynham, John 208
——— William 210
Beake, Sir Nicholas 63
Bealing, Richard - Arundel 221
Beaton, Sir David 100
Beaumont, Sir Thomas 229
Bechard, John 73
Beckwith, Leonard 57
Bective, Earl of 298
Bedford, Duke of 266
——— Earl of 91
Belhaven, Lord 95, 97, 123
Bellew, John 37
——— Lord 179
Bellamont, Earl of 136
Belinge, Richard 47
Bellingham, William 70
Belvidere, Earl of 146
Bendysh, Henry 201
Bennet, Sir John 83
——— Anthony - Purlton 254
Bennyon, Thomas 16
Berenger, Moses 231
Beresford, Tristram 296
Berkeley, George 139
——— Doctor 179
——— Lord 239, 242, 243
——— Sir John 269, 283
Bermansel, John 4
Bermingham, Sir William 31
Bernaval, Sir Nicholas 30
——— Sir Ulpram 30
Berry, William 251
——— Richard ib.
Berwick, Duke of 26, 43
Bertie,

INDEX.

Bertie, Lady Bridget 28
———— William *ib.*
———— Richard 262
Befsborough, Earl of 291
Beverwaert, Lord of 68
Bingham, John 115, 174
———— Henry 183
———— Sir Richard 269
Bird, John 263
Blackwell, John 182
Blayney, Lord 183
Blenerhaffett, Sir John 139
———————— John 141
Bligh, Thomas 139
Blunt, Edward 273
Bodvile, Sir John 66
Bodychan, John 25
Bohemia, King of 83
Bold, Sir Robert 31
Bolney, Thomas 207
Bolton, Duke of 80, 167
———— Family of Brazeel 141
———— Edward 141, 178
———— Sir Edward 141, 163
———— Sir Richard 141
———— Robert *ib.*
———— Theophilus *ib.*
Bond, William 217
———— Sir Thomas *ib.*
———— Henry-Jermyn 223
Booth, Sir William 17
———— George 18
———— Thomas 250
———— Hugh 280
Borlace, Doctor 238
Borough, Lord 25
Boftock, Sir Ralph 17
Bofvile, Sir Thomas 249
———— Sir Anthony 250
Bofwell, Robert 185
———— Sir John 188
Bothwell, Earl of 101
Bouchier, Thomas 247

Boudler, John 300
Bourke, Sir John 38
Bovey, John 267
Bovile, William 257
Bowden, William 267
Bowes ———— 227
Boyde, Sir Thomas 110
———— Lord 111
Boyle, John 168
———— Michael 19
Boyne, Viscount 110, 172, 174, 177
Boye, Sorley 267
Brabazon, Lord Treasurer 36
———— George 140
Braddock, General 224
Broderick, Sir Thomas 159
———— Sir Allan 160
———— Sir St. John 161, 162, 163, 164, 168
———— Laurence 163
———— Doctor Laurence 163, 170, 292
———— Thomas 171
———— Henry *ib.*
———— William *ib.*
———— John *ib.*
Brandon, James 32
———— Sir William 258
Bray, Edmond 9
Brechin, Lord of 92
Brereton, Randal 17
———— Sir Randal 17, 60, 62
———— Sir William 17, 59
———— John 19
———— Andrew 41
———— Ralph 62
———— Randolph 151
———— Hugh 295
———— Sir Andrew 295
Brett, Richard 17
Breufe, Sir Paul 268

Brews,

INDEX.

Brews, Sir Richard	255, 256, 261	Bulkeley, Family of, Baronets		20
Bridgham, George	189	——— Rowland	21,	24
Bringfield, Colonel	143, 145	——— William		21
		Bulmer, Sir Ralph		57
Bristol, Earl of	216	Burdet, Sir Robert		12
Bromley, Sir Thomas	10	Burgoyne, Christopher		201
——— Robert	16	Burguillon, John		227
——— John	59	Burrowes, Robert	168,	169
Brome, Viscount	187	——— Erasmus		273
Bromflete, Sir Thomas	72	Burton, William	77,	226
Brooksby, William	282	——— John		293
Brooke, Earl of	125	Bury, William		180
——— Sir Henry	178	Buswell, Eusebius		260
——— Sir Basil	216	——— Sir Eusebius		ib.
Browne, Sir Anthony	209, 210	Butler, Sir William		2
		——— Thomas		15
——— Lady Anne	35	——— Richard		34
——— George	116	——— Edward		47
——— Captain	186	——— Henry		140
——— General	ib.	——— Sir Richard		168
——— Robert	291	——— Sir Edmond		267
Brownejohn, ———	140	——— Pierce		290
Browning, Davidson	197	Bysse, John Lord Chief Baron		
Brownlow, William	124			23
Bruce, Lord	196	——— John	133,	134
Buckton, Robert	250			
Bucknall, John Askell	199	**C.**		
Buckhurst, Lord Treasurer	62			
		Cadogan, Earl of		69
Buckingham, Duke of	129, 131, 208, 266	Caernarvon, Earl of		127
		Calverley, Sir George		62
——— Earl of	150	Cambden, Viscount		85
——— Marquess	231	Cambridge, Earl of		105
Bulkeley, Viscount	14, 20	Campbell, Sir Matthew		111
——— Family of Eaton	15	Canterbury, Archbishop of	3, 209,	241
——— John	16	Capel, Sir Gamaliel		196
——— Sir William	ib.	Carbery, Lord	31,	139
——— Family of Porthamell	18	Carbonel, William		257
		Carden, Sir John Craven		183
——— Sir Richard	18, 22	Carew, Sir George		267
——— Daniel	18	Carpenter, General		145
——— Robert	19	Carter, Thomas		239
				Carysfort,

INDEX.

Carysfort, Lord 186
Caffilis, Earl of 105, 106
Castledurrow, Lord 242, 285, 287
Castleman, Rev. John 170
——— Jonathan ib.
Castlehaven, Earl of 263
Cathcart, Lord 111, 125
Cavan, Earl of 178, 183
Cavendish, Lord James 69
Cavil, Sir John 249
Caulfield, Toby 287
Cecil, Secretary 233
——— Richard 260
Chamberlain, Leonard 58
——— Sir John 212
——— Sir William 259
Chandos, Duke of 3
——— Lord 9
Chaplin, 247
Charlemaigne, Emperor 90
Chatelherault, Duke of 102
Cheadle, Roger 17
——— 26
——— Richard ib.
Chedworth, Lord Family of 81
——— Lord 82
Cheney, Sir John 59
Chester, Earl of 2, 54, 55, 56, 225, 252
Chesterfield, Earl of 299
Chetwood, Knightly 201
——— John ib.
Chetwynd, Viscount 148, 153, 155
——— Richard 149
——— Thomas 151
——— Sir William ib.
——— Walter 153
Chichester, Edward 22
——— Viscount ib.
Cholmondeley, Family of Chorley and Whitby 56

Cholmondeley, Family of Vale-Royal 63
——— Thomas 65
——— Seymour ib.
——— Sir Hugh 17
——— Viscount 17, 64, 66
——— Hugh 17
——— Lord 67
——— Earl of 55, 63, 66, 67
——— John 56
——— Roger 57
——— Sir Richard ib.
——— Sir Henry 58
——— Robert 64
Choppoyne, Robert 182
Churchill, John 73
——— Sir Winston 161
Clanbraffil, Earl of 96
Clare, Earl of 9
——— Viscount 26
Clarendon, Earl of 159, 193, 195, 211
Clarges, Thomas 205
——— Sir Thomas ib.
Clarke, Humphrey 79
——— James 137
——— Sir Edward 229
Clanrickard, Earl of 269
Claypole, Adam 262
Clayton, Sir Randal 162
Clifford, Sir Roger 3
Clifton, Lord 114
Clotworthy, James 296
——— Sir Hugh 297
Clover, ——— 198
Cloyne, Bishop of 139, 171
Cradock, George 66
Craifford, Matthew 111
Craige, Sir James 21
Crawford, Earl of 97, 98, 105
Crespie,

INDEX.

Crespie, Count 90
Creythin, Robert ap Hugh 24
Crofts, General 145
Crooke, Sir George 194, 195
────── Sir John 201
Crompe, William 36
Cromwell, Oliver 115
────── Lord 260, 272, 273
Cropley, John 301
Crosbie, William 298
Cobham, Lord 231
────── Viscount 232
Cock, William 234
Cockburne, Patrick 96
Cocton, Sir Simon 4
Colclough, Rev. Thomas 138
────── Cæsar ib.
Coleraine, Lord 195
Colley, Henry 124
────── Anthony 282
Cole, John 138
Colholme, Sir John 188
Colt, ────── 44
Colooney, Lord 136
Colquhoon, Alexander 111
Colvile, Sir Robert 242
Compton, Lord 25
Coningsby, Sir Thomas 8
Connell, Richard 19
────── Michael 124
Conolly, William 86
Constable, Sir Robert 57
────── Fulke 188
────── Marmaduke 189
Constant, Colonel 145
Conway, Sir John 9
────── Lord ib.
────── Sir Edward ib.
────── John 18
────── Pierce 27

Conyers, Lord 57
Conyers, Sir George 74
────── Reginald 282
Cooke, Edward 161
────── James 198
Cooper, Lord Chancellor 10
────── Joshua 183
Coote, Sir Charles 115
Cope, Sir Edward 152
────── Sir Jonathan 158
Copley, Sir John 126
────── Sir Thomas 211
Copinger, Ralph 192
Corbet, Sir Roger 60, 227
────── Miles 237
Cork and Orrery, Earl of 169, 253
Cornwall, Earl of 13, 19, 127
Cornwallis, Earl of 187
Cossart, David 140
Coventry, Bishop of 155
Courthorpe, Sir Peter 170
────── John ib.
Courtney, Edward 22, 23
────── Sir Peter 299
Coward, Colonel 123
Cowse, Kanton 124
Cox, Thomas 10
────── Sir Richard 165, 178
Coytmore, Robert 26
Culme, Hugh 5
────── Sir Thomas ib.
Culpeper, Lord 120
────── Sir Thomas 120, 121
Cumberland, Earl of 58
Cunyngham, Sir William 112
Cusack, James 32
────── Sir Thomas 38
────── Christopher 41
────── Henry 46
Curson, Penn Ashton 87

Dacres,

D.

Dacres, Sir Thomas	12
Daeth, Sir Thomas	75, 76
Daines, Sir William	204
Dakine, John	189
Dalby, William	281
Dallifon, William	73
Dalton, Theobald	263
Daly, Peter	53
Danby, John	250
Danett, Lawrence	228
D'anney, Sir Edward	72
———— Sir Nicholas	ib.
Danvers, Sir Henry	238
Daquila, Don Juan	269
D'arcy, William	37
———— Lord	74
Darell, Henry	215
———— Sir John	73
———— Thomas	73
———— Sir George	ib.
Darlington, Countefs of	85
Darnley, Lord	98
———— Earl of	139
Darrell, George	260
Dartmouth, Earl of	33
Davenport, Sir John	15
———— Sir William	25
———— John	59
Davidfon, William	233
Dawney, Sir Paine	72
———— Sir John	72, 73
———— Sir Nicholas	72
———— Roger	73
———— George	74
———— Doctor	76
Dawfon, Jofhua	178
Deane, Sir John	263
———— Jofeph	293
De Beauchamp, Simon	91
De Bellamont, Humphrey	89
———— Robert	92
De Beefton, Henry	55
De Belward, William	54
De Bermingham, Sohn	150
———— Thomas	151
De Berneval, Reginal	30
———— Sir Wilfranus	30
De Befeicke, Sir Macy	3
De Braybroke, Gerard	128
De Broderick, George	159
De Brueil, Lewis	259
De Burgo, Hubert	188
De Burton, John	56
———— Simon	ib.
De Caen, Robert	91
De Capenhurft,	59
De Chetwynd, Adam	148
———— Sir John	ib.
———— William	ib.
———— Roger	149
De Cholmondeley, Sir Hugh	55, 56, 59
———— Richard	59
———— William	59
De Clermont, Hugh	2
De Clifford, Robert	ib.
De Coéton, William	4
De Cogan, Anna	30
De Dreux, John	66
De Egerton, Wion	55
De Gauder, Ralph	91
De Glanville, Sir Gilbert	256
De Golbourne, Sir William	55
De Grandmefnil, Hugh	92
De Grendon, Ralph	148
———— Robert	149
———— Sir Ralph	ib.
De Grimfton, Silvefter	188
De Hamilton, William	92
De Harecourt, Richard	148
De Harling, Sir Robert	259
De Haftings	

INDEX.

De Hasting, Sir John 63
De Henhall, Richard 59
De Holme, Gilbert 128
De Horn, Count 68
De Ipston, William 63
De Kearnie, Count 124
De Kingsley, Richard 56
——— Randal ib.
Delafeld, John 34
Delahyde, George 32
——— Christopher 37
——— Richard 47
Delapole, 256
De la Spencer, John 92
De la Spine, Sir Guy 4, 6
——— William 4
De la Roche, Thomas 150
De Laverer, Thomas 57, 58
De Lerges, Monsieur 101
De Levinston, Alexander 96
De Lovayn, Sir Nicholas 207
——— Nicholas ib.
Delves, Henry 60
——— Sir Thomas 62
——— Sir Henry 268
Delvin, Lord 32, 39
——— Lady 168
De Maigne, Walter 2
De Malpas, Sir William 55
De Mitton, Philip 148
De Molesworth, Sir Walter 127, 128
——— John 127
De Montalt, Lord 140
De Monte Morisco, Harvey 289
——— Jeffrey ib.
De Munsale, Edmund 56
De Nassau, Lewis 68
Denbigh, Earl of 105
Denny, Sir Anthony 267
Denton, Sir Thomas 229

Derby, Earl of 16, 57, 60, 61, 309
Dering, Sir Edward 58, 161
——— Sir Cholmondeley 58
De Rode, Winthianus 295
——— Henry ib.
——— Randolph ib.
Derwentwater, Earl of 221, 222
De Rowley, Roger 295
Desbouverie, Sir Edward
De Shamsbury, Thomas 55
Desmond, Earl of 217
De Spurstow, William 56
De Sudeley, John 2
——— Ralph 3
De Temple, Henry 227
——— Nicholas ib.
——— Richard ib.
De Tilley, Henry 128
De Totneis, Alured 1
De Trrei, Henry 1
——— William 3
De Trogoze, Robert 2
De Velci, Viscount 124, 234
Devon, Earl of 72, 84
Devereux, Nicholas 47
——— John 217
Dewes, Sir Symonds 218
De Weverham, Hugh 55
De Wingfield, John 255
Dewyas, Robert, 2
Dickson, David 179
Digby, Sir Simon 9
——— John 302
Digley, Sir Roger 94
Dillon, Sir Robert 32
——— William 33
——— John 296
——— Sir Bartholomew 35, 37
——— Martin 42
Dillon,

Dillon, Gerald	116
———— Viscount	119
———— Francis	263
———— Theobald	ib.
Dirleton, Earl of	106
Dixwell, Sir Basil	242
Dolliffe, George	248
Dolman, George	61
Domville, Matthew	16
Doneraile, Viscount	183
Done, John	62
Dongan, Sir John	42
Dorset, Marchioness of	210
———— Duke of	214
Dover, Earl of 217,	218
Dowdall, Lancelot	22
———— Edward	33
Dowdeswell, William	10
———— Charles	11
Downe, Viscount	72, 73, 75
Downes, Roger	60
Downing, Sir George	24
Douglas, Sir James	96
———— Earl of	97, 98
———— Marquess of	106, 109
———— Duke of	109
Draicot, John	46
———— Sir John	47
———— Sir Henry	ib.
Drake, Lady Maude	30
———— Sir Nicholas	ib.
Drury, William	90
———— Sir Drue	263
Drayton, Sir Simon	128
Drogheda, Earl of	168
Drummond, Lord	100
———— Sir John	111
Dublin, Archbishop of 19, 20, 37, 145, 270
———— Archdeacon of	21
Dumferling, Earl of	109
Duminelle ————	247
Dunboyne, Lord	31
Dungannon, Viscount 274, 291, 292, 294
Dungarvon, Viscount	169
Dunn, Charles	284
———— Barnaby	ib.
Dunsany, Lord 32, 40, 47
Dupass, Samuel	185
Durrow, McDonagh	283
Durward, ————	264
Dutton, William	7
———— John 17, 59, 80
———— Thomas	18
———— Sir Thomas 55, 59
———— Sir Richard	58
Dysart, Earl of	64

E.

Eastcourt, Thomas	199
Eaton, James	20
Eccles, Hugh	239
Eden, Thomas	76
———— Sir Robert	ib.
Edward, Prince	209
Edwards, Sir Francis	70
Eglinton, Earl of 105, 106
Egerton, Philip	15
———— Sir Philip 27, 66
———— Sir Rowland 27, 66
———— Lord Chancellor	62
———— Sir John	63
———— John 64, 66
Elliott, Richard	125
Ellis, Edward	285
———— ————	218
Elphin, Bishop of	183
Elphinston, James	111
Ellyott, Thomas	267
Ely, Lord Chancellor	270
Empson, Sir Richard	7
Esmond, Lord	172
———— Lady	273

Essex,

INDEX.

Essex, Earl of 170, 209, 233, 260, 262, 272
Ethelbald, King 225
Ethelred, King 225
Evandale and Ochiltree, Lord 100
Evans, General 231
——— Sir William 290
Everard, James 32, 44
——— Thomas 36
——— Sir Richard 196
Everton, Henry 228
Evers, Lord 101
Eure, Lord 74
Eustace, Sir Richard 31, 37
——— Christopher 37
——— Lord Chancellor 160
Eurieux, Earl of 90, 92
Eyton, Thomas 56
Eyre, Robert 252

F.

Fade, ——— 291
Fagan, Christopher 115, 116
Fairfax, Sir Thomas 74
Falconberg, Viscount 52
Falstaffe, John 255
Farmer, John 229
Ferdinand, Prince 187
Ferrard, Lord 134, 140
Ferrers, Earl of 14, 252
——— Sir Thomas 252
——— Lord 150
——— Humphrey 252
Fettiplace, Robert 86
Finch, Lord Chancellor 239
Fineux, Sir John 74
Fingall, Earl of 51
Finglass, Thomas 46
——— John 47
Fitton, Hamon 55

Fitz-Allen, John, 258
Fitz-Eustace, ——— 267
Fitz-Gerald, Thomas 31
——— William 33
——— Sir Edward 41, 46
——— Philip 50
——— Robert 184, 297
——— Maurice 289
Fitz-Gibbon, John 168
Fitz-Harding, Viscount 156
Fitz-Hugh, Robert 54
Fitz-Leons, Patrick 37, 39
Fitz-Lewis, Sir John 261, 268
Fitz-Nigel, Robert 55
Fitz-William, Sir William, 8, 214, 268
——— Earl of 131
——— William 189, 214
Flatsbury, James 36, 48
Fleming, James 37
——— Sir John 48
——— Robert 73
——— Lord 101, 106
Fletcher, Walter 138
Flinton, Robert 188
Flower, Captain William 284, 285
——— Lieutenant-Colonel Henry 284
——— Thomas 242, 285
——— William 278, 286
——— Sir Richard 282
Folliott, Lord 274
Folkstone, Viscount 216
Ford, Major John 124
——— Matthew 120
Forrester, Lord 199
Forster, John 139
——— John Hill 139
——— General 144
Fortescue, Henry 173

Y 2   Fortescue,

Fortescue Sir John,	229	Gage, Robert	296
Forth, James	123	Galloway, Viscount Lord	
Forthingham, Robert	189	——— Earl of	92
Fountayne, John 251,	252	Galway, Viscountess	183
Fowlds, Sir William	76	——— Viscount 249, 251,	
Fowler, Sir Richard	301		252
Fox, James	17	Galtrim, Baron of	32, 37
——— Sir Patrick	ib.	Gape, Thomas	199
Frasier, Sir Alexander	95	Garnish, John	190
Fraunces, Sir John	282	Garraway, Sir Henry	58
Freke, Family of	169	Gascoigne, William	18
——— Sir John	ib.	——— Henry	57
——— Francis	ib.	Gayer, Robert	300
——— Robert	ib.	Gedney, Thomas	228
——— Thomas	ib.	Geering, Richard	139
——— Raufe	ib.	Geoghegan, Kedagh	33
Frensham, Rev. Mr.	139	Gerard, Sir Francis	244
Frith, John	6	——— Sir Gilbert	272
Frobisher, John	17	Germany, Duke of	159
Frodsham, William	149	Gibbs, Sir Henry 229,	230
Froggett, Godfrey	17	Gideon, Sir Sampson	224
Frowick, John	188	Giffard, Sir John	3
Fryer, Sir John	244	——— Sir Thomas	238
Fuller, Doctor	4, 229	——— Lady	240
Fyan, Richard	38	Gill, George	190
——— William	38	Ginkle, General	175
——— Lady Anne	39	Girlington, Nicholas	189
		Glasgow, Bishop of 96, 99,	
G.			108
		Glammis, Lord	105
Gage, Viscount 206,	218	Glencairn, Earl of 100,	105
——— John 207, 210,	217	Glerawley, Viscount	299
——— Sir John 207,	213		301
——— Henry	210	Gloucester, Earl of	1, 91
——— Rev. John	ib.	Godfrey, William 75,	223
——— Family of Healing		Godolphin, William	243
	211	Golding, ———	264
——— Colonel	212	Gomeldon, William	301
——— Sir Edward	213	Good, James	51
——— George	216	Goodmaghan, Sir John	188
——— Family of Hengrave,		Gordon, Lord Adam	94
Baronets	217	——— Duke of	106
——— Count Joseph	220	——— Lord	ib.
——— General Thomas	223	Gore, Frederick	142
——— Hodgson	277	——— Sir Ralph 167,	179
			Gore,

INDEX.

Gore, Sir William 175
—— Sir Paul 276
—— Sir Arthur ib.
—— Ralph 290
—— William ib.
Goring, John 153
—— Sir Henry 218
Gormanston, Viscount 43, 50
Gosford, Viscount 110
Golding, —— 84
Goutell, Sir Robert 258
Grammont, Count 119
————— Duke ib.
Grant, Captain John 141
Gregor, Hugh 130
Green, Major 186
Grenville, Richard 231
————— Hester 232
Gresham, Paul 260
Grey, Lord Deputy 36, 267
—— Lord 66
Griffith, Guilliam ap 18
——— Sir William 19, 62
——— Owen 20
——— John ap 18
——— John 27
——— Sir Edward 48
Grimston, Sir Harbottle 79, 192, 193, 197, 205
————— Viscount 188,
————— Sir Thomas 188
————— Sir William ib.
————— Sir Gervais ib.
————— Edward 190, 191
————— Sir Samuel 195, 196, 197, 205
————— William 199
Grosvenor, Sir Richard 63
Grove, Richard 302
Grubham, Nicholas 78
————— Sir Richard 78, 79

Guldeford, Sir Richard 208
————— Sir Thomas 215
Guise, Sir John 83
—— Duke of 100, 190

H.

Hadley, Benjamin 180
Haddington, Earl of 94
Hales, John 149
Hall, Edward 7
—— Roger 124
—— Sir Philip 197
—— William 199
—— Benedict 223
Halifax, Marquess of 196
Hamilton, Sir John 93, 100
————— Sir William 93, 109, 111
————— Count 51
————— Sir Thomas 94
————— Lady Susan 12
————— Sir Archibald 95
————— Sir James ib.
————— Sir Alexander 97
————— Lord 96, 100
————— Duke of 12, 101, 105, 106, 124
————— James 103
————— Marquess of 105
————— Lord John 105, 107, 108
————— Dutchess of 106
————— Lord Claude 107
————— Sir Claude 109, 111
————— Sir Robert 109
————— Sir George 110, 114, 116, 118, 121
————— Sir Frederick 110, 114, 172, 173
————— William 120, 174
————— George 120
————— Richard 121, 179
Hamilton,

INDEX.

Hamilton, Lord Archibald 124
────── John James 126
────── John *ib.*
────── Rev. Gustavus 141, 178
────── General Richard 175, 43
────── Major Gustavus 175
────── Lord Baron 176
────── Gustavus 178, 179
────── Henry *ib.*
────── Joshua *ib.*
────── Sackville *ib.*
────── Charles 180
Hammond, Thomas 234
────── John 238
────── Doctor Henry
Hanbury, Capel 13
────── William 301
────── John 247
Handasyd, Colonel 137
Handcock, Gustavus 234
Hanmer, Peter 19
Hapsburg, Count 159
Hapson, Major-General 204
Harbottle, John 191
Harcourt, Sir Simon 10
Hardell, Sir Thomas 158
Harland, Robert 218
Harefoot, Harold 225
Harrington, Sir John 153, 282
────── Sir James 267
Harrison, Robert 234
Hartopp, Chiverton 87
Harvey, Daniel 27
────── George 28
────── Thomas 190
Harvey, Sir William 216, 217
────── Captain 283

Harvey, Sir Nicholas 266
────── Lord 267
Haselrig, Bertin 153
Haselwood, William 250
Hastings, Sir Hugh 258
Hatbean, 131
Hay, Sir Thomas 100
Haydocke, Joshua 290
Hedges, 248
Hely, Sir John 286
Hender, John 129
Hereford, Earl of 2
────── Viscount 12
────── Bishop of 243
Herick, 268
Heriott, James 94
Hertford, Earl of 101, 250
Heritage, John 228
Hill, Thomas 61
────── Edward 139
────── Arthur 141, 163, 294
────── Michael 170, 292
Hilliard, William 78
Hillsborough, Earl of 157, 292, 294
────── Viscount 168
Hoare, Richard 199
Hoby, William 9
Holbein, Hans 209
Holden, Ralph 12
Holford, Christopher 62
────── Thomas 15, 17, 62
────── Sir George 17
────── Sir John 62
────── George 63
Holland, Owen 25
────── Edward 65
Hollis, Gervais 131
Hollingshead, Ralph 16
Holmes, Richard 137
Holt, Thomas 190
Home, Lord 100
Honeypot 256
Hook, Alderman Thomas 132
Hope,

INDEX.

Hope, Sir Roger 117
Hopkins, Sir William 25
Hotham, Sir John 249
Houblin, Abraham 243
Hovendon, Robert 79
How, Viscount 78, 80, 84, 204
——- Henry 78
——- John 78, 81, 86
——- George Grubham 79
——- Sir Richard Grubham ib.
——- Family of Cold Berwick, Baronets ib.
——- Sohn Grubham ib. 80
——- Sir Thomas ib.
——- Lady Annabella 81
——- Sir William 86
——- Earl of 87
——- Sir George Grubham 195
Howard, Lieutenant General 70
——- Lord 98, 262
Howdenby, Robert 73
Howth, Lord 46, 51
Hudson, Sir Roger 12
Humble, Sir William 216
Hume, Sir John 175
——— Sir Gustavus ib.
Hungate, Sir Philip 58
Hunsdon, Lord 80
Hunter, Thomas Orby 261
Huntingdon, Earl of 91, 152, 153
Huntley, Earl of 99, 101, 106
——— Marquess of 106, 114
Hurland, Thomas 130
Huson, Colonel John 160
Hussey, Meyler 35
——— Patrick 37
——— George 250

Hutchinson, Alderman Daniel 132
——————— Ephraim 291
Hutton, Sir Richard 74

J.

Jackson, Richard 169
Jacob, Sir John 263
Jeffreys, Sir James 168
——— James St. John ib. 285
Jekyl, William 228
Jermyn, Lord 217, 218
——- Sir Robert 217
Jennings, Richard 51, 119
———— Sir John 210
Jephson, John 234
Jervorth, Goth Gryffith 15
Inchiquin, Baron 272
Jones, Griffith 26
——- Sir William 113
——- Theophilus 141
——- Michael 284
——- Richard 285
Johnston, Robert 185
Johnston, Captain 137
Itchingham, 261
Julien, William ib.

K.

Kay, Robert 282
Keating, Maurice 141
Keck, Sir Anthony 11
——- John Tracy 12
Keith, Sir William 95, 97
Kells, Viscount 54
Kelly, Joseph 139
Kemble, Peter 224
Kemp, Anthony 215, 219
Kendal, 229
Kenly, John 35
Kenn, Christopher 57

Kerry,

INDEX.

Kerry, Lord 12
―――― Earl of 90
Kent, Earl of 2
―――― Rev. Mr. 65
―――― Duke of 242
―――― Earl of 262
―――― Countess of 264
Keyt, Sir William 12, 13
―――― Sir John 13
―――― Sir Thomas Charles ib.
―――― William ib.
Kielmansegge, Baron 85
Kildare, Earl of 35, 50, 184
―――― Countess 210
Killala, Bishop of 276
Killeen, Lord 32
Kilmarnock, Earl of 111
Kinderton, Baron 15, 63
King, Sir Henry 270
―――― Matthew 41
―――― Charles 242
―――― Luke 243
Kingsland, Viscount 29, 31, 32, 35, 43, 49
Kingston, Earl of 276
Kington, Anthony 9
Kirk, General 121
Kirkcudbright, Lady 296, 297
Kitson, Sir Thomas 216
Knap, Mr. 231
Knapton, Lord 124, 234
Knowles, 267

L.

Lambert, Charles 178
―――― Sir Oliver 270
―――― Robert 302
Lanark, Earl of 106
Lancaster, Duke of 149
Langford, Viscountess 295
―――― Sir Hercules 297

Langham, Sir John 231
Langley, Thomas 227
Langton, John 73
Latimere, Lord ib.
Larkton, John 15
Lawson, Sir Henry 219
Le Cave, Peter 72
Leicester, Earl of 88, 89, 90, 91, 92, 225, 236
Le Cooper, David 26
Ledgiard, Sir Richard 74
Lee, Henry 79
―――― Sir Henry 28
―――― Edmund 229
―――― Colonel 244
Legard, John 74
―――― Sir John ib.
Legge, Colonel, 33, 82
Le Grosse, Raymond 90
Leigh, Lord 11
―――― Sir Thomas 12
Leinster, Earl of 65, 66
―――― Countess of 85
―――― Duke of 289, 297
Leitrim, Lord 38
Leman, Thomas 190
Lennox, Earl of 98, 104
―――― Duke of 105
Lenthall, William 114, 117
―――― Sir John 230
Leslie, Charles Powel 293
Leveson, Sir Richard 230
―――― Sir John ib.
Levingston, Sir Alexander 97
―――― Sir Robert 100
Lewen, Sir William 24
Lewis, Thomas 129
Lewellin, Hugh 18
Le Wolfe, Thomas 295
Lhuellin, Jenkin ap Griffith ap 20
Licelor, John 295
Limerick, Earl of 42, 52
Limerick

INDEX.

Limerick, Viscount 179
——— Lady 243
Lincoln, Earl of 25
Linlithgow, Earl of 97
Lisle, William Clapcott 70
——— John 79
——— Lord 236
Litchfield, Bishop of 149
——— Earl of 244
Locke, ——— 135
Lodge, Francis 290
Loftus, Sir Adam 30, 159, 160, 236
——— Nicholson 141
——— Viscount 297
London, Bishop of 80, 266
Londonderry, Earl of 64, 230
Long, Philip Parker 82
Longford, Lord 298
Longueville, Duke of 100
——— John de Sutton 128
——— Sir Henry 230
Lovell, Henry 198, 205
Lovibond, Edward 180
Lound, Sir Alexander 73
Louth, Lord 36, 47, 51
Lowther, Sir Gerard 134
Lloyde, William 18
——— Robert 19, 25
——— Edward 19
——— David 20
——— Hugh ib.
——— Pierce ib.
——— Piers 26
Lucas, ——— 146
——— Robert 250
Luckyn, Sir Capel 195, 196
——— William 196
——— Sir William ib.
——— Robert ib.
Lucy, Sir Thomas 7
Lumm, Sir Francis 139

Luvel, Lord 148
——— John ib.
Lynch, Sir Thomas 129
Lyons, Hugh-Montgomery 180
Lyster, Christopher-Kirwan ib.
Lyttleton, John 10
——— Sir Thomas 231
——— Sir William ib.
——— Christian 232

M.

Macdonnell, Lady Anne 48
Macclesfield, Earl of 220
Mac-Carthy, Florence 283
Mac-Glanigh, Caher 173
——— Rory ib.
Mac-Hugh, Pheogh 267
Mackworth, Sir Henry 125
Mac Lelan, Robert 297
Ma-Mahon, 51
Mac-Murray, Owen Mc Manney 173
Mac-William, 265
Mac-Williams, Henry 65
Madden, Robert 235
Magnus, Hugh 90
Magrath, John 172
Maguire, William 301
——— Richard ib.
Maltavers, Lord 258
Manchester, Duke of 267
Mangey, 129
Manwaring, Edward 16
——— Henry 22, 295
——— Sir Randal 60, 62
——— Randal 60
——— Sir Thomas 62
——— Charles 63
——— Sir William 79
Mar, Earl of 107, 144
Marishal, Earl of 97
Marlborough,

Vol. V. Z

INDEX.

Marlborough, Duke of 86, 142, 143, 231, 248
——— Dutchess of 119
Martin, Henry 22
——— Robert 43
——— Anthony ib.
——— Richard ib.
——— Sir Joseph 300
Mary, Queen of Scotts 98, 209
Mason, Robert 140
——— Thomas 192
Massareene, Viscount 296
Masterson, Roger 22
——— Sir Richard 47
——— John 60
Mathew, George 124, 219
——— Daniel 254
Maule, Thomas 138
Maxwell, Lord 105
Meath, Bishop of 22, 36, 145, 300
Meautys, Sir Thomas 195
——— Hercules 195, 210
Medows, Sir Philip 163, 170
Mee, Benyamen, 244
Mellent, Earl of 88, 89, 90
Melross, Abbot 96
Mercer, Robert 285
Mercia, Earl of 2, 225
Meredyth, Robert 18
——— Sir William 64
——— Rev. Charles 124
——— Sir Robert 236
——— Sir Amos 284
Merry, Henry 216
Meverell, Robert 172
——— Lewis 151
Meyler, Robert 250
Meyrick, William 64
Middleton, Sir Thomas 63
——— Thomas 137, 142

Middleton Viscount 159, 163, 166, 167
——— Sir William 250
Middlemore, Robert 152
——— Thomas 219
Minshull, John 17, 63
Misset, Richard 39
Mitchell, Knight 137
Molyneux, Sir Richard 16
——— Sir Francis 83, 135
Monroe, Sir George 174
Montacute, Viscount 210
Montagu, Sir James 10
Moore, Rev. William 22
——— Mr. 124
——— Capel 168
——— William Henry 234
——— Acheson 276
Mordaunt, Colonel Charles 85
——— Sir John 69
——— John 65
Morgan, Sir Edward 81
——— Sir Richard 286
Morin, Robert 78
More, Colonel Roger 48
——— Cressacre 216
——— Sir Thomas ib.
——— Basil ib.
Moss, Philip 7
Mostyn, Sir Roger 26, 27
——— Sir Thomas 27
——— William 250
Mohun, Lord 124
Molesworth, Viscount 127, 128, 134, 136, 140, 141, 143, 147
——— Sir Roger 128
——— Sir Hender 129
——— Sir John 129, 130
——— William 130
——— Colonel Guy 131
Molesworth,

INDEX.

Molesworth, Captain 144
——— Lieutenant Colonel James 146
——— Lady ib.
——— Coote 147
——— John 282
Molyns, John 153
Monck, George 138, 140
——— Charles 138, 139
——— Henry 139
——— Charles-Stanley 140
——— Henry-Stanley ib.
——— George-Paul ib.
——— General 193
Monckton, Thomas 249, 250
——— John 250, 251
——— Anthony 250
——— Marmaduke 250
——— Sir Philip 251
——— Sir Francis ib.
Monmouth, Earl of 80
Montander, Marquess of 146
Monteith, Earl of 97, 101
Monford, Hugh 90
Montgomery, Count 101
Montrose, Duke of 97, 100
——— Earl of 101
Mornington, Earl of 124, 293, 298
Morres, John 289
——— Sir William Evans 290
——— Sir Haydocke Evans ib.
——— Sir William Ryves ib.
——— Redmond ib.
——— Lodge Evans ib.
——— Rev. Redmond 291
——— Francis-Harvey ib.
——— William ib.
Morrice, Sir Nicholas 130
Mortimer, Sir Thomas 128

Morton, E. of 96, 104, 107
Mount-Alexander, Earl of 34
Mount-Garret, Viscount 43, 47, 221
Mount-Joy, Lord Deputy 269
——— Lord 277
Mount-Morres, Viscount 289, 290, 291, 293
Mountrath, Earl of 123
Moyle, General 137
Mugg, Captain 84
Mundy, Edward-Miller 171
Mure, Sir Adam 95
Murphy, John 116
Murray, Earl of 93, 97, 103, 107
——— Colonel John 183

N.

Nagle, Peter 31
Needham, Thomas 19
——— George 25
——— Sir Robert 56, 234
Nesbitt, William 173
Netterville, ——— 33
——— John 35
——— Viscount 42, 46, 51
——— Lucas 48
Newcastle, Duke of 253
Newcomen, Sir Robert 22
Newhaven, Lord 186
Newton, Sir Peter 60
——— Brigadier 69
——— John 73
——— Alexander 268
Neville, Sir Henry 74
——— Gervais ib.
——— Sir Thomas 268
Nicholas, Sir Ambrose 7
——— Sir Oliver 159

Nichol,

INDEX.

Nichol, Rev. John 288
Nithsdale, Earl of 105
Noel, Andrew 282
—— Sir Verney *ib.*
Noon, Henry 268
Norborough, Sir John 75
Norfolk, Duke of 61, 258
—— Lord Treasurer 209
Normandy, Duke of 8, 88, 89, 90, 91, 188
Norreys, Sir William 18
Norris, Sir John 268, 269
Northampton, Earl of 58, 212
Northumberland, Earl of 2, 58, 62, 89, 131, 209
Nottingham, Earl of 196
Nugent, Christopher 31, 42
—— Thomas 31, 32, 33
—— John 31
—— Robert Oge *ib.*
—— Oliver 32
—— Richard *ib.*
—— James Moyle *ib.*
—— Lady Catharine 39
—— Sir Christopher *ib.*
—— Sir Robert 41
—— Michael 42
—— Lady Mary 51
—— Earl 231
Nutt, Edward 79

O.

Oakwell, Francis 285
O'Brien, Sir Donagh 119
—— Tiege 272
—— Donagh M'Conner *ib.*
O'Campo, Alphonso 269
Ochiltree, Lord 261
O'Conner, Carbry 283
O'Conolly, Owen 297
O'Doghertie, Sir Cahir 270, 274, 277

O'Donel, Sir Neil 270
Offley, Richard 201
Ogle, —— 230
—— George 293
Oldfield, Samuel 251, 252, 260
Olney, Sir Robert 6
O'Neil, Shane 37
—— Sir Phelim 114, 115, 174
—— Charles 168
—— John *ib.*
—— St. John 168
Onflow, Richard 126, 142
—— Lord 126
Orange, Prince of 84, 134, 185, 230, 120, 252
Orford, Earl of 70
—— Countess of 266
Orkney, Earl of 142
Orme, —— 75
—— Garton *ib.*
Ormond, Duke of 34, 118, 120, 125, 164, 175, 184, 231, 286
—— Earl of 44, 118, 236
—— Marquess of 132, 284
Ormsby, John 298
O'Rourke, Terman 173
Orrery, Earl of 274, 276
Osborne, Sir Peter 240
O'Shaghnassey, Roger 176
Ossory, Bishop of 286
Ossulston, Lord 83
Owens, John 18
—— Lewis 28

P.

Packinton, Sir John 13
Page, Thomas 85
—— Sir Francis 131
Paisley, Lord 109, 117, 162, 172

Paisley,

INDEX.

Paisley, Francis	161
Palmer, Sir Henry	197
———— Roger	276
Palmerston, Viscount	225, 228, 238, 241, 243, 285, 287
Palmes, Bryan	74
———— Sir Francis	131
Panmure, Earl of	138
Pargeter, Sir Henry	208
Parker, Sir Henry	13
———— John	214
———— Sir Nicholas	229
Parsons, Sir William	236
Patterson, Colonel	178
Pauncefoot, Sir John	5
Payne, Thomas	210
Peachy, Sir John	255
Philips, John	22
———— Sir Thomas	109
Phipps, Lord Chancellor	135
Pelham, Lord	171
———— Thomas	244
Pembroke, Earl of	85, 90
Penston, Sir Thomas	230
Penteney, William	48
Penruddock, George	220
Perceval, Sir Philip	46
———— John	183
Perche, Earl of	89
Percy, Henry	140, 185
Perkins, Richard	50, 115
———— Captain John	114
Perrott, Sir John	32, 38, 41
Peterborough, Earl of	85
Petre, Sir Thomas	216
———— Henry	217
———— Lord,	ib.
Petty, John	160
Pery, Viscount	234
Pigott, John	16, 124
———— Southwell	124
———— Alexander	141, 163
Pigott, Thomas	284
Pitchcroft, ——	216
Pitt, George	77
———— William Augustus	86
Platen, Count	85
Plessington, Sir Henry	281
Pleydell, Robert	76
Plunket, Sir John	31, 37
———— Patrick	31
———— Oliver	ib.
———— Sir Thomas	32, 35
———— Sir Oliver	32, 42
———— Sir Alexander	35
———— Thomas	ib.
———— George	37
———— John	46
———— Sir Nicholas	120
———— Nicholas	285
Plummer, John	125
Plumpton, Sir William	73
Pointz, John	18
Polwarth, Lord	202
Ponsonby, Henry	140
———— William Brabazon	147
———— Sir John	274
Poole, Sir Francis	244
———— Henry	264
Pope, Alexander	232
Popham, Sir John	18
Pordage, Sir Thomas	216
Porter, Sir Thomas	25
Portington, Sir John	189
Portland, Duke of	139
———— Earl of	242
Power, Sir Henry	20
Powerscourt, Viscount	255, 260, 268, 271, 272, 275, 277, 289
Powis, Marquess of	221
Povey, John	284
Poynings, Edward	260
Praers, William	16
Pratt, Sir John	10, 11
———— John	11

Pratt,

Pratt, Dr. Benjamin	124	Rookwood, Thomas	218
—— Rev. Joseph	291	Roos, Lord 188, 190, 259	
Prestland, Richard	60	Roper, John	74
Preston, Rev. Nathaniel	179	Rose, ——	138
Price, William	7, 28	Ross, Earl of 95, 97, 175	
—— Ryse Wyn ap Wil-		—— Viscount	119
	19	Roscomon, Earl of	47
—— Roger	27	Rotney, James	173
—— Robert	205	Rous, Sir John	229
—— Uvedale	ib.	Rowlands, Thomas	28
—— John	286	Rowley, Hercules, 278, 298	
Primate, Lord	273	—— Hercules - Lang-	
Prior, Andrew	291	ford 295, 298	
Puleston, Roger	17	—— Randolf	295
Purefoy, William	149	—— John 295, 296,	
Pyne, Sir Richard	165	297	
		—— William 295, 296	
Q.		—— Hugh 296, 297	
		—— Edward 296, 297	
Quarles, George	260	—— Sir John	297
Queensbury, Earl of	105	—— Clotworthy	298
Quinn, Henry	139	Ribbesford, Sir John	227
		Rich, Thomas	79
R.		Richmond, Duke of 114,	
		117, 212	
Radnor, Earl of		Ridge, ——	288
Railton, Thomas	25	Risby, Thomas	191
Raleigh, Sir Walter	131	Risdon, William	129
Rainsford, Sir Mark	141	Risley, Paul	229
Rambouillet, De Plesses	240	Rivers, Earl of 69, 80, 216,	
Ramsden, Mr.	75	266	
Randolph, Sir James	93	—— Lord	86
Ratoath, Baron of	31	Riverston, Lord	51
Rawson, Sir John	47	Ruish, Sir Francis	172
Reading, Sir Robert	122	Rundal, ——	76
Reeps, Henry	190	Rupert, Prince 82, 212	
Roche, James	118	Russell, Sir John 258, 269	
Rochfort, John	36	—— Sir Thomas	57
Rockliffe, Guy	73	Russia, Czar of	90
—— Sir Guy	ib.	Rutland, Duke of 70, 253,	
Rolle, Henry	129	254	
Romney, Earl of	43	—— Earl of 80, 84	
Rooke, Sir George	79	Ruytenburgh, Baron	68
—— Sir Richard	259	Rysom, Sir John	189
		Sackville,	

INDEX.

S.

Sackville, Sir Richard	214
Saint Asaph, Bishop of	20
Saint Albans, Duke of	205
——— Earl of	217, 218
St. Andrew, Bishop of	92, 99, 107
St. Aubyn, Sir John	130
St. Clare, Thomas	207
——— Sir Philip	ib.
St. George, Sir George	178
St. John, Sir Walter	64
——— Viscount	ib.
——— Lord Deputy	233
St. Leger, Sir John	167
St. Piere, Bryan	15
St. Quinton, John	250
Salisbury, Earl of	89, 261
——— Bishop of	205
——— John	283
Saltby, Richard	281
Salter, Sir John	151
Saltmarsh, ———	73
——— Robert,	189
Salton, Lord	95
Saltonstal, Richard	197
Sambroke, Sir Jeremy	216, 248
——— John	248
Samon, Thomas	250
Sands, Sir Thomas	230
——— Sir Michael	ib.
Sandys, Sir William	266
——— Sir Edwin	26
——— Sir Samuel	ib.
——— Lord	ib.
——— Miles	229
Savage, Sir John	19, 62
——— Sir Arthur	284
——— William	ib.
Savile, John	58
——— Thomas	251
Saunders, Edmund	215
Saunders, Edward	229
Saxe Weismar, Duke of	131
Say and Sele, Lord	229
Scarborough, Earl of	171
Scardeville, Rev. Henry	131
Scrope, Baron	10
——— Lord	58, 80, 259
——— Gervais	201
Searle, John	247
Sedgrave, Christopher	38
Sedley, Sir Charles	12
Selkirk, Earl of	106
Semple, Lord	107, 112
Serjeant, Sir John	31
Seton, Lord	109
Seymour, Thomas	128
——— Sir Edward	ib.
Shaftesbury, Earl of	135
Shaftoe, Robert	76
Shakerley, Sir Ralph	7
Shee, Richard	42
Sheldon, Dominick	175
——— Edward	219
——— Ralph	282
Shelleto, George	25
Shelly, John	214
——— Sir John	219
Shepey, William	227
Sheppard, Philip	76
——— Anthony	182
Sherle, Patrick	46
——— John	ib.
Sherratt, Richard	16
Sherrington, William	197
Shirley, Sir Thomas	10
——— Lady Selina	14
Shovel, Sir Cloudesly	76
Shrewsbury, Duke of	165
Shute, Christopher	200
——— Benjamin	201
——— John	202
Sidney, Sir Henry	61
——— William	173
Singleton,

INDEX.

Singleton, Rev. John 123	Stanley, Sir Rowland 220
Simnell, Lambert 35	———— Sir Ralph 227
Skelton, John 31	St. pylton, Henry 158
Skeffington, Sir William 282	Stanton, John 38
	Steed, Edwin 121
Skipwith, Ralph 22	Shephens, Sir John 240
Slane, Lord 32, 33, 48	Stewart, Lady Sophia 26
Slaning, Sir Richard 130	Still, John 79
Slingsby. Sir Thomas 66	Stockdale, George 49
———— Sir Francis 283	Strabane, Viscount 88, 122
Sloane, William 301	———— Baron 111, 112,
Smith, John 13	Stradling, Sir John 214
———— Sir Piercy 169	———— Sir Edward 215
———— Sir Edward 161	Strafford, Earl of 81, 181, 251
———— Edward 273	
———— Sir William 27	Strangways, James 58
———— Sir Walter 151	Stratford, 79
———— William 296	Strickland, Sir William 58
Smyth, James 130	Staremberg, Count 112
———— Thomas 197	Strathern, Earl of 92, 97
Somerset, Duke of 102, 195, 163	Strathmore, Earl of 105
	Strode, 79
Somerville, William 10	Strongbow, Earl 189
———— Sir Quaile 180	Style, Sir Charles 278
Sorrell, Henry 217	Sudeley, Baron 2, 3
Southwell, Edward 81	Sudgrove, John 207
Spain, Prince 265	Suffolk, Duke of 209, 259, 262, 265, 266
Sparke, John 129	
Spencer, Thomas 228	———— Earl of 256, 257
Spilman, Sir Anthony 190	Sulyard, Edward 217
Spooner, James 285, 286	Sunderland, Earl of 8, 248
Spotswood, Archbishop 104	Surry, Earl of 56
Springe, Sir Thomas 218	Sussex, Lord Deputy 37
Sprinuall, Sir Adam 188	———— Earl of 56
Squire, Simon 128	Sutton, Lord 189
Stafford, Earl of 63, 119	———— Francis 251
———— Edward - Francis 293	Swaine, Arthur 169
	Sweden, King of 173
Stanhope, Lord 65	Swynerton, Sir Robert 63
Stanihurst, James 46	Sydney, Lord 33
Stanley, John 60	———— Lord Deputy 267
———— Sir Thomas 139, 220	———— Sir Philip 233
	Sykes, Francis 254
———— Sir Humphry 151	Synnott, Walter 47
	Taaffe,

INDEX.

T.

Taaffe, Stephen 51
Talbot, Richard 51, 47, 51, 182
——— William 31
——— John 35, 157
——— Thomas 39
——— Lord 157
——— John-Chetwynd *ib.*
——— Earl of 83
——— Sir Gilbert 265
Tankerville, Earl of 83
Tarah, Viscount 33, 43
Tasbourgh, George 223
Tath, Richard 37
Tatton, General William 287
Taylor, John and Mary 240
——— Richard 35
——— Sir Thomas 140
Telling, Richard 32
Temple, Thomas 129
——— Richard 228
——— Paul *ib.*
——— Peter 228
——— Viscount Cobham Family of 228
——— Lady 229
——— Robert 234
——— Gustavus-Handcock 234
——— Family of Waterstown 234
——— Family of, Baronets 239
——— John 240
——— Sir John 241, 285, 286
——— Sir William 242
——— Henry 244
Tessington, Sir John 282
Teynham, Lord 220
Thanet, Earl of 196

Thatcher, John 210
——— James 215
Thirkeld, Marmaduke 189
Thirleston, Lord 106
Thomas, Richard ap 18
——— Sir Edmund 81
Thomond, Earl of 269, 270
Thornton, William 189
Thorold, ——— 260
——— Sir Edmund *ib.*
Thoroton, Doctor 79
Thwenge, John 189
——— Marmaduke *ib.*
Throckmorton, Sir Thomas 6, 9
——— Sir Arthur 230
Thurles, Viscount 118
Thwaites, Marmaduke 189
Thynne, Sir Henry Frederick 80
——— Henry-Frederick 82
Tilbury, Baron 9
Tiptoft, Lord 80, 190, 259
Titchbourne, Sir William 134
——— Captain William 140
Tolmach, Sir Lionel 64
Tottle, Thomas 129
Townshend, Marquess of 171
——— Thomas 170, 264
——— Sir Roger 9
——— Viscount 169, 171
Traci, Sir William 3
Tracy, Viscount 1, 4, 8
——— Family of Stanway, Baronets 6
——— Paul 7
——— Ferdinando 8, 11

Vol. V.   A a   Tracy,

INDEX.

Tracy, Robert 10
——— Thomas ib.
——— Sir John 11
Traun, Count 221
Tredenham, John 129
——————— Sir Joseph ib.
Tresham, Lawrence 3
——————— Sir William 216
Sir George Trevilian 297
Trevor, Sir Thomas 10
——— Sir John 170, 292, 293, 294
——— Edward 274
——— Arthur 291, 292
Trimbleston, Lord 31
Trenchard, Sir George 34, 35, 36, 39, 48, 50, 52
Tuffenell, George 139
Tufton, Sir Richard 129
Turnbull, Bishop 97
Tunstall, Sir Marmaduke 74
Turenne, Duke of 97
Turpin, Jane 268
Turnville, William 228
Tuscany, Duke of 142
Tynte, James 23
——— James-Worth 24
Tyrawley, Lord 187
Tyrconnell, Earl of 50, 52
——————— Duke of 119
Tyrone, Earl of 140, 272, 277, 296, 302

U.

Unton, Sir Edward 153
Upton, Thomas 185
——— Henry 297
——— Arthur 298
——— Clotworthy ib.
Usher, Rev. William 146
——— Christopher 278
——— Sir William 284

V.

Valentia, Viscount 20, 299
Valois, Countess 90
Vanhoohan, Mr. 132
Vassal, Florentius 204
Vasserot, Monsieur 121
Vavasor, Sir Charles 131
——————— William 189
Vaughan, Rev. Stephen 19
——————— Sir Henry 74
——————— Sir John 174
Veell, Sir John 235
Venables, Thomas 17
——————— George 60
——————— Peter 63
Vere, Sir George 262
Vermandois, Count 92
Vernon, Sir Thomas 64
Ville Real, Mr. 253

W.

Wale, Garrett 290
——— William 291
Wales, Prince 70, 76, 101
Walgrave, Princess 85
——————— Thomas 264
Walker, Charles 138
Walpole, Sir Robert 70
Walsh, John 78
——— Pierce 290
Walter, Richard 141
——— Edward 199
Ward, Job 49, 235
——— John 199
——— Charles 242
——— Rev. Charles 300
Wannup, Rev. Mr. 64
Warburton, Sir Geffery 17
Warbeck, Perkin 56
Warren, Sir Lawrence 17
Warren,

INDEX.

Warren, Sir George 28, 69
—— Henry 32
—— Edward 69
—— William Paul 185
—— Richard ib.
—— Earl of 258
Warwick, Earl of 18, 89
Watkins, 217
Waters, Lady 43
—— Major 251
Weaver, Thomas 15, 60
Weldon, Arthur 183
—— Walter 284
Wenman, Sir Thomas 162
Wentworth, Matthew 250
—— Sir William 251
—— Lord 263
—— Sir George 273
West, Doctor 231
Westcote, William 128
—— Lord 231
Western, 247
Weston, Peter 73
—— Samuel 132
—— John 221
Westmeath, Earl of 51
Westmorland, Earl of 9, 62
Westenra, Henry 183, 253
Wetenhall, Robert 16
Weymouth, Viscount 80, 82
Wharton, Earl of 265
White, Henry 27
—— George 31
—— Charles 51
Whitefield, Thomas 22
—— Henry 24
—— William 162
Whitmore, William 78
Whittingham, Thomas 9
Whitwell, 227
Wilbraham, Thomas 62

Wilbraham, Sir Richard 62
Wilford, Thomas 25
Williams, William 19
—— Sir William 28
—— Edward ib.
—— John ib.
—— Sir Hugh ib.
Wilson, John 174
Winchester, Earl of 92, 252
—— Marquess of 211
Wingfield, Sir John 255, 256, 260, 264, 268
—— Robert 255, 268
—— Sir William 255
—— William 257
—— Families of Upton and Tickencote 259
—— Sir Robert 260
—— John 260, 268
—— Mervyn 261
—— Sir Henry ib.
—— Family of Letheringham ib.
—— Sir Richard 262, 270
—— Sir Edward 262, 264, 271, 272
—— Sir Anthony 263
—— Henry 264
—— Family of Kimbolton 265
—— Jaques 267
—— Sir Edward Maria ib.
—— Humphrey 268
—— Lewis 268, 272
Winter, Sir John 263
Wise, Sir Thomas 130
—— Thomas ib.
—— Edward ib.
Wiseman, 268
Wyatt, Francis 140
Wybrants,

INDEX.

Wybrants, Peter 132, 284
Wybrow, Richard   182
——— John   ib.
Wyld, Thomas   11
Wyndham, Sir William 156
Wyn, Rowland ap   18
Wynne, Maurice   19
——— Sir John   ib.
——— Owen 114, 145, 174
——— Sir William 198
Wyse, William   32

Y.

Yardley, Richard   296
Yarner, Abraham   238
——— Sir Abraham   241
Yates, Sir Charles   219
Yeamans, Henry   201
York, Duke of 18, 27, 64, 83, 120, 160, 230, 238, 280
——— Archbishop of   94

FINIS.

www.ingramcontent.com/pod-product-compliance
Lightning Source LLC
Chambersburg PA
CBHW021153230426
43667CB00006B/369